Friendly Divorce Guidebook for Colorado
How to Plan, Negotiate, and File Your Divorce

FIFTH EDITION

M. Arden Hauer, M.A., J.D.
S.W. Whicher, M.A., J.D.

BRADFORD PUBLISHING COMPANY
Denver, Colorado

PLEASE READ

This book, *Friendly Divorce Guidebook for Colorado*, is intended to provide general information with regard the subject matter covered. It is not meant to provide legal opinions or offer advice, or to serve as a substitute for advice by licensed, legal professionals. It is sold with the understanding that Bradford Publishing Company and the authors are not engaged in rendering legal or other professional advice.

Bradford Publishing Company and the authors do not warrant that the information herein is complete or accurate, and do not assume and hereby disclaim any liability to any person for any loss or damage caused by errors, inaccuracies or omissions, or usage of this book or its forms.

Laws, and interpretations of those laws, change frequently and the subject matter of this book contains important legal consequences. It is the responsibility of the user of this book to know if the information contained in it is applicable to his or her situation, and if necessary, to consult legal, tax or other counsel.

Library of Congress Cataloging-in-Publication Data

Hauer, M. Arden.
  Friendly divorce guidebook for Colorado : how to plan, negotiate, and file your divorce / M. Arden Hauer, S.W. Whicher.-- 5th ed.
       p. cm.
Includes bibliographical references and index.
  ISBN 1-883726-94-8
  1. Divorce--Law and legislation--Colorado--Popular works. 2. Divorce mediation--Colorado--Popular works. I. Whicher, Susan Wendall II. Title.
  KFC1900.Z9H38 2003
  346.78801'66--dc22

                                        2003020958

The "Bunky" artwork © by M. Arden Hauer, used here by permission.

To those who, at the most difficult of times, find and create
ways to talk, to cooperate, to keep talking, to resolve differences
to honor agreement—peacemakers all.

M. Arden Hauer

For my re-discovered birth son, who used this book for
clients without knowing it was written by his mother, and
his extraordinary family — complete with grandchildren —
who have seamlessly included me.

S. W. "Wendy" Whicher

TABLE OF CONTENTS

INTRODUCTION

Welcome to the fifth edition of the Friendly Divorce Guidebook for Colorado. Five editions in just under nine years illustrates the fast-changing nature of the divorce process in Colorado. Change means we must revise in order to keep up our commitment to you to provide accurate and current information for doing your own divorce in our beautiful state. This edition is updated for legal, tax, and procedural changes through the 2003 Colorado Legislative Session and the 2003 federal income tax reduction. We have also added information about the ending of a living together relationship, where a couple ceases to be partners, and where the law and procedure is sometimes the same as, and in many places significantly different from, that for dissolution of marriage.

This Guidebook is particularly useful in conjunction with mediation. You and your mediator can work through this book together. It also provides useful information for people whose attorneys are negotiating for them, and who want to better understand and particiapate in their own settlement process. It can also be used by the spouse who is alone, where the other spouse cannot participate in the process because he or she has disappeared, is ill or otherwise unavailable.

You can read the Guidebook chapter by chapter, in order, going through every step in the contemporary, amicable Colorado divorce. You can also begin anywhere in it. Each chapter contains a complete topic. Look up specific questions as they occur to you. You can use the index and treat this book like an encyclopedia.

This Guidebook can also be used for specific stages on the long road to being single. Pick it up as needed over time as your situation changes. For example, when you are just starting out and everything is too raw and confusing to even contemplate an entire divorce, just read the beginning chapters, especially Chapter 3 Taking Care of Yourself, and Chapter 4 Moving From One Household to Two. If you are ready to divorce and eager to begin, read Chapters 5 through 12 if you have children or Chapters 5 through 7 and 10 through 12 if you do not have children. If you are concerned about whether your final agreement will be kept or how changes in your life will be affected, read Chapters 2 and 13.

As a practical matter, it takes two to have a marriage, and only one to have a divorce. Either spouse, or both, may opt out of the marriage, and there is no legal penalty for being the one who makes this choice.

"From pro's and con's they fell to a warmer way of disputing." Miguel de Cervantes, *Don Quixote*.

Regardless of who is making the choice to end the marriage, you each continue to have options about how to carry it out. The choice to end the marriage does not control the manner in which you go about it. This Guidebook shows you how to end your marriage in a cooperative way—which can be a sound foundation for the next part of your life.

This Guidebook is not likely to be useful in litigation—a trial in court—Cooperation and the adversarial process have very different consequences, although the results may be the same. The terms of a privately developed or a mediated agreement may be virtually identical to those a court would order, or lawyers would negotiate for you. It is possible that these methods might arrive at the same outcome for property division, parental responsibilities, child support and maintenance as a mediated agreement, but each method has very different emotional consequences. In the court-ordered divorce, the terms are dictated to the parties by the judge, based on law and precedent. In the lawyer-negotiated settlement, the provisions are likely to be given to the parties as law or legally-acceptable compromise. The parties may not fully understand the terms— they may feel ambivalent about them and each other, and they are statistically less likely to carry them out as written. Privately developed and mediated agreements which come from the parties themselves are more likely to be honored because the parties understand, endorse and are committed to, each provision.

This book contains
- Discussion of divorce and its alternatives (Chapter 1).
- A list of all the facts and figures you must collect in order to undertake and conclude a fair and complete settlement (Chapter 5).
- A helpful outline of how to plan you separation, and make other temporary arrangements and agreements   (Chapter 4).
- An overview of divorce in the legal system and the role of law in your divorce agreement (Chapter 2).
- Information about some of the indirect results of divorce in areas such as taxes and credit (Chapters 7, 11 and 13).
- Instructions for the court forms and for the procedures necessary to obtain a dissolution of marriage (a divorce) or legal separation in Colorado (Chapters 6 and 12).
- Instructions on obtaining your final Decree (Chapter 12).
- Instrucions on how to transfer title to property between you, and how to put into effect other aspects of your agreement (Chapters 7 and 13).
- Occasional information about partners in similar or parallel situations (throughout).

"There is truly a magical quality about conflict which can call out the best in us, that which is not summoned under ordinary circumstances." Thomas F. Crum, *The Magic of Conflict*.

"When they [people] no longer trust themselves, they begin to depend upon authority." Lao-Tzu, *Tao Te Ching*.

- Information about a new Simplified Divorce Procedure taking place in some Colorado courts.

The Guidebook format combines a complete discussion of each topic with illustrative examples, charts, checklists, questionnaires, resources and full-size sample forms. There is a bibliography at the end, and the major technical, legal, and tax terms used in the divorce process are defined in sidebars throughout the book.

We have incorporated certain symbols in the text— called icons— to set apart categories of information.

 Indicates tax information

 is a caution, or something of particular importance not to be overlooked;

 is a warning about something with dire consequences;

 indicates the definition of a legal term;

 indicates information for partners, those in relationships without marriage (new in this fifth edition)

Lastly, we introduce Bunky:

A Bunky is an opinion or belief that is, in whole or part, not quite accurate. Some are more fiction than fact. Bunkies abound in the area of marital difficulty and divorce. We discuss many of these widespread views in order to "debunk" the inaccuracies that can really cause harm, as well as to clarify what is true.

Our purpose is to provide the information you will need as you go through the divorce process. This Guidebook is not a substitite

 "My spouse won't give me a divorce"

You don't need each other's permission to get a legal divorce. If either of you declares to the court in a written petition that the marriage is irretrievably broken, you have established sufficient legal grounds for the divorce process to begin. This does not prevent you from working together to complete it.

"This Guidebook is the only help you will need with your divorce."

This is not true. In addition to the information provided in this Guidebook, you may need to consult with an attorney, a counsellor or therapist, accountant, appraiser, pastor, family and friends in order to be able to make clear and wise choices yourself.

for a lawyer's advice to you about your particular situation. Remember, you are legally responsible for whatever assumptions and agreements you make in your divorce, so be sure you obtain all the information and advice you need in order to be secure in your choices. Do not rely on your spouse to do this for you.

This Guidebook is designed to give you a broad and detailed sweep of the cooperative divorce process. It will help you gather all the data you will need to consider, and organize it so that you can make informed decisions. It will assist you in developing an agreement that makes optimal sense of your situation now and into the future.

Our special thanks to Pam Gagel of the Colorado Judicial Department for her very knowledgeable, kind, and timely assistance.

CHAPTER 1

THE INITIAL DECISION

How Do You Know if You Should Get a Divorce?

Every marriage ends in either death or divorce.

Violence and Abuse

If your marriage is experiencing physical or serious emotional abuse it is important to get physicially separated as soon as possible—regardless of what you are deciding about legal separation or divorce.

If you need help with this, you can call your local police or sheriff's office and ask for Victim's Assistance or the Domestic Violence Unit. Most communities have a domestic violence victims assistance organization which will help every step of the way, from providing a Safehouse, to reporting, investigation, and trial. Many will help you terminate an abusive marriage or relationship with free or low-cost legal advice.

How to Find a Marriage Counselor

- Get a referral from a friend you trust who can make a recommendation based on personal experience.

- Ask your pastor, social worker, lawyer, or mediator to make a recommendation.

- Look in the Yellow Pages under the following headings:
    Marriage and Family
     Counseling
    Psychotherapists
    Psychologists
    Physicians – Psychiatrists
    Divorce Services

- Inquire at your local mental health center.

THE INITIAL DECISION

How Do You Know if You Should Get a Divorce?

Most of us said "Till death us do part" when we married, and meant it. The prospect of divorce is unsettling and threatening as an earthquake for some of us; the welcome end of an intolerable situation for others; somewhere between these two extremes for most. Throughout this critical time, both what you do and especially how you do it are important to the present and future well-being of you and everyone in your family.

Options for the Marriage in Difficulty

When a marriage begins to experience serious difficulty, it sometimes seems impossible to step back and take a serious and rational look at the possible alternatives. Some of the available options are marriage counseling and the possibility of reconciling (staying together and working on the relationship); marital mediation; physical separation (often called trial separation); legal separation; dissolution of marriage (divorce); or annulment. Following is a short discussion of each of these.

Marriage Counseling

Every spouse thinks about separation and divorce once in awhile. Is the cause of your current marital discord a single incident or an acknowledged problem? Do you both want to stay married if you can resolve the difficulty? If so, you might want to hold off on any legal filing and seek marriage counseling.

Some common marital problems which can be helped through marriage counseling are:

- Situation stress: loss of job, death of a loved one, major illness or injury of a family member, new child, disabled child, or elderly relative in the home, child at difficult age or sudden major expenses.

- Ongoing quarrels over money, or difficulty in budgeting.

- Sexual dissatisfaction or dysfunction: this is often a specialty within the field of marriage counseling. If this is the type of problem you are experiencing, ask specifically about expertise in this area during your first contact with any professional you are considering.

If you are thinking of divorce, it is a good idea to explore all reasonable possibilities for continuing the marriage—so you're not plagued with guilt later. Marriage counseling can be of help with this, regardless of whether you decide to continue your marriage.

Marital Mediation

Mediation is a process for resolving conflict and coming to agreement. A mediator helps you reach your own agreement. Mediation can be appropriate for clearing things up so that the marriage can continue, or for reaching an agreement for separation or divorce. If you are looking at staying married and doing some problem solving, mediation can be particularly helpful. In marital mediation, it is not unusual for couples to enter into marital agreements which contain understandings about money management and house rules similar to those in pre-marital agreements.

Marital mediation will help you reach your own agreement based on your unique needs. You can use marital mediation as much or as little as you need. You may only need help in clarifying an understanding you already have. You may need help in learning how to bargain collaboratively, or in understanding a complex financial situation.

Some common marital problems which are especially appropriate for marital mediation are:

- Ongoing money problems.

- Major changes in fortune, such as finishing school and getting the first big job, significant inheritance, losing one's job.

- Changes in family structure: new baby, in-law moving in, children leaving home, illness or injury requiring long term attention, retirement.

Be sure you look for a mediator who specializes in family matters. See Chapter 2 for information about mediation for divorce.

Physical Separation (Trial Separation)

Most people use this term to mean getting physically—especially sexually—away from each other. In most cases, one spouse moves out. Some people separate within the same house by one of them moving to the finished basement, to another bedroom, or to the mother-in-law apartment. Working out a schedule of different

How to Find a Marital Mediator

- Ask friends or professionals whom you trust for a personal recommendation or referral.

- Look in the Yellow Pages under "Mediation Service."

 PARTNERS Relationship counseling and relationship mediation are both available for the partnership in difficulty.

 DEFINITION **Mediation** A process in which a neutral third person helps people develop their own agreement.

 DEFINITION **ADR:** Alternative Dispute Resolution. This is the title the legal profession has given to cover all methods of resolving conflicts outside of court. It includes mediation, arbitration, a hybrid called med-arb, negotiation, shuttle diplomacy, even flipping a coin.

"Once you are physically separated you are legally separated."

This assumption is incorrect, and can be very costly. You are legally separated only if and when you receive a signed decree of legal separation from a court. **Physical separation is not legal separation.**

kitchen and laundry room times can help create a feeling of separateness, and is a way to avoid difficult surprises. Many people need to be further apart.

The question of whether to physically separate ultimately comes down to whether one or both of you is so uncomfortable being around the other that he or she cannot function well. Sometimes physical separation brings with it the insight needed to work on resolving serious differences and prompts a renewed commitment to the marriage. Other times, however, it awakens the realization that you really want the marital relationship to end.

PHYSICAL SEPARATION HAS BOTH LEGAL AND TAX CONSEQUENCES

Unless you agree otherwise, the legal consequences of your marriage continue after you separate. The law presumes that any property or debts either of you accumulates are marital – joint. For example, during a long separation the husband continues to contribute to his retirement account, and the wife incurs substantial credit card debt. The increase in the retirement amount is marital property and the increase in credit card debt is marital debt, i.e. joint property and joint debt even if only one name appears on the account.

Your tax filing status may be affected by the date of your physical separation, as may the tax status of your home as your personal residence. See Chapter 7.

It is often a very good idea to write out in detail the agreements you make with each other about your physical separation. This is what makes a physical separation into a trial separation—it is a time to try out your ideas about parenting, support, and meeting marital obligations. See Chapters 2 and 4 for how to plan your separation.

Legal Separation

Legal separation is the same as dissolution of marriage except that neither party is free to re-marry, and the right to inherit is not terminated except by written agreement.

A decree of legal separation declares that you and your spouse, as well as your financial assets and obligations, are legally separate. The decree requires everyone, including creditors, financial and other institutions, to treat the two of you as separate persons. You can no longer file your income taxes as married taxpayers, either jointly or separately. After the decree of legal separation is

"If you leave the family home, your spouse can 'get' you for desertion or abandonment."

Not any more. It is not a crime to leave a marriage. 1972 saw the end of fault grounds for divorce in Colorado, but leaving the family home may impact your discussion of parenting.

Legal Separation: The legal process which declares marriage partners to be separate persons not responsible for each other.

entered, you are no longer responsible for each other's debts or actions, no longer entitled to each other's earnings or property. You are also no longer obligated to support each other except as provided in your separation agreement. (A decree of dissolution of marriage does all this too.)

Before the court can enter a decree of legal separation, you or the court must divide your marital property and debts, determine your parenting plan, and set child support and/or maintenance (alimony/spousal support), just as you must do for a divorce. In practice, the procedure and timing in court for a legal separation is generally the same as for a dissolution. **This Guidebook is about how to reach these decisions yourselves.**

WHY WOULD YOU WANT A LEGAL SEPARATION?

Some couples aren't sure they want to divorce. A legal separation is a way to separate, to divide property, to end mutual responsibility for each other's support and debts except as agreed, and to take a good look at the relationship—while making divorce one easy step away.

Some religions forbid or frown on divorce. Legal separation permits you to lead separate lives without divorcing.

There may be some kinds of health insurance, and some survivor benefits or life insurance connected with retirement plans, which still cover or benefit legally-separated persons while they cut off people who are divorced.

Social Security can be figured on the basis of a former spouse's earnings instead of one's own if the marriage lasted 10 years or more and, if at the time, you are not married to someone else. If you are close, it might be good planning to do a legal separation until you reach 10 years, then convert to a divorce.

If you are unsure of whether to do a legal separation or a divorce, one place to start to ask questions is the benefits and/or personnel office where each of you works. Find out which benefits, if any, apply to the non-employee spouse after either a legal separation or a divorce. Find out what your respective Social Security benefits are now, and are projected to be. Some careful research now may save you thousands of dollars in benefits later.

CHANGING FROM LEGAL SEPARATION TO DIVORCE

After you begin a court action for legal separation, (but before the decree for legal separation is signed), either or both of you may change your request to one for dissolution of marriage.

"Possession is nine-tenths of the law."

Not true. You do not give up your rights to ownership in your home or other property by moving out. Marital property is presumed to be anything you acquired during your marriage, except by gift or bequest. You don't lose it by letting the other spouse use or occupy it.

During the first six months, you can convert it to a decree of divorce only if you both sign the request. But after the six months passes, and a decree of legal separation has been granted, either spouse may have it converted to a decree of dissolution. You only need to ask and prove to the court that you told your spouse you want the conversion to happen. The terms of your agreement—about property, debts, parenting, support, maintenance—stay the same unless you specifically change them at this time. If neither of you ever asks to have your legal separation converted to a divorce, you can remain legally separated for life.

Annulment

Annulment: The legal process which declares that a marriage never existed.

Declaration of Invalidity: The Colorado term for an annulment.

If your marriage was prohibited—not valid right from the start—then you may ask the court to annul your marriage, called a Declaration of Invalidity in Colorado. In this procedure you are asking the court to "declare" that your marriage never happened. A marriage may be annulled because one of you was already married, you are siblings or close relatives, you are underage, or the marriage was never consummated or was based on fraud or "gross misrepresentation."

Annulment is a legal action that requires "grounds" which must be proven—unlike a dissolution of marriage. Consult with a lawyer if you think this is what you need.

Dissolution of Marriage (Divorce)

Dissolution of Marriage: The Colorado term for divorce.

Dissolution of marriage, more commonly known as divorce, can only be obtained through a court action.

Divorce: The legal process which ends a marriage; dissolution of marriage.

The marriage is dissolved—ended—when the judge signs the decree of dissolution of marriage. The decree ends the mutual obligation spouses have to support each other—to provide the necessities of food, shelter, and clothing—and ends conjugal rights, although you may continue a sexual relationship if you wish. The divorce also ends a person's right to any part of his or her spouse's estate at death. The moment a divorce decree is signed by the court, the spouses are each free to marry again.

"You're automatically divorced if your spouse has been gone for 7 years."

This is not true. There is no "automatic" divorce, even if your spouse has disappeared.

Before the court can sign the decree ending your marriage, you or the court must establish that the marriage is irretrievably broken, divide the property and debts, determine a parenting plan, and set child support and/or maintenance (alimony, spousal support). **This Guidebook is about how to reach these decisions yourselves.**

COMMON LAW MARRIAGE IN COLORADO

"Common law" refers to laws of conduct which evolved from custom and usage, as well as opinions of the Colorado Court of Appeals and the Colorado Supreme Court rather than laws written by a legislature. Common law marriage and a marriage with a license and a ceremony are legally equal. They are both marriages.

You have a common law marriage in Colorado only if:

1. You have lived together ("cohabited") in Colorado (or in another state which recognizes common law marriage) while "holding yourselves out" as being married, meaning that you acted as though you were married. Typical proof of this is that you introduced each other as wife and husband, had the same last name, held joint accounts or filed married/joint income tax returns; *and*

2. Neither of you was still married to someone else, either by a marriage license and a ceremony (called a statutory marriage), or by common law.

If you introduced each other as fiancees or some other term besides husband, wife, or spouse, and talked about getting married some day later, then you are not common law married, no matter how long you have been living together.

Your Other Divorces

The ending of a marriage is much more than a legal event. It is the letting go of dreams. It is the dissolution of a financial partnership. It is the forming of a new relationship with the other parent of your children. It usually involves profound emotional upheaval.

The legal divorce, no matter how final that process may be, may do little or nothing toward taking care of your "other divorces." Some people wake up the morning after the final decree has been signed to find they don't feel divorced at all.

Working through this Guidebook from the first to the last page is a good way to ensure that all your divorces happen together.

Common Law Marriage: A marriage in which the parties did not obtain a license or go through a recognized ceremony, but lived together as married, openly manifesting your intention that your relationship is that of husband and wife.

"We don't need to go through court for our divorce, we're just common law married."

There is no such thing as common law divorce. If you are common law married and you want a divorce or legal separation, you can only obtain it from the court.

The ending of a long term, or even not so long term, living together partnership, like a divorce, can involve a profound emotional upheaval, even when done with understanding and cooperation. Be sure to take care of yourself during this difficult time to help ensure a peaceful conclusion and the ability to move on. See Chapter 3.

CHAPTER 2

DIVORCE AND THE LEGAL SYSTEM

"The court will automatically grant our divorce on day 91."

Nothing occurs automatically at the end of 90 days. You have to take action to request that the court finalize your divorce.

How long will it take for my divorce?

The volume of cases that a court has to process, and the number of staff, varies from court to court. Many courts have a high number of cases at all times, but have staff limitations based on the economy and state budgets. You can ask the clerk of your Court how long you have to wait to get an appointment on the docket for the court to decide something for you—a contested hearing. The quickest way through the Court process is for the two of you to come to complete acceptable agreement, so that the Court's only involvement is to read it and approve it, usually a ten to fifteen minute process—a non-contested hearing.

P Partners don't need a statement or decree from a court to end their partnership.

DIVORCE AND THE LEGAL SYSTEM

The Court Aspect of Divorce – An Overview

Divorce is a legal matter. It can only be obtained through court.

You begin the legal process by filing a petition with the clerk of the district court. The present cost of filing a petition for dissolution of marriage is $184.00; filing a petition for legal separation presently costs $179.00.

The waiting period of 90 days, required by law, begins once you have filed the petition and have obtained jurisdiction over your spouse, by either filing jointly as co-petitioners or completing service of process, both of which are explained in Chapter 6. The reasoning behind the 90-day wait is that a marriage should not be ended without serious thought. The law therefore imposes this "cooling off" time for the couple before the judge has the power to grant a divorce.

During the period from the time of filing until the judge signs the decree, couples must exchange complete financial information. They usually make a temporary separation agreement about who lives where, uses what property, and pays which bills while their divorce or legal separation is pending. This may be an informal, unwritten understanding between them. It may be written and signed. It may be submitted to the court for approval by the judge, in which case it becomes a temporary order. You decide how formal you must make your temporary arrangements. A discussion of temporary agreements and orders is found in Chapter 4.

SEPARATION AGREEMENT

Most couples use the waiting period between filing and decree to work out their final divorce plan which, when written, is called the separation agreement. Whether you are seeking a decree of dissolution or a decree of legal separation, the final agreement is called a separation agreement. Chapters 7 through 11 discuss all the necessary elements for writing your own separation agreement.

Your separation agreement must cover all the following: property division (real estate, cars, household goods, art, sporting equipment and other personal property, investments, businesses, retirement plans and pensions, and the like), payment of debts, maintenance (spousal support, alimony), allocation of parental responsibilities, parenting time and support of children, taxes, and medical and life insurance.

Your separation agreement may also include: a detailed plan for sharing the children, payments agreed to now but to be paid later, future higher education costs for each other or for your children, career plans or goals for each or either of you, and financial planning for the future. Your separation agreement may also anticipate the "Oh My God!"s—such as one parent losing a job, leaving the state, or the death or prolonged illness of a family member.

You can choose to file, or not file, your completed separation agreement with the court (see about privacy and enforcement), but you must at least show it to the court when you ask for your final decree. Some people prefer to get everything worked out, written up, and even signed before they file the petition. Most people file the petition first and then use the waiting period to work things out. Use this time wisely. Provisions and agreements which are acceptable when you have just separated may not be workable months later. It is very hard, and not always possible, to change your agreement after it is approved by the court. You may therefore want to make tentative agreements at the time you file and then use the mandatory waiting time to try living with them—to "get the bugs out."

You must also show the court affidavits (sworn statements) detailing the financial circumstances of each of you before you ask for your final decree. These affidavits provide the basis for the court to *find* your separation agreement to be *fair*, and to *enter* a decree of dissolution of marriage or legal separation.

OBTAINING YOUR FINAL DECREE

You may obtain your final decree in one of two ways:

1. By sending in a signed *Affidavit For Decree Without Appearance of Parties* along with your other final papers. To qualify for this *divorce by affidavit*, you must agree on how to divide your debts and property and either have no minor children, or, if you do, then you must each be *represented by counsel*—each have your own attorney.

2. Those who do not qualify for divorce by affidavit, and those seeking a decree of legal separation, must appear at a final hearing in court.

THE COURT'S CONTINUING JURISDICTION

After your divorce or legal separation has been granted, the court retains *continuing jurisdiction* over your children (allocaton of parental responsibilities, child support). If you have filed your

Dismissal for Failure to Take Action

Some courts will dismiss your divorce or legal separation case if you fail to take action towards finalizing it within a reasonable time, sometimes very soon after the waiting period is over. The dismissal notice gives you 30 days to send in the final papers and proposed decree, or set your case for a non-contested hearing or a contested trial. If you don't do one of these, your case will be dismissed by the court.

There is no body of law for the dissolving of personal relationship partnerships, as there is the Dissolution of Marriage Act for divorce. When dissolving partners go to court, one or the other is usually suing on contract, written and signed, or verbal, or even implied, and a legal theory called unjust enrichment. There is no right to an equitable portion of what is acquired during the relationship, as there is in marriage and divorce, unless you have made a prior agreement that says so.

D
DEFINITION
Continuing jurisdiction: The ongoing power of the court where you obtained your divorce to hear requests to enforce or change its orders made at the time of the decree.

separation agreement, the court also keeps jurisdiction over any future payments and promises which are contained in it, such as a payment due when the house is sold or open-ended maintenance (spousal support). If after your divorce you wish to change one of the provisions of your separation agreement, the court keeps jurisdiction over that too. Even if one or both of you moves out of the state, the original court keeps jurisdiction until another court formally takes over.

The court will not interfere in your personal family matters unless one of you asks it to. If you can cooperate with each other, and be reliable—keeping all your agreements, in spirit and letter—neither of you will have to ask the court to do anything but approve your agreement.

Chapters 5 through 12 of this Guidebook cover each step of the non-contested court process, from first papers through the final decree. Most forms for this process are found in this book and on the enclosed CD-ROM.

"Simplified" Divorce Procedures

The simplest way for your divorce to go through the Court is to come to full and acceptable agreement, put it in writing, and to complete all your court forms accurately. Then when you file your papers, the court's only involvement is to read and approve them.

Many courts are now introducing, and some requiring, a new *"simplified procedure"* for divorces—not simpler than the above, but definitely simpler than the traditional procedure. The simplified procedure is a case management process designed to provide early contact with the court; minimize the use of the adversarial system; resolve conflict; be faster, cheaper and simpler; and maintain the responsibility for decision-making in the family.

When a case is designated to be under the simplified procedure, typically you will be given a written order at the time you file your petition that will give you several obligations and deadlines. The order will require you to exchange financial information; in most jurisdictions, take a parenting-after-divorce class; and set a date and time for a *status conference*, usually within 45 days of filing the petition. This status conference is an informal meeting where you both, along with your lawyers, if any, will meet with a judge, magistrate, or family court facilitator, to discuss how you are progressing in your divorce process.

Have you reached agreement about temporary matters, final agreement about parenting, child support, maintenance, property division, responsibility for debts? What are your sticking points, if any? What are you going to do to resolve them? If you need an expert opinion about something, whether financial or parental or some other area, the court can encourage you to hire only one, rather than multiple, competing experts. If you have all issues resolved at the time of the status conference, then the court can set your final orders hearing, or set time frames for you to file for divorce by affidavit. If not, you will set a date and time for other status conferences or hearings to resolve your case.

If you or the court finds that you don't belong in this simplified procedure, you can "opt out" by making that request to the court at the initial status conference. Usually there is no need to "opt out" as the court will consider requests for formal discovery, motions, additional experts and formal hearings at the status conference.

A Word About the Law

Many people, both lay persons and lawyers, assume that all parts of the law apply to everyone. In family matters this may not be true. The question of how much of the law of divorce applies to people doing their own divorce in a friendly way is unsettled.

Statutes—bills that are passed by the Legislature and signed by the Governor—apply differently to different people. According to the divorce statute (The Uniform Dissolution of Marriage Act, Colorado Revised Statutes 14-10-101, et seq.), if you want a divorce you must go through the court system. That applies to everyone. There is no other way to obtain a divorce. There is common law marriage, but there is no common law divorce.

The divorce statute lists the factors that the judge must consider when dividing property in a divorce. The statute does not say that you must consider those same factors when you divide your property yourselves. What the judge must consider is the law that applies if you and your spouse cannot agree. For example, the statute defines *marital* and *separate* property. You may agree to define these terms the way the statute does, but you are free to define them your own way. For another example, the Dissolution of Marriage Act tells the court the factors it must listen for in allocating parental responsibilities. You may consider these same factors, if you wish, or decide for yourselves what factors are important to you.

The court system produces a second part of the law called case law or precedent. If, after a trial, one or both parties are unhappy with the judge's decision (juries are not used in family law

"But to live outside the law you must be honest…" Bob Dylan, "Absolutely Sweet Marie".

How to Win in Court – Not!

Since this Guidebook is about friendly and cooperative divorce, it offers no advice or tips about how to "win" in court.

"The notion that most people want black-robed judges, well-dressed lawyers & fine-paneled courtrooms as the setting to resolve their disputes is not correct. People with problems, like people with pains, want relief, and they want it as quickly and inexpensively as possible." Warren E. Burger, Chief Justice, United States Supreme Court

matters in Colorado) they may appeal to the Colorado Court of Appeals. If they challenge the results from the Court of Appeals, they may further appeal to the Colorado Supreme Court. The appeal process reviews only the transcript of the trial, and hears arguments by the lawyers. The appellate court then decides whether the trial court made an error, or *abused its discretion*, meaning that the trial judge wandered too far beyond the boundaries of other similar cases. The appellate court either *affirms* the trial court's decision, *reverses* it, or sends it back *(remands)* to be tried again. The appellate courts publish their rulings in those cases they decide are significant. These published opinions are what lawyers call "precedent."

In the area of divorce, these opinions are law in that they create legal *presumptions* for people in similar circumstances. Since most of these precedent cases arise from trials, and not from cases in which the parties reached agreement, there is a very real question whether such case law applies to people who do their own divorce.

Occasionally, however, cases settled by the spouses themselves are appealed. This usually occurs when the court does not approve the proposed separation agreement or when one of the spouses has a change of heart immediately after the agreement is approved. For example, there are a number of cases where the parents initially agreed to no child support, the trial court would not approve it, and the parties appealed. The Colorado Court of Appeals affirmed, refusing to permit the parties' agreement. The same thing has happened to agreements which do not provide for parenting time for both parents. Both trial and appellate courts agree that support from, and time with, parents are rights of the child—even the parents cannot take them away.

This Guidebook distinguishes between legal definitions and procedures which you, *if you do this divorce yourself*, must follow, and those areas in which you can make your own definitions and agreements.

Privacy

The United States conducts its legal business in public. All courts are open to the public, except juvenile court and certain specific cases which are closed due to especially sensitive testimony. Some trials are broadcast live on television. Many small towns in Colorado still publish a list of just-granted or just-filed divorces in the local newspaper.

A little-known result of this openness is that your divorce file may be asked for, read, and even copied by anyone—including the media, credit reporting agencies, real estate brokers, insurance salespersons, and your children. Many courts are limiting who may have access to court files. Check with your court if you are worried about this.

Even in a non-contested, non-adversarial divorce the court must review the economic circumstances of the spouses in order to determine if their separation agreement should be approved. What do you do if you do not want your financial circumstances to become public knowledge? The way to keep your privacy and still be sufficient in your divorce papers is to provide the minimum amount of specific information for the court to understand your agreement and why you think it is a good one.

Following are some suggestions that may help you keep your private matters private while still providing necessary information to the court:

- Consider not including bank account or credit card numbers anywhere in the papers you will file with the court. Describe things instead, such as "Wife's account at US Bank", Husband's VISA card".

- Consider bringing necessary but sensitive documents with you to the final hearing for the court to review, but ask that they be returned at the end of the hearing, i.e., you do not file them. Psychological evaluations, profit and loss calculations for your business, trust account data, medical reports, criminal actions involving you, all are examples of things you may wish returned to you, and not left in a court file which is open to the public.

- Consider not incorporating into the decree all or part of your separation agreement. See Chapter 12, page 298, for how to do this. If you do not incorporate an agreement into the decree, you lose your right to enforce your agreement through the divorce court. You will have to decide how much your privacy is worth when measured against ease and sureness of enforcement. See Chapter 13 for more on enforcement.

- Consider asking the court to seal your file, or parts of it. To do this, you must satisfy the court that your, or your children's, need for privacy outweighs the public right to know. Such confidential sealing is routinely done with parenting evaluations filed with the court.

"The human animal needs a freedom seldom mentioned, freedom from intrusion. He needs a little privacy quite as much as he wants understanding or vitamins or exercise or praise." Phyllis McGinley, "A Lost Privilege," *The Province of the Heart.*

 Whether or not you incorporate your agreement into the decree, a) the decree will indicate your parenting arrangements, and, b) the support order will recite the amount of child support being ordered. This is because the court keeps jurisdiction over minor children.

Most people find that their divorce file contains nothing which they do not want the public to know. You can determine how much you wish to be revealed about you.

How Do You Want to Conduct Your Divorce?

Most people want to end their marriage as inexpensively as possible and not make difficult matters worse. At a time when there may not be enough money to support a family in two homes, no one wants to make unnecessary payments to parenting evaluators, lawyers, appraisers, tax accountants, career counsellors, business consultants, mediators, arbitrators, or fact-finders.

Money isn't the only issue. How do you want to conduct your divorce? How do you want it to be conducted? Here are some examples of how a divorce can be done, from the simple to the complex, from the friendly to the more adversarial, as well as from the inexpensive to the costly.

DIVORCE PROCESS OPTIONS

DO IT YOURSELVES

There is a list of all the published forms you might need for non-adversarial divorce in Chapter 6 of this Guidebook. You can print out any or all of these forms from the CD found in the back of this book, or fill out the forms on the screen. You must fill out the forms correctly, file them in the correct sequence and pay the correct filing fee.

You must negotiate and prepare a separation agreement for the court to review at the time of your decree. You can negotiate your separation agreement at home.

- You will need to create you own agreement, perhaps using the sample language in Chapter 12, or by using one of the Separation Agreement forms on the CD.

If you have no children and little property or debts, you may have a separation agreement of only a few lines or paragraphs which you can create on a separate sheet of paper and attach to the decree, or you can use the form, JDF 1215. Not many qualify for this simple method since most married couples have some joint obligations or separation-year tax filings that require a more detailed written understanding between them.

"Should I use an Agreement Form?"

When we wrote the first edition of this book in 1990-1993, we decided not to include a sample separation agreement, and for good reason. On the one hand, forms are attractive because they make a difficult thing look relatively simple, and offer the opportunity to get a painful process over with quickly. But on the other hand, any separation agreement form that just requires you to fill in the blanks has already made some decisions for you, either by what is implied in the words of the form and how it is set up, or by what is not said. In truth, you have much more latitude and many more choices than is implied in any separation agreement form.

Use any such form, including our sample wording at the end of Chapter 12, with caution. It's always wise to have a separation agreement read by an attorney—one for each spouse—before you sign it.

ASSISTANCE FOR DO-IT-YOURSELFERS

If you need some help in working out the separation agreement, there are some low-cost resources available to you.

There are a number of books and manuals which will help you complete the forms and the process. This Guidebook is one.

There are classes on do-it-yourself divorce in most counties, and at many of the community colleges and adult education centers.

There are legal centers and a few private attorneys who will, for a flat fee, fill out the forms and review your agreement to see that it is complete and in a form acceptable to the court. Generally these flat fees include consultation, and sometimes filing of the forms in court—but they do not include negotiating your agreement for you.

DO IT YOURSELVES WITH MEDIATION

In mediation the two of you negotiate with each other in the presence of the mediator—who is neutral. After you gather all the papers that show your incomes, assets and debts, you bring them to the mediation meeting, put all the cards on the table, so to speak, and then negotiate with each other to form your agreement and your parenting plan, if you have children. The mediator's function is to help focus the conversation, explain the process, show you different ways to do things so you can consider a variety of options, and help each of you hear what the other is saying. But YOU make the decisions. Mediation is a good way to stay in charge of making your own decisions, and at the same time to get help on how to put an agreement together.

As the two of you begin to come to agreement and the agreement begins to take shape, the mediator puts your agreement in written form, so you can see how it looks in writing, and to give you further opportunity to consider it. You can go through as many drafts as you need as you become progressively clearer about what you want to do, until it finally says exactly what you want. Usually only one or two drafts are needed, but some couples require several. The written agreement that emerges from mediation is usually called a *Memorandum of Understanding* and you can use it as your separation agreement in court.

It is always recommended that each of you have the agreement reviewed by your own attorney, before it is signed. Sometimes those reviews raise issues that need to be further discussed in mediation. If decisions are changed, then the *Memorandum* is revised.

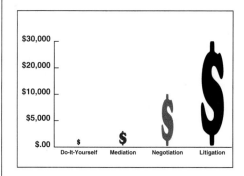

A partnership can end far more quickly and abruptly than a marriage, and often does, leaving feelings wounded and often financial matters unresolved. Mediating the untangling of your blended personal and financial matters can help you to come apart without increasing the amount of baggage you already have.

How do we know if we can mediate?

If you can trust each other to be forthcoming about all your facts and circumstances, and not hide anything, and if you can communicate with each other reasonably well, with the assistance of the mediator, you may be good candidates for the mediation process.

Working together with a mediator allows you to be directly involved in the process of arriving at every decision. Sometimes if you are not in the thick of the decision-making process yourself, the results may not fit you. The agreement someone else may reach on your behalf may be the best they can envision – but they do not see with your eyes. If you want to have an agreement which is uniquely suited to you and to which you will commit with your whole heart, you will have to feel that YOU negotiated it. You are more likely to be satisfied with your agreement—and with yourself—and more likely to abide by the agreement if YOU BOTH walk through each step and negotiate each issue.

When to Use a Mediator

You can hire a divorce mediator to work with you both right from the beginning of your decision to separate to help you make your decision about who will move out and where, who will be responsible for what expenses and bills, and how you will manage the children from two locations, until you make some final decisions. Once temporary agreements are made—your agreed upon holding pattern, so to speak—you can move forward to working on long term solutions.

Some people come to mediation after they discover that the attorneys they have hired are more contentious than they are, and they decide to take back being in charge of their divorce. Still others, having begun a contentious divorce process, change their minds, and are able to instruct their lawyers to shift gears to assist them in the mediation process. Still others, doing their divorce themselves, discover that with only a few weeks to go they can't seem to manage it themselves, and so they go to mediation to get assistance in putting their final agreement together. Mediation can be an excellent choice in all these different situations.

Choosing a Divorce Mediator

There are many different kinds of divorce mediators with different kinds of backgrounds. While most are lawyers or mental health professionals, you will find a wide variety of other backgrounds.

A divorce mediator can help you decide how you are going to approach and do your separation and divorce. For example, whether to be petitioner and co-petitioner, or petitioner and respondent. A divorce mediator who is trained in law, can help you understand the forms and how they fit into the process you have selected. A divorce mediator can help you throughout to evolve a collaborative bargaining process which you can use well into the future.

Do I have to mediate?

Many courts now order mediation in nearly every case where parenting or change of parenting is an issue, or for modification (change) of child support or maintenance. If you wish to be excused from a court ordered mediation, due to recent domestic violence or fear of it, you must bring a motion to the court.

In mediation, are we in one room or two?

Usually both spouses are in the same room, at the same table with the mediator. Occasionally the mediator may find it helpful to talk with you individually for a few minutes, to *caucus* with each of you separately, and then go back to all three of you together. Sometimes that's all it takes to get through a sticking point. In more hostile cases, sometimes the husband and wife are in different rooms and the mediator goes back and forth. But most mediations occur in one room.

The mediator is not an expert to tell you the "right things to do." There is no right or wrong answer in divorce. There are probably a number of possible solutions, many of which would work for both of you.

Consider the two basic styles of divorce mediation. One is based on problem solving, which is the style of mediation we have described here. The other is more structured, focusing more on reaching specific agreements around what they believe to be the likely outcome in court. This style is more narrow, the former more broad in focus.

Select a mediator who has experience in the areas that you are discussing, such as parenting plans and their relation to child development, divorce taxation, financial planning, business or pension valuation and division. The more expertise the mediator has in the areas you are negotiating—especially those areas where you are unsure—the more efficient and less expensive your mediation is likely to be.

Questions to Ask a Prospective Divorce Mediator

Ask the following questions of any mediator you are considering until you find one who answers them to your satisfaction.

- Are you a specialist in family matters? How many families have you assisted in the divorce process? How long have you been a mediator?

- How much do you charge? Do you charge per couple per hour, or per person per hour? Do you meet with the parties together or separately? How long does the average divorce mediation take in your practice?

- How available are you? How quickly do you return phone calls? How long does it take to schedule an appointment?

- Do you mediate within the legal context of the outcome in court? How important is it to you that the results in mediation be similar to the probable results in court?

- Do you have a problem-solving style, or it is more outcome oriented?

How to Find a Divorce Mediator

- Ask friends or professionals whom you trust for a personal recommendation or referral.

- Look in the Yellow Pages under "Mediation Services."

- Ask at your local courthouse if they maintain a list of mediators available in your judicial district.

"If we don't work everything out in mediation, the mediator will decide for us."

A mediator does not make any decisions for you. Rather, he or she works with both of you to help you come to agreement. You keep your power to decide in mediation.

Arbitration is a very different process where you each present your "side," and the arbitrator decides.

Med-Arb

Some mediators offer a hybrid process called *med/arb.* You initially work with the professional as a mediator, then, after a time, if you do not reach agreement on any given issue the mediator becomes an arbitrator and makes that decision for you. If you are interested in med/arb, be sure you make that clear to the mediator you hire.

Arbitrators

An arbitrator, like a judge, makes the decisions for you. You argue, the arbitrator decides. An arbitrator can decide your whole divorce for you, or any single issue on which you get stuck. You can make the decision binding, that is, it becomes a court order immediately as though you had gone to court on that issue. Or, you can make the decision of the arbitrator advisory, so that you are not bound by it, but you incorporate it into your thinking as you work on developing your final agreement.

Fact-Finder, Special Master

You can ask the court to approve a person, often a lawyer with special expertise in the area in which you are stuck, to investigate and collect data and then recommend a decision to the judge or to you about these issues. Sometimes this will save you the cost of lengthy litigation, in part because you can ask for this service very early on and then use the recommendation as the starting point for building the rest of your settlement. Lawyers who specialize in family law are probably the best source for knowing who provides these services.

HIRE AN ATTORNEY

You can hire an attorney to conduct your divorce right from the beginning. You can learn the lawyer's view of the law as it applies to you and your situation. An attorney can relieve you of having to meet face to face with your soon-to-be-ex; protect you if you feel you need it; sue the blankety-blank for everything you can get, if that's what you want to do.

There are several ways to use a lawyer in divorce, but they can be classified into two fundamental categories: lawyer as *consultant*, and lawyer as *representative*. Within these two categories you have further options. Ask yourself, how much authority, responsibility, and control do I want my attorney to have? Here are some examples.

Should I Hire an Attorney?

In Colorado, whether and how you use a lawyer in your divorce is up to you. The statutes allow you to conduct your divorce "pro se" – the Latin phrase for "for yourself."

The question of whether to hire an attorney is not, in and of itself, the same as whether you are going to be friendly or adversarial, or whether you are going to keep control through the divorce process. These are determined by which lawyer you hire, and what you ask your lawyer to do for you.

Lawyer As Consultant

- You can learn a lawyer's view of the law as it applies to you and your situation before you start the legal process, or during it, including the likely outcome in court should you ask the court to decide any issues for you.

- You can do the paperwork yourselves, including your separation agreement and each run it all by a lawyer before you finalize and file your agreement.

- If you have reached agreement in mediation, you may want a lawyer to review your agreement before you sign it. The lawyer can tell you if he or she believes it to be sound and in your best interests, and make suggestions for additions and changes.

- In some instances an attorney can fill out the official court forms for you without becoming your representative. Many lawyers aren't willing to do this.

- You can work out an agreement yourselves, and one or both of you hire an attorney to do the paperwork. This may or may not include translating your agreement into legal language. Depending upon how much you ask the attorney to do for you, this could be consultant or representative. Most lawyers will not work for both of you, but only for one, which can lead to some unwanted one-sidedness in the writing. Many in this situation prefer to have a law-trained mediator, a neutral who works for both of you, prepare the written agreement.

Lawyer As Representative

- Having a lawyer as your representative means he or she is your official representative to the Court. Anything you want to file with the Court must be filed by your lawyer. Your representative must be present with you any time you appear in Court.

- A lawyer as representative will speak to your spouse's attorney, or your spouse directly if he or she is not represented, and negotiate with them for you.

- Some lawyer representatives require you not to speak to your spouse to ensure that all communications are through lawyers. This may or may not be what you need or want, so make your wishes known before you hire someone.

"I'll wait until we have our agreement signed and sealed, and then show it to an attorney."

Noooooo! It's best to do all your consulting and information gathering before you sign something. Find out about your mistakes before you make them.

Partners can hire attorneys to handle their financial separation.

"That's just my lawyer talking."

Don't kid yourself. If you hire an attorney, he or she becomes your representative. You are responsible for the way your divorce is conducted, including what your lawyer says, as well as how, when and where it is said. Your lawyer works for you.

**How to Find a Lawyer
for a Family Matter**

- Ask everybody you know who has hired a family law lawyer recently if they recommend anyone. Word of mouth from a person you trust is still the best recommendation a family lawyer can have.

- Ask your marriage counsellor, mediator, social worker, or pastor to make a recommendation.

- Look up "Lawyers" or "Attorneys" in the Yellow Pages, under the sub-heading "Divorce" or "Family Law".

- Call Metropolitan Lawyer Referral Service: (303) 831-8000.

- To check out the lawyers you are considering, call the Colorado Supreme Court, Attorney Registration Office. They will tell you if the lawyer is registered (which is mandatory for lawyers) and whether there is a public censure (discipline) on his/her record. This is the equivalent of a Better Business Bureau for lawyers.

- Look up the lawyer's name in the Martindale Hubbell lawyer directories available at your library. Lawyers and firms are rated by other lawyers for experience and expertise.

- A lawyer as representative will require you to bring in all the papers from the Great Hairy Checklist (Chapter 5), although in a more formal way, and require your spouse to produce them too. This can be helpful if you fear someone is hiding something.

- Mediation is still available for those with lawyers representing them. You and your attorney can decide whether it's important for your attorney to attend mediation sessions with you.

- You can each hire a lawyer as a representative who is specially trained in Collaborative Law, a recent innovation in legal representation. Attorneys who practice collaborative law agree, in writing, at the time they accept the case that they will work together towards settlement, and they work together with you as a team. If there is a need for 3rd party opinions or experts, such as an appraiser, or parenting evaluator, they are retained by the team and not by one side. If later it becomes clear that the matter should go to court, the attorneys and the experts are disqualified from the case and must resign.

- As your representative, a lawyer can direct operations right from the start all the way through your Decree. A lawyer can argue in court as your advocate, for your rights and interests, to maximize your outcome.

Helping Your Lawyer Work For You

The information in this book about separation agreements and divorce will help you help your attorney work for you. Knowing about many of the details in advance will save your attorney time in explaining things to you. That will save money on hourly fees. Your knowledge of the tax rules and divorce procedure will also increase your attorney's bargaining power because more options will be understood by you. Thoroughly reviewing the chapters that deal with your most difficult points can put you in a position to understand and contribute to the negotiations.

Which functions do you want your lawyer to fill for you? How much control do you wish to have over your divorce and your role in it? Before you begin interviewing attorneys, clarify what you want and expect from a legal professional. Following are some suggestions about things to consider.

Questions to Ask Any Lawyer You Are Considering

Ask the following questions of any lawyer you are considering until you find one who answers them to your satisfaction.

- Are you a specialist in family law? How many family law cases have you handled? How long have you been a lawyer?

- How much do you charge? Hourly? Retainer? Additional rate for paralegal, associate or clerical staff?

- How available are you? How quickly do you return phone calls? How long does it take to schedule an appointment?

- How adversarial or non-adversarial are you?

- Are you supportive of the mediation process? How much experience do you have assisting clients in mediation?

- Are you willing to work with me as a consultant rather than a representative? Will you allow me to negotiate directly with my spouse?

- Do you practice Collaborative Law?

Divorce Services and Consultants

Whatever process you choose to achieve your divorce, there are a number of services you can hire to help make the final result more complete and workable. Some of these services may help you with the process of coming to an agreement. They range from those who work with you both to develop your own solutions, to those who decide some of the outcome for you. You may or may not need any of them, but read through the entire list to see if any of them might be helpful to you.

PARENTING CONSULTANTS

There are many resources and services available to help you with issues concerning your children. The following are some things you can do, as well as kinds of professionals and resources concerning children:

- Speak with a co-parenting coordinator or parenting consultant about how your children are doing and for assistance in working together as parents.

All of these services and consultants are available to partners who need these kinds of professional input.

You can divorce a spouse but you cannot divorce a child.

MANDATORY PARENTING CLASS

Nearly all jurisdictions in this state require divorcing parents to attend a three to four hour parenting-after-divorce class to learn the latest on the effects of divorce on children at different developmental levels. The cost is about $50 for each parent.

- There are a number of excellent books that may help both you and your children. See the bibliography at the end of this Guidebook for some suggestions.

- Speak to the school psychologist about how your children are doing. Also ask about the kinds of difficulties which other children experience when their parents separate.

- Find a divorce recovery group for your children through your school, church, community center, local mental health center, or one of the services—public or private—which specialize in assisting children when their parents divorce.

- If your child or children are experiencing protracted difficulty adjusting to the divorce, you might hire a therapist for them.

- Hire a parenting evaluation team to advise you and your spouse, your lawyer, or the court, about what kind of parenting plan is best for your family.

- Ask the court to appoint an attorney to be a representative of your children to advise the court as to what he or she determines is in their best interest.

- Ask the court to appoint a special advocate for your children to investigate, report, and make recommendations on any issues that affect their best interest. This may be an attorney, a mental health professional, or a layperson.

- Hire an attorney for the child. This is a legal representative for your child to advocate your child's wishes.

Decide what you want from a professional. Do you want advice about your children to go directly to you? To the children? To your attorney? To the court? Do you want a professional to help you make your decision(s), or do you want someone to decide for you?

FINANCIAL CONSULTANTS

This category includes various experts who can help you unravel your money issues. You can find financial consultants by asking for recommendations from friends, lawyers, mediators or other financial consultants; through the yellow pages; or through the classified section of your local newspaper.

- Certified Public Accountant. A CPA experienced in divorce taxation issues can be a tremendous help in planning your settlement. Having an experienced CPA review several proposed settlements may save you money in the future by avoiding errors or inadequate tax planning.

• Certified Financial Planner. A CFP can project any settlement you are considering, to give you an idea of your earnings and net worth years from now. Some are certified divorce planners. This can be especially useful for those who have income-producing assets that one or the other plans to live on, or a long-term debt to pay after the divorce.

• Employment Counselor: If either or both of you are re-entering the job market after being away for some years, or are changing careers during the divorce process—whether or not by choice—some employment testing and counseling can be very useful. There are resource centers in a number of community colleges available to both men and women, which will assist you in aptitude testing, skills evaluation, resume writing, and other job-seeking skills. $5.00 of your divorce court filing fee funds these centers.

• Employment Evaluator. This service can evaluate your current skills and training and can estimate the cost of, and increased earnings from, additional training and education. Lawyers who do personal injury work are probably the best source for finding these services.

ASSET EVALUATORS

• Real Estate Appraisal. Real estate appraisers determine the value of your home, or other real estate, based on current construction costs as well as comparable properties which have sold recently. An appraiser adjusts the sold values of comparable properties by using certain industry standards, for example, a certain amount for a garage, so much for brick vs. wood, etc. Real estate appraisers are certified for certain specialties, such as residential, commercial, or agricultural. Ask their fee before they begin their work.

• Real Estate Market Analysis. A real estate salesperson or broker provides this service. He or she will review the properties sold recently in the same area and compare your property in a less formal and technical manner than the appraiser. The market analysis is usually much less expensive than an appraisal, and is often free.

• Personal Property Appraisers. These are specialists who will appraise anything from antiques to fine art, pin ball machines and beer can collections, juke boxes, pedigreed livestock, and

If you request a real estate market analysis, consider asking for three values:

• High sales value (also often the recommended listing price) the most you can get if you are willing to wait for just the right buyer.

• Fair market value – the probable value of your property if you and a willing buyer are able to compromise.

• Fire sale value – the quick sale value.

beer steins. Sometimes it is useful to ask for the same three values suggested in the real estate market analysis.

- Business Appraisers: These are ususally CPAs who specialize in valuing sole proprietor businesses or closely-held corporations. This is often the only way to obtain a value for the goodwill of a busines—what it is worth above and beyond assets minus liabilities. See Chapter 7 for more on this.

- Pension Plan Evaluators. These services are necessary only if you need to know the present value of a future income stream. For example: what is the present value of a pension which will pay only when you retire or after you reach a certain age? What is the present value of the matching portions of a defined contribution plan? See Chapter 7 for a more complete discussion of the division of future assets such as retirements, pensions, and annuities and for more about property and valuations. There are computer programs available that can evaluate a future income stream. Many lawyers and mediators have these programs.

As you can see, there is a great range of choices in how you conduct your divorce and who you select to help. The choices you make now will determine cost, duration and the over-all tone of your transition to single lives. Keep all these options in mind as you work through your own situation.

CHAPTER **3**

TAKING CARE OF YOURSELF

"It is a common tendency for us to misinterpret spiritual or relationship hunger for physical hunger. When we are 'unconscious' of the distinction, we move like robots to the refrigerator every time we feel a lack of something." Thomas F. Crum, *The Magic of Conflict.*

 This chapter is just as relevant for partners as it is for married couples.

TAKING CARE OF YOURSELF

Keeping Yourself Together So You Can Work Together

Now that you have a better understanding of the legal system and your options for navigating through it, you will soon be taking some life-changing steps to plan for the future. As you go through this process, it is important to keep track of how you are doing.

Disconnecting a marital relationship is not easy, whether you are the initiator of it, the receiver, or even when it is mutual and simultaneous. No matter which way you do it, feelings abound. Grief, hurt, fear, a sense of loss, a sense of failure, guilt, and of course anger. Many also feel relief, sometimes even joy that it's over, or that they have at last stopped denying that it's over. It's not unusual to feel grief and relief or joy at the same time.

People in divorce are much more accident prone, injury prone, and illness prone, than the general population. Be careful. Feeling edgy? Don't drive. You don't even have to be drinking for driving to be dangerous for you. Avoid other potentially dangerous activities, too, such as using knives and other sharp objects, heavy machinery, heavy anything, fast skiing or cycling. This is not the time to try bungee jumping or sky diving. Be careful around alcohol, medicine, and drugs. Even your ordinary day-to-day tasks that you take for granted can become challenging, if not dangerous, as you may find yourself forgetful, or easily distracted.

Take good care of yourself. Be patient with yourself. Try a relaxing warm bath, a cup of herb tea, soothing music, a massage. Don't be afraid to ask your friends to drive and for other help, until you calm down. Often, much of your physical and emotional energy can be so consumed by coping with the separation – actual or impending – that there is almost no energy left for taking care of yourself.

"When people fall in deep distress, their native sense departs." Sophocles.

Working out your own divorce plan with your spouse requires some important skills, such as the ability to focus and concentrate, to understand the issues – especially about money and property – and to learn more about them. You will also need the ability to communicate in ways that do not close off discussion, and the ability to take responsibility for your participation and whatever you agree to without creating the foundation for future anger and regret. These skills are all needed at a time when you feel ready to explode with some of the most difficult and intense feelings ever.

The information in this chapter about knowing yourself and understanding your feelings will help you to think clearly and participate effectively in your negotiations. If any position you take or compromise you make is based on anger, or hurt, or intimidation, or revenge, or guilt, or determination to be a victim, you are likely to conclude the divorce process with far more emotional baggage than you entered it with. It is better to do your divorce well now so that you don't remain stuck in it for years after it's over.

Just about everyone going through divorce could use psychotherapy at least part of the time. If you answer YES to any of the following questions, you might consider consulting a professional:

- Am I having trouble taking adequate care of myself (bathing, buying groceries and eating, putting gas in the car, and the like)?

- Am I having trouble meeting my obligations to my family?

- Am I having trouble carrying out my responsibilities at work?

- Am I having trouble sleeping?

- Am I having trouble starting and finishing my tasks each day?

- Do I experience anger or sadness that is out of proportion to the apparent cause?

- Do I hear myself saying things that I don't believe, or I know to be untrue, but I can't stop myself?

- Am I taking physical chances like driving too fast, not using potholders, not wearing warm enough clothing, and the like?

- Am I drinking more than usual, or does using drugs sound inviting?

Whether or not you are seeing a professional therapist, consider finding someone to talk to during this time – a friend, neighbor, pastor, or find a divorce group to join for awhile.

How to Find a Divorce Therapist

1. Get a referral from a friend you trust who can make a recommendation based on personal experience.

2. Ask your pastor, social worker, lawyer, or mediator to make a recommendation.

3. Look in the Yellow Pages under the following headings:

   Marriage and Family Counseling

   Psychotherapists

   Psychologists

   Physicians – Psychiatrists

   Divorce Services

4. Inquire at your neighborhood or county mental health center.

The Emotional Divorce Sequence

For most people, the emotional divorce follows a fairly typical pattern. The timing of the phases may be very different for each spouse, but everyone goes through them all.

1. First is the crisis, the critical point in time when the relationship is coming apart – one of you leaves or announces that it's over, or you both decide that it's over. This recognition may be experienced by one spouse significantly before the other.

2. The second phase is the reaction to the initial crisis, which frequently just feels "crazy." This phase usually extends over several months, and has identifiable stages of its own. Knowing these stages and their sequence can help you through them. See below.

3. Then, at last, comes the recovery – the healing, the sense of peace. Now, you can get on with your life.

The middle reactionary phase has five recognized stages, which are actually the stages of grief. As you read them, see if any of them seems to be where you are. (This information is from *Rebuilding*, and *When Your Relationship Ends*, by Dr. Bruce Fisher. Dr. Fisher has found that the stages of the emotional divorce parallel the five stages of grief as outlined originally by Dr. Elizabeth Kubler-Ross. Used here by permission.)

"Give sorrow words; the grief that does not speak / Whispers the o'er-fraught heart and bids it break." Shakespeare, *Macbeth.*

Grief has many faces besides full blown sorrow. It frequently appears as a feeling of loneliness, difficulty in concentrating, and a sense of being weak and helpless. Sometimes it will bubble up as a kind of anger, not so much anger at the sorrow but at the inability to "be yourself" and get things done like you usually do. When you feel unable to control your mood swings or your ability to be responsible and productive, it can be frightening.

"We cannot direct the wind but we can adjust our sails." *City of Hope.*

Stage 1: The first stage of grief is emotional shock. "This isn't happening to me." "This isn't real." There is a numbness about it. We suppress the anger and hurt and act as though nothing has happened. We put on our best manners. We keep it all inside and don't tell anybody, and put up walls and protect ourselves.

The next four stages are each steps toward accepting the end and letting go.

Stage 2: Anger appears in the second stage – anger turned outward towards others. It's easy to lash out angrily and inappropriately in a variety of situations. Much of the anger, about "how terrible it was to be married to him/her," is expressed to friends and others and not to the spouse. The anger, however, is a "Catch 22" because of fear that if we are too angry at the departing spouse (or the one we are leaving or think we should leave) there will be no getting back together. The emotional door is usually still open at this stage – there is strong ambivalence about wanting the spouse back.

Stage 3: The third stage is yet another attempt to prolong the relationship. We repeatedly bargain and compromise – we try to make deals with our spouse, in thought if not in action. This can be a "teddy bear" stage (see chapter 3) where we are willing to accommodate almost anything in order to have the relationship continue. This can be a dangerous stage because many couples get back together at this point by agreeing to be teddy bears, yet most of us can't stay that way for very long before emerging angrier than before. Frequently people get back together at this point because they can't stand the loneliness and the unhappiness of ending the relationship – choosing the spouse again as the lesser of two evils.

Stage 4: The fourth stage is the "blahs," a kind of depression and internal questioning: "Is this all there is to life?" This is the darkness before the dawn. It's a stage of growth where we build a stronger identity, and find life more meaningful, more purposeful. However, some people in this stage become suicidal when they find themselves discouraged at having worked so hard on this relationship which they now must let go. This stage frequently comes a long time after the actual separation – we are often surprised to find ourselves depressed about it all over again. Research has found that people who are aware of this stage get through it more easily.

Stage 5: The last stage brings acceptance of the loss of the love relationship. We are finally free of the pain of grief. The end of grief is the acceptance of the end of the relationship. We find internal peace, become centered, and once again move on in our lives.

It's wise to get through all five stages of grief before entering a new relationship. You may experience them in a different order, and they may overlap. Many who work professionally with people in the divorce process say the grief process takes eighteen months to two years for most people.

Look in The Mirror

If you feel tempted to blame your present misery on your spouse, look in the mirror and pretend you see your spouse there as your reflection. You might notice that when you think or say, "I hate it when you do that" is really code for "I hate it when I do that, and I keep doing it."

Peggy Lee sang: "Is that all there is? If that's all there is, then let's keep dancing."

Rate Your Fears

Directions: Each of you list the fears you have relative to your separation or divorce, and rate each on a scale of 1-10.

My worst fears are: Rating

My worst fears are: Rating

Distinguish between a good belly laugh and cynicism. Cynicism is not funny.

Paste your favorite family or divorce cartoon here:

Staying Sane Under Insane Conditions

Passing through the five stages of grief is like navigating your ship through a storm in the Twilight Zone. Try to recognize where you are in relation to these stages. Pay close attention to yourself throughout, and expect to be surprised. Here are some tips to help you along the way.

- *Fear* is often the trigger for doing some of the craziest or most hurtful things. It can lure you away from your deepest sense of yourself. Tell your worst fears to someone, or write them for yourself. To ensure that the fears do not control your choices, examine each fear. Rate just how realistic or likely an eventuality it is, on a scale of one to ten (ten being the most likely). For those fears you've rated over 5, ask yourself what you can and should do to minimize the risk. For example, as a marriage ends we might harbor a deep fear of "being a bag lady/bum." To minimize this risk, be responsible for budgeting your post-divorce life style and realistically assessing how much of that you can earn.

- *Let them flow*, strange as it may seem, is the way to deal with grief and its component emotions. Cry, weep, wail, however it is you do it, in ways that don't hurt yourself, or anyone else. Avoiding these emotions takes all our available energy, like trying to hold the door shut in a tornado, leaving us exhausted and depressed. Acknowledging them is the only way to release them. You must let them pass through, like opening both the front door and a window so the breeze can flow through. You can maintain yourself in your job, and perform better at work, by actually allocating time before or after, for expressing strong emotions in a non-destructive manner, without making anyone wrong. You can do this in a number of ways. Play music that helps you weep. Write a letter expressing your anger, but do not send it. Write or call a close friend. Therapy can help too.

- *Find your sense of humor,* even if you think there isn't anything in your situation to laugh about. Think back to the last ridiculous thing you did. If you cannot find anything to laugh about in yourself, find something out there, somewhere, that will help you have at least one good belly laugh. Find something to laugh about at least once a day. Cartoons, comedy videos, animals, pets, children – all of these can be of help.

- *Blame is a black hole.* Allow your feelings to flow without placing blame for them – especially on your spouse. Keep acknowledging your emotions (grief, anger, hurt, fear, etc.) within yourself, without focusing on your spouse, or anyone else.

- *Guilt is the desire to blame yourself.* Take responsibility for whatever you did or didn't do in your relationship without judging any of it as wrong. Figure out what you need to learn from it. Try to see your own actions and omissions in terms of their results, both in your relationship and inside yourself. This step is vital to moving on to a new relationship, one that won't be a repeat of the one that's ending.

- *Be patient.* The phases of the emotional divorce, although easily described, take time to live through. To rush through them is to try to push the river or rush the harvest. Allow each stage the time it needs.

- *Celebrate when you can.* Give yourself exactly what you want for birthdays and Christmas, Hanukkah, or Kwanzaa. Recognize your wedding anniversary. Don't set yourself up to receive nothing on important occasions. Don't abandon yourself. Celebrate your successes, no matter how small.

- *Create your own support system.* Maintain connection with several people with whom you can discuss anything. Be sure you find people who are genuinely caring, compassionate, and not just blindly militant on your behalf.

Being a Good Parent is Part of Taking Care of Yourself

Part of taking care of yourself is to be sure that you do your very best as a parent at this difficult time. It goes without saying, children need and deserve good parenting. Your own sense of self-esteem will plummet if you feel in any way that you are neglecting or harming your children. See How to be a Good Parent Through the Divorce Process in Chapter 8.

Whining doesn't solve anything.

Healing Has its Ups and Downs

Healing, or recovering, from the pain of separation and divorce would be so much easier if it were a steady and consistent improvement from miserable to "feelgood". But it's not. You might have one really good day followed by three depressing and confusing downers. Sometimes when you're feeling buffeted about by emotions you don't understand, you think you're going nuts. Know that progress from misery to complete recovery is a zigzag, not a straight line. Whether you're feeling better or worse than yesterday, or a few minutes ago, know that even as you feel like you're bouncing around, your recovery is under way.

You can divorce a parent, but you cannot divorce a child.

Automatic Injunction:
(From the Petition in Chapter 6)

Both of you are bound by the terms of the following injunction the moment your case is filed and served (see Chapter 6). If you are filing as co-petitioners, you are *presumed* to be bound by it as soon as you sign the Petition.

AUTOMATIC TEMPORARY INJUNCTION

1. Both parties are restrained from transferring, encumbering, concealing, or in any way disposing of, without the consent of the other party, or an order of the Court, any marital property, except in the usual course of business or for the necessities of life and requiring each party to notify the other party of any proposed extraordinary expenditures and to account for all extraordinary expenditures made after the injunction is in effect;

2. Both parties are enjoined from molesting or disturbing the peace of the other party; and

3. Both parties are restrained from removing the minor child(ren) of the parties, if any, from the state without the consent of the other party or an order of the Court.

4. Both parties are restrained, without at least fourteen days' advance notification and the written consent of the other party or an order of the Court, from canceling, modifying, terminating, or allowing to lapse for nonpayment of premiums, any policy of health insurance, homeowner's or renter's insurance, or automobile insurance that provides coverage to either of the parties or the minor children or any policy of life insurance that names either of the parties or the minor children as a beneficiary.

How to Handle Potential Violence and Other Stressful Encounters

Fear, panic, feeling frozen emotionally and intellectually, are all results of relationships which are on the edge of violence. Both spouses may feel these, and both or only one may react with violence. Such violence, the experts say, is very often a result of feeling out of control (not necessarily that someone else is controlling you, but that you aren't in control of you). Some people use violence to make their partner feel helpless, in order to feel powerful.

If you feel, at any time in the course of your separation, that you or your spouse are to the point of violence or abuse, whether physical or extreme verbal assault, then do the following:

*   *Get physically separated.* Go to solid friends or family. Some may need to go to the nearest safehouse.

*   *If there is a neutral place where your children can go,* take them there. Grandparents can be a Godsend or a real curse. If they will defend the children's peace against both of you, they are the ones to go to. Neutral, mutual friends with children your children's age are often best. Sometimes, if you leave and take the children with you – especially to a secret place – that, too, can feel violent to the person left behind.

*   *Do not destroy, sell, give away, or secret any property* which the other party is likely to feel is marital. Such unilateral action often feels like violence at the receiving end and generally escalates hostility.

*   *Do not try to move the divorce along too fast.* Jumping into the adversarial process or even forcing yourself into mediation or counseling when you are still hurt and fearful may only convert anger to rage and rage to more violence.

*   *Establishing certain agreements will go a long way* toward helping you get back in control of your individual lives: mutual agreements to stay apart, pay certain debts, preserve certain property; agreements about seeing the children without seeing each other; mutual promises of no violence or derogatory comments about each other. Try writing down what you yourself are willing to do along these lines. Make no demands about what you expect your spouse to

do. Then sign it and give it to a trusted friend to give to your spouse. Such a proposal may open a door to settlement.

If none of these suggestions works or is even possible, and you fear that violence is imminent or inevitable, then you may need to use the courts to protect you. You should know that, in practice, a court order is a piece of paper. Sometimes it can push someone over the edge, so they no longer can be controlled by law. Sometimes the order is ignored.

There is a county court procedure for dealing with domestic violence. Forms and instructions may be obtained through the county court or Bradford Publishing.

Protection orders are also available through your divorce action in district court. If you need more information on this subject, take care of yourself by consulting with an attorney who has expertise in the area of domestic violence and abuse.

If violence happens, or is threatened, call the police to report it immediately, and be willing to follow through with your charges. When it gets to this point you must seek intervention.

Spouses in marriages in which there has been actual violence may still be able to have a friendly divorce, usually with the assistance of a mediator with experience in this area. A great deal of self-knowledge and insight on the part of both spouses has to occur, however, before this is possible.

Protection order: Written action by a court which prohibits a person from doing certain acts, for example from entering a certain property. Doing the prohibited act is then punishable by the court.

Restraining or protection orders are available to partners through a county court procedure under the Domestic Abuse statute.

Beware the Eternal Return

Statistics show that without some introspection, self-reflection, and change, most of us will form a relationship with someone almost exactly like the person we just ended with. We all repeat patterns we have learned, especially in childhood. One of the keys to peace with yourself is knowing when you do it.

MOVING FROM ONE HOUSEHOLD TO TWO

MOVING FROM ONE HOUSEHOLD TO TWO

If you have decided to move apart—whether you are doing a trial separation, a legal separation, or a dissolution of marriage—you will be faced with a number of immediate choices. There will be some choices which you will want to make, but shouldn't; there will be others which you will not want to face, but should. This chapter is designed to help you to choose wisely for the short term.

You must make sure that as you separate nothing falls through the cracks. The children must be cared for on a daily basis; your bills must get paid; your property must be maintained. It is vital that at this difficult time you keep your communications open so that you can make clear agreements about all of these matters.

A useful first step is to decide the time frame for each of your interim agreements. You may make an agreement about paying the bills, for example, for three or six months, and an agreement about managing the children day to day for only one month or six weeks until you see how it works for everyone. Now is a good time to try different schemes to discover what works and doesn't work for you.

If you are planning a legal separation or divorce, and will therefore be filing papers in court, the interim agreements you make in this chapter may be made into a temporary order of the court, as explained at the end of this chapter. Many couples do not need to write down their temporary arrangements because their communications are clear and there is complete trust and reliability. Others want something written, more formal or official.

Your financial separation should be carefully planned. A common problem results when, sensing an imminent separation, one spouse fears that the other will do something that will cost a lot of money. So, to "protect" the money, he or she closes the joint account and puts the money in a separate account. The other spouse then panics, matters get out of control, and the legal fees soar.

Sometimes instead of fear, anger takes over. The working spouse will disallow the non-working spouse from using credit cards or bank accounts. This will nearly always result in bad things happening to the targeted spouse's credit rating and ability to survive financially. Judges usually frown on that.

Temporary agreement: Formal accords, usually written, between spouses concerning use of property, payment of debts, children and their support, temporary maintenance and taxes, to govern or affect the time stated in the agreement, which is generally from the time of the agreement until the final decree.

Temporary orders: Court orders which affect divorcing or legally separating spouses from the date of the order until their final decree; may be the result of a court hearing, status conference, or trial, or an order approving the spouses' temporary agreement.

"Once you are physically separated you are legally separated."

This assumption is incorrect, and can be very costly. You are legally separated only if and when you receive a signed decree of legal separation from a court.

Temporary Responsibility and Use, Not Permanent Ownership

Your temporary agreement does not decide who ultimately gets what, only the use of property, responsibility for keeping it up, and who will make what payments. Even the court is cautioned by statute not to let temporary agreements dictate the way things should be permanently. Temporary agreements are opportunities for you to experiment and try out ideas.

Partners can avoid much difficulty, and save money too, by carefully planning your separation so that neither of you gets in over your head, and no one is out on the curb either. You can make temporary agreements between you, as suggested in this chapter, making clear to each other just how long you mean temporary to be.

Residence Checklist – Short Term

Fill in the property address, occupant and the amount of the payment in the appropriate column for which of you will be responsible for making the payment in the short term. At this point the person who occupies a residence does not necessarily have to be the one responsible for all its expenses. Make two copies so you can repeat for a 2nd home or for non-residence real estate, such as rentals, or a vacation condo.

Address: _____

Occupant: _____

	Husband	Wife
Mortgage/ Rent	_____	_____
Mortgage (2nd)	_____	_____
Property Tax (if not in mtg.)	_____	_____
Insurance (if not in mtg.)	_____	_____
Homeowners Dues	_____	_____
Repairs	_____	_____
Capital Improvements	_____	_____
Regular Upkeep and Maintenance	_____	_____
Utilities	_____	_____
Appliance & Utility Repair	_____	_____

If you feel the need to have a written agreement, transfer the agreements on this checklist, as you reach them, to the Sample Temporary Agreement at the end of this chapter or to JDF 1109 on the CD-ROM.

These and other kinds of unilateral actions, without discussion or notice—let alone agreement—usually escalate the situation from very warm, to a mild simmer, to a fast boil. Suddenly your separation is no longer a private change of life, but a very expensive and public war. The more your early actions are based on joint decisions, made ahead of time, the more chance you have of finishing your divorce in peace, if not in harmony.

Who Uses What and Who Pays for It

In order for a couple to begin to live apart as satisfactorily as possible, they need a clear understanding of who will get to use what property, who will live in the home, how the mortgage or rent will be paid, who will drive which car, and who will be responsible for the car and other expenses. There are usually several major items of personal property about which you need understandings. For example, the computer, the washer and dryer, the ski condo time-share, the camping gear. Even if you are separating within the same residence, you will need to face these same questions.

You are not deciding ownership at this point, only temporary use. Do not try to resolve the entire property picture right at the beginning. Just settle who uses what, and who makes what payments for now.

Be certain that you plan clearly how long your temporary agreement is to last. Having a definite cut-off point (3-6 months is a likely term) helps you stay focused on finishing the final agreement. Be certain to define what circumstances will send you back to the bargaining table (loss of job, for example).

HOMES

Who will stay in the family home and who will move out? The answer to this question has serious financial consequences, both short term and long term. This chapter is about the short term.

If one or both of you wants to keep the house in the long term, test this plan for at least a month or two before committing to it. Use your temporary period to experiment. This is especially important if you're not sure whether you want to do this "for the sake of the children," or because you love the house so much.

For example, the lower income spouse may want to stay on in the house since this spouse might have difficulty qualifying for a new home loan. If the house is very large, very expensive or difficult to keep up, the burden may not be worth it. If the spouse who wants to keep the home is not the one who usually did the repairs or tended the lawn, the amount of headache involved may be an unpleasant surprise.

How will you as a couple finance the additional expense of a new home or apartment along with the expenses of the family home? Some people find they have to spend savings, sell stock, or take out a loan. If so, begin thinking about who will repay the loan, or whose share of your property the repayment will come from.

Even for the short term, be sure you list all the expenses of a family home, plus those of a new second home for the spouse who is moving.

You may wish to consider whether either of you may have another adult living with you to help with the expenses. Are there any restrictions between you as to who this person may be? Do any of your children contribute anything toward the costs or the upkeep of either home in money or in labor?

CARS AND OTHER MOTOR VEHICLES

Make clear agreements with each other about who will drive which car for the time being. Nothing needs to be done at this point about changing the names on the title. Car loans and automobile insurance should be unchanged and payments must be kept current. You may need to talk about joint use of a single car. Think in terms of problem solving—what's going to work—and a reasonable sharing of comforts and conveniences along with burdens and inconveniences.

In the permanent property division, the spouse who gets the car ordinarily gets the loan on it too. But you do not have to do it that way in the short term. You can usually keep both cars on the same insurance policy until the date of the divorce or until the next time the premium comes due after the date of the divorce. Discuss who will be responsible for paying the premium, or whether and in what proportion it will be shared. Once your case is filed, the Temporary Injunction is the petition restricts you from canceling insurance without following a detailed procedure.

OTHER PROPERTY AND OTHER REGULAR EXPENSES

You may wish to clarify which of you gets to use other items during this period, such as the computer, sound system, TV or home theater, pets, RV, microwave, camping and other sports equipment. Make an agreement that whoever gets to use these items for now will maintain them until you reach a final decision. Remember, you are not deciding ownership, only use.

Motor Vehicle Checklist – Short Term

Directions: Fill in the vehicle year and make and the amount of each expense in the appropriate column for which of you will pay it in the short term. At this point the person who has the use of a vehicle does not necessarily have to be the one responsible for its expenses. Repeat for additional vehicles.

Year & make of vehicle _____

	Husband	Wife
Loan/lease payment	_____	_____
Insurance	_____	_____
Gas & Oil	_____	_____
Maintenance	_____	_____
Other	_____	_____

Year & make of vehicle _____

	Husband	Wife
Loan/lease payment	_____	_____
Insurance	_____	_____
Gas & Oil	_____	_____
Maintenance	_____	_____
Other	_____	_____

If you feel you need a written temporary agreement, transfer the agreements on this checklist, as you reach them, to the Sample Temporary Agreement at the end of this chapter or to JDF 1109 on the CD-ROM.

Other Property Checklist – Short Term

Directions: List in the left hand column those items of property which are important to both of you. Then put a check in the "Husband" or "Wife" column to indicate which of you will have the use of it for the time being, and be responsible for maintaining it.

Item	Husband	Wife
_____	____	____
_____	____	____
_____	____	____
_____	____	____
_____	____	____
_____	____	____
_____	____	____
_____	____	____
_____	____	____
_____	____	____
_____	____	____
_____	____	____
_____	____	____

Similarly, you must decide who will make your fixed payments, such as life and medical insurance, installment loans and credit cards, and student loan payments. Once you file your case, you must follow the Temporary Injunction regarding cancellation of any insurance.

 It is essential at this time that you either agree not to use any credit cards except together, or that you each choose one or more credit cards to use and be responsible for their payment. For example, you may wish to retain the use of an oil company credit card for your car expenses.

Whatever your agreement about use and payment of credit cards or payment of debts, creditors are not bound by your agreement. They will still have the right to "come after" both of you for any missed payments. See Temporary Teeth, page 63.

Fixed Payments Checklist

List your creditors in the left column. For each creditor, write the amount of the payment in the column of the spouse who will be responsible for making the payment. Be sure to indicate the time period for any payment that is not monthly.

Creditor	Husband	Wife
_____	$ _____	$ _____
_____	$ _____	$ _____
_____	$ _____	$ _____
_____	$ _____	$ _____
_____	$ _____	$ _____
_____	$ _____	$ _____
_____	$ _____	$ _____
_____	$ _____	$ _____
_____	$ _____	$ _____
_____	$ _____	$ _____
_____	$ _____	$ _____

If you feel you need a written temporary agreement, transfer the agreements on these checklists, as you reach them, to the Sample Temporary Agreement at the end of this chapter or to JDF 1109 on the CD-ROM.

NECESSARY PURCHASES

Whenever a family expands from one household to two, some items will need to be duplicated. Such items might be: children's furniture, couch, bed, washer/dryer, towels, sheets, coffee pot, iron, tools, stereo, TV.

 Purchasing these items could easily swallow your budget. You may need to limit this list to essentials, with each household bearing some burden of doing without. You might color-code different items—red for essentials needed right away; green for things needed soon, etc.

Consider sharing instead of duplicating. Alternate times with the washer/dryer. Use the camper on alternate weekends. Mow your lawns on different days with the same mower.

Share the burden of being without or being inconvenienced. For example, if one of you has no washer/dryer and must use the laundromat, perhaps the other could do without the stereo. Some couples prefer to separate within the same residence in order to save on these items and not have to incur this expense right at the beginning.

Agree that neither of you will make major purchases other than those on the DIN List below. This will help you build trust in one another's sense of what is necessary. Agree that neither of you will borrow any money, or use any credit cards, without the consent of the other.

Duplicate Items Needed List ("DIN" List)

Directions: List in the "Item" column those things which you will want to acquire to make your two households complete. Work together on this. Under the heading "Husband" or "Wife," list the maximum cost for each item that you agree needs to be duplicated for that person's household.

Category	Item	Husband	Wife
Furniture			
	_____	_____	_____
	_____	_____	_____
	_____	_____	_____
	_____	_____	_____
	_____	_____	_____
	_____	_____	_____
Linens			
	_____	_____	_____
	_____	_____	_____
	_____	_____	_____
	_____	_____	_____

Category	**Item**	**Husband**	**Wife**
Appliances			
	_____	_____	_____
	_____	_____	_____
	_____	_____	_____
	_____	_____	_____
Kitchen items			
	_____	_____	_____
	_____	_____	_____
	_____	_____	_____
	_____	_____	_____
	_____	_____	_____
	_____	_____	_____
	_____	_____	_____
Children's things			
	_____	_____	_____
	_____	_____	_____
	_____	_____	_____
	_____	_____	_____
Other			
	_____	_____	_____
	_____	_____	_____
	_____	_____	_____
	_____	_____	_____
	_____	_____	_____
Total Cost		_____	_____

This DIN list is an example of a private agreement between you and your spouse that will probably not find its way into a formal Temporary or Permanent Agreement or form.

YOUR CREDIT AND YOUR DIVORCE

Without credit, you can't get a credit card. Without a credit card, you cannot rent a car, make hotel or travel reservations, buy a truck or furniture on time, or have that margin of borrowing power for emergencies. In short, it is very important that you protect your credit in your divorce. This section is about how to emerge from a divorce with the highest possible credit ratings for each of you.

You should each immediately obtain your individual credit rating as soon as you decide to separate. This way you have ample time and the legal right to remedy any errors between you, and to add any missing accounts for either of you. Look under "Credit Reporting Agencies" in the Yellow Pages and call at least one. A recorded message will tell you how to obtain your credit report. Be sure that you request your individual reports, not your joint report, and that you each give any previous name(s).

Credit ratings are the history of the way you pay your bills. This history is kept by a number of credit reporting agencies to which the individual creditors (credit card companies, department stores, banks, credit unions) report the relative regularity and promptness of payments by those who owe them money. Marriage and divorce affect credit ratings indirectly, but profoundly.

If the debt or credit card was applied for by both of you and based on both your incomes, then it is a pretty good bet that it has been reporting in both your names and contributing to both your individual credit ratings. You will see the debt on both your credit reports.

If, however, one of you had the card or debt before the marriage, or it was applied for by one of you based on only that one income, then the credit may not be reporting in both names. This often happens when one spouse is the primary wage-earner. In such cases, the non-wage-earning spouse may well not have a credit rating at all or have an inadequate one because it does not contain some of the major credit accounts used during the marriage. You will know this is the situation if your credit report comes back blank, or does not contain any information about debts you know were paid on jointly.

The only way an account that is in one name only will report into both your credit ratings is if the person to whom that card was issued requests in writing, before the divorce is final, that their spouse receive credit on that account. The spouse who wants the credit cannot do this. So, if you are agreeing to finish paying off a

"I signed all the checks which paid the bills and they were all written on our joint account, so I know I have good credit."

The correct information: Credit is reported automatically only in the name of the person who applied for the account or loan and on whose income it was based. If you did not sign the application, then this record of payments on your marital debt may not be reporting in your name at all.

Notes:

debt or credit card as part of your settlement, be certain that particular debt or credit card is reporting on your own credit rating. Otherwise, you may pay off a bill which will not establish or benefit your own credit.

You may build up a credit rating for a low- or non-income spouse by making certain all the high-rated credit cards are reporting in his or her name before the divorce. Then, pay off the balances on these cards at the time of the divorce. Have the low-income spouse keep at least one of the best-rated cards—with a provision that he or she will 1) use the card for small purchases that will be paid off quickly, 2) apply for a card in his or her own name within a certain number of months or years after the final decree, and then 3) close the old joint account.

If you close any high-rated credit card accounts before the divorce, or notify the issuing bank to "take my spouse off the card," you may have sabotaged your spouse's ability to build a satisfactory credit rating. A better arrangement is to put all the credit cards in a sealed envelope and leave it with a trusted friend or in a safe deposit box out of sight, and agree not to charge anything until you finish your agreement. Then make clear agreements about all the cards as part of your temporary agreement. See the bibliography to read more about credit.

Notes:

Children

The time when parents begin living apart is one of the most stressful for children. Their worst fear is of losing a parent. They need both parents to stay actively involved in their lives at this time. Children can readily adjust to the separations and transitions involved in two-household parenting. They adjust better when their parents work together to support each other's relationship with them. You might wish to read through the information about how children react to the divorce process in Chapter 8 of this book. It is full of useful tips about putting together a parenting plan that will work for your children.

HOW TO BE A GOOD PARENT THROUGH THE DIVORCE PROCESS

Children feel more secure when they are confident that their parents can take care of themselves. If they feel you are not doing that, they will try to take care of you, and the parent-child relationship becomes reversed. Therefore taking care of yourself at this difficult time is not only good for you, it is in the best interest of your children.

Critical to good parenting throughout the divorce process is insulating the children from any hostilities between the parents. This means managing your own conflict well. Work toward strengthening your children's sense of security while they navigate their own choppy waters as you separate and divorce. It's a time to be very careful what you say, and to whom you say it. Think your conduct through carefully.

WHO MAKES WHAT DECISIONS ABOUT THE CHILDREN

The two major kinds of decision-making about children are day-to-day decisions, and major decisions. Day-to-day decisions—menus, schedules, bed times, transportation—are made by the parent who has the children at the time.

The divorce statute suggests that the major decisions include "the health, education, and general welfare of the child." Most divorcing parents find this definition unworkably inclusive. It is important that the two of you evolve your own more specific list of decisions which you agree you must share during this interim period. Some examples are:

- activities of our children which will take place on both parents' time with them.

- major expenses for our children which we expect the other parent to share.

"Divorce always hurts children." "You just can't possibly be a responsible parent and get a divorce."

The truth, shown by extensive research, is that divorce does not necessarily hurt children. What does hurt them is ongoing hostilities between their parents, whether or not there is a divorce. Research shows that children of divorcing parents who stopped fighting were as well adjusted as those raised in successful marriages. The same research also shows that children of parents who stayed together, but who continued to fight, had as much trouble adjusting as children of the continually hostile divorce. So it's not the divorce that hurts the children, it's the ongoing anger and hostility that are harmful.

"Children have never been very good at listening to their elders, but they have never failed to imitate them." James Baldwin, "Fifth Avenue, Uptown." *Nobody Knows My Name.*

Parenting-After-Divorce Classes

Just about all Colorado courts now require divorcing parents to attend a one-time class about the effect of divorce on themselves and their children. These classes teach coparenting skills and strategies. The court will require a certificate of completion to be in the file before determining parenting issues and before it will enter a final decree. Usually the parties are responsible for mailing or bringing the certificate to the court. In some jurisdictions, the instructor will take care of this. The cost of the class is usually $35 to $50 each, which can be waived by the instructor upon a showing of serious need.

Temporary Parenting Plan: Parental Responsibility. Designates the way parents will make the major decisions about their children during the time between their separation and divorce.

They can agree that one parent will be responsible for making the decisions or that both parents will share all major decisions. Or, parents may select certain decisions to be made by one parent and certain other decisions to be made by the other parent—with or without negotiation beforehand. Other decisions may be made jointly.

Partners who are parents have all the same concerns and responsibilities as married parents when moving from one household to two. You probably won't be ordered to take a parenting-after-divorce class, but you aren't prohibited from taking one, and you might find it helpful.

- major planned elective medical or dental care, but not emergency medical care.

- how we will share or divide birthdays and holidays which occur during this interim period.

Shared or mutual decision-making means you keep talking until you reach agreement. You may agree that some or all of the major decisions, or categories of decisions, will be made by one or the other of you. Even if you are agreeing that one parent alone will make particular decisions, you may list matters about which the decision-maker must consult with the other parent. This means you must discuss it beforehand, even though the decision-maker still makes the final decision. For example, one parent might make all the clothing purchases, but discuss ahead of time the limit on spending and how to pay for it.

Naming one parent to make certain decisions and the other parent to make others allows some parents to share this important aspect of parenting without creating endless confrontations. If one of you has historically made the decisions about medical care, and the other has always had the last word about education issues, you can continue this way of doing things in your temporary agreement.

Whatever your choices, being clear about who makes what decisions about your children helps them feel secure, and to know that you are in control.

Notes:

Temporary Parenting Decisions List

Directions: List in one of the categories below, the decisions concerning your children which you anticipate must be made during this interim period.

We will make the following decisions together, jointly:

1. X-mas gifts,
2. Classes – Emily's music is paid thru May
   Ryan – Rock climbing?
3. Extra activities – golf, climbing, skiing
4. Extra medical
5. How often Emily might stay at aftercare
6. When the kids go to NH (Feb, July)
7. Work schedules, pick up + drop off

Mother will make the following decisions:

1.

2.

3.

Mother must consult Father on (all) (#   ).

Father will make the following decisions:

1.

2.

3.

Father must consult Mother on (all) (#   ).

If you feel you need a written temporary agreement, transfer the agreements on this list, when completed, to the Sample Temporary Agreement at the end of this chapter or to JDF 1109 on the CD-ROM.

Temporary Parenting Plan: Physical Residential care.

Where the children of separated parents live between the time of separation and final decree.

"Children should have only one home."

Research shows that children adjust better to divorce when they continue to have stable and loving relationships with both parents. This can be accomplished in two homes.

"Children get confused when their parents' lifestyles are too different."

Not necessarily. Some experts do say that for two households to work well together, they shouldn't be too terribly far apart in value systems. For example, if one parent lives a "laid-back" lifestyle and the other household uses linen napkins, the child may begin to wonder whether to be like Mom and her household, or Dad and his. Studies show that children can make these transitions – but not frequently and with support and preparation from their parents in every transition.

WHERE WILL THE CHILDREN STAY

The temporary period is an excellent time to try out various parenting plans. Put together a consistent schedule for six weeks or so, try it out, and then assess it. You may discover that some aspects of your plan do not work well for your family. Talk about it with each other; then listen to the children's input; reach agreement and make the needed changes and adjustments. Don't expect to know right away what arrangements are going to be best for your children in the long term. Your first plan may well not be your final agreement. You will need flexibility.

Some parents want equal time sharing when it may not be in the children's best interest at this time. For example, infants and very young children may not be developmentally ready for two homes on a 50-50 basis. Small children may be better served by gradually expanding the overnights with the other parent, with a goal of reaching 50-50, or roughly equal time sharing by a certain age, such as 5, or 6, or 7. However, a younger child may do quite well in equal time sharing if his or her connections have been strong with both parents, and/or if there is an older sibling making the same transitions on the same schedule. Teenagers, who can do well with equal time sharing, need to have a great deal to say about where and how they spend their time.

For more on the significance of your child's developmental age for your parenting plans, see Chapter 8. This would be an excellent time to read *Children of Divorce*, by Baris and Garrity, or any other books listed in the bibliography at the end of this Guidebook which relate to your circumstances.

HOW TO TELL THE CHILDREN

How do you tell your children about your separation? Have both parents there, if possible, and tell the children not only your decision to separate, but also your plan. Help them understand that you are not separating from or "divorcing" them. Tell them that you will always take care of them, no matter what. Tell them how important it is to both of you that they continue to have both of you. Be concrete with them about your plans.

When appropriate, share your six-week calendar with your children and ask for their input. Listen to their concerns about the mechanics: "Where will my bicycle live?" "How will my ice skates get from one house to the other?" "I only have one computer, how will I do my homework?"

If you can, discuss in advance the physical plans for your separation with the children. Involve them in the doing—take them with you to see possible new apartments or homes so they can participate in the creation of their second home. They will have their own ideas about which toys and books should be at which place and how they want their spaces to look. You may have to override some of their choices, but they should be allowed to participate and to express themselves, and even to carry out some of their wishes in their own way.

Notes:

Six Week Parenting Plan and Calendar

Directions: Using the material from the following page, fill in your parenting time for the next six weeks. This calendar ends the week with Saturday and Sunday together. Most published calendars divide the weekend by placing Sunday as the first day of the week, and Saturday the last—a picture which is generally confusing when working out parenting times.

Mon.	Tues.	Wed.	Thurs.	Fri.	Sat.	Sun.

USING YOUR SIX-WEEK CALENDAR

Fill in the following information on the calendar on the previous page. Make several photocopies first for your rough draft(s). (Sometimes it is useful to use different colored pens for each parent, or each member of the family.)

1. The dates for the six-week period you are planning, and any holidays or other special days, such as a child's birthday.

2. Parents' fixed schedules. For example: work hours, fixed meetings and appointments.

3. Children's fixed schedules, such as school hours, and planned regular activities such as soccer practice, piano lesson, Cub Scouts. Discuss whether a change in the children's day care schedule is desirable. On the one hand it may be just the time to make a needed change; on the other hand, if both of you are moving, keeping the day-care schedule the same may help a young child feel more secure at this difficult time.

4. Appointments (doctor, dentist) and special events already committed to (recital, track meet, reunion).

5. Looking at the six-weeks as a whole, begin to discuss and even pencil in some possible parenting times. For example, school nights with one parent, weekend or vacation nights with the other; alternating weeks with each parent; dividing each week 4-3, 5-2, or 6-1; dividing each two week period in half with a 4-3-3-4 schedule; dove-tailing with one or both parents' variable work schedule.

6. Be sure you take into account your children's ages and stage of development. Your time plan for an infant will be very different from the plan you would make for a teenager.

7. Indicate on the calendar who will provide the transportation each time, who will pick-up or drop-off. The further apart you live, the more important the transportation issue will become. Whenever you bring your children to their other parent, you demonstrate your support and willingness for your children to leave you and to relate to their other parent.

8. Write or at least discuss any items which must move back and forth with the children, such as clothing, boots, homework, and musical instruments.

If you feel the need to have a written temporary agreement, transfer the agreements you make about the residential physical care of your children into the Sample Temporary Agreement at the end of this chapter or use JDF1109 on the CD-ROM.

The Budget Crunch

Two together still live more cheaply than one. Two apart are more expensive than one. Negotiating early through the stark reality of the high cost of two households is a major key to keeping peace throughout the separation and divorce process. As you separate, it is important that you and your spouse have a complete understanding of which income will pay for which expenses.

The purpose of this section is to help you keep track of your incomes and budget your expenses as your family moves from one household into two.

TRACKING YOUR INCOMES

The word "income" can mean very different things to different people. To the worker it probably means spendable earnings. To the IRS it means what is taxed. In the Colorado Child Support Guideline, it can mean potential earnings that are not actually coming in, and even imputed income nobody actually receives.

Using the "Income Tracker," write down the income each of you expects to receive during the interim period you are planning for. List both incomes you are certain of receiving, and that which you might receive. Definite income includes your base pay before commission, salary, draw, guaranteed hours, required overtime, regular bonuses. Possible income may include commissions, bonuses, one-time sales or liquidation, irregular overtime, irregular bonuses.

Write down both your gross and net incomes. The gross is the larger number, before anything is withheld. The net number is the amount you bring home, after all the withholding and deductions from your paycheck. This number may change as you make agreements about tax planning and saving for your futures, but use the present actual numbers for now.

If you are self-employed, your gross income is your business net, i.e., your total business receipts less your total necessary business expenses. The information on your Schedule C from your last several income tax returns is an excellent place to start. In most instances, the bottom line on that form, your business income, will be your own personal gross income—the number to use for figuring family support during this period.

Income Tracker

Husband *expects* to receive the following regular income (averaged per month) for the next _____ months:

$_____ gross; $_____net.

Husband *may* receive the following additional income (averaged per month) over the next _____ months:

$_____ gross, $_____net.

Wife *expects* to receive the following regular income (averaged per month) for the next _____ months:

$_____ gross; $_____net.

Wife *may* receive the following additional income (averaged per month over the next _____ months:

$_____ gross, $_____net.

Look at a Week Instead of a Month?

Cheryl had managed the household, but had never been responsible for paying the bills. When she and Mike separated, she was starting at the beginning when it came to thinking about a monthly budget. In fact a month was too large for her to start with. So they began with a weekly budget. After a few weeks of experience, Cheryl, was ready to begin looking at the monthly picture.

EXPENSES

The purpose of this section is to budget your expenses as your family changes from one household to two. You will have the on-going expenses of both households, plus any debt payments you may have.

The ongoing expenses for two households can be divided into three categories:
1. bare bones: necessary expenses during this period of time ("survival");
2. discretionary: expenses which either of you could live without, albeit with difficulty ("lifestyle"); and
3. children: expenses which are directly for the children.

The Informational Family "IF" Budget is the 3-page chart located in Chapter 5. It lists your expenses in the three categories described above. Make several photocopies of the IF Budget and complete one for each household. You may need some now for your rough drafts, and to prepare again toward the end of your interim or temporary period (at the time of your decree), as your circumstances change.

Be sure that between your two spouse's IF Budgets, you include all your expenses and debts for both households, and that you do not duplicate any of them. Do these budgets separately even if you are physically separating within the same residence. You will still have to decide how to share the expenses of the home.

Notes:

BUDGETING YOUR SEPARATION

Now you are ready to compare your expected incomes with your expected expenses for this interim period.

Directions: Have in front of you the following:

1. Your DIN (Duplicate Items Needed) List, page 43-44.

2. Your Income Tracker, page 54.

3. Both of your IF Budgets (from Chapter 5). Use them to complete the following chart. You may want to make several photocopies of this for rough drafts.

Budget Analysis Chart

HUSBAND:

Basic Income (Inc. Tracker)	$ _____	Extra Income (Inc. Tracker)	$ _____	Total $ _____ Income
Bare Bones Expenses (IF Budget)	$ _____	Discretionary Expenses (IF Budget)	$ _____	
Children's Expenses (IF Budget)	$ _____	DIN List Expenses (IF Budget)	$ _____	Total Expenses $ _____

WIFE:

Basic Income (Inc. Tracker)	$ _____	Extra Income (Inc. Tracker)	$ _____	Total $ _____ Income
Bare Bones Expenses (IF Budget)	$ _____	Discretionary Expenses (IF Budget)	$ _____	
Children's Expenses (IF Budget)	$ _____	DIN List Expenses (IF Budget)	$ _____	Total Expenses $ _____

BUDGET ANALYSIS

Step 1. A Look at your Combined Picture.

Add your combined total incomes: $ _____

Add your combined total expenses: $ _____

Subtract expenses from incomes: +/−$ _____

If your result is a positive number, this means that you have enough take-home money at the present time to meet the total short term expenses for both households. Make a clear agreement about what you will do with the surplus, so that the whole family can benefit from it during this time. You are not unusual if you have a negative number here. Most people do not have enough income to meet the total "wish lists" of two households.

Step 2. One Household Shortfall.

If you have a combined negative number, go to Step 3. If you have a combined positive number, you must now check if you individually have a positive number. Subtract your individual total expenses from your individual total income as follows:

Husband's Total Income $ _____	Wife's Total Income $ _____
Husband's Total Expenses $_____	Wife's Total Expenses $ _____
Difference: +/−$ _____	Difference: +/−$_____

If one of you has a positive difference, and the other a negative, some money must change hands between you to enable both households to meet all expenses. It is possible to increase the net income to your whole family by decreasing income taxes in this situation. In principle, this type of planning lowers the tax burden of the higher income spouse by allocating some of his or her income to the lower income spouse who is in a lower tax bracket. This can generate significant savings from which you can both benefit. See the next section of this chapter and Chapter 10 (Maintenance) and Chapter 11 (Taxes) for more about this.

Step 3. Mutual Belt-Tightening.

If the result in your Budget Analysis is a negative number, there is not enough combined income to meet your total combined expenses. Look at both of your IF Budgets and your DIN List. What can you agree together to cut back on? The discretionary column on your IF Budget is the most likely place where you can cut. If by doing this you can break even in your combined numbers, then go back to Step 2.

Step 4. Rethinking Your Budgets.

If Step 3 does not bring you back to break-even or a positive number, then you will probably need to take a hard look at the assumptions underlying your two-household IF budgets:

- Can either of you increase your income by decreasing your withholding, working additional hours, or taking interest or dividend incomes which you would normally not do?

- Is this the time for either of you to go from part time to full time employment, or to find employment?

- Is this the time to sell the house?

- Is this really the time to buy the second home? Can one or both of you rent or lease-with-option-to-buy for a time?

- Is this the time to sell an asset, or use a savings account?

- Is this the time to borrow against an asset: take a second mortgage on the house, borrow against your life insurance, or your car?

- Are there friends or relatives who will help you through this interim period?

- If your short-fall is primarily due to large debts or bill payments, is this the time to call Consumer Credit Counseling, or to consider a Chapter 13 Bankruptcy?

This is a difficult time for everyone who faces these circumstances. This may be the time when you are most tempted to give up working together and let someone else take over. Don't panic. Be careful not to lose yourself in fear about money. Keep focused on the good that will come to your family by separating cooperatively.

If you can agree on a solution like the suggestions above, thereby bringing your combined totals to break-even, then go back to Step 2.

Step 5. "Oh My God!"

If there is nothing you yourselves can do to make your two-household budgets happen, then ask:

- Must you separate at this time? Can you put off the separation until one of you finishes school, or is no longer laid off? Is this the time to reconsider sharing the house "upstairs/downstairs?"

- Can you resolve the situation itself: place the disabled child or elderly family member in a care facility, or delay your separation until the difficulty is resolved?

- Is this the time for a Chapter 7 Bankruptcy?

- Is there a source of community, church, or family assistance? (Food Stamps, Unemployment Compensation, Social Security, Supplemental Security Income?)

Temporary Support Between Spouses

TEMPORARY MAINTENANCE

If your budget analysis on the previous page shows that some money needs to change hands between you in order that you may both meet your on-going living expenses, you may need to agree on temporary support. Here are two basic ways.

1. *Higher income spouse pays some or all of lower income spouse's expenses directly.* One expense may be the mortgage. If the mortgage is still in the paying spouse's name and he or she doesn't have another primary residence, and you file separate returns (including married filing separately), this spouse can take the tax deduction for the home mortgage interest. Other expenses might be insurance, credit card bills and utilities.

   The paying spouse can also pay directly some of the children's expenses, such as day care, babysitting, medical and dental bills. The child care credit, available to single working parents, may then be taken by the paying spouse IF AND ONLY IF you file separately (including married filing separately), the paying spouse has been separated for more than 6 months before the end of the year, and has sufficient parenting time to qualify as head of household. This is an easy rule to miss and a costly one.

2. *Higher income spouse pays temporary maintenance, each party pays their own bills.* If you structure your agreement so that the bills the lower income spouse is paying are tax deductions (like the mortgage interest and property tax) or lead to a credit (like work-related child care), then the receiving spouse off-sets these against the taxable payments from the paying spouse. And everyone saves money. If the lower income spouse is the primary residential care parent, remaining in the family home, this way of doing things may be tailor-made for you.

As you move towards a decision on the amount of your temporary maintenance, if any, and your combined annual gross income is less than $75,000, there is a statutory formula which the court must follow if you asked the court to decide it for you (see sidebar). You may wish to include this as part of your thinking.

Once you have decided on the amount of your temporary maintenance, whether it's a fixed amount throughout or one amount for certain months and another amount for other months, or

Alimony

Same as maintenance. Also called Section 71 payments, referring to the section in the Internal Revenue Code.

Temporary Maintenance

Payments made by one spouse to the other, prior to the final decree, are deductible from the income of the paying spouse, included in the income of the receiving spouse, and are subject to federal and state income tax, but not Social Security taxes.

Tax filing status during separation.

If there are no children, you must file Married (jointly or separately). As long as you remain married, if one of you qualifies as Head of Household, (see Chapter 11 Taxes), the other must file as Married Filing Separately, unless he or she also qualifies as Head of Household.

When married taxpayers file separate returns, both must either itemize or use the standard deduction. If one spouse itemizes and the other does not, the second spouse's deduction will be zero.

Temporary Maintenance Formula

Higher monthly gross income
x 40% _____

minus lower monthly gross income
x 50% - _____

Result is Temporary Maintenance
= _____

If 0 or minus number, no presumed payment

If partners choose to pay some short term support, there is no tax effect. The paying partner pays in after tax dollars, and the receiving partner may owe income tax on it. Nevertheless this is a solution for some, often until the receiving partner obtains employment. The word "temporary" meaning "before the Decree" in the divorce process, has no parallel meaning for partners.

simply one lump sum, you must decide whether you want it to be a private agreement between the two of you, or a court order.

1. Temporary maintenance by private agreement. Write an agreement that states your names, that you are husband and wife, the date of your marriage, and the date of your separation—you must be living apart in order to have a temporary maintenance agreement. Then write the amount of the maintenance, whether it's per month, per quarter, one lump sum, and when it is due to the receiving spouse—for example "on or before the 4th day of each month starting in February 2004", and how long you want it to go—often "until entry of our Decree". Then each of you sign it in front of a notary, and each keep a copy or the original in your tax file. Such an agreement must be signed and dated before you make any of the maintenance payments in order to shift the taxes. Temporary maintenance paid according to a private agreement IS NOT an exception to the steep stair-step recapture rule test calculations (see Chapter 11). Read the rule and decide whether it makes any difference in your situation.

2. Temporary maintenance by Temporary Order of the Court. Temporary maintenance paid according to a Court order IS an exception to the steep stair-step recapture rule test calculations (see Chapter 11). Check the rule to see if you need to go this route. If so, you will find the court forms (numbers 1210 and 1211) for this on the CD-ROM. If your combined annual gross income is less than $75,000, you will have to show the calculation of maintenance according to the statutory formula and either use that number, or explain why a deviation from the formula is fair in your particular circumstances. If you have children, you will also need a child support worksheet and an agreement about temporary child support. Calculate maintenance first, then child support.

TAX CONSIDERATIONS

The date of your physical separation affects the options you have about your filing status, as does the date of your final decree.

If it is less than 90 days between your time of filing for dissolution or legal separation and the end of the calendar year, you must file married filing jointly or married filing separately. (You cannot file as Single.) If you wish to have temporary maintenance that is taxable, you must file married filing separately. If your temporary maintenance is non-taxable, you can file married filing jointly.

If you have been separated for more than six months before the end of the year (i.e., you physically separated before July 1 of this year) you have another option. Any separated person who has provided a home for his or her dependant child for more that six months of the year, may file as head of household. If you have more than one child and are sharing residential care parenting time, you might each have this option and each get the child care credit for that child. This may save money over filing jointly. If only one parent can qualify as head of household, the other must file married filing separately while you are still married.

If your 90 day waiting period will finish before the end of the year, then you have the option of completing your final decree in this tax year, and will be able to file as single or head of household for the tax year.

Agreeing to temporary maintenance can help you avoid the "recapture problem" if you have one (see Chapter 11). If you can reach agreement quickly about high-end temporary maintenance—even large lump-sum maintenance—ask the court to approve your written agreement as an order of court, then any amounts will not count in the steep stair-step recapture rules.

Temporary Child Support

If you wish to have the court approve your temporary agreements you must use the Colorado Child Support Guideline to calculate child support and include a child support worksheet and financial affidavits. See chapters 9 and 12 for instructions on these forms. This means that some of the money changing hands will probably have to be labeled child support, thus losing some of the tax planning opportunity of calling it maintenance. You can still do some tax planning by subtracting the amount of temporary maintenance from the income of the paying spouse and adding it

---

Checklist of Temporary Maintenance and First Year Filing Status.

☐ **We plan to obtain our final decree of dissolution of marriage (legal separation) this calendar year.**

We will file our taxes this year as:

Wife: ☐ Single   ☐ Head of Household

Husband: ☐ Single   ☐ Head of Household

_____ (paying spouse) will pay $ _____ per month as temporary maintenance to

_____ (receiving spouse) starting _____ (date), until the decree. _____ (paying spouse) will pay $ _____ per month as maintenance between the final decree and the end of the calendar year, for a total of $ _____.

We ☐ will ☐ will not make our temporary maintenance agreement into a court order, so that the total paid before the decree ☐ will ☐ will not be counted in the first separation year maintenance total for testing under the recapture rule (see Chapter 11).

☐ **We don't plan to obtain our final decree this calendar year.**

We will file our taxes this year as follows:

☐ Married filing jointly.

☐ Married filing separately.
  ☐ Wife   ☐ Husband

☐ Head of Household.
  ☐ Wife   ☐ Husband

_____ (paying spouse) will pay to _____ (receiving spouse) $ _____ per month for temporary maintenance ☐ by ☐ not by court order for a total of $ _____ which ☐ will ☐ will not be our first separation year for maintenance recapture test calculations (see Chapter 11).

If you feel you need a written temporary agreement, transer the agreements on this checklist, when completed, to the Sample Temporary Agreement at the end of this chapter. If using the formula to calculate temporary maintenance, use Bradford forms 1210 and 1211 on the CD-ROM.

to the income of the receiving spouse on the child support work-sheet. This will alter the ratio of your incomes, thereby reducing the child support of the paying spouse—often significantly.

If you are bargaining between yourselves about how to get the bills paid, and you feel no need to have your temporary agreement made into a court order, you do not have to follow the Colorado Child Support Guideline in calculating support.

Once you have agreed to an amount for temporary support and other temporary arrangements and if you prefer a written agreement, you may transfer the information to the sample Temporary Agreement at the end of this chapter or to form JDF1109 on the CD-ROM.

The Temporary Agreement

HOW FORMAL DOES OUR TEMPORARY AGREEMENT
NEED TO BE?

Many couples do not need to write down their temporary arrangements. Others want something more formal, or official. This is your call, but remember any temporary maintenance arrangement must be in writing and signed by both of you.

If you want to make your arrangements very firm, write down your temporary agreements. You may have your signatures notarized to show the strength of your intent. Once your agreement is written and signed, you are bound by it as you would be by any contract, such as the contract for the purchase of real estate, car, or sofa. Also, once it is written in this way, the IRS must honor any designation of payments as maintenance—even if you don't file your petition—so long as you file separate returns.

WHAT IF YOU DON'T HAVE AN AGREEMENT ABOUT
TEMPORARY ORDERS?

If your spouse will not agree to work out a temporary plan with you, or has chosen not to be involved in the divorce negotiations at this stage, you can still obtain some temporary orders. Use JDF 1109 on the CD-ROM as "Information for the Court." Also use Motion for Temporary Orders (JDF 1106), Temporary Orders (JDF 1110), Notice of Hearing Date (JDF 1108) and Bradford form No. 1195, Notice to Set. See Chapter 12. JDF forms are available from Bradford Publishing. If you are under the simplified procedure, you would ask for temporary orders at your status conference, and the Motion and Notice forms will not be needed.

File the Petition First

In order to make your Temporary Agreement a Temporary Order of the Court, you *must* file your Petition so that you have a case number and an action in court. See Chapter 6. You may file your Petition and your Temporary Agreement at the same time if you wish.

TEMPORARY TEETH

If you are worried that the agreement might not be kept by either or both of you, consider writing in some "teeth". In a maintenance agreement, for example, some teeth to help the paying spouse keep his or her promises would be to agree that if a payment is missed, that money, when paid, is not counted as maintenance.

The paying spouse loses the tax deduction, and the receiving spouse does not pay tax on it. (The IRS permits you to say whether or not something that looks like maintenance to the IRS will receive the deductible/taxable treatment.) In this case, make the tax consequences strictly contingent on prompt payments.

Teeth to help the receiving spouse keep his or her promises would be to agree that if the money he or she receives from the paying spouse is not used to pay for the home or car, as agreed, that asset will be immediately placed on the market. It may or may not be appropriate for you to put such strict punishments in your own agreement. That's your decision. But, if you begin right away treating your agreement as a very serious bargain between you, there will be less chance that you will be tempted to take it lightly later on.

You may also give your temporary agreement legal teeth by making it an order of the court. If you do this, your agreement is then enforceable directly by the court. When you make your agreement an order of the court, the obligations in the contract become court orders, and therefore enforceable through judgments and contempt. See Chapter 13.

Notes:

"My object all sublime I shall achieve in time – To make the punishment fit the crime." Sir William Schwenk Gilbert, *The Mikado.*

Sample Wording for Temporary Agreements

Directions: To write your own temporary agreement, use your notes and agreements from this chapter. Following are samples of how you might word a variety of arrangements. If you use any of these samples, be sure to change them to express your own agreements precisely.

General Statements and Agreements

1. We, _____ (full name, how you will be referred to in this

    agreement), and _____ (full name, how you will be referred to

    in this agreement), agree to the following:

2. We were married on _____ (date) and separated on _____ (date).

    Our current addresses are (as stated in the petition) _____ ,

    and _____ , respectively.

3. Our children are: _____ (name), _____ (age),

    _____ , _____ , and _____ , _____ .

4. We intend this agreement to stay in effect from the date we sign it until our final decree of _____

    or (for _____ months/days) or (until _____ [date]). We will agree to any changes in

    writing, signed and dated.

5. We agree to the following ground rules for conduct between us during this interim period:

6. We agree that the terms of this temporary agreement are fair to both of us and in the best interests of our children.

Who Uses What and Who Pays for It

7. _____ will remain in the family home at

    _____ (address), and will be responsible for

    paying the following expenses at that address (list the expenses that you agreed to in the Residence

    Checklist – Short Term):

_____ *(other spouse)* will be responsible for the following expenses

at the family home _____ and/or will be solely responsible

for all living expenses at _____ *(address) (Repeat here*

information from your Residence Checklist – Short Term):

8.   We will separate within our residence as follows: _____ will occupy the _____

bedroom and _____ bath / the finished basement / the _____ floor and _____

(Repeat for other spouse).

9.   We will share the common areas of the house as follows:

10.   _____ will drive the _____ automobile(s) and will be

solely responsible for paying the following expenses for it (them) *(list from Car Checklist – Short Term):*

(Repeat for other spouse.)

11.   The next premium for car insurance is due _____ *(date)* and _____

will be responsible for paying it.

12.   We agree to be responsible for our bills and other expenses during this period as follows:

13.   _____ will be responsible for paying the following during the period covered by this

agreement *(list credit card and loan payments not listed above; children's expenses such as school, day care,*

medical and dental; family expenses such as health and life insurance, and any other expenses either of you

is paying from your IF Budgets): (Repeat for other spouse.)

14. _____ will have the exclusive use of the following credit cards and may use them only for the following purposes: *(Repeat for other spouse.)*

15. _____ agrees to contact the following creditors and ask to have _____ *(other spouse)* designated as a person to receive credit on this account: *(Repeat for other spouse.)*

16. Neither of us will sell or mortgage any of our assets except as we specifically agree in writing.

17. We specifically agree to sell or mortgage the following for the following purpose:

Item:

Anticipated Sales/Mortgage Proceeds:

Money to be Used for:

18. Neither of us will incur any debt, including charging anything else on our credit cards, except as we specifically agree in writing.

19. We specifically agree to borrow $_____ from _____ , for the purpose of _____ on the following re-payment terms: _____ .

Children: Parental Responsibilities, Decision Making
Transfer here the decisions you made working through this chapter

20. We will share the following decisions about our children:

21. _____ , mother, will make the following decisions about our children: Mother will consult with father on (all) (#   ).

22. _____, father, will make the following decisions about our children: Father will consult with mother on (all) (#   ).

23. For the purposes of the IRS, school registration and interstate custody laws, we designate _____ (*parent*) as the residential home of_____ (*child*) and_____ (*parent*) home as the residential home of _____(*child*)

24. We will use the following process if we can't reach agreement:

Residential Care, Parenting Time.

25. We agree to the following schedule of time with our children during the period covered by this temporary agreement (*copy or re-write the schedules, including holidays, which you agreed to in your Six-Week Calendar extending it, if necessary, to cover the whole period of your temporary agreement*):

26. We agree to the following about transporting the children between us, changing the schedule, notifying of significant events, etc. (*copy or re-write here any other agreements you have reached about your children*):

Budgeting Your Separation

27. _____ expects to receive regular income of $_____ per month from _____ (*source*). _____ (*same spouse*) may also receive occasional income of $_____ per month from _____ (*copy or re-write here your information from the Income Tracker*). (*Repeat for other spouse.*)

28. We agree that _____ need not seek employment outside the home at this time (in order to be at home with our children) (in order to complete school or training at _____) (due to _____ [illness] or _____)

29. _____ will pay as Temporary Maintenance (*spousal support, Section 71 payments*) to _____ (*other spouse*) $_____ per (month)(quarter)(lump sum). This is to be paid on _____ (*dates*), by _____ (check) (direct deposit) (money order) (voluntary income assignment)(other). (*If applicable*) Our motion for Temporary Maintenance is attached. We agree that this maintenance will be deductible from income by _____ and taxable as income to _____ for income tax purposes.

30. _____ will pay to _____ $ _____ per (month) (week) (twice monthly) (every other week) as temporary child support. This amount will be paid on _____ *(dates)* and/or by (check) (money order) (direct deposit) (voluntary income assignment) (other).

31. _____ will pay $_____ per _____ to (child) (other parent) (institution) as post-secondary education costs for our child _____.

32. _____ *(other parent)* will pay $_____ per _____ to (child) (other parent) (institution) as post-secondary education costs for our child _____.

33. In addition to the above child support, we agree that we will share the following extraordinary expenses for our children which are not included in the calculations for child support *(indicate each category of expense and who will pay it, or in what proportion you will each pay it.*

34. We anticipate that we will file as separate taxpayers beginning with the year_____. We anticipate that _____ will file as Head of Household for _____ *(child)*, and may claim the Child Care Credit for this child. *(Repeat for other spouse if applicable.)*

35. _____ may claim _____ *(child)* as tax exemption and receive the child care credit for the____ tax year. *(Repeat for other spouse as agreed.)*

36. _____ may have as a deduction _____% of the mortgage interest and property taxes on the family home for the year_____.

37. We   ☐ agree   ☐ do not agree   to ask that this Temporary Agreement be made an order of the court.

38. *(Add any additional agreements you have made at this time.)*

Add your signatures, the date you sign, and a notarization.

MAKING YOUR AGREEMENT INTO A COURT ORDER

Before you can ask the court to approve your temporary agreement, you must have already filed your case. See Chapter 6 for how to do this. Be sure you put your case number on everything.

If you want to ask the court to approve your temporary agreement and make it into a court order, you should:

1. Copy the caption from page 297 onto a blank sheet of paper, type your agreement, both sign it in front of a notary, and write "Exhibit 1" on the first page.　OR
2. Complete and sign JDF 1109
3. Fill out the top of the Temporary Orders, JDF 1110 and attach the original of your own typed agreement or JDF 1109, and take or mail it to the clerk of the district court along with:
   a) your completed, signed and notarized Affidavits with Respect to Financial Affairs (see Chapter 12), and Child Support Worksheets (see Chapter 9);
   b) two additional photocopies of the Temporary Orders; and
   c) two stamped envelopes (one addressed to each of you).
   d) your Petition and other first papers if you are filing everything at the same time.
4. Be sure you each keep a signed copy of your temporary agreement.

CHAPTER 5

GREAT HAIRY CHECKLIST
OF THINGS TO GATHER

GREAT HAIRY CHECKLIST OF THINGS TO GATHER

The following "Great Hairy Checklist" lists all the items you will need to pull together in order to understand your complete financial picture, to negotiate with each other, and to prepare your separation agreement and financial affidavits.

Your agreement should not be based on guesswork. Knowing that the balance in your spouse's IRA is $13,857.95 as of December 31, 2003, gives you much more confidence in your discussions than estimating it's somewhere around $10,000 or $15,000. Your statement will have the most accurate numbers. You should have clear and accurate paperwork to back up every number you use in your final settlement.

The Income Chart and the Informational ("IF") Budget at the end of this chapter will help you gather the information you need to discuss maintenance and support and to fill out your financial affidavits. Your check register and credit card statements are good sources of information about your monthly expenses and spending habits.

P Partners should review this checklist for whatever information would help them deal fully and honestly with each other.

Some people keep track of their household expenses using software like Quicken, TurboTax, and portfolio software to keep track of their investments. Many people keep records by throwing receipts, canceled checks, and statements of all kinds into a shoe box or file folder, sometimes marked "House", "Car", "Bills", "Taxes", or "Kids". Important papers like Deeds and Wills, and insurance policies are often kept in a fireproof box or the safety deposit box at the bank.

Records

It is better to assemble everything, unsorted, into a single box or grocery bag, even if you don't have time to organize it, than to halt your negotiations for lack of a piece of paper.

Assemble all of these things ready to take to wherever you are going to begin talking—around the kitchen table, mediator's office, or lawyer's office. Gather as much of this information as possible before you begin any discussions. You might find it helpful to make two photocopies of everything, one for each of you. This will give you something to make notes on as you continue working through this book and as you begin your negotiations.

Property, Debts, Insurance, and Income

Assemble all documents you have showing the current fair market value of your major assets and any balance. This includes items titled in either of your separate names, titled in your joint names, or titled to either or both of you jointly with others. If you still own assets you entered the marriage with, you should also document their value at the time of your marriage. As you will see in Chapter 7, you are free to make your own distinctions between marital and separate property. Gathering this data, **if you have it**, will help you focus on your specific situation.

REAL ESTATE

1. Home.
   a. Your Warranty Deed.
   b. Purchaser's closing statement, or cost of construction.
   c. Documentation of your cost of any capital improvements.
   d. Current balance of mortgage(s).
   e. Market analysis or bank appraisal showing current market value.
   f. County tax assessment valuation.
   g. IRS form 2119 for all previous primary homes sold by you during this marriage showing any capital gain rolled over into this home or, if you don't find any 2119s, your purchaser's closing statements and your seller's closing statements for the purchase and sale of any previous homes, and record of any capital improvements and cost of sale on those homes. Don't obsess over this one if your primary residence (home) has increased less than $250,000 in value (including any amount rolled into it).

2. Other real estate.
   a. Warranty deed or other deed to you.
   b. Amounts owing against the property.
   c. Any depreciation taken by you if you have been renting the property or using it for business.
   d. The cost of any capital improvements, or cost of construction if you built it.
   e. Market analysis or bank appraisal showing current market value.
   f. County tax assessment valuation.
   g. Purchaser's closing statement or 1031 documents to ascertain purchase or "start-up" value.

PERSONAL PROPERTY

1. Furniture, appliances and household goods. List every item of significant value—you decide what significant value means to you. Remember, value may not be monetary: something may be valuable to you because of its utility or that it reminds you of a person, or the place where you acquired it. It is often useful to make your list with columns: "I want," "You want," "Both want," "Nobody wants." You can make a fifth column for value or comments if you wish. You can make columns for whether something was yours before the marriage or was a gift or inheritance or for some other reason feels more like "mine" than "ours." An interesting way to gather this information is to each do a list and compare them. Be sure you leave time to walk through the house individually (or together if you wish) to prepare the list. If you are separated, walk through each other's homes, listing the items you acquired together.

   Many people do not detail their division of these assets in their settlement. It is possible to keep this as a written private agreement. Therefore, this is an early agreement you can be working on while you gather data necessary to complete your larger settlement.

   If you use a monetary value for these items in your settlement, use street value—what you would get for an item if you sold it yourself.

2. Art, antiques, collectibles. Start making a detailed list of these items with enough description so there is no question which item is which. If you agree any of these were your pre-marriage property or a gift to one of you

(not to both of you), list these separately. If you don't agree on this, or think you might not agree, find proof of when you acquired the property and under what circumstances.

3. Necessary purchases of duplicate items needed for two households. As the two of you move from one household to two, inevitably you will need to acquire some new furniture and household goods. If you envision some necessary purchases in this vein, complete the Duplicate Items Needed ("DIN") List in Chapter 4.

MOTOR VEHICLES

Look at the NADA *Blue Book* or *Kelley Blue Book* online *(kelleybluebook.com)* for retail and wholesale values and/or ads for similar cars from the newspaper classifieds. List loan balances owed and how titled. Unless your lender is holding it, provide the title(s).

CASH ON HAND

If you keep on hand more than small amounts of pocket money, list it here, whether it's in a safe, mattress, or buried in the back yard.

STOCKS, BONDS, AND OPTIONS

1. Stocks and Bonds. If all of your securities are in a brokerage account or an employee stock purchase plan, provide a current statement. For each security that you own provide the following:
    a. Name of company, and type and number of shares or bonds.
    b. How titled now.
    c. Value/cost at acquisition, value now.

If you have a large portfolio, it is sometimes simpler to value the portfolio at acquisition (or, at the date of the marriage, if some of it is pre-marital) and the value of the whole portfolio now. Again, if you claim any of it is yours by gift, then bring whatever proof of that you can find, or at least the value at the time you received it.

2. Options
    For options, provide the document granting them and list the following information about each grant:
    a. Name of the company.
    b. Name of the person the options are granted to.
    c. Date of the grant.
    d. Number of shares optioned.
    e. Exercise or strike price.
    f. Vesting schedule.
    g. Expiration date.
    h. Number vested during marriage.
    i. Number that will not vest during marriage.
    j. Are they qualified or nonqualified?
    k. Will the company permit you to transfer them at divorce?

HEALTH AND LIFE INSURANCE

Most of the information you need to answer the questions in this section is in a *benefits booklet* from your employer. If you do not have a benefits booklet, ask your employer to provide the information to you in writing.

1. Provide the most recent health benefits booklet you have. Answer the following with regard to your health insurance coverage:
    a. Who is covered?
    b. What is the premium for each person or category of person?

   c. What is the coverage for each kind of medical expense? Dental? Eye glasses? Chiropractic? Preventive care? Office visits? Prescriptions?

2. Does your medical insurance require that your children be the legal dependent of the employee in order for them to be covered? Some companies, for example, permit stepparents who have not adopted children to include them.

3. Must the employee claim any covered person as a dependent exemption on his or her income tax return? Some insurance companies still accept this as the only proof that the covered person is a dependent. This can cause havoc in your tax and other planning if you don't know about it ahead of time. See Chapter 11.

4. Must the insurance company and/or the employee authorize any non-emergency expenses before they can be covered?

5. Obtain the details on the *COBRA* option which permits a former spouse to purchase separate coverage, as though they were an employee, for up to three years after the divorce.(See Chapters 10 and 12 for more on this.)

6. For each life insurance policy you have, summarize:
   a. Is it whole life, term, or decreasing term, hybrid (mixture of several kinds), universal life? What is the current cash value or cash surrender value? What is the balance of any loan against the policy?
   b. Which policies cover whom? Spouse? Children?
   c. Who is the named beneficiary (get copies of the actual beneficiary designations).

7. Does the insurance company have any special rules about how this life insurance coverage will be affected by a legal separation or dissolution of marriage?

PENSION, PROFIT SHARING, AND RETIREMENT FUNDS
INCLUDING 401KS AND IRAS

1. Your employer, plan administrator, or trustee has been giving you, or should have been giving you, the following documents regarding your pension, profit sharing, retirement, 401K, thrift savings, and IRAs. Provide the most current:
   a. A benefits statement telling what kind of retirement, pension or tax-deferred benefit you have.
   b. A current statement of the amount which is vested for you or in your name.
   c. If there is a formula to determine the amount of your monthly benefit at retirement, obtain a copy of the formula and the current projected monthly amount.
   d. Is your plan subject to a Qualified Domestic Relations Order ("QDRO")? If so, are there written information and "in house" forms available from your employer or plan administrator? If so, provide them.

2. Check the accuracy of the factual data in the plan (since small discrepancies can create huge problems, including with the Social Security Administration). Not all this data will appear in every plan, but check your plan for the accuracy of the following data:
   a. Participant's name, address, Social Security number, birth date, and the exact date you began participating in the plan.
   b. The exact name of the surviving spouse or alternate payee, and his or her address.
   c. The date of your marriage.

3. Make a photocopy of this question for each retirement, pension or tax deferred savings plan, IRA, 401K, thrift savings and the like, either of you has. Then, for each plan, answer the following questions. If you don't know the answers to these questions, you can get help from the benefits office at work, or your account executive.
   a. Does the plan continue, or pay, at the death of the participant?
   b. Does the plan have a separate death benefit? (Yes or No) If so, state the exact name and address of the named beneficiary.

c. How is the plan funded? Does participant contribute? Does the employer contribute? If so, how much, and when?

d. How and when does the plan vest?

e. When and under what circumstances does the plan pay out?

f. Is the plan subject to divestment? Total? Partial? If so, when and how?

g. Does the plan have a surviving spouse provision? If so, what are its terms?

h. Does the plan have a separate death benefit? If so, what are its terms?

i. What portion of the funds held in this plan are tax-deferred?

j. What portion of the funds held in this plan have already been taxed?

k. Can the participant receive a lump sum payout? If so, when, and under what circumstances?

l. Is any benefit or amount available to the participant now? Is there a "hardship" clause which permits a partial payout for
    1) purchase of a primary residence
    2) college or higher education (self, spouse, or children)
    3) medical emergency
    4) divorce
    5) other

m. May the participant borrow from the plan? If so, under what circumstances?
    1) purchase of a primary residence
    2) college or higher education expenses (self, spouse, or children?)
    3) medical emergency
    4) divorce
    5) other

n. What is the participant's expected date of retirement?

o. What is the participant's earliest possible date of retirement?

p. What change in benefits, if any, results from early retirement?

q. Is any portion of this plan in lieu of Social Security (i.e., participant does not pay F.I.C.A. and does not have F.I.C.A. paid on his/her behalf)?

r. If the answer to the previous question is yes, what is the value of the portion of the plan which is in lieu of Social Security?

s. Are the benefits described above in questions h, i, and p affected by participant's Social Security benefits, estimated or received? If so how? In what amount?

t. Is the participant presently eligible for Social Security benefits? If so, what is the present anticipated monthly benefit? If not, how many more quarters are needed.

4. If you have worked for 40 full-time quarters (10 years), you will probably be eligible to receive Social Security — unless you work for a public entity which has a plan in lieu of Social Security, such as P.E.R.A. Call the local Social Security office and ask them to send you a statement of your present earned credits and probable benefit.

MISCELLANEOUS ASSETS

The rest of your assets may include tools, sports equipment, pedigreed animals, craft supplies, country club memberships, rights to season tickets, and frequent flyer miles. Start gathering titles, descriptions, and costs to acquire or maintain. The paper work should be ready to give to whoever will keep that asset after the divorce. Now is the time to start assembling everything so you avoid lost documents and nerve-wrenching last minute scrambles.

UNSECURED DEBTS AND CREDIT CARDS

1. Assemble all the current debt, credit card, and loan statements you have, including those since your separation. If you had debts at the time of the marriage that you think will be important in your bargaining, find out what the balance was then – especially if the item purchased still exists.

2. Write out, in a manner you can refer to quickly, the present balance, minimum payment, and number of months left to pay on every debt either of you are legally responsible for, whether or not you are, or want to be, the one paying it.

3. Write out, in a similarly clear manner, all the payments and charges you have made since your separation.

INFORMATION ABOUT INCOME

The word "income" can mean different things to different people. To the worker it probably means spendable earnings. To the IRS it means what is taxed. In the Colorado Child Support Guideline, it can include potential earnings that are not actually coming in, or even imputed income nobody actually receives (for example, capital gains on an asset you sold such as stocks, or a rental property). The list of items to be gathered and the Income Chart that follows are designed to help you assemble and organize all your various kinds of income.

1. If you have a salary or regular pay (whether or not you receive additional income from commissions, tips, or performance-bonus), provide the following:
    a. Employment contract or letter, if you have one, which states what your salary or hourly pay is and what you must do to earn it.
    b. A current basic paycheck stub. If your income is hourly and you can earn overtime, be sure you select a paycheck without any extra time. Similarly, if you are paid hourly, be sure you select a paycheck stub with a full week—whether that is 32 or 40 hours—whatever is required to earn your base pay. This will give you a baseline for your minimum earnings.
    c. Paycheck stubs for the last 3-6 months (depending on how variable your income has been), added and averaged, to show average monthly income actually earned by each of you, including overtime.

2. If you are self-employed, put together, summarize, and average monthly:
    a. Gross business receipts.
    b. Necessary expenses to earn this income. (For some ideas about categories see IRS Schedule C. Do not factor in depreciation on business assets, but consider allocating something for replacing equipment and/or repairs.)
    c. Estimated tax payment and tax rate you are using.
    d. Average take home. Remember to keep and provide copies of all the paperwork on which you base your averages.

3. If your business is a corporation or limited liability company, provide the last year's corporate or company tax return. Your gross (before tax) income should appear under officer's pay, while your benefits (insurance, retirement, etc.,) will appear as corporate expenses. The corporate tax return will also show any income you received from the profits as an owner.

4. If your business is a partnership, provide the IRS Schedule K-1 form, Partner's Share of Income, Credits, Deductions, etc., to show your actual income received, if any.

5. If you have supplemental (not primary) income from any of the sources in 3 or 4 above, you still need to obtain the tax returns mentioned above.

6. If you have primary or supplemental income from investments, assemble at least a year of monthly or quarterly reports. Summarize the earnings, even if you left them in the account, and any expenses, and average them monthly. Do the same for any interest on bank accounts.

7. If your income for this last year included a one-time windfall such as profits from the sale of a home or stock, lottery winnings or an inheritance, assemble all the information about this income, including any taxes paid at the time or which you expect to pay.

8. Put together documentation (as above) of any additional income, other than that listed above, which you received during the last year.

9. Provide the last three year's income tax returns (the complete returns), including any business schedules or corporate returns on which your income was based.

Directions for Completing Income Chart

There are two copies of the Income Chart in this Guidebook—one for **each** of you. Use it to show your respective incomes from all sources. Read each numbered paragraph before completing the corresponding section of the chart.

There are references in each step to the relevant chapters of this Guidebook and to the Affidavit With Respect to Financial Affairs ("financial affidavit") in Chapter 12, which you **each** must prepare for the court along with your signed separation agreement.The information in the Income Chart and IF Budget can be transferred to your financial affidavit.

1. Write your gross *monthly* income from your primary employment, base pay, or salary only. If you are paid every two weeks, multiply the paycheck gross times 26 and then divide by 12.

2. List any bonuses, overtime, or commissions, and describe how often you receive them and how certain they are. For example, "I am guaranteed at least _____ hours of overtime per month," or "My bonus depends on company performance, it is not certain."

3. Write your total gross income from your primary employment. This should be #1 plus #2, especially if #2 is fairly certain. (If #2 is not so certain, you may wish to hold it for step #7.) This information will go on line 4 of page 1 of your financial affidavit.

4. Write your withholding classification. For example, "M-3" means filing Married claiming 3 exemptions. See your paycheck stub or the most recent W-4 which you filed with your employer. This will go in section 5 of your financial affidavit.

    If your paycheck stub does not show your withholding classification, obtain the W-4 form you filed with your payroll office. If you changed your W-4 when you separated, or in anticipation of separation, then obtain one basic or typical paycheck under each designation. Ask your payroll office to calculate for you what your paycheck would be at your present rate if you filed Single, claiming 1. This will give you a worst case scenario baseline for your tax planning (see Chapter 11).

 This information is important. Your tax status and the number of exemptions will change with your divorce. Understanding the effect of this change is vital to your budgeting. See Chapter 11.

5. What is being taken out of your *monthly* pay? You will need the following for both your basic pay and your average pay. If you are paid every two weeks, multiply the deduction amount times 26 and then divide by 12.

    a. Federal, State, and FICA (Social Security) taxes being withheld;
    b. Required minimum retirement contribution;
    c. Optional retirement, pension and/or savings;
    d. Spouse or family health and/or life insurance premium. Be CERTAIN you distinguish any amount you pay specifically for children, if this is available.
    e. "Cafeteria Plan" pre-tax amounts for day care, family medical, etc.

    f.   If your entire Social Security taxes are taken out in the first ten months of the year, be sure you provide at least one typical paycheck each with and without this amount withheld.

    g.   List any other deductions.

Later on, you will list these deductions in section 4 of your financial affidavit.

6.   Add #5 a and b together and subtract that total from #3. This will be line 6 of your financial affidavit.

7.   a.   List any additional income you receive, such as interest on savings or retirement accounts, or dividends (whether or not you actually collect them at this time), paper route, cash flow from rentals, any second or third job, or income from any small service or sales company (Amway, Mary Kay), or uncertain additional income from your primary employment (see step #2). This information will go in section 7 of your financial affidavit.

    b.   Write the profits or income to you from your business or self-employment. Subtract your actual out-of-pocket expenses of doing business from the actual business gross receipts. Do not calculate depreciation or subtract expenses which are fully reimbursed. (Unreimbursed expenses will appear on your budget.) This amount is not the same as the bottom line on Schedule C of your tax return. This information will go in section 7 of your financial affidavit.

8.   Write your deductions and/or estimated tax on income listed in #7 a and b. Most people do not have taxes withheld from their secondary incomes. If you do not, you should estimate the probable tax on this income and pay it to the IRS quarterly, or put it into a savings account. For most people, this additional income is likely to be taxed at 25% in federal tax, and 4.63% in Colorado state tax.

Include in this number your Social Security tax (if any) on this income, currently 7.65% (which includes Medicare tax, currently 1.45%). Social Security tax is not usually paid on unearned income, such as interest and dividends. Be sure to check whether the income you list here is subject to Social Security tax. If you are self-employed, you will need to calculate your Social Security amount as *Self-Employment Tax,* which is presently 15.3% and includes Medicare. The Medicare amount (2.9%) applies to total earnings (amount is unlimited) while the Social Security and Self-employment tax phase out of $87,000 in 2003. This information will go in section 8 of your financial affidavit.

9.   Subtract #8 from #7. This step will be line 9 of your financial affidavit.

10. List your total take-home pay from all sources. This should be #6 plus #9 on your Income Chart. This step will be reported on line 10 of your financial affidavit.

Income Chart

1. Monthly gross base pay from primary employment $ _____

2. Extra income from primary employment (averaged over _____ months) $ _____

    a. Overtime $_____/ month. Describe:

    b. Bonus: $_____/ month. Describe:

    c. Commissions $_____/ month. Describe:

3. Add #1 plus #2. $ _____

4. Rate of withholding: Married/Single claiming _____ exemptions.

5. Deductions from paycheck:

    a. Federal withholding   _____

        State withholding   _____

        F.I.C.A. (Social Security)   _____

        Insurance   _____

        Credit Union   _____

        Pension/Retirement   _____

        401K   _____

        Other: _____   _____

        Other: _____   _____

        Other: _____   _____

        Total deductions $ _____

    b. Monthly amount for Cafeteria or Flex Plan (day-care, medical) $ _____

6. Subtract #5a and b from #3. $ _____

7. List any additional interest or earnings:

    a. Interest   _____

        Dividends   _____

        Cash flow from rentals   _____

        Second (and third) job   _____

        Other   _____

        Total additional income $ _____

    b. Net income from your business or self-employment (Note: Be sure to read Instruction #7b.) $ _____

8. a. Estimated tax on #7a $ _____

    b. Estimated tax on #7b $ _____

9. Subtract #8a and b from #7a and b $ _____

10. Add #6 plus #9. $ _____

Income Chart

1. Monthly gross base pay from primary employment $ _____

2. Extra income from primary employment (averaged over _____ months) $ _____

    a. Overtime $_____ / month. Describe:

    b. Bonus: $_____ / month. Describe:

    c. Commissions $_____ / month. Describe:

3. Add #1 plus #2. $ _____

4. Rate of withholding: Married/Single claiming _____ exemptions.

5. Deductions from paycheck:

    a. Federal withholding   _____

        State withholding   _____

        F.I.C.A. (Social Security)   _____

        Insurance   _____

        Credit Union   _____

        Pension/Retirement   _____

        401K   _____

        Other: _____   _____

        Other: _____   _____

        Other: _____   _____

        Total deductions $ _____

    b. Monthly amount for Cafeteria or Flex Plan (day-care, medical) $ _____

6. Subtract #5a and b from #3. $ _____

7. List any additional interest or earnings:

    a. Interest   _____

        Dividends   _____

        Cash flow from rentals   _____

        Second (and third) job   _____

        Other   _____

        Total additional income $ _____

    b. Net income from your business or self-employment (Note: Be sure to read Instruction #7.b.) $ _____

8. a. Estimated tax on #7a $ _____

    b. Estimated tax on #7b $ _____

9. Subtract #8a and b from #7a and b $ _____

10. Add #6 plus #9. $ _____

Monthly Household Expenses

The purpose of this section is to budget your expenses as your family changes from one household to two. You will have the on-going expenses of both households, plus any debt service payments you may have.

The ongoing expenses for two households can be divided into three categories:

   a)   bare bones: necessary expenses during this period of time ("survival");

   b)   discretionary: expenses that are in addition to bare bones items that either of you could live without, albeit with difficulty ("lifestyle"); and

   c)   children: expenses which are directly for the children.

About the Informational ("IF") Budget

The "IF" Budget is the 3-page chart that begins on page 84. There are 2 provided in this Guidebook—one for each of you. The IF Budget lists your expenses in the three categories described above. It is designed to help you organize your information for your negotiations, and to prepare the information so that it can be transferred to your financial affidavit. You may want to make several copies for your rough drafts now, and to prepare them again toward the end of your interim or temporary period as your circumstances change. You may want to prepare these separately and then share them with each other. As you do so, try not to let this process become an opportunity to tell each other how to spend. Write down the information that is true for you, or as best you can project for the expenses in your future households.

If you have not yet separated or have recently separated, much of the information will be based on your expenses when you were together. If you have been separated for some time, the information will be based on some individual experience.

Directions for Completing the IF Budget

Make several copies. You will probably do several rough drafts to look at different possibilities. Be sure that between your two IF Budgets, you include all your expenses and debts for both households but that you do not duplicate any of them. Do these budgets separately, even if you are physically separating within the same residence. You will still have to decide how to share the expenses of the home.

1.   Using your check register(s), list all the expenses you have had in each of the categories on the IF Budget over a period of time (6 months to 2 years), then divide the total by the number of months. Write the number in the appropriate place on the IF Budget, allocating it, if necessary, among bare bones, discretionary, and children. For example, the base rate for your telephone is bare bones; long distance and other services are probably discretionary; a second telephone line may be for the children.

2.   Include the monthly cost of paying for items from the DIN List (Duplicate Items Needed) from Chapter 4.

3.   If you have no experience with an expense on this Budget, do some investigation:

   a.   To determine rent or a mortgage, drive around the area you want to live in, and call about homes for rent or sale. Be sure you ask about the average monthly cost of utilities. One way to find your children's portion is to ask about the difference in cost between one and two bedrooms, or one and three.

   b.   Buy a simple budget book at your local office supply or discount store. Each day, write down every penny you spend.

c. Super market spending is rarely limited to groceries. Decide whether to keep the cleaning supplies, panty hose, and toiletries grouped with the groceries in your budget. These are real expenses. Be sure you know where you have allocated them in your budget.

d. Obtain information regarding the balance you can expect to pay for any ongoing treatment for any members of your family, such as dental care, mental health, physical therapy, and the like.

e. Find out about one-time children's expenses such as prom, yearbook, school pictures, school trips, summer camp.

4. Don't forget to include expenses which might not be paid monthly or weekly, such as car insurance, life insurance, or property taxes if they are not included in the mortgage payment.

5. Be sure you average expenses which vary with the time of year: heat, water, birthday expenses, Christmas gifts, summer activities, school clothes in the fall.

6. If you included your entire expense allowance as received from your employer in your Income Chart, include your actual expenses on this Budget. Similarly, if you participate in a "cafeteria plan" pre-tax medical or day care expense program, then either put the entire monthly amount on this budget, with a notation that this is "pre-paid" and do not add it into the total expenses, or list the amount from the cafeteria plan in your Income Chart and put the amounts you actually spend for these services (averaged monthly, for example including summer day care) here and add them into your expenses. Be sure to include any copay amounts or deductibles that you pay for medical expenses that are not covered by your insurance.

7. Be sure that between your two IF budgets you have listed all your debts and debt payments. Debts are those bills which are not paid in full within the month such as most credit cards and signature loans. Do not list debts that you have already listed above such as mortgages and car loans.

Informational Family (IF) Budget

	BARE BONES	DISCRETIONARY	CHILDREN
HOUSING: Mortgage/Rent			
Second Mortgage			
Insurance and Taxes (if not included in the mortgage); renter's insurance; condo fees			
DIN List Items (averaged monthly)			
Other			
UTILITIES: Public Service/ Gas/Electric			
Water/Sewer			
Phone			
Trash			
Yard care/snow			
Other			
FOOD: Groceries			
Eating Out			
School Lunch			
MEDICAL:* Cafeteria plan			
Medical Insurance			
Dental Insurance			
Doctor			
Dentist			
Prescriptions and Medications			
Other			

*Read instruction No. 6 on previous page. List here out of pocket amounts only.

	BARE BONES	DISCRETIONARY	CHILDREN
LIFE INSURANCE: Minimum required at work or to secure child support or maintenance			
TRANSPORTATION: Car payment			
Fuel			
Maintenance			
Insurance			
Parking/Bus (less reimbursement)			
Other			
CLOTHING:			
LAUNDRY/CLEANING:			
CHILD CARE: Work-Related (Less Fed. Credit – unless Cafeteria Plan			
Not work-related			
EDUCATION: Tuition			
Books & Fees			
Other			
CHILD SUPPORT:			
MAINTENANCE:			
RECREATION:			

	BARE BONES	DISCRETIONARY	CHILDREN
MISCELLANEOUS:			
DIVORCE EXPENSES: (Mediators, lawyers, etc.)			
TOTAL EXPENSES:			
DEBTS: (list individually; do not repeat those listed above – car payment or mortgage)	Creditor Bal. Pmt.	Creditor Bal. Pmt.	Creditor Bal. Pmt.
	Creditor Bal. Pmt.	Creditor Bal. Pmt.	Creditor Bal. Pmt.
	Creditor Bal. Pmt.	Creditor Bal. Pmt.	Creditor Bal. Pmt.
	Creditor Bal. Pmt.	Creditor Bal. Pmt.	Creditor Bal. Pmt.
TOTAL DEBTS			
TOTAL DEBT PAYMENTS			
TOTAL EXPENSES & DEBT PAYMENTS			
GRAND TOTAL: ALL EXPENSES PLUS ALL DEBT PAYMENTS			

Informational Family (IF) Budget

	BARE BONES	DISCRETIONARY	CHILDREN
HOUSING: Mortgage/Rent			
Second Mortgage			
Insurance and Taxes (if not included in the mortgage); renter's insurance; condo fees			
DIN List Items (averaged monthly)			
Other			
UTILITIES: Public Service/ Gas/Electric			
Water/Sewer			
Phone			
Trash			
Yard care/snow			
Other			
FOOD: Groceries			
Eating Out			
School Lunch			
MEDICAL:* Cafeteria plan			
Medical Insurance			
Dental Insurance			
Doctor			
Dentist			
Prescriptions and Medications			
Other			

*Read instruction No. 6 on previous page. List here out of pocket amounts only.

	BARE BONES	DISCRETIONARY	CHILDREN
LIFE INSURANCE: Minimum required at work or to secure child support or maintenance			
TRANSPORTATION: Car payment			
Fuel			
Maintenance			
Insurance			
Parking/Bus (less reimbursement)			
Other			
CLOTHING:			
LAUNDRY/CLEANING:			
CHILD CARE: Work-Related (Less Fed. Credit – unless Cafeteria Plan			
Not work-related			
EDUCATION: Tuition			
Books & Fees			
Other			
CHILD SUPPORT:			
MAINTENANCE:			
RECREATION:			

	BARE BONES	DISCRETIONARY	CHILDREN
MISCELLANEOUS:			
DIVORCE EXPENSES: (Mediators, lawyers, etc.)			
TOTAL EXPENSES:			
DEBTS: (list individually; do not repeat those listed above – car payment or mortgage)	Creditor Bal. Pmt.	Creditor Bal. Pmt.	Creditor Bal. Pmt.
	Creditor Bal. Pmt.	Creditor Bal. Pmt.	Creditor Bal. Pmt.
	Creditor Bal. Pmt.	Creditor Bal. Pmt.	Creditor Bal. Pmt.
	Creditor Bal. Pmt.	Creditor Bal. Pmt.	Creditor Bal. Pmt.
TOTAL DEBTS			
TOTAL DEBT PAYMENTS			
TOTAL EXPENSES & DEBT PAYMENTS			
GRAND TOTAL: ALL EXPENSES PLUS ALL DEBT PAYMENTS			

Recent Transactions

The period of the break-up of a marriage, and especially the physical separation, are times of high stress when people are likely to be less careful than usual – including about finances. Keep track of all your recent transactions.

Provide documentation of any large withdrawal from, or sale of, an account or asset you made during this last year, especially since or around the time of your separation. If you can show the money you received went into a current asset (for example: home, car, furniture) then also provide that documentation (for example: bank statement, sales receipt, closing statement). If the money went into your own account, try to show what you used it for through your check register or other written records.

Loans and Gifts Received

If anyone gave you a gift or loan of money during the last year, or especially since or around the time of your separation, then obtain a written statement from the person who gave you the money showing their understanding of the amount and whether they expect it to be paid back, and the interest rate if any.

If anyone gave you a gift of an item of significant value since or at about the time of your separation (car, jewelry, antiques, pedigreed animal), then obtain written proof of the gift and the value.Obtain your individual (not joint) credit reports. Look under "Credit Reporting Agencies" in the yellow pages and call at least one. A recorded message will tell you how to obtain a copy of your credit report(s). See "Credit and Your Divorce" in chapter 4 for why this is important.

Credit Report

Obtain your individual (not joint) credit reports. Look under "Credit Reporting Agencies" in the yellow pages and call at least one. A recorded message will tell you how to obtain a copy of your credit report(s). See "Credit and Your Divorce" in Chapter 4 for why this is important.

One More Thing on Your Checklist...

Sorting out the details of your financial past and future can take its toll on your emotions. This might be a good time to go back and reread Chapter 3 and do something nice for yourself.

THE FIRST COURT PAPERS

THE FIRST COURT PAPERS

Who May File in Colorado

In order for you to obtain a Colorado divorce or legal separation, one of you must have been domiciled in Colorado for at least 90 days before filing your first papers with the court. "Domicile" is "residence" (you live here), plus the intent to make it your primary residence. If you are new in Colorado, you may file your divorce on day 91 after your arrival in the state. Voter registration or transferring your driver's license to Colorado indicates your intention to make Colorado your home. If you are leaving Colorado and you want to keep jurisdiction in this state, file your divorce before you go.

Where to File

Where do we file? The legal term for this is venue. Divorces take place in the state court, as distinguished from federal or municipal court. The state court in Colorado is divided into 22 judicial districts. Each judicial district contains at least one county, and maintains both district and county courts. Divorce cases are filed and heard in the district court.

Which district should you file in? In legal terms, this is also a *venue* question. As a practical matter, you may file your case in any district court in Colorado. Your case will stay where you file it unless your spouse or the court disagrees. Civil cases (divorce is a civil rather than a criminal matter) are supposed to be heard in the judicial district where you both live, where the respondent lives, or where the marital home was, or is. Sometimes, court administrators "clean house" and try to move all "alien" filings. It's best if the two of you agree on which district you will use before you file. You may pick the court that is most convenient for both of you. If your divorce remains friendly and cooperative, you won't have to spend much time in court anyway.

Venue: The location where a case will be heard; often refers to a choice of several available courts, those with ties to this family.

To Locate Your Court

To locate your court, see the "District Courts" list in Appendix B in the back of this book, or look in the blue pages of the phone book for the county where you want to file. Then find the sub-heading "District Court – Civil Division." Larger judicial districts may have a special Domestic Relations Division or Clerk. Asking for the Domestic Relations Clerk when you call, or addressing your correspondence to the Domestic Relations Clerk is likely to be helpful, even if there is not a specific clerk or court for divorces in your particular district.

Applicaton for Waiver of Court Costs

If your financial situation is such that the filing fee is too much for you to pay, then you may apply to the court to waive (not pay) the filing fee. Ask the clerk of the court when you go to file your case for a form for you to fill out called Application for Waiver of Court Costs in Civil Cases. The judge will review your application and decide if you should be relieved of paying.

If you are filing with the court for Parental Responsibility, it may be helpful to read the information in this chapter about where to file, understanding jurisdiction, and types of service. Depending on your circumstances, you may need a Summons or Petition in Paternity, or a form for Allocation of Parental Responsibilities. Forms for these procedures can be found at Bradford Publishing.

What Forms Do We Need?

You will need some, but not necessarily all, of the forms on the list below. Read the entire list and check off the ones you think you will need. Practice copies of each form are printed in the chapters indicated, along with line by line instructions for completing them. Actual forms that you can fill in, print and file are found on the CD-ROM in a PDF format. PDF forms cannot be saved to your computer, but the CD will allow you to print each form up to 4 times. Print a blank form, pencil in your information, and fill in the form on the screen. If you close the document, your information will be deleted. So it is best to modify your penciled drafts until you are ready to print the final form.

☐ **Petition:** Every action for divorce or legal separation needs this. Bradford Publishing form No. 248A if you have children, and 248B, if you don't. See this chapter.

☐ **Summons:** You will need this if you are not filing as co-petitioners, i.e. if you are not both signing the petition. Bradford Publishing form No. 254. See this chapter.

☐ **Waiver and Acceptance of Service/Return of Service:** One spouse can sign the waiver and acceptance of service if the other spouse filed the petition. Use the return of service—to be filled out by the person who the spouse the papers—if the spouse will not sign the waiver and acceptance of service. Bradford Publishing form No. 254-back. See this chapter.

☐ **Petitioner's Verified Motion and Order For Publication:** You will need these if:
a. you are not filing as co-petitioners, and
b. your spouse will not sign the waiver and acceptance of service, and
c. you are unable to have your spouse served personally.
Bradford Publishing form Nos. 250 and 250A. See this chapter.

☐ **Response:** If both of you signed the petition, you don't need this form. If only one spouse signed and filed the petition, the spouse who did not sign may use this. Bradford Publishing form No. 249. See this chapter.

☐ **Required Disclosure: Certificate of Compliance with C.R.C.P. 16 and 26.2.** Both parties are required to prepare, sign and file JDF 1104, certifying that they have exchanged the required information. See this chapter.

☐ **Worksheet A – Child Support Obligation: Sole Physical Care** (for 273 or more overnights per year). You will need this if your children spend less than 25% of the overnights (92 or less) per year with the other parent. Bradford Publishing form No. 1170. See Chapter 9.

☐ **Worksheet B – Child Support Obligation: Shared Physical Care:** You will need this if you have a shared physical care arrangement—93 or more overnights per year with each parent. Bradford Publishing form No. 1171. See Chapter 9.

☐ **Decree:** Everyone needs this. Bradford Publishing form No. 251. See Chapter 12.

☐ **Affidavit with Respect to Financial Affairs:** Everyone needs this, one for each spouse, unless one spouse is not available and not participating in the divorce. Bradford Publishing form No. 253. If you do not have children and are not agreeing to maintenance as part of your agreement, you may use a simplified form, JDF 1112. See Chapter 12.

☐ **Affidavit for Decree Without Appearance of Parties:** You must use this form if you are obtaining your decree "by Affidavit" rather than by a court hearing.
You qualify to avoid a hearing if:
a. there are no minor (under 21) children of this marriage; or
b. you have minor children and each of you is represented by your own attorney.
c. you agree on how to divide your property and debts.
Bradford Publishing form No. 252. See Chapter 12.

☐ **Support Order (Attachment to Decree):** Use this form if you will be paying, or receiving, child support or maintenance. Bradford Publishing form No. 251A. See Chapter 12.

☐ **Notice to Withhold Income for Support:** You will need this if you want to pay child support and/or maintenance by means of an income assignment. Bradford Publishing form No. 1155. See Chapter 12.

☐ **Notice to Employer to Deduct for Health Insurance:** You will need this if your agreement requires a working parent to provide health insurance for the children as a deduction from pay. Bradford Publishing form No. 1162. See Chapter 12.

☐ **Notice to Insurance Provider of Court-ordered Health Insurance Coverage:** You will need this if your agreement requires that a parent provide insurance for children when he or she is not currently covered. Bradford Publishing form No. 1164.

☐ **Temporary Orders Agreement, Temporary Orders:** JDF 1109 and JDF 1110. You may use these to summarize your interim agreements and to make them into a court order. See Chapter 4.

☐ **Notice to Set for Non-Contested Hearing**, and **Notice of Hearing Date:** Use Bradford Publishing form No. 1195 and JDF 1108 to set your case for hearing. See Chapter 12. In the simplified procedure, these forms will be replaced with a notice of the status conference. Ask your court about this form.

☐ **Separation Agreement:** Everyone needs this in non-contested cases. You may write your own agreement using the sample at the end of Chapter 12, elements of which can be found in Chapters 7 through 11, or use JDF 1115, (with children) or JDF 1215 (without children), or have a mediator or attorney write it for you.

☐ **Parenting Plan:** You will need this form if you have children, or you may include this information in your separation agreement. Sample form is in Chapter 8. See JDF 1113.

☐ **Qualified Domestic Relations Order:** There is no pre-printed form for this. You'll find a sample in Chapter 7. You may use this to transfer an interest in certain retirement plans from one spouse to the other when agreed to in your final separation agreement.

Keeping Track of Your Case in Court

No one except you is going to keep track of the progress of your case. If you want to know if a certain form has been filed, or a certain thing done, you have to ask. Here's an easy way to keep track of your case. If you file something in person, include two photocopies and obtain the court filing stamp on them. Keep one and give the other to your spouse. Now you both have a record of the date and time of what was filed. If you file something you want the court to sign, or file something by mail, keep two copies of what you filed, but give the clerk two more copies and two stamped, self-addressed envelopes to mail copies back to you.

Case Number

When you file your petition with the court there will be a case number, or "docket" number on your receipt. Example: 04 – DR – _____ , followed by division or courtroom number, or the judge's initials. The first two digits represent the year you filed your petition, and "DR" means Domestic Relations. *Be sure to make note of your case number because you must write it at the top of any correspondence and all forms and papers you file with the court about your case.* This is the only way to be sure that your document will find its way into your file, and not get lost.

Preparing Your Papers for the Court

You must file original forms with the court, keeping photocopies for your records. The forms you will need are located on the CD-ROM in the back of this book. Extra or additional forms are available from many office supply stores, directly from Bradford Publishing in Denver, or on their website at www.bradfordpublishing.com.

There are some procedures which vary with each district, and some which vary by county. The best way to be certain you are doing things correctly for your particular court is to find out what information they provide and if they require any specific forms or instructions.

TYPING

Papers to be filed with the court should be typed, if possible. The courts will accept forms that are printed neatly in black ink.

TRUTH

On any paper you file with the court, write only what you know or believe to be true. If the form asks for something not part of your case, write "not applicable" or "N/A" next to that question. Deliberately not telling the truth to a court, especially if signed under oath, is a crime.

Filing Your Petition

Give the clerk of the district court where you have chosen to file your case:

- Your completed petition, signed by you and notarized, or signed by both of you and notarized if you are co-petitioners. If you are signing at different times, there can be two notarizations. If you submit two copies of the Petition and stamped envelopes, the clerk will sign, date, and return the copies for your records.

- The filing fee (as of the publication of this Guidebook— $184 for dissolution of marriage, $179 for legal separation). Most courts prefer cash, money orders, or certified funds, but many will accept your personal check. Call ahead to be safe.

When you file your Petition, if this court is using the simplified procedure, the clerk will give you an Order detailing the next steps you must take. Be sure to read it carefully.

District Court, _____**①**_____ County, Colorado

Court Address:

②

③ **In re the Marriage of:**

Ⓐ **Petitioner:**

v.

Ⓑ ☐ **Respondent** ☐ **Co-petitioner:**

Attorney or Party Without Attorney (Name and Address):

④

Phone Number: E-mail:

FAX Number: Atty. Reg. #:

⑤

▲ COURT USE ONLY ▲

Case Number:

Division: **⑥** Courtroom:

PETITION FOR DISSOLUTION OF MARRIAGE OR LEGAL SEPARATION AND AFFIDAVIT AS TO CHILDREN

⑦ 1. This Petition is for ☐ Dissolution of Marriage ☐ Legal Separation.

2. The Marriage is irretrievably broken.

3. Information about the Wife: ☐ Petitioner ☐ Respondent/Co-Petitioner Check if in Military ☐

Date of Birth _____ Social Security No. (if there are children) _____

Current Mailing Address _____

City, State, Zip _____ Length of Residence in Colorado _____

⑧ Home Phone No. _____ Work Phone No. _____ Cell No. _____

4. Information about the Husband: ☐ Petitioner ☐ Respondent/Co-Petitioner Check if in Military ☐

Date of Birth _____ Social Security No. (if there are children) _____

Current Mailing Address _____

City, State, Zip _____ Length of Residence in Colorado _____

Home Phone No. _____ Work Phone No. _____ Cell No. _____

⑨ 5. Date of the Marriage _____ Place of Marriage _____

⑩ 6. Date the parties separated _____

⑪ 7. The Wife is ☐ pregnant ☐ not pregnant.

⑫ 8. The following children were born or adopted of this marriage: (attach a second sheet, if necessary).

NAME   PRESENT ADDRESS   SEX   DATE OF BIRTH   SOC. SEC. NO.

No. 248A. Rev. 7-03. PETITION FOR DISSOLUTION OF MARRIAGE/LEGAL SEPARATION/AFFIDAVIT AS TO CHILDREN (JDF 1101-A) (Page 1 of 4)

Bradford Publishing, 1743 Wazee St., Denver, CO 80202 — (303) 292-2500 — www.bradfordpublishing.com

13 A. The children have lived at the following addresses during the last five years:_____

_____

_____

14 B. The names and present addresses of the persons with whom the children have lived during the last five

years are: _____

_____

15 C. I participated as a party or witness, or in any other capacity, in the following proceeding concerning the allocation of decision-making responsibility or custody of, or visitation or parenting time with, the children (court, state, case no., date of child-custody determination, if any):_____

_____

16 D. The following proceedings for enforcement, domestic violence, domestic abuse, protection orders, restraining orders, adoption, or termination of parental rights could affect the current proceeding (court, state, case no., date, nature of proceedings): _____

_____

17 E. The following people, not a party to this proceeding, have physical custody of the children or claim rights of parental responsibilities, legal or physical custody of, or visitation or parenting time with, the above children (name and address of such persons): _____

_____

Each party has a continuing duty to inform the Court of any proceedings in this or any other state that could affect the current proceedings.

18 8a. ☐ Disclosure of information concerning children is subject to a pending *Verified Motion for Non-disclosure of Identifying Information Pursuant to §14-13-209(5), C.R.S.*

19 9. REQUIRED NOTICE OF HUMAN SERVICES INVOLVEMENT.

Check ☐ Yes OR ☐ No to the following statement:

The parents or dependent children listed on this petition have received within the last five years, or are currently receiving benefits or public assistance from the state Department of Human Services or the county Department of Social Services.

If you checked yes, answer the following:

NAME OF PERSON RECEIVING BENEFIT   NAME OF COUNTY OR STATE   CASE NO.

20 _____   _____   _____

10. REQUIRED NOTICE OF PRIOR PROTECTION/RESTRAINING ORDERS.

21 Have any civil protection/restraining orders to prevent domestic abuse, criminal protection/restraining orders, or emergency protection orders been issued against either party by any court within two years prior to the filing of this Petition? ☐ No ☐ Yes If yes, complete the following: The Protection/Restraining

22 Order was ☐ Temporary ☐ Permanent and issued against _____ **A**_____

in the County of _____ **B**_____ State of _____ **C**_____ in case number **D**_____

No. 248A. Rev. 7-03. (Page 2 of 4)

What was the subject matter of the Protection/Restraining Order or Emergency Protection Order?

23 _____ **E** _____

24 11. The following agreements, if any, as to allocation of parental responsibilities, support, maintenance, property and payment of debts have been made:

25 The Relief Requested is that the Court enter orders regarding the following:

A ☐ A Decree of ☐ Dissolution of Marriage ☐ Legal Separation

B ☐ Allocation of parental responsibilities: _____

C ☐ Child support:_____

D ☐ Maintenance: _____

E ☐ Property and/or debts: _____

F ☐ Attorney fees and costs: _____

G ☐ The name of the _____ be restored to _____

H ☐ Other orders the court finds appropriate (Use additional sheets if necessary):

NOTICE: Colorado Revised Statutes §14-10-107, provides that upon the filing of a _Petition for Dissolution of Marriage or Legal Separation_ by the petitioner or co-petitioner or by a legal guardian or conservator on behalf of one of the parties, and upon personal service of the petition and summons on the respondent, or waiver and acceptance of service by the respondent, a temporary injunction shall be in effect against **both parties** until the final decree is entered or the petition is dismissed, or until further Order of the Court.

AUTOMATIC TEMPORARY INJUNCTION

26 1. **Both parties are restrained from transferring, encumbering, concealing, or in any way disposing of, without the consent of the other party, or an order of the Court, any marital property, except in the usual course of business or for the necessities of life and requiring each party to notify the other party of any proposed extraordinary expenditures and to account for all extraordinary expenditures made after the injunction is in effect;**

2. **Both parties are enjoined from molesting or disturbing the peace of the other party; and**

3. **Both parties are restrained from removing the minor child(ren) of the parties, if any, from the state without the consent of the other party or an order of the Court.**

4. **Both parties are restrained, without at least fourteen days' advance notification and the written consent of the other party or an order of the Court, from canceling, modifying, terminating, or allowing to lapse for nonpayment of premiums, any policy of health insurance, homeowner's or renter's insurance, or automobile insurance that provides coverage to either of the parties or the minor children or any policy of life insurance that names either of the parties or the minor children as a beneficiary.**

NOTHING IN THIS INJUNCTION SHALL PROHIBIT EITHER PARTY FROM APPLYING TO THE COURT FOR FURTHER TEMPORARY ORDERS, AN EXPANDED TEMPORARY INJUNCTION, OR ORDERS MODIFYING OR REVOKING THIS INJUNCTION.

Petitioner and co-petitioner, if any, acknowledge that he or she has received a copy of, has read, and understands the terms of the Automatic Temporary Injunction above.

VERIFICATION AND ACKNOWLEDGEMENT

I swear/affirm under oath that I have read the foregoing petition and that the statements set forth therein are true and correct to the best of my knowledge.

27 _____
Petitioner   Date

State of _____

_____ County of _____ ⎫ ss.

Subscribed and affirmed, or sworn to before me on

(date) _____ .

My commission expires: _____

☐ Notary Public   ☐ [Deputy] Clerk of Court

29 _____
Signature of Attorney for Petitioner

28 _____
Co-petitioner   Date

State of _____

_____ County of _____ ⎫ ss.

Subscribed and affirmed, or sworn to before me on

(date) _____ .

My commission expires: _____

☐ Notary Public   ☐ (Deputy) Clerk of Court

_____
Signature of Attorney for Co-petitioner

The Petition

The Petition for Dissolution of Marriage or Legal Separation and Affidavit as to Children is the first document that you must submit to the court. It is your official request for a dissolution of marriage or legal separation.

INSTRUCTIONS FOR FILLING OUT THE PETITION (form 248A, with children). If you do not have children, use form 248B, and skip instructions 12-23.

1–6 of the instructions contains the information the court requires to keep track of your case. It goes in the top portion of the form known as the "Caption." You will fill out the caption on every form the same way.

1. Fill in the county in which you are filing.

2. Insert the mailing address for the court where you are filing. To find this, see Appendix B in the back of this book.

3. A. Type the full name of one of you. This person is now the "petitioner" (the person petitioning for a dissolution or separation).

    B. If one of you is not joining in the initial petition for dissolution or legal separation, check the Respondent box. If you both want to join in asking the court for the dissolution or separation, check the Co-petitioner box. Type the full name of the other of you.

4. Type the name, address and phone number, including area code, of the petitioner. Include your fax number if you have one at home. Leave the e-mail and Att. Reg.# blank or put N/A.

5. Leave this space blank for the court stamp.

6. The case number and the division, courtroom, or judge, will be assigned to you when you give the petition to the clerk of the district court and pay your filing fee. Put this information on all subsequent forms.

7. Check the appropriate box, depending on whether you are seeking a dissolution of marriage (divorce) or legal separation.

     Be sure you understand the difference between a Dissolution of Marriage and a Legal Separation (see Chapter 1).

    If you are asking for a legal separation, and your reason is that you are not convinced the marriage is irretrievably broken, you may draw a line through line #2 on the petition.

8. Fill out this information for each of you. Check the applicable box for each of you for Petitioner or Respondent/Co-Petitioner and if you are in the military. Insert your dates of birth. If you are filling out form 248A, with children, insert your social security numbers (this is required for child support purposes). Fill in your current mailing addresses. If you both still have the same address, type it in both places. If you do not know your spouse's current address type "unknown" in the lines for address and city. In most cases, the "length of residence in Colorado" is simply how long you have lived here. If this is less than one year, type the number of months and the abbreviation "mos". Insert home and work phone numbers for each of you, and cell phone numbers if you have them.

9. For "Date" and "Place of Marriage" indicate the date of the ceremony, and the city, county and state (or country, if you were married outside the U.S.A.) where your marriage ceremony was performed.

10. "Date of Separation" is the date you stopped living with your spouse. If you are still living together, type "We are not yet separated."

11. Check the appropriate box if the wife is pregnant.

If the Wife is Pregnant

A child conceived during the marriage is presumed, by law, to be the child of that marriage. If the child the wife is expecting is not the husband's child, you must tell the court. Be certain your final agreement and decree say that this child is not from this marriage. Some people also make a notation to this effect right on the petition, next to the box which tells the court that the wife is pregnant, to say "but expected child will not be child of this marriage".

---

12. List all children of the marriage, natural and adopted, even if they are now adults, and provide all the information requested. If they are married, put their married name too. If there are no living children of this marriage write "None."

13. List all the names and addresses where each of your children has lived, except for vacations or visits, for the past 5 years.

14. List the names and present addresses of any persons, other than you (the parents) who have had physical or legal custody if any of your children at any time during the last five years. This may include, for example, grandparents or other relatives, social service agencies, residential treatment centers, Department of Institutions, natural or foster parents if the child has recently come to you. You do not list camps, day care centers, babysitters, or other child care providers. Write none if this does not apply.

15. Fill in information about any legal action in which you participated concerning any of the children of this marriage. This could include a custody or visitation case, allocation of parental responsibilities, an adoption, or a non-support, delinquency, or dependency and neglect action. If the case was closed or dismissed, be certain to include this information. If there has been no such legal action, type "None".

16. Fill in the requested information about any case that could affect this court case.

17. If someone other than you (the parents) has cared for your children for any significant length of time (such as a grandparent who has always kept the children for the summer), you should list them here. In Colorado, grandparents have a right to visitation. They are sometimes given consideration in determining parenting time. If you are fairly certain there is a relative or former caretaker who will wish to be considered for parenting time or physical care of your children it is probably wise to anticipate it here. If no one fits this category, write "None."

 This information is required by both federal and state law. You will be signing this affidavit under oath and therefore swearing to the truth of this information. Be sure that it is accurate and complete to the best of your knowledge and belief.

18. You would check this box only if you have ALREADY FILED a Motion to ask the court to seal the information in this petition. If you have reason to believe that the health, safety or liberty of you or your children will be at risk by disclosing the information in this petition, such as your current address, you should STOP, call an attorney, or ask the court about how to seal this information.

19. Tell the court whether you or any of your children have received any benefits or public assistance from either the state Department of Human Services or any county Department of Social Services.

20. If you answered "yes" to number 19, you must list the name of the person receiving that benefit, his or her relationship to you, the location (county and state) of the agency that paid it, and the case number.

21. Check the appropriate box to indicate whether either of you has had any protection or restraining orders issued against you in the last 2 years.

22. If you answered "yes" to number 21, you must check whether the protection/restraining order is temporary or permanent.
    A. Write the name of the person it was issued against.
    B. Put here the county that issued it.
    C. Write the state in which it was issued.
    D. Write the case number in which the protection/restraining order was issued. Attach a separate piece of paper if there is more than one restraining order, providing the same information about each of them.

23. Write here what actions or behaviors are restrained or prohibited in the order.

24. This is where you summarize any temporary agreement you may have. Leave this blank if you don't. If you want to file it with the court, write "see attached." If you don't have a written agreement, but you are doing things in a fairly consistent way (for example, the child lives during the school week with husband, wife is making the car payment, and the two of you are sharing the mortgage 2/3 – 1/3), then describe these agreements here. You may have temporary agreements about some things, but not others. If you don't yet have any agreement, then write "no agreement."

25. This is where you tell the court what you want the court to order for you at your final hearing or after 90 days when the court reviews your final agreement. If you and your spouse have worked these things out, whether or not it is in writing, give that information to the court. If you and your spouse have not come to a complete agreement, fill in those things you have agreed to or are consistently doing. If you don't have any idea what would be fair or what you need, put words instead of dollar amounts (for example, you might type "in a fair amount", "if need is found", "whatever we agree to later", or "to be determined." These will tell the court you did not overlook this section. Check only the boxes which apply to you.

    A. Same as instruction # 7.

    B. If you have minor children, check this box. If you are co-petitioners, type in the parenting arrangement you both have agreed to, if any. If you have not agreed, write "to be determined." If you are the petitioner, type in the parenting arrangements you wish the court to order.

    C. If you have minor children, check this box. Fill in the amount you both have agreed to and who will pay it, or write "to be determined," or the amount you wish.

    D. If you are co-petitioners and you have agreed that one of you will pay maintenance to the other, check this box and fill in the amount agreed to and who will pay it. You may want to check this box, but fill in words such as "if we agree," to leave this issue open during your discussions. If you are the sole petitioner and you want to either receive maintenance from or expect to pay maintenance to your spouse, check this box. In this case you may or may not wish to fill in an amount.

    E. Check this box if there are any assets or debts of your marriage. You might want to write in "be approved as we have determined them." This way you keep control.

    F. You will probably not check this box if you are doing your divorce together. If you are the sole petitioner and you want your spouse to pay your lawyer or the costs of the case (like the court filing fee, appraisals, counseling professionals, financial advisors, mediators), then check this and complete it.

    G. Check this box if one or both of you wants to return to your name before the marriage. Type "Petitioner" or other designation in the first space, then type in the complete restored name(s) in the second space. The final decree will reflect the restored name(s) and, when signed by the judge, becomes the official document which you may use to change your Social Security card, your drivers license, bank accounts, etc. You may use the divorce proceeding to restore your name before the marriage, but not to change to an entirely new name. To do that you must file an action for change of name in the county court where you live.

    H. Check this box if you want the court to have the power to enter other orders about things you may have omitted, or which you learn about later. If you are doing your divorce together you will probably not check this box.

26. Read the Temporary Injunction carefully. It applies to both of you the instant the court has jurisdiction in the case.

27. and 28. You must sign in the presence of a notary. Be sure to include the date. If you are co-petitioners, you both sign in front of a notary or notaries, and fill in the date.

29. If either or both of you is represented by an attorney who wants to sign the petition, they may sign here.

Jurisdiction: Power of the court to enter orders; can also refer to which court is the proper place for this kind of case (i.e., juvenile court has jurisdiction over persons under 18 years); can also refer to the parties having been properly notified of the court action (see "Service of Process," this chapter).

Personal jurisdiction: Power of the court to enter orders which must be personally carried out; derives from the person(s) affected having received personal notification of the case.

In rem jurisdiction: Power of the court to enter orders only concerning a legal status; derives from those affected having received no personal notice of the case.

Quasi-in-rem jurisdiction: Power of the court to enter orders affecting some limited in-state property; derives from the request for title to that property having been specifically described in the initial

Jurisdiction

If you and your spouse are filing as *petitioner and respondent,* the information in this chapter applies to you.

If you and your spouse are *co-petitioners* and each signed the petition in front of a notary, the court already has jurisdiction. You may wish to read this section to more fully understand jurisdiction, or you may skip it and go to Chapter 7.

Jurisdiction is the legal word for the power of the court to take action about something. The court's jurisdiction in a divorce or legal separation case usually begins when both spouses file jointly as co-petitioners, OR when one spouse (petitioner) files with the court and completes service on the other spouse (respondent).

How you serve your spouse determines the type of jurisdiction (power) the court gets over your divorce case. Most cases result in either, **in personam** (personal jurisdiction), or **in rem** (jurisdiction over the matter, in this case over the legal marital status). The court has personal jurisdiction when the spouse has been served personally. The court has **in rem** jurisdiction when the whereabouts of the spouse is unknown and he or she cannot be served personally.

If the court has personal jurisdiction it can order either of you to transfer property, make payments on debts, or pay maintenance or child support. If the court has only **in rem** jurisdiction it cannot order these things. Whether Colorado courts, without personal jurisdiction over both parents, can enter orders granting custody of children located in Colorado is an unsettled legal question. Courts generally enter custody orders anyway and sometimes order support or transfer of property with the reminder that the absent spouse could come in later and re-open the matters that require personal jurisdiction.

If the court has entered such an order in your case and your spouse reappears, immediately serve him or her with all the court papers that have been filed, or ask him or her to sign the waiver of service and then ask the court to deal with the personal jurisdiction matters it could not determine earlier.

If the court has only *in rem* jurisdiction, and you must have clear title to real or other property, you must get **quasi-in-rem** jurisdiction. This procedure has specific requirements explained briefly in this chapter, and in Chapters 12 and 13.

Notifying Your Spouse/Service of Process

In the American civil legal system, the court cannot enter an order against anyone unless the court is certain that the person had notice of what was going on. If you decide to file for a divorce and your spouse does not go along with it, then you are responsible for proving to the court that your spouse was properly notified about what you filed and what you are asking for. The paper which notifies your spouse of what you have filed is the summons. Proving to the court that your spouse got a copy of the summons and petition is called service of process.

There are several ways to notify your spouse of what you have filed. To determine which procedure you should follow, complete the following checklist.

JURISDICTION AND SERVICE OF PROCESS CHECKLIST

Directions: Check the statement which fits your situation. Then, see the instructions in this chapter for that procedure.

☐ **Co-petitioner filing:**
You and your spouse are co-petitioners and each signed the petition in front of a notary. You do not need to "serve" a summons. The court has personal jurisdiction over both spouses, the children and all your property and can enter any order. You may go to Chapter 7.

☐ **Only one spouse is filing the petition and you know the whereabouts of your spouse:**
You will need to fill out the summons and then choose one of the two following methods of service:

    ☐ **Waiver and Acceptance of Service:**
You may ask your spouse to "sign" for the papers. This means that your spouse waives his or her right to be handed the papers by a third party and acknowledges receipt of a copy of both the petition and the summons. The court has jurisdiction over both parties, the children and all your property even if the respondent is out of state or in the military. If you use this procedure, your spouse must complete and sign the waiver on the back of the summons. You may then skip the section on personal service and go to Chapter 7.

    ☐ **Personal Service:**
You may have your spouse personally served with the papers and then prove to the court how service was completed. See "Personal Service" (page 110) and complete the return of service (page 113) on the back of the summons. The court has jurisdiction over both parties, any children and all property unless you served out of state on a non-resident, in which case the jurisdiction may be limited to *quasi-in-rem* (previous page). You may then go to Chapter 7.

☐ **Only one spouse is filing the petition, and you do NOT know the whereabouts of your spouse:**
If you have only a post office box or general delivery address for your spouse, or you absolutely do not know the whereabouts of your spouse, you must fill out the summons and serve your spouse by constructive service (see page 114). You must obtain permission from the court to serve in this manner by filing a Verified Motion and Order (see page 117).

☐ **Response filing:**
If your spouse filed the petition, but you do not agree, see page 120 for issues that you may respond to. Filing of a response gives the court personal jurisdiction even if the manner of service of process did not, unless the response is specifically limited to the jurisdictional issue.

District Court, _____ County, Colorado

Court Address:

❶

In re the Marriage of:

Petitioner: **❷**

v.

Respondent:

Attorney or Party Without Attorney (Name and Address):

❶

▲ COURT USE ONLY ▲

Phone Number: E-mail:

Case Number:

❸

FAX Number: Atty. Reg. #:   Division: Courtroom:

SUMMONS FOR DISSOLUTION OF MARRIAGE OR LEGAL SEPARATION AND TEMPORARY INJUNCTION

TO THE RESPONDENT NAMED ABOVE:

You are summoned and required to file with the Clerk of this court a Response to the attached Petition within twenty (20) days after this Summons is served on you in the State of Colorado, or within thirty (30) days after this summons is served on you outside of the State of Colorado, or is published.

After ninety (90) days from the date of service or publication, the Court may enter a decree affecting your marital status, dividing marital property, and addressing parental responsibilities, child support, maintenance, attorney fees and costs to the extent the Court has jurisdiction.

If you fail to file a Response or enter your appearance in this case, any or all of the matters above, or any related matters which come before this Court, may be decided without further notice to you.

❹   This is an action to obtain a decree of: ☐ Dissolution of Marriage ☐ Legal Separation   as more fully described in the attached Petition, and for orders regarding the following children of the marriage:

❺

and for title to the following in-state property:

❻

NOTICE:

Section 14-10-107, Colorado Revised Statutes, provides that upon the filing of a Petition for Dissolution of Marriage or Legal Separation by the Petitioner or Co-petitioner or by a legal guardian or conservator on behalf of one of the parties, and upon personal service of the Petition and Summons on the Respondent, or upon waiver and acceptance of service by the Respondent, a temporary injunction shall be in effect against **both parties** until the final decree is entered or the Petition is dismissed, or until further order of the Court. Either party may apply to the Court for further temporary orders, an expanded temporary injunction, or modification or revocation under §14-10-108, C.R.S. or any other appropriate statute.

AUTOMATIC TEMPORARY INJUNCTION

❼ **BY ORDER OF THE COURT, YOU AND YOUR SPOUSE ARE:**

1. **Restrained from transferring, encumbering, concealing or in any way disposing of, without the consent of the other party or an Order of the Court, any marital property, except in the usual course of business or for the necessities of life, and requiring each party to notify the other party of any proposed extraordinary expenditures and to account to the Court for all extraordinary expenditures made after the injunction is in effect;**
2. **Enjoined from molesting or disturbing the peace of the other party; and,**
3. **Restrained from removing the minor child or children of the parties, if any, from the State without the consent of the other party or an Order of the Court.**
4. **Restrained, without at least fourteen days' advance notification and the written consent of the other party or an order of the Court, from canceling, modifying, terminating, or allowing to lapse for nonpayment of premiums, any policy of health insurance, homeowner's or renter's insurance, or automobile insurance that provides coverage to either of the parties or the minor children or any policy of life insurance that names either of the parties or the minor children as a beneficiary.**

❽

☐ Signature of the [Deputy] Clerk of Court   Date   ☐ Signature of the Attorney for the Petitioner   Date

No. 254. Rev. 5-02. SUMMONS FOR DISSOLUTION OF MARRIAGE OR LEGAL SEPARATION AND TEMPORARY INJUNCTION

Bradford Publishing, 1743 Wazee St., Denver, CO 80202 — 303-292-2500 — www.bradfordpublishing.com — 6-03

The Summons

If you and your spouse are co-petitioners you do not need this form or service of process. Go to Chapter 7.

The summons for dissolution of marriage or legal separation and temporary injunction is the official document used to notify your spouse of your request (petition) for a divorce or legal separation. In legal terms you are the "petitioner" and your spouse is the "respondent." This means that you are the one who is initiating the request to dissolve the marriage and that your spouse chooses not to join in the request from the beginning. This does not necessarily imply that your spouse is contesting or disagreeing with your request. For more information on responding, see the end of this chapter.

INSTRUCTIONS FOR FILLING OUT THE SUMMONS

1. Fill out these lines the same as you did on the petition.

2. Type your name in the space for petitioner and your spouse's name in the space for respondent, just as you did on the petition.

3. Leave these spaces blank until you take your petition to the clerk of the district court. Once the clerk has assigned you a case number, it is a good idea (although not technically required) to include the case number on the summons before it is served.

4. Check the appropriate box, depending on whether you are asking for a dissolution of marriage (divorce) or a legal separation.

5. List only minor children (under 21) who are not married or in the military service. If you do not have any children from this marriage (born or adopted), write "none".

6. If you have no marital property write "none." If you have already divided your marital property and transferred title, type "as completed." **If** you have agreed how title will be changed but are waiting until after the decree to do it, **if** you can only serve by publication, **or if** you are cooperating in your divorce but have not yet divided your property and you want the court to have the power to enforce your agreement about the property, fill in this section by listing the big items of property such as your automobile, home and other real estate (giving the location of each parcel)—basically things with titles. If you are dealing with an absent spouse who will not participate in your divorce process, then you can obtain *quasi-in-rem* jurisdiction over larger items of in-state property by means of *constructive service*. Part of that process **requires** you to specifically describe those large items of property here.

7. Read the Temporary Injunction carefully (also on the petition). It applies to both of you the instant the court has jurisdiction in the case.

8. Do not date or sign the summons. These spaces are for the signature of the clerk of the court or your attorney, if any. Obtain the signature of one or the other.

Waiver: The giving up of a legal right. In waiver and acceptance of service, the respondent is giving up the right to require the petitioner to have the papers personally delivered by a third party to him or her.

"If I sign the Waiver, I am signing away all my rights."

Not so. What you give away in signing the Waiver, is your right to make your spouse hire the sheriff or process server to give you the papers. You still have the right to participate in every phase of the negotiations.

"My 90-days started when I filed the Petition."

Not necessarily. The 90-days begins only when both filing and service of process are complete. Both are completed at the same time when you file as co-petitioners, but at different times in all other circumstances.

WAIVER AND ACCEPTANCE OF SERVICE

If your spouse does not want to be a co-petitioner, but is willing to accept service by "signing" for the papers, then your spouse is said to be "waiving" (giving up) the legal right to be "served" (handed the papers by the sheriff or a neutral third person). In signing the waiver, your spouse is not agreeing to the truth of anything you wrote in the petition—including arrangements you say have been already made and the "relief" you requested. By signing the waiver, your spouse only acknowledges receipt of a copy of both the petition and summons and acknowledges and accepts the court's power (jurisdiction) to issue a decree that will be binding on both of you. If your spouse is not living in Colorado, using the waiver can substantially decrease the time involved to obtain a divorce or separation because you can avoid time-consuming out-of-state service. A signed waiver may also give the court personal jurisdiction over the Respondent, where even personal out-of-state service might not.

If Your Spouse Is In the Military Service

If your spouse is in the military service, he or she is protected by the Soldiers and Sailors Civil Relief Act. This law provides that military personnel cannot have orders or judgments entered against them if they cannot attend the hearing because they are in the military. The serviceperson, his or her spouse or any dependent can receive counseling and legal advice from the Judge Advocate General's (JAG) office where they are stationed. This includes advice to the serviceperson about the jurisdictional meaning to him or her of signing the waiver and acceptance of service. If you check the box on the form to indicate that this is a military waiver, you should expect that your spouse will have it reviewed by the JAG office. If your spouse is on active duty, away from home and will not sign the waiver, your divorce case may be very difficult to accomplish at the present time. You may wish to consult an attorney if this happens. In practice, most mililtary persons sign and return the waiver promptly.

90 Days Begins

If your spouse signs the waiver, the 90-day waiting period begins the date the waiver is signed in front of a notary, provided that you have already filed the petition with the court or do so within 10 days of the signing of the waiver. In practice, the signed waiver may become void if your petition has not been filed within ten days of the signing of the waiver.

WAIVER AND ACCEPTANCE OF SERVICE

I declare under oath that I am the Respondent in this case; that I received and accepted service of the Summons and Petition in this case; that I waive any other service, and consent to the jurisdiction of this Court to determine all issues raised in the pleadings as if I were served by personal service within the State of Colorado.

Check one:

□ I am not in the military service. This waiver of service is not to be construed as an admission by me of the truth of the allegations in the Petition and I reserve the right to receive notices of settings and the right to respond and appear in person if I wish.

1

OR

□ I am in the active military service of the United States of America. After consultation with the base legal officer or other counsel of my choice, I waive the provisions of the Soldier's and Sailor's Relief Act of 1942, as amended, including my right to court-appointed counsel, and permit the action to proceed without further notice to me.

Signed under oath before me on _____

2 _____
Signature of Respondent

My commission expires _____

Address: _____

_____

_____
Notary

INSTRUCTIONS FOR FILLING OUT THE WAIVER AND ACCEPTANCE OF SERVICE

1. Have your spouse check the appropriate box.

2. Your spouse must sign in the presence of a notary. Once your spouse signs and returns the waiver, you may go to Chapter 7.

Personal service: Having legal papers handed to and left with a party or witness. Must be served by a *disinterested* (not connected to the case) person over 18.

Not So Friendly

It is not a good idea to have your new "significant other" or a close personal friend serve the papers on your spouse. It may create hard feelings which could add to an already difficult time and make a friendly settlement less likely.

PERSONAL SERVICE

If you know where your spouse is and he or she did not sign as co-petitioner, and did not or will not sign the waiver and acceptance of service, you must have your spouse served with the summons and petition. If your spouse is in Colorado, you may use a friend to serve, or use a private process server in the same locale. Whether your spouse is in Colorado or some other state, you may use the sheriff in the county where your spouse lives.

Using a Friend to Serve Your Spouse

You may ask an acquaintance to give your divorce papers to your spouse. This is a lot to ask of a friend. To serve this way, give your friend a **COPY** of the Petition, and a **COPY** of the Summons, marked (with pencil, or with a sticky note) "to be served." Also give the friend the **ORIGINAL** Summons, showing on the back where the friend will fill out the Return of Service.

Using the Local Sheriff or Private Process Server to Serve Your Spouse

If you are having your spouse served locally, check the government section of the phone book for the sheriff's number or the yellow pages for a "process server." If you are having your spouse served out of town or out of state, call directory assistance in that area code and ask for the sheriff's office for that county. Call and obtain their rates for Civil Service of Process. Then send a **COPY** of the petition, and a **COPY** of the summons, marked (with pencil, or with a sticky note) "to be served." Also send the **ORIGINAL** summons, indicating on the back where the process server is to fill out the return of service. Enclose a stamped envelope, addressed to you, and a check for the amount they charge for service. You may write a cover letter to the process server like the following sample. Including the Spouse's Whereabouts Information Sheet, which follows, will give the server valuable information.

Sample Cover Letter to Process Server

Your name
Your address
Date of your letter:

Dear Sheriff/Process Server,

Please serve the enclosed copies of a Petition for Dissolution of Marriage or Legal Separation, and the Summons on _____ (name of your spouse).

Information for locating _____ (name of your spouse) is on the attached Spouse's Whereabouts Information Sheet.

I have enclosed a photograph to help you identify him/her.

After you have completed the Return of Service on the back, please return the original Summons to me in the enclosed stamped legal size envelope.

My check to you for $_____ is enclosed.

Sincerely,

Enclosures:

   Original Summons
   Photocopy of Summons
   Photocopy of Petition
   Spouse's Whereabouts Information Sheet
   Your check to the Process Server
   Stamped legal size envelope addressed to you

---

90 Days Begins

If you serve your spouse by personal service, the 90-day waiting period begins on the date personal service is completed, provided that the petition has already been filed with the court or is filed within 10 days of the personal service. If you have not previously filed your petition with the court, you must do so within ten days of personal service, or the service becomes void.

SPOUSE'S WHEREABOUTS INFORMATION SHEET

If you are using personal or constructive service, you will find it useful to complete this form. It will help you to gather and clarify the information needed for personal or constructive service. Copy this form, complete the information, copy the information onto the Motion if doing constructiove service, or give it to the server if doing personal service. It is helpful to include a recent photograph of your spouse for the server. Any sheriff will charge by the number of attempts to serve and mileage so efficient service is much less costly.

Spouse's full name:_____

Other names used by spouse: _____

Last known address: _____
Street, Apt. #

_____
P.O. Box

_____
City, State, Zip

When there: _____

Work information:

    Company name: _____

    Company office address: _____

    _____

    Position/title _____

    Hours: _____

    Supervisor: _____

Physical Description: _____

_____

Family members who might know where spouse is:

Name _____   Relationship _____

Address _____

Phone: Work _____   Home _____

Name _____   Relationship _____

Address _____

Phone: Work _____   Home _____

RETURN OF SERVICE

State of _____ **①** _____ }
County of _____ **②** _____ }

I declare under oath that I served this Summons and a copy of the Petition in this case on the Respondent in County of
_____ **③** _____ on _____ **④** _____ (date) at _____ **⑤** _____ (time) at the following
location:. _____ **⑥** _____
Check one:

☐ By handing it to a person identified to me as the Respondent.
⑦ ☐ By leaving it with the Respondent who refused service.
☐ By leaving it with_____who is over the age of 18
and is designated to receive service for the Respondent.
☐ I am over the age of 18 years and am not interested in nor a party to this case.
⑧ ☐ I attempted to serve the Respondent on _____ occasions but have not been able to locate the Respondent. Return to the Petitioner
⑨ is made on _____ (date).

Signed under oath before me on _____
⑩   ☐ Private process server **⑪** _____
My commission expires _____   ☐ Sheriff,_____ County

_____   Fee $ _____ Mileage $ _____
Notary Public

INSTRUCTIONS FOR FILLING OUT THE RETURN OF SERVICE

The person who serves the papers must fill out the return of service to show how he or she delivered, or attempted to deliver, the papers (petition and summons) to your spouse. The steps below should be followed by the person serving or attempting service on your spouse, **NOT BY YOU.**

1. Indicate the state in which service of the summons (and petition) was actually made or attempted.

2. Write the county in which service of the summons (and petition) was actually made or attempted.

    Complete steps 3-7 *only* if service was accomplished. If service was not accomplished, go directly to step 8.

3. Same as step 2.

4. Indicate the date the summons and petition were served.

5. Indicate the time (including a.m. or p.m.) of delivery.

6. Write the address or other description of the exact location where you served the Respondent.

7. Check the appropriate box.

8. Check this box.

9. This should be filled in *only* if it was not possible to locate respondent.

10. Leave blank. This must be filled in by a notary.

11. Make sure that the person who served your spouse, or attempted service, signs in this space and dates his/her signature, in the presence of a notary, and checks the correct box.

Constructive service: Serving papers when papers can't be served, a "legal fiction," refers to publishing notice of the case in a newspaper and/or sending the papers to a post office box or other non-specific address.

 If you can only do published or mailed service, the court only gets jurisdiction over the marital status and sometimes over in-state property. The same is true for out of state service on a spouse with "no contacts" with the state of Colorado.

 "It's okay to tell the court that you don't know where your spouse is, even when you actually do know or could easily find out."

This is not only a bad idea, it's also a crime, which is why it requires a Verified (sworn) Motion to get permission to serve your case by constructive service. Lying about this might get you a divorce without initial hassle, but your divorce is null and void (can be wiped out) if your spouse finds out about it and can prove to the court that you knew his or her whereabouts all along, or could have discovered it.

CONSTRUCTIVE SERVICE – DIVORCING THE ABSENT SPOUSE

There are three ways to get jurisdiction for the court so your divorce can proceed even if you cannot actually serve your spouse personally.

Certified Mail allows you to send the petition and summons to your spouse's last known address.

Publication by Consolidated Notice permits the court to include your names and docket number in a group publication in a local paper so you can obtain a decree of dissolution.

Publication of Summons (Individual) enables you to publish your whole summons in a local paper so that the court can give you not only the final decree but also title to in-state real estate, cars, and other titled assets. Some of the larger courts have their own instructions about how they want this done. Ask about this when you file your petition.

Why Should I Bother With Constructive Service?

If you can serve your spouse only by constructive service, the court only gets jurisdiction over the legal marital status and if you follow some additional procedures, over certain in-state titled property. So, why bother? Why not stay married?

Marital Obligations Continue After Separation

So long as you are legally married, you are potentially obligating each other on every debt you make and arguably sharing all property you acquire, regardless of the names on either. Any children born or conceived by the wife are presumed to be fathered by the husband, even if the real father is present at the delivery and wants the child to carry his name.

Certified Mail

If you have only a post office or general delivery address for your spouse, you will need to get permission from the court to serve by certified mail. To do this, prepare the Verified Motion shown below. Take or mail the original and a photocopy of your verified motion along with a stamped envelope addressed to you, to the clerk of the district court where you filed your case.

Different courts handle service by certified mail in different ways. Some courts do the certified mailing for you, and some ask you to do it yourself. You must ask which procedure your court uses.

1. *If your court does the mailing,* then you must pay the court a small fee to do this for you. The court will then mail back to you, in the envelope you provide, a receipt showing the dates the petition and summons were mailed to your former spouse. Sometimes the court will post notice of your divorce on a bulletin board or other public place at the courthouse, so do not be startled if you see it there.

2. *If your court does not do the mailing for you,* then you should expect to receive, from the clerk, the copy of the verified motion and order showing the date the judge signed the order. You then send your spouse, by certified mail, RETURN RECEIPT REQUESTED (forms available at the post office), one copy each of the petition, the summons, and the verified motion and order as signed by the judge. You will eventually receive in the mail either the green receipt card signed by your spouse, or the original envelope you mailed showing that it was never picked up. Be sure you put your case number on everything, including both post office forms.

If you get back the signed green card, file it with your case in the court file, and you have completed service sufficiently to obtain a final decree of dissolution of marriage. **For service by certified mail, the 90-day waiting period begins the date your spouse signed the certified envelope.**

If the entire envelope is returned to you, this indicates that certified mail was not accomplished, and that you did not get service on your spouse. You must file another verified motion and order asking this time for permission to publish, which is covered in the next section.

Publication by Consolidated Notice

For publication by consolidated notice, the clerk groups together all the cases for divorce filed that week or month which request service by publication, and runs them in a "consolidated notice" in the newspaper. To participate in this, give the clerk the original and a copy of the verified motion and order, the original summons, a stamped envelope addressed to you, and the amount of money the clerk requests. The clerk will publish the consolidated notice, sign a certificate of publication, put the original of this in your file, and send you a copy. **In consolidated notice publication, the 90 day waiting period starts on the last date of publication.**

Service by Certified Mail: The Clerk of the Court mails a copy of the summons and petition to the respondent's last known address, or to an address such as a post office box or general delivery, when no address for service of the respondent is known. Requires court permission.

Service by Publication (Consolidated Notice): clerk of the court supplies a general notice to newspapers listing all similar actions filed in that court on or by a certain date. Lists only names of parties and case numbers of all actions for dissolution of marriage, etc. Requires court permission.

Service by Publication (Individual)

DEFINITION

Publishing your entire Summons in a newspaper, usually in the county where the case is filed, once a week for four weeks. Necessary to obtain *quasi-in-rem* jurisdiction.

Publication of Summons (Individual)

There are several reasons why you might want to serve your spouse by publication of summons (individual).

a) If you want the court to have jurisdiction over title to in-state property (see Jurisdiction, this chapter), then you must publish your whole Summons, individually, not a consolidated notice with other cases.

b) If you are reasonably certain of your spouse's whereabouts, but do not have an exact address, then you may want to publish the summons in a newspaper in that locale. The consolidated notice is published only in the county where the case is filed.

c) The jurisdiction where your case is filed may not have a consolidated notice option.

To do service by individual publication, complete the verified motion and order for publication and give the original and a copy and a stamped envelope addressed to you, to the clerk of the district court. Ask the clerk to send the copy back to you indicating when the judge signed the order which gives you permission to publish.

You must publish your entire summons in a newspaper of general circulation four times one week apart. The newspaper may be located either where the respondent is located or in the county where your case is filed. As a general rule, local papers are much less expensive than the big dailies. Call and find out what they charge. You may choose the least expensive if you wish. Send the newspaper a copy of the summons and petition and a copy of the signed order for publication, along with their fee, and a stamped envelope addressed to you. After the publication is completed, the newspaper will send you "proof of publication" in the envelope you provided. Send the proof of publication and the original summons to the court for filing in your case. (You have already filed the petition.) **In individual publication, the 90-day waiting period begins on the last day of publication.**

① District Court, _____ County, Colorado

Court Address:

In re _____ :

Petitioner:

v.

Respondent:

Attorney or Party Without Attorney (Name and Address):

Phone Number: _____ E-mail: _____

FAX Number: _____ Atty. Reg. #: _____

▲ COURT USE ONLY ▲

Case Number:

Division: _____ Courtroom: _____

② **PETITIONER'S VERIFIED MOTION:** ☐ **PUBLICATION OF SUMMONS**
☐ **SERVICE BY CERTIFIED MAIL**
☐ **PUBLICATION BY CONSOLIDATED NOTICE**

The Petitioner moves for an Order to serve the Respondent by the method checked above for the following reasons:

③ 1. Petitioner has filed for a: ☐ Dissolution of Marriage ☐ Legal Separation
☐ Other _____

☐ Petitioner has been unable to locate an address for service of Respondent despite diligent efforts consisting of:

_____

_____

④ 3. ☐ Respondent's known address is a post office box.

☐ The last known address of the Respondent is: _____

⑤ _____

⑥ 4. Petitioner last saw Respondent on _____ (date) at _____

_____(place)

5. ☐ Property located in the state of Colorado, in which the Respondent has an interest, is the subject of this action by *quasi*

⑦ *in rem* jurisdiction, and is specifically described in the Summons.

☐ Minor children, if any, who are the subject of this action, are listed in the Summons.

⑧ _____   _____
Petitioner   Attorney for Petitioner

⑨ Subscribed and affirmed, or sworn to before me in the County of _____, State of _____,

this _____ day of _____, 20_____.

My commission expires: _____   _____
                                                                              Notary Public/Clerk

CERTIFICATE OF MAILING AND POSTING

⑩ I certify that on _____ (date), I posted a copy of the Summons ☐ and Petition in this case, from

_____ to _____ and on _____ (date) I mailed a

copy of the Petition and Summons to the Respondent at Respondent's last known address, as follows:

TO: _____

_____

_____   _____
                                                                      (Deputy) Clerk of Court

No. 250. Rev. 9-03. PETITIONER'S VERIFIED MOTION (JDF 1301-A)

Bradford Publishing, 1743 Wazee St., Denver, CO 80202 — 303-292-2500 — www.bradfordpublishing.com

District Court, _____ County, Colorado

Court Address:

11 **In re the Marriage of:**

Petitioner:

v.

Respondent:

▲ COURT USE ONLY ▲

Case Number:

Division: Courtroom:

ORDER FOR PUBLICATION

12 This Matter comes before this Court on Petitioner's:

☐ Verified Motion for Publication of Summons

☐ Verified Motion for Service by Certified Mail

☐ Verified Motion for Publication by Consolidated Notice

The Court is satisfied that the Petitioner has used due diligence to obtain personal service upon the Respondent and that all such efforts have failed.

Therefore, the COURT ORDERS:

☐ That the summons in this case shall be published, including the description of the property located in the state of Coloradoand the names of any children of this action, for four (4) weeks, and that the Clerk of this Court send a copy of the Petitionand Summons to the last known address of the Respondent.

☐ That the Petition and Summons shall be served on the Respondent by certified mail.

☐ That the Clerk of this Court shall include this case in the consolidated notice pursuant to Section 14-10-107(4), CRS,as amended.

BY THE COURT

Date: _____   _____

                                          Judge/Magistrate

The *Petitioner's Verified Motion and Order for Publication* are to be used to meet the service requirement only if, with due diligence, you have been unable to locate your spouse after a good faith effort to find him or her. You will have summarized this information if you filled out the Spouse's Whereabouts Information Sheet.

Instructions for Filling Out the Petitioner's Verified Motion and Order For Publication

1. Fill out these lines the same as on the petition. Be sure to include the case number and the division or courtroom number. Fill in your name for petitioner and your spouse's name for respondent as they appear on the petition.

2. Check the correct box: "Publication by Consolidated Notice" or "Publication of Summons," depending whether you need the court to have the power to give you title to property; "Service by Certified Mail" if you know your spouse's mailing address or post office box but can't get a street address.

3. Check the appropriate box depending on whether you are asking for a dissolution of marriage or a legal separation. Write N/A in the space for "Other".

4. Check the appropriate box. If you have not been able to locate your spouse's address, describe in detail all efforts you made to determine his or her whereabouts. IF YOU KNOW YOUR SPOUSE'S OUT OF STATE ADDRESS, YOU MUST PERSONALLY SERVE HIM OR HER IF POSSIBLE.

5. Type your spouse's last known address.

6. Fill in the date, city, state, and address, if possible, of the place where you last saw your spouse.

7. Check the first box if you have listed any property in the summons; check the second box if you have listed any children in the summons.

8. Sign and date in the presence of a notary.

9. Leave blank. This is for the notary to fill in and sign.

10. Leave blank. The Certificate of Mailing and Posting will be completed by the court.

11. Fill out the caption the same as on the Motion, except that the information for attorney or *pro se* party is not needed.

12. Leave blank. The order will be completed by court personnel.

The Response

This form is for the spouse who did not sign the petition.

When the petitioner asks the court for a dissolution of marriage, he or she says to the court that the marriage is "irretrievably broken." But, what if you really do not want the divorce, and instead believe the relationship can be reconciled? In that case, you may wish instead to be a respondent (responding to the petition).

You may use the response to say any of the following:

- That you disagree that the marriage is irretrievably broken. If you are using the Response to urge the court to find that the marriage is not broken, and that there is a chance for reconciliation, then you MUST sign the Response in front of a notary.

- That you think any of the factual data on the petition is incorrect.

- That you disagree with what the petition said were temporary arrangements.

- That you want results different from those requested in the final paragraph of the petition.

If you are using the response for any purpose except to urge that the marriage is not irretrievably broken, your signature does not have to be notarized. But, you may wish to do so anyway, to show the seriousness of your intent.

If the response asks for a reconciliation, the court may postpone signing the decree for up to an additional 60 days and order the spouses to try marriage counseling. If the court does so and the petitioner still wants the divorce at the end of 60 days, the divorce will go through.

To file the response, send or give the original response to the clerk of the district court along with the current filing fee ($70) in cash, certified or cashier's check, or money order. Give or send a copy to the petitioner. To prove to the court that you have given or mailed a copy of the response to the petitioner, fill out the Certificate of Service/Mailing on the original response form to show when you gave your spouse a copy or mailed one to him or her or the petitioner's lawyer. Use certified mail, return receipt requested, to prove to the court that you did this. File the green card, which the post office returns to you, or take it personally to your final hearing. Be sure to write your case number on it.

Contradiction?

Is it contradictory to file a Response asking for a reconciliation of your marriage while at the same time using this guidebook to reach a settlement? Not necessarily. You may feel strongly against the divorce, but still be sufficiently realistic to know it will happen, and sensible enough to want to keep control over how it happens. The initial papers to the court, the Petition and Response, tell the court and anyone who reads your file, how you each felt at the time the petition was filed.

District Court, _____ County, Colorado
Court address:

In re the Marriage of:
Petitioner:

1 v.

Respondent:

▲ COURT USE ONLY ▲

Attorney or Party Without Attorney (Name and Address):

Case Number:

Division: Courtroom:

Phone Number: E-mail:
FAX Number: Atty. Reg. #:

**RESPONSE TO THE PETITION FOR
DISSOLUTION OF MARRIAGE OR LEGAL SEPARATION**

The Respondent states that:

2   ☐ The marriage is irretrievably broken.

OR   ☐ The marriage is not irretrievably broken.*

☐ There is a possibility of reconciliation.

☐ The parties should seek counseling.

The information in number(s) _____**3**_____ of the Petition is incorrect. The following information is correct:

4 The Relief Requested is that the Court enter orders regarding the following:

A ☐ A finding that the marriage is not irretrievably broken

B ☐ That the Court suggest to the parties that they seek counseling

C ☐ A Decree of ☐ Dissolution of Marriage ☐ Legal Separation

D ☐ Allocation of parental responsibilities: _____

E ☐ Child Support: _____

F ☐ Maintenance:_____

G ☐ Property and/or debts:_____

*Sign before a notary if you deny that the marriage is irretrievably broken.

H ☐ Attorney fees and costs: _____

I ☐ The name of the Respondent be changed to: _____

J ☐ Other orders the Court finds appropriate:

Date: _____ **5**   _____
                                          Respondent

                                          _____
                                          Address

                                          _____
                                          City, State, Zip

                                     6 _____
                                          Attorney for Respondent

7 STATE OF COLORADO
      _____ County of _____ } ss.

      Signed under oath before me on _____.

      My commission expires: _____

                                          _____
                                          Notary Public

---

8   **CERTIFICATE OF SERVICE**

I certify that on _____ (date) a copy of the *RESPONSE TO THE PETITION FOR DISSOLUTION OF MARRIAGE OR LEGAL SEPARATION* was served on the other party by

☐ Hand Delivery OR

☐ Faxed to this number _____ OR

☐ placed in the United States mail, postage pre-paid, and addressed to the following:

TO: _____

    _____

    _____

                                          _____
                                          (Your Signature)

INSTRUCTIONS FOR FILLING OUT THE RESPONSE

1. Fill out this entire top section of the form the same as the top of the petition. If there are misspellings or other errors in this material, include your corrections under number 4 below.

2. If you agree that your marriage is irretrievably broken, check the first box. If you do not agree, check the second box, then check the third box if you think there is a possibility of reconciliation, and the fourth box if you think you and your spouse should seek counseling.

3. If the petitioner has made any factual errors in paragraphs 3 through 11 of the petition, write the number of the paragraph you are correcting in the space indicated and any corrections or missing information you want the court to know in the space below. Repeat as needed for every paragraph for which there is a correction.

4. This is where you tell the court what you want the court to order. If you and your spouse are in agreement, check only those boxes that are consistent with those that your spouse checked on the petition.

   A. If you believe your marriage is not irretrievably broken and you want the court to agree, check this box. This will probably not apply if you are doing your divorce together.

   B. If you want the court to suggest that you and your spouse seek counseling, check this box.

   C. If you want the court to enter a decree of dissolution of marriage at your final hearing, check the first box. If you want the court to enter a decree of legal separation at your final hearing, check the first and third boxes.

   D. If you have minor children, check this box. If you and your spouse have agreed to your parenting arrangements, type that information in the space provided, which should agree with the parenting arrangement requested in the petition. If you do not agree with what is stated in the petition, write either "to be determined," or the parenting arrangements you wish to have, such as "the respondent," "the petitioner," or "the parties mutually."

   E. If you have minor children check this box and fill in the amount you have agreed to and who will pay it, or write "to be determined", or the amount you wish.

   F. If you want to either receive maintenance from or expect to pay mainenance to your spouse, check this box and fill in the amount you have agreed to and who will pay it, or write "to be determined", or the amount you wish and who will pay it.

   G. Check this box if there are any assets or debts of your marriage. Fill in the blank with what is on the petition if you agree with it.

   H. You will probably not check this box if you are doing your divorce together. If you want your spouse, the petitioner, to pay your lawyer or the costs of the case (like filng fee, appraisals, counseling professionals, financial advisors, mediators), then check this box and complete it.

   I. Write your former name if you want it back.

   J. Check this box if you want the court to have the power to enter other orders about things you may have omitted, or which you learned about later. If you are doing your divorce together you will probably not check this box.

5. Put your signature here and write the date in the space provided. If you have written in step 4 that you do not agree that your marriage is irretrievably broken, you must sign this line in front of a notary. Otherwise you do not need a notary.

6. If you have a attorney representing you, he or she signs here.

7. The notary will fill out this part, if necessary.

8. Complete the Certificate of Service on the back of the Response to prove to the court that you have given or mailed a copy of the Response to your spouse.

What If You and/or Your Spouse Have a Change of Heart?

What if you wake up the morning after filing your case with a heart full of regrets? What if you feel you might not need a legal separation or a divorce after all?

If your case has not been served yet, you can call the sheriff and tell him to hold off while you re-think. He will send you back your papers and your down payment—with a bill for his time.

If the case has been served, you filed jointly, there are no lawyers, and you are *not* under the simplified procedure, your case will not come to a hearing unless *you* take some action to set a hearing or file the final papers. If your case has languished in the court-house with nothing happening for several months, the clerk will contact you by mail saying that your case will be dismissed unless you take steps to activate and conclude it. This way of dismissing your case for "failure to take action" has the advantage of giving you a few months, in some courts, to see if the changes in behavior you and your spouse have promised each other will actually take place. If you decide to go ahead, you will not have to pay any additional fee and can take up exactly where you stopped.

If you and your spouse both agree that the divorce is a bad idea at this time and want to have it dismissed—knowing you will have to start all over if the reconciliation does not work out—you may ask the court for the forms you need to accomplish this.

If you, the Petitioner, want to drop the divorce before the other side has filed a response, double check yourself to be sure that this is what you truly want. In many families, expecially those experiencing domestic violence or abuse, the morning after remorse and guilt may be very powerful. If you are the victim, you may be under tremendous pressure from your spouse, friends and family to drop the divorce, forgive, and give the abuser another chance. Only you have the right to determine how many chances are enough. Statistically, sadly, the odds are not with reformation.

Discovery

Now that you have begun the Court process and established the Court's jurisdiction over both of you, your marriage, and any children, it's time to uncover, and make available to each other, all the information about your financial circumstances. You can make your own checklist of all the documents for your situation or use the Great Hairy Checklist in Chapter 5. You will both need to have all this information before beginning to negotiate your agreement about division of debts and assets, how to raise and support your children, or help each other out financially.

◆ CAUTION

Dismissal for Failure to Take Action

Some courts will dismiss your divorce or legal separation case if you fail to take action towards finalizing it within a reasonable time, sometimes very soon after the waiting period is over. The dismissal notice gives you 30 days to send in the final papers and proposed decree, or set your case for a non-contested hearing or a contested trial. If you don't do one of these, your case will be dismissed by the court.

Required Disclosure

Parties to a domestic case in Colorado must exchange certain information—whether or not they have lawyers. You must give each other the following within 20 days of when you both signed and filed the Petition as Co-Petitioners, or within 40 days of when your case was served in-state (50 days if served out-of-state). (See the earlier part of this chapter for kinds of service.)

- Completed Affidavit With Respect to Financial Affairs for EACH of you (see Chapter 12)

- 3 years of personal income tax returns with all schedules, attached W-2's, 1099's, and K-1's

- 3 years of business returns, if any

- Paycheck stubs, or proof of income, for 3 months

- Any available information relating to retirement-type assets

Once you have exchanged this information, you will each prepare, sign and file the Certificate of Compliance, JDF 1104 found on the CD-ROM.

Checklist of Required Disclosure:
(initial when done)

	Completed	Exchanged
Financial affidavit	Initials/Date	Initials/Date
3 years personal tax return	Initials/Date	Initials/Date
Paystub/proof of income	Initials/Date	Initials/Date
3 years business tax return, if any	Initials/Date	Initials/Date
Retirement account info	Initials/Date	Initials/Date

 "That's just my lawyer talking."

Avoid the temptation to try to get your spouse to agree to something before you provide all the information, or before he or she has had time to digest and understand it all. On the other side of that coin, it's also wise to avoid allowing yourself to be talked into something before you feel you have grasped the whole picture. Review Chapter 3 about fear, and how to steady yourself through a time of great change. You can practice saying "I'll give that some thought," and/or "I don't feel like I'm ready to make that decision yet." Then get the input you need—discussing it in mediation, or with counsel. Take the steps you need to take in order to be able to make appropriate and wise choices.

CHAPTER 7

ASSETS AND DEBTS
SEPARATION AGREEMENT – PART I

Separation Agreement: The written (typed) instrument, filed with the court that sets out how the parties are dividing assets and debts, planning to parent their children, paying support and maintenance, and any other agreement between them which they want the court to approve.

**Separation Agreements–
By other names...**

"Separation agreement" is a generic term that refers to the writing that details your agreement about property and debt division, maintenance, child support, as well as parental decision-making and parenting time. In recent years some professionals put their agreement about parental responsibilities in a separate document called a "Parenting Plan," while others include the Parenting Plan as part of their Separation Agreement. Sample forms for each are on the CD-ROM in the back of this book. When you develop your agreement in mediation, the mediator prepares a "memorandum," usually called a "Memorandum of Understanding," or "Memorandum of Agreement". This book assumes that your parenting plan is part of, or included in, your separation agreement.

Partners can make their own rules about what is separate property and what is joint, and therefore to be divided, whether or not it is in separate or joint names.

ASSETS AND DEBTS
SEPARATION AGREEMENT: PART I

Introduction to the Separation Agreement

Before the court can give you a final decree of dissolution of marriage or legal separation, you must resolve and put in writing all the financial and parental issues remaining from your marriage. This written summary is called the separation agreement whether you are obtaining a divorce or a legal separation. It must be read and approved by the court.

Your separation agreement must include the following:

1. Assets you have accumulated must be accounted for and divided (this chapter).

2. All debts, including taxes, must be acknowledged and paid or the responsibility for paying them allocated between you (this chapter, and Chapter 11, Taxes).

3. You must establish a parenting plan for your children—decision-making and parenting time—and make commitments about their support (Chapter 8, Children, Chapter 9, Child Support, and Chapter 11, Taxes).

4. If either spouse is to assist in supporting the other—spousal support, maintenance—the amounts and duration must be set (Chapter 10, Maintenance, and Chapter 11, Taxes).

5. You must arrange to pay for any costs of the divorce itself: the court filing fee, mediators, lawyers, accountants, recording fees, and the like, if any (this chapter).

6. You must agree when and under what circumstances any of your agreements change or terminate (Chapters 7-10 and Chapter 13).

The five separation agreement chapters (7-11), plus Chapter 13, designed to help you write your separation agreement, are full of technical terms and legal requirements. The information you will need for your separation agreement is listed in the Great Hairy Checklist, Chapter 5. Gathering this information now will make all your bargaining more effective and more complete. Using the Great Hairy Checklist will ensure that you don't omit anything vital to a comprehensive agreement. Much of the information you gathered in Chapter 5 will be especially helpful for this chapter.

Chapter 12 contains sample wording for a wide variety of options in writing a separation agreement, drawn from the topics discussed throughout this Guidebook. As you complete your agreement about each topic, you might wish to read the relevant sample wording in Chapter 12 for ideas about writing your own agreement.

Assets—Marital and Separate

Nearly anything of value is considered an asset. Assets may include: real estate, furniture, household goods, art, musical and sporting equipment, any personal items, cars, trucks and other motor vehicles, cash, bank accounts, stocks and bonds, investments, retirement and pension plans, profit sharing, business interests including accounts receivable, furniture and fixtures, and good will. You must divide all your marital assets in your separation agreement. Similarly, you must divide all your marital debt.

Your first task is to distinguish separate from marital assets. By definition, separate assets belong to one of you only. Marital assets belong to both of you together. The only assets that must be allocated or divided between you in your divorce are what you determine to be marital. You may define separate and marital assets any way you wish. If you do write your own definitions, they must be included in your separation agreement. If you choose **not** to distinguish between separate and marital assets, you must say so in your separation agreement.

Similarly, you must distinguish between marital and separate debts. For example, you might agree that any debts incurred by either of you after your physical separation are the separate debt of that person; or, agree that these are still marital. Most couples agree that a debt related to a separate asset is a separate debt.

Bear in mind, an asset or debt may be part marital and part separate. For example, a spouse may have a retirement plan, part of which was accumulated before the marriage. A credit card may have been used for both marital and separate purposes.

If you do not use your own definitions of marital and separate assets and debt, or state that you do not want to distinguish between them, the court will presume you used the following definitions:

Separate Assets:

Marital Assets Division is Not a Taxable Event

Division of assets in a divorce does not result in taxable income for anybody, even if one spouse pays off the other in cash, as long as the transfers are directly between the two spouses, either before the divorce is final, or after, according to the terms of a written separation agreement. The transaction is seen by the IRS as the division of something you already own, not as a taxable "sale."

"We have to divide our assets equally. That's the law."

Nowhere is it written in Colorado that your marital assets must be divided equally. The word used in the statute is "equitable" which means fair.

Pre- and Post-Marital Agreements

If you and your spouse have a signed agreement written before or after your marriage which defines "marital" and "separate" assets and/or debts, it will control your definitions of these terms, unless you agree otherwise now. This is especially true if you were both represented by counsel.

Gifts to Each Other

While a gift to one of you from a third party is treated as separate property, recent legislation now makes gifts to each other marital property. This ticklish area may well be one in which you would rather make your own definitions.

Anything brought into the marriage.

Anything acquired during the marriage by gift or inheritance, except gifts to each other.

Anything purchased with the sale or trade of separate assets.

Marital assets:

Anything acquired during the marriage, regardless of whose name is on it or who paid for it.

Increase in the value of separate assets during the period of the marriage.

Gifts to each other

Marital debt:

Any debt incurred during the marriage, regardless of whose name is on it (remember your marriage continues until the court approves your separation agreement and signs your Decree).

Notes:

BRAIN TEASER
MARITAL OR SEPARATE? YOU BE THE JUDGE

How would you define the following assets (remember, there is no right or wrong answer here).

A. Wife's aunt brings over a rocking chair with a card that says: "Dear kids, this is wife's grandmother's chair. Thought you should have it." Is the chair

_____ Separate   _____ Marital   _____ Other _____

B. A 5-year marriage. Husband quits job he had for ten years, and therefore keeps only his contribution to his retirement. He takes it out in cash. Is it

_____ Separate   _____ Marital   _____ Other _____

C. Wife's previous divorce "awarded" her the house in which she and present husband have been living. Three years ago they re-financed, putting the home in both names. Is the home

_____ Separate   _____ Marital   _____ Other _____

D. Husband uses a credit card in his name to pay for furnishings for his new home on the day of physical separation. Is the debt

_____ Separate   _____ Marital   _____ Other _____

A strict reading of current statutes and case law would probably suggest the following answers:

A. Marital gift to both husband and wife. Not an inheritance, unless you agree otherwise.

B. Part marital, part separate. The portion earned during the marriage is marital, the rest is separate. An accurate way to determine the portions would be to find out the amount (value) of husband's contribution as of the date of the marriage. That much is his, the rest is marital.

C. Marital? A strong, much-quoted case Moncrief, Colorado Court of Appeals, July 1975, says putting assets into joint tenancy makes it a "gift to the marriage." But the Rhodes case, Colorado Supreme Court (the higher of the two courts), same month and year, says that separate money put into the home at the time of marriage is separate and comes back to the spouse who contributed it.

D. Marital, unless you agree otherwise.

OUR AGREED-UPON DEFINITIONS OF MARITAL AND SEPARATE

Directions: Write your own agreed-upon definitions of marital and separate assets and debts:

Marital assets are:

Separate assets are:

Marital debts are:

Separate debts are:

MARITAL OR SEPARATE ASSETS AND DEBTS ORGANIZER

Directions: You may photocopy the chart below, or copy it onto a larger piece of paper if you need more room. List each of your assets and debts, by **name** (not value), in one or more of the columns below. For example, the Marital column may include "Husband's retirement during marriage," and the Husband's separate column may include "Husband's retirement before marriage." The Marital column may include "Wife's student loan during marriage," while Wife's Separate column may include "Wife's student loan before marriage."

ASSETS and any SECURED DEBT	WIFE'S SEPARATE	HUSBAND'S SEPARATE	MARITAL
Real Estate			
Personal Items			
Motor Vehicles			
Cash			
Bank Accounts			
Stocks, Bonds, and Other Securities			
Retirement, Pensions, Profit Sharing			
Business Interests			
Other Assetss			
UNSECURED DEBTS			
Loans			
Credit cards			
Tax Debt			
Divorce Expenses			

Valuing Your Assets

You may list your division of assets and debts on the 2-page Division of Marital Assets and Debts Chart near the end of this chapter. The value of an asset, or the amount of a debt, will probably be an important part of this division. The next section of this chapter describes each kind of asset that may be part of your marital estate. Each discussion contains suggestions about how to find values for that particular kind of asset. Following are some thoughts about value to keep in mind as you read this chapter.

What if the two of you are unable to agree on a value? This is not a reason to give up, or to stop negotiating. Put down both values and agree that the value of that asset falls somewhere in between. It is possible to put together an asset settlement in which several assets are assigned range-values only. Some assets are extremely difficult to value, such as a small business. Bringing in a professional to tell you a value could cost hundreds, if not thousands of dollars. You may list the value of such an asset for now as simply "unknown," and decide later, if your negotiations necessitate, to hone in on a precise number or range.

You have the right to decide to allocate any or all of your assets between you without regard to monetary value at all. Value is not always monetary. The value an item has for you may be the memories it contains, its usefulness, or its beauty. Value to you may mean your need for an asset. For example, you might decide that certain items of furniture, such as the washer and dryer, may need to remain in the home with the children. You do not have to inventory and place values on such items.

Kinds of Assets

REAL ESTATE

Real estate includes your family home, condo, vacation home, time-share, commercial real estate, raw land, and real estate partnerships, as well as a contract for the purchase of real estate. Most people value real estate at current fair market value (the amount a willing buyer would pay a willing seller). There are three resources which may help you in determining fair market value: real estate appraisal, market analysis, and county tax assessment value. To help you decide whether you need either of the first two of these, see Asset Evaluators in Chapter 2. The tax assessment value, which is an appraisal done by the county for determining the property tax, may be a reasonable approximation

"If we can't agree on values, we can't agree on anything. We'll never be able to settle."

This is not true. You may elect to divide anything and everything without regard to monetary value. There are many kinds of value; dollars is only one of them. You are only required to divide your assets "equitably" – in a fair manner.

Real Estate Gross Equity Calculation

(Complete for each asset)

Fair Market Value
(FMV)   _____

Less: 1st
Mortgage Balance   _____

Less: 2nd (& 3rd)
Mortgage(s)   _____

Gross Equity   _____

of fair market value if it is not more than a year old. You can obtain it at no cost.

Getting the fair market value of your real estate is only the beginning. This is not the value to you in the divorce. You must take into account what is owed against the property: mortgages, liens, etc. The fair market value minus the amount owing is the gross equity. This is the most this asset could be worth to the two of you.

You may wish to adjust the gross equity value of your real estate for selling costs and capital gains taxes.

Selling Costs

Selling costs typically include real estate sales commission, title insurance, and fix-up and repairs to make the property saleable. If the property is to be sold immediately, or in the near future (especially if the selling costs would wipe out the equity and the person keeping the property is not certain whether he or she can hold on to it for very long), it makes sense to take out the costs of sale in arriving at what the value really is for you. Some selling costs to consider are:

- *Real Estate Sales Commission.* To estimate this, multiply the probable sales price times 7%—or other rate (the commission on farm, ranch, mountain, or commercial properties may be as high as 10%). There are services which will assist you in selling your home yourself so that the real estate commission may be as little as 2-3%.

- *Points, if any, when the seller pays them.* These represent seller's agreement to discount the sales price by a percentage —one point is one percent. Points are likely in some markets, especially if you need a quick sale.

- *Title insurance and deed recording fees.* $500-$1000 is a good ball-park for these last two items, but you should check with professionals in your area.

- *Cost of fix-up for sale.*

If the spouse receiving the property is likely to keep it for a number of years, for example until the children are grown, then you may not wish to subtract future selling costs now.

Whether or not you subtract the costs of sale to determine the equity is up to you. Making a clear agreement about selling costs is one of the ways in which you can fine tune your settlement.

"I don't have to worry about capital gain because I'm not going to make any money on the sale."

This belief could be fatal to your financial health, particularly with regard to investment real estate. The warning signs of this disease are: equity loan, rolled over capital gain from previous exchange, second mortgage, depreciation over many years. Your capital gain may be many times larger than your "profits."

The tax on capital gains is a "hidden" cost of real estate sales.

Capital Gains Taxes on Real Estate

The capital gains tax is a real cost that stays with a piece of real estate and that will have to be paid when the property is sold, unless you fit into one of the exclusions. Whoever keeps the property will ultimately be responsible for this tax. If you sell the property now, the persons whose names are on the deed are responsible for this tax.

Capital gain is the difference between the adjusted selling price and your investment in the property. You will pay income tax on the gain as though it were additional income earned by you in the year of sale. The amount of your investment for tax purposes is called the *basis.*

If you bought your property, your original basis is the purchase price. If you acquired the property by means other than a purchase (built it yourself, hired someone to build it for you, or received it as a gift or inheritance), see IRS Publications 523 and 551 for how to determine your original basis. The bibliography at the end of this Guidebook will tell you how to obtain these publications.

While you owned the property you may have increased or decreased your basis. You may have *increased* the basis by additions or capital improvements; you may have *decreased* the basis by rolling over a prior capital gain, or depreciation. The lower your basis, the greater your gain, and the greater your tax on the gain. See IRS Publication 551 for a detailed discussion of these, and other adjustments to basis.

To determine your likely capital gain, subtract your adjusted basis from the fair market value. Then you may adjust for probable selling costs. Next step, figure your tax on it.

1) If the real estate is your personal residence:

The capital gain exclusion on the sale of your personal residence may also apply to partners. Each partner whose name is on the deed may exclude up to $250,000 as a single taxpayer.

1997 legislation effectively eliminated capital gains tax on the sale of a personal residence for most individuals. Married homeowners may exclude up to $500,000 of gain from the sale of a principal residence; $250,000 for single taxpayers. There is no age requirement and the exclusion is reusable every two years. You can claim the exclusion if, during the five year period ending on the date of the sale, you have: 1) owned the home for at least two years (the ownership test), and 2) lived in the home as your main residence for at least two years (the use test). This tax break allows most homeowners to sell a more expensive home and purchase a less expensive one, or even to sell and not repurchase, without incurring a capital gains tax, and relieves most homeowners of the burden of keeping paperwork on capital improvements.

If there is any question in your mind that this new rule might not apply to you; your gain might exceed these limits (including any rolled over gain); you are concerned about property other than your personal residence; or you don't know enough about capital gains to know whether you qualify or not, then read the rest of this section. Making a mistake about capital gains tax can be very costly. Consult your tax lawyer or accountant for clarification abour your situation.

2) If the real estate is not your personal residence, or if you have gain on your residence beyond what can be excluded:

A good rule of thumb is that your tax is approximately 1/5 (19.63) of your capital gain 15% for federal tax, plus 4.63% for the State of Colorado). If your total taxable income for the year of sale has not filled the 10% and 15% tax brackets, the tax on your capital gain will be less. See Chapter 11 Taxes.

It is crucial that you take into account the tax consequences of the eventual sale of real estate before you make decisions about it in your property settlement.

The following worksheet is for investment or rental property. Do one worksheet for each piece of real estate you own that is not your personal residence—whether or not you plan to sell. Take the worksheet line by line, reading the instructions as you go. If you get frustrated, stop and come back later, or consult an accountant.

Even if you're not selling the property right now, you can use these forms to estimate how much you would clear after a sale, taking into account capital gains tax. Naturally, you'll be estimating certain items and some items may not apply if you're not going to actually sell the property now.

NOTE: Use only the total column now and fill in the Husband's and Wife's shares after you determine how you will divide your assets and debts using the chart at the end of this chapter.

To Estimate the Capital Gain on Your Personal Residence

Selling price	_____
Less:	
Brokerage fees	(_____)
Closing costs	(_____)
Original purchase price	(_____)
Original closing costs	(_____)
Cost of improvements	(_____)
Depreciation deducted on previous returns	(_____)
Capital Gain	_____

A zero or negative number means no capital gain. If you have a positive number, determine whether you qualify for the exclusion ($250,000 or $500,000), and if so, reduce your gain accordingly. If you do not qualify for the exclusion, or still have a positive number then calculate your tax, if any, at 15% if you are in the 25% tax bracket or above, and 5% if you are in the 10% and 15% tax brackets until those brackets are filled, and the rest at 15%.

Capital Gains Tax Worksheet for Rental or Other Investment Real Estate

The Property	Total	Wife's Share	Husband's Share
1. Selling Price of this Property			
2. Brokerage commission (usually 6%):			
3. Closing Costs on sale (usually ±1%):			
4. Amount Realized for Capital Gains Tax purposes (Line 1 minus Lines 2 and 3):			
5. Mortgage Balance and any other liens: *(Not part of capital gain calculation)*			
6. Net cash before taxes (Line 4 minus Line 5):			
CAPITAL GAINS TAX			
7. Original Price of this Property:			
8. Improvements and Original Closing Costs on purchase or refinance:			
9. Depreciation deducted on previous returns:			
10. Adjusted Basis of Property Sold (Line 7 plus Line 8 minus Line 9):			
11. Capital Gain (Line 4 minus Line 10):			
12. Capital Gains Tax (multiply Line 11 by your est. tax rate):			
13. Net cash after taxes (Line 6 minus Line 12):			

Instructions for Equity and Capital Gains Tax Worksheet for Rental or Other Real Estate

Line 1: Estimate a realistic sales price, or use the actual price if you have already sold this property.

Line 2: This item is optional if there's no actual sale contemplated. But some people still include it if they think a later sale is inevitable.

Line 3: Closing costs for a sale usually include title insurance and recording fees. They may include advertising, a survey, and mortgage points paid by you. This item is also optional if there's no actual sale contemplated. But some people still include it if they think a later sale is inevitable.

Line 5: Mortgage amounts are not included in capital gains tax calculations.

Line 7: Put in the total price you paid for this property.

Line 8: Improvements are things that add to the permanent value of the property, such as additions, paving a driveway, a new roof, or an intercom system. Usually, maintenance and repairs of existing features do not count as improvements. Also include here the closing costs you paid when you bought this property.

Line 9: If you took any depreciation on this property, put it back here.

Line 11: If this is zero, or a negative number, there's no capital gain and no tax, and no problem. Line 6 is your actual net.

After you have calculated your costs and any capital gains tax, decide for each piece of real estate the value which you will use in negotiating your total marital assets division. This information will be helpful in deciding how to divide your real estate using the chart at the end of this chapter.

WHAT TO DO?

If one of you retains real property in your divorce settlement, consider decreasing your equity—the value you are working with in your settlement—by the estimated tax on the capital gain to date, or some portion of it, for the person who takes this property.

Different Ways to "Divide" Real Estate

Before you take out the chain saw or sign the listing agreement, think about all the possible ways you might "divide" real estate. There are many workable options:

1. Sell it together now, and determine how you will handle the capital gain (see previous section).

    Divide the proceeds. Dividing responsibility for the capital gain does not mean you have to divide the proceeds in the same proportion. Responsibility for tax on your share of any gain is an IRS requirement. This has nothing to do with how you choose to divide the proceeds. You may:

    • Give more than half to the spouse who needs more down payment in order to qualify for a mortgage; and/or

    • Off-set some or all of the proceeds with some other kind of asset to the other spouse, business interests for example, or savings, stocks, or present value of retirement; and/or

    • Use the proceeds to pay off marital debts.

2. One of you keeps the home or other real estate.

    • The other gets some other asset of like value; or

    • The other gets cash or other liquid assets; or

    • The other gets a promissory note (with or without interest) promising to pay at some later date (a balloon payment), due on sale, or even amortized over a period of time (months or years). This promise to pay may be secured by a deed of trust (to the public trustee) which would be recorded with the clerk and recorder in the county in which the assets is located, and then become a mortgage or lien against the home. Although the principal

The IRS Never Gives Anything Away
If you have maintained a rental home or business property during your marriage, you have probably been depreciating it. (Even if you haven't, the IRS may.) The total amount of the depreciation for all the years you have rented the property becomes a capital gain which is taxable at the time of sale.

Allocating real estate equity between partners is much more difficult than between spouses. A transaction between partners is deemed a sale, and that is a taxable event. You must report it on your tax return, and pay any resulting tax on the capital gain, if any.

Difference Between Joint Tenancy and Tenancy In Common
Joint tenancy means that you each own an undivided 50% interest in the property, and the whole property comes to the survivor upon the death of the other joint tenant. Tenancy in common is a divisible interest, presumed to be 50-50, unless otherwise specified (60-40, 72-38) and each owner's share passes at death with his or her estate (does not go automatically to the other owner). Most couples own their family home in joint tenancy.

Personal Assets Checklist

Directions: Check or complete those statements below which are true. Use a separate piece of paper for any itemized lists.

☐ We will divide our personal assets by value.

☐ We will divide our personal assets by need.

☐ We have set aside the separate personal assets for each of us.

☐ We have agreed to walk through the house together on _____ (date).

☐ We will create THE LIST of items we both want by _____(date).

☐ We will divide the items on THE LIST by means of _____ _____, on _____(date).

These personal assets have debts against them:

Item	Amount of Debt

We need to research the values for the following items of personal assets:

Who will do it? When will it be done?

☐ We have completed our DIN List (see Chapter 4), or will complete it by _____(date).

amount of these payments is not taxable, the interest on them is taxable to the recipient in the year it is received.

3. You can retain the home or other real estate together.

    • If the property is your personal residence, one of you can live in the home, and you can agree to keep it for a time, even for many years, and then sell it and share the profits at a later time.

    • You can rent it to a third party and wait for a better market, both can depreciate your share of the home, and pay tax on the capital gain when the property is sold. If the property is not your personal residence, you have the option of continuing joint ownership of it after your divorce is final.

In either case, be sure you make clear agreements about who will pay the following: the mortgage, property taxes, insurance, homeowners association dues, day-to-day upkeep and repairs, major repairs, capital improvements, selling costs. Be sure you agree about how to share the profits when you sell, taking into account who has been paying what.

If you have now decided how you want to divide all or some of your real estate, write the appropriate information on the Division of Marital Assets and Debts Chart at the end of this chapter. You may do this even if you are not certain this is your final agreement. Noting your interim thinking in pencil is a good idea. You will probably look at several different assets divisions before you reach final agreement.

PERSONAL ASSETS

Your personal assets include furniture, appliances, stereo system and TV, linens, all your kitchen items, musical instruments, art, collections, sporting equipment, pets and animals, and all the stuff in the basement and the garage. This section is about how to allocate these things.

Personal assets usually do not include your personal clothing and jewelry. Yours is yours, and your spouse's is your spouse's. An exception might be if you choose to treat certain gifts to each other as marital property. Another exception might be if you have treated gems, jewelry, or furs as an investment or as a collection, and therefore as marital assets. Personal assets do not include business personal assets, such as the computer or the copier or the desk that is part of one's business. Business personal assets are included as part of Business Interests below.

The division of personal assets is often a discussion one spouse wants to avoid completely. "He/she can have it all! I just want out!" This is usually a great mistake. Both of you probably need some continuity with your things, even though the thought of having any of them may be painful at first.

Sometimes things become "larger than life." An item can become a metaphor for your time together, or for your marriage or divorce. If you feel yourselves stuck on items of personal assets, it is probably because this has happened. Take a little time to figure out what this hard fought-for item really represents for one or both of you.

Some people list all their personal assets, place values on them, and then divide the value in some agreed upon proportion. Most people who do this use fair market value, which for most of us is the likely price at a garage sale. For more expensive items, such as musical instruments, art, antiques, collections of any kind, you may want to pay for an appraisal. The importance you put on the value of items is up to you.

Another approach is to divide things by need. Walk through the house together and see if you can agree on who gets what with a view to setting up two households that are as complete as possible. Inevitably some new purchases will be necessary. See the "DIN" list in Chapter 4. Many people try to find an equitable way to bear that burden/benefit too. It's a burden because you have to spend money, and can be a benefit or a burden because one of you gets the "new" item while the other gets the used one with all the memories. Remember, the replacement cost of an item is probably much higher than the fair market value of the existing one.

There may be items you don't agree on. You can always sell what neither of you wants, but what to do about items you both want? First of all, just list them—don't argue about them. When you have allocated everything else to your satisfaction, you can begin to deal with "The List." See if you can strike a bargain about any of those items. "You can have #4 if I can have #3." "I'll give you $40.00 if I can have #6." Agreements like these can shorten The List. Finally, you can flip a coin to decide who goes first to pick one item off The List. The other then takes the next two items from The List (in exchange for not being first). You then take turns until nothing remains on The List.

If you have now agreed to your division of personal assets, you may enter the appropriate information on the Division of Marital Assets and Debts Chart at the end of this chapter. If you have

George's Tools

Mary thinks George spends all his time in the garage tinkering with small motors which appear to propagate overnight. She proves, through a review of the check register, that they have spent over $5,000 on his tools and equipment. She wants to value his things in the garage at the original cost. He says they "might be worth $500 on a good day," if he could find someone who wanted them.

Louise's Dining Room

Louise and Charles bought a Chinese Chippendale dining room set for $8,000, fifteen years ago, because it was "just like" the one Louise grew up with—and her parents gave to her sister when they retired. Charles has no objection to Louise keeping it, but wants to be allocated $8,000 to buy his dining room set. Louise says that it might bring $800 at a garage sale.

Motor Vehicle Checklist

Provide the following information for each of your motor vehicles:

Make and Model:

Blue Book Value:

   Wholesale:

   Retail:

Loan balance:

How titled:

Make and Model:

Blue Book Value:

   Wholesale:

   Retail:

Loan balance:

How titled:

Liquid Assets Checklist

Bank name:
Type of account:
Name(s) on the account:
Balance:
Date of balance:

Bank name:
Type of account:
Name(s) on the account:
Balance:
Date of balance:

Bank name:
Type of account:
Name(s) on the account:
Balance:
Date of balance:

Bank name:
Type of account:
Name(s) on the account:
Balance:
Date of balance:

agreed not to value your personal assets monetarily, there is no need to enter the information. If you have not yet reached agreement, just read on.

CARS AND OTHER MOTOR VEHICLES

Motor vehicles include: car, pick-up, RV, boat, cycle, trailer, and aircraft. You may divide these by value, need, or any other measure you agree to.

If your vehicle is leased, you do not own it, and therefore you cannot divide it. You should state in your agreement who will be responsible for the remainder of the lease payments and who owns the buy-out option.

To divide by economic value, you may start with the automobile values obtained from the NADA (National Automobile Dealers Association) *Blue Book,* available at any Public Library, car dealer, bank, or lending institution or from the Kelley Blue Book. Both of these are online. This will give you three different values that parallel the retail, wholesale, and loan values. "Retail" in the Blue Book is often slightly higher than fair market value to you, since it is the price a dealer would get. Likewise, "wholesale" is probably too low, as it is the price a dealer would pay. The value of your automobile is probably between these. You can further refine these values by looking for used cars like yours in the weekend classified ads of your local newspapers.

For other motor vehicles, you can call and survey dealers and brokers, especially of used items like yours, and find out what they are asking. You can find these dealers and brokers through the yellow pages, under the type of item you are valuing, such as "Aircraft," or "Boats." You may also compare your vehicle with those offered for sale in classified ads in local newspapers. To get a professional appraisal, you can start your search by looking in the yellow pages under "Appraisers." See also Asset Evaluators in Chapter 2.

If you have now agreed on how you are going to divide your motor vehicles, you may enter the appropriate information on the Division of Marital Assets and Debts Chart at the end of this chapter. If you have agreed not to value your motor vehicles monetarily, there is no need to enter the information. If you have not yet reached agreement, just read on.

LIQUID ASSETS: CASH AND BANK ACCOUNTS

Cash, the most liquid of assets, is easiest to value. Bank accounts and certificates of deposit, are also "liquid" assets. You may include money market accounts here too. Savings accounts, certificates of deposit, and some checking accounts earn interest, and money market accounts increase in value. See your most recent statements for their current values. Remember to take into account amounts that are in a form which has not yet matured, bonds and certificates of deposit for example. You may want to adjust your valuation of these assets in your settlement if the person keeping them will have to cash them out soon—therefore realizing less than face or full value.

If you have now agreed on how you are going to divide your liquid assets, you may enter the appropriate information on the Division of Marital Assets and Debts Chart at the end of this chapter. If you have not yet reached agreement, just read on.

STOCKS, BONDS, AND OPTIONS

If your holdings are in an investment account at a brokerage, then the current fair market value will be given in your most recent statement. For individual stocks, bonds, and some limited partnerships, look up their values in the *Wall Street Journal.*

If stocks (or bonds) have increased in value during the time you have held them, then the spouse who keeps them will face a capital gains tax when they are sold. The top capital gains rate, for most assets, has been lowered to 15% for those in the 25% tax bracket or higher, and to 5% for those in the 10% and 15% tax brackets. This change is effective May 6, 2003 and the regular holding period for long-term capital gains is now 12 months. You must decide whether to factor this tax burden in your bargaining. If you have been carrying a loss on investment assets from year to year, you now must stop doing so at the time of divorce and factor the loss into the value of the asset. This may increase your capital gain considerably. Consult your tax lawyer or accountant for how this affects you.

Bonds carry a similar built-in capital gains tax burden. The face value of a bond is the amount it will pay on its maturity date. Before that date, bonds are usually worth less than the face amount; after that date, more.

Limited partnerships may be especially tricky to value. Some enable the owner to take depreciation year after year. This lowers the basis. The more the basis is lowered, the greater the gain when sold—and the higher the tax on the sale. Some call this "phantom income." You must investigate each limited partnership interest you own to discover its fair market value (what a willing buyer would pay for it currently), plus whatever the tax burden will be upon sale.

Stocks Checklist

Repeat as necessary, for each stock held.

Company:
# of shares:
Value per share:
Date of value:
How titled:
Who holds certificate:

Bonds Checklist

Repeat as necessary, for each bond held.

Name on bond:
Face value:
Date of maturity:
Estimated current value:
How titled:
Who holds the bond:

 As with real estate, a transaction between partners of stocks, bonds, or other securities, is a taxable event. You must report it on your tax return, and pay any resulting tax on the capital gain, if any.

Options Checklist

Repeat as necessary for each grant.

1. Company:

2. Person granted to:

3. Date of grant:

4. Number of shares/options:

5. Exercise price:

6. Vesting schedule:

7. Expiration date:

8. Number vested during marriage:

9. Number that will not vest during marriage:

10. Are they qualified or non-qualified?

11. Will the company permit you to transfer them at divorce?

Life Insurance Checklist

Complete the following for each life insurance policy on either of your lives, or owned by either of you on anybody's life.

Company:

Person insured:

Death benefit:

Accidental death benefit?

Beneficiary(ies):

Type of policy:

Cash value:

Surrender value:

An option is a right to purchase a stock at a stated price, called the exercise price. The majority of these are typically granted by a company to an employee as an incentive, vest over a period of time, and are given an expiration date after which they may no longer be exercised. Usually options that vest before the end of the marriage are marital, and those, which vest later, are not. Vesting means you own it, but it will expire on the expiration date, or if the employee leaves the company. There is a method for determining the present marital value of unvested options, and if this is of concern to you, you need to consult counsel. There are qualifying and non-qualifying options, the former receiving more favorable tax treatment than the latter. Options may be transferable to your spouse, if the company that granted the options agrees—be sure to get any such agreement in writing. If you want to divide non-transferable options between you, the spouse they are granted to must hold the other spouse's options for him/her, and pay that spouse any net profit, or transfer the actual shares when the options are exercised. You will need to agree on who will decide when they will be exercised and who will pay the exercise price.

If you have now agreed on how you are going to divide your stocks, bonds, and other securities, you may enter the appropriate information on the Division of Marital Assets and Debts Chart at the end of this chapter. If you have decided to divide some or all of your stocks, bonds, and options according to some value other than monetary, you do not need to make an entry on the chart. If you have not yet reached agreement, just read on.

LIFE INSURANCE

There are two basic kinds of life insurance policies, "whole life," and "term." And there are many hybrids. Whole life policies have cash value, which is an asset. The value is often stated in the policy, or can be learned by asking your insurance agent. Usually two values will be given: the cash value which is the actual value of the policy in place, and the lesser surrender value, which is the amount of money you would receive if you cashed in the policy.

Term policies, including most group policies offered by employers, have no cash value and are not valued in the division of assets. These policies are useful to "secure" or "underwrite" your agreements about child support, and/or maintenance (see Chapters 9 and 10).

Many so-called insurance policies are really annuities, similar to a retirement plan. You may want to include these policies, or portions of these policies, in your discussion of retirement.

If you have now agreed on how you are going to divide your insurance policies, you may enter the appropriate information on the Division of Marital Assets and Debts Chart at the end of this chapter. If you have decided to divide some or all of your insurance policies according to some value other than monetary, you do not need to make an entry on the chart. If you have not yet reached agreement, just read on.

RETIREMENT, PENSIONS, AND PROFIT SHARING

If you have completed the Great Hairy Checklist, Chapter 5, you will have gathered all the information you will need to allocate or divide your retirements. If you have not done this, you may wish to refer to the "Pension, Profit Sharing, and Retirement" section of Chapter 5 to gather the information regarding your specific plans.

Retirement plans are of two general types: those **defined by the benefit paid** at retirement, and those **defined by the contributions made.** Many plans combine both these elements.

A plan defined in terms of its benefits is usually called a **pension.** It tells you what it will pay you at retirement, usually based on a percentage of your highest earnings at the time of retirement. Typically the employer contributes directly to this benefit, and nothing, as a rule, is withheld from your paycheck for this purpose. Sometimes these benefits are lost completely if you leave the employment before retirement age. Others vest over a period of years. Vesting means you own that portion and it cannot be taken away. If a plan vests gradually, you might own 20% of your plan after one year of employment, 40% after two years, etc.

Examples of this kind of retirement are: pensions, Civil Service Retirement System, Federal Employee Retirement System, Military Retirement, most Railroad Retirements, and many municipal and state employee group plans such as firemen, policemen.

A plan defined in terms of its contribution means there is a set amount which you contribute from your gross pay—often a combination of a required percentage of your pay plus an optional amount. Then your employer may "match" the amount you put in. The employer's contribution frequently does not occur until you retire, however, or may vest over time.

Sometimes there is a vesting schedule, similar to that in the defined benefit plan. The employer can provide a schedule or formula of their matching as well as of the vesting. If you leave employment before retirement, sometimes you lose a portion or all of the employer's contribution, but you do not lose your own.

Retirements Checklist

Complete the following information for each retirement or pension plan either one of you has.

Name of Plan:

Kind of plan, if known:

Name of participant:

Vested?

Current vested value:

Date of vested value:

Future benefit?

At what age?

Monthly amount, lump sum or formula?

Reductions for early retirement?

Subject to divestment?

Divisible by QDRO?

Loans available?

Early payout option?

Preretirement survivor benefit?

Survivor benefit?

Name of Plan:

Kind of plan, if known:

Name of participant:

Vested?

Current vested value:

Date of vested value:

Future benefit?

At what age?

Monthly amount, lump sum or formula?

Reductions for early retirement?

Subject to divestment?

Divisible by QDRO?

Loans available?

Early payout option?

Preretirement survivor benefit?

Survivor benefit?

For additional retirements, repeat on a separate sheet of paper.

The amount of your total contribution, plus accumulated interest, is yours when you leave the company, even if you do so before retirement. The amount in your account is shown at least once a year in a statement from your employer or the trustee or institution which manages your account or plan.

Examples of this kind of plan are: PERA, IRA, SEP, 401K, Profit Sharing, ESOP, Tax Sheltered Annuities, Money Purchase Plans, Keogh, 403(b), TIAA-CREF, (and TRASOP and PAYSOP which are no longer available).

The first step in negotiating about retirement plans is to find out exactly what you have. Most of us don't really know. Today's plans are often complex hybrids of the simple plans that existed only a few years ago. There are tax pitfalls to be wary of, some of very recent origin.

How Do We Value Our Retirements?

There are two ways of looking at the value of a retirement plan. The first applies to defined contribution plans, taking the actual amount of your contributions, plus those of the employer which are vested to you (if any), plus accrued interest to date. This is the most readily obtainable value because it is on the periodic statement from the plan administrator, trustee, or agency holding your account.

The second way is to figure the present value of a future flow of payments—a pension, a defined benefit plan. For example, you will receive $680 per month starting at age 65. This amount can be translated into a current cash value: the amount of money you would need now, invested at 6% (or other interest rate), which would pay you your monthly pension amount, starting at age 65, for 16.9 years. This is the life expectancy of men and women at age 65, according to the Colorado Mortality Table (C.R.S. 13-25-103). (Mortality tables differ, show longer life expectancies and are different for men and women.) Some of these plans include other valuable rights, such as cost of living increases, or the right to purchase certain health insurance. Most also have the opportunity for a joint and survivor annuity at retirement, so that payments to the survivor will continue after the death of the retiree, as well as a right to a preretirement survivor annuity in the event of the death of the employee prior to retirement. WARNING: These benefits are widely misunderstood by both professionals and lay people in dividing retirement benefits between spouses. If either of you has a defined contribution plan, be sure to discuss it with an attorney or CPA who specializes in retirements before making your decision about it.

Death Benefit

There are two kinds of death benefits often attached to retirement or pension plans. The first is the remainder of the retirement (if any) after the death of the participant, usually payable to the surviving spouse. The second is a separate amount, often about $10,000, which, like a life insurance policy, is payable in a lump-sum upon the participant's death to the designated beneficiary. Be certain your agreement is clear about what happens to any death benefit. Does it stay with the current spouse, or will it be available to a future spouse, if any?

Tax Status of the Money in the Plan

For the most part, contributions—whether yours or your employer's—will be carried in your account in tax-deferred status. This means that you did not pay income tax on this money, but that you will pay tax on it when you receive it—typically at retirement. Since you will usually be in a lower tax bracket at retirement than you are in now, you save money by deferring or putting off tax on this money until later. By contrast, some of your or your employer's contributions may have already been taxed, or be tax-free, and they should not be taxed again when those dollars are paid out to you. If you are considering an early payout, when you examine the present value of the plan be sure you understand which dollars are in which tax status because it will substantially change the value to you of each dollar.

The plan administrator may or may not tell you the present value of your account. If it is provided to you, be sure you know what interest rate was used to determine it. (A low interest rate means a higher present value, and vice versa.) If your plan administrator does not provide the present value, you may need to hire a CPA, an actuary or an attorney who specializes in this kind of valuation, or there are computer programs which do this (see the bibliography at the end of this Guidebook). The values determined by any of these professionals may vary considerably since they are based on the evaluator's choice of what interest and discount rates to apply. (The discount rate is a number representing the probability that you will not exceed the life expectancy from the table, or that you will not continue in your job until retirement. Figuring this for a 35 year old is different from figuring it for a 55 year old.) Large amounts of time and money are being spent in divorce cases figuring out the present value of these assets which may or may not ever get paid. Sometimes it seems like so much smoke and mirrors.

There are other ways to factor your retirement into your negotiations than dividing it by present value. See the "How to Divide" section below for ways to divide such plans without spending money on present-day valuations.

EARLY PAYOUT OPTIONS

There are three typical early payout options: lump-sum, hardship, and loans.

1. *Lump-sum.* Some plans offer a lump-sum payout at retirement, or on the occurrence of certain events, such as leaving the job. The lump-sum options on defined contribution plans are usually available at either retirement, leaving the employment, or at death. It is important in your bargaining and in your planning to know the options in your plan. Even if your periodic statement about your account gives your balance in projected monthly payout, or account balance, don't assume that this is the only option for you.

2. *Hardship.* Some plans offer a lump-sum payout of all or a portion of the balance on the occurrence of certain events. Most common are purchase of a primary residence, second mortgage for capital improvements, college or higher education expenses, medical emergency, and sometimes divorce. The payouts, if available, are taxable as additional income in the year you receive them. Some hardship option clauses allow you to get money out, but you have to pay a penalty. Be sure you know which kind of hardship clause you have, if any.

 In some defined contribution plans, it is possible for an employee spouse to distribute retirement assets to a non-employee spouse as current taxable income at the time of the divorce or legal separation, but without a 10% penalty. The penalty on early withdrawal of funds does not apply to certain "qualified" plans when the distribution is made to the non-participant spouse under a divorce court order, and within 60 days of distribution by the plan administrator. If this would fit your situation, be sure to consult with your plan administrator to see if your plan qualifies for this exemption.

3. *Loans from the Plan.* Some plans, especially those with actual present value, permit you to borrow against the balance, similar to borrowing against a whole life insurance policy. Often you must prove need. The terms are strict—usually repayment within five years but the interest rate is usually low. This can be a valuable planning tool for you to meet short-term emergency needs at the time of your separation or divorce.

SOCIAL SECURITY

To be eligible for Social Security benefits, a worker must accumulate 40 full-time working quarters (3-month periods, 40 of them equals 10 years) in which the worker paid F.I.C.A. or Self-employment taxes. Until you have 40 quarters, you are not eligible for Social Security retirement in any amount. Once you become eligible, the amount of your benefit payable at retirement depends on your earnings during your working lifetime.

These payments represent a future income stream which may not be the same for each spouse. Most people use their estimated Social Security incomes when discussing whether maintenance or child support payments should survive or be payable after retirement of either the recipient or the payor. Some people, however, do ask for a present value of their future Social Security benefits, and treat it like an asset.

PLANS IN LIEU OF SOCIAL SECURITY

Some retirement plans take the place of Social Security. Common examples are P.E.R.A., Civil Service, Military Retirement, and some specific plans for groups of public employees, like firemen and police. The difficulty in valuation of these plans is that there is usually no way to accurately determine the equivalent Social Security portion. If, in your bargaining you choose to treat pension and other retirement benefits as assets but not Social Security, then set aside some part of any plan in lieu of Social Security as though it were Social Security. A ballpark way to do this is to take 7% of your salary over the time of your contribution to the plan, plus interest. (The present Social Security rate is 7.65%, 15.3% if you are self-employed.)

How May We Divide Our Retirements?

This section shows you the mechanics of how to divide your retirements if you choose to do so in your final separation agreement. You may choose, alternatively, not to "divide" them at all, but simply to allocate them—"You keep yours, and I'll keep mine." Some plans are divisible directly, some require a Qualified Domestic Relations Order (QDRO), some are divisible by written agreement, and some are really not divisible at all.

Divestment

Whatever the nature of your retirement (defined contribution, defined benefit, or a hybrid) all or some of it may be subject to divestment (you may lose it) under certain circumstances. The most likely of these is if you leave the employment before your retirement date—by quitting, being fired, or death. If your retirement is subject to divestment, you may want to consider dividing it with an agreement that goes into effect only if it pays.

 IRS regulations withhold 20% if YOU take money from an IRA, or other tax-deferred plan even for the purpose of transferring it into another IRA for yourself or your spouse. The trustee must take out the 20% and send it to IRS. You must then replace the 20% out of your own pocket to transfer to the new IRA, or pay tax on that 20% as though you had received it as income that year. You therefore not only lose this money from the IRA, but you also pay tax on it. If you do replace the 20% out of pocket, the IRS will then return the 20%, without interest, if you request it as a tax refund on your next income tax return. If you put it back into the IRA, you won't pay tax on it. The only way to avoid this 20% is to never let YOUR HANDS touch it. Have it transferred by the trustee, DIRECTLY to the trustee of another IRA for yourself or your spouse as part of your divorce agreement.

PLANS WHICH ARE DIVISIBLE DIRECTLY

The most immediately divisible plans are those which are really tax-deferred savings plans, such as IRA's and SEP's. These may be divided by directly transferring all or some of the balance to a similar account in the name of the other spouse.

If you decide to withdraw money from the account to help finance your separation, you will pay a 10% penalty to the IRS plus federal and state income taxes on it, unless your withdrawal is permitted under the "hardship clause." The IRS has been permitting "hardship" withdrawals which, if returned within 60 days, will avoid the 10% penalty for withdrawing money from a tax-deferred account. An IRS rule requires 20% withholding of federal tax from withdrawals from tax-deferred accounts which is intended to cover your federal income tax on the amount plus your 10% penalty.

Many plans are not required by law to permit division on divorce. Nevertheless, an increasing number which are not required to do so are now permitting such division. The largest of these are the various military and civil service retirements. TIAA-CREF has permitted division for 30 years. An increasing number of private plans are also offering their own process for dividing retirements at divorce, whether or not they are required to do so by federal law.

CSRS (Civil Service Retirement System and FERS (Federal Employee Retirement System) are divisible under the Civil Service Retirement Spouse Equity Act of 1984.

For all of these, contact the accounting office for the military service in question, the plan administrator for TIAA-CREF, FERS, and CSRS, or your employer. Request information about the procedure and forms, if any, for division of your retirement at divorce, and talk to an attorney or CPA who specializes in this area to prepare the documents for you, including the appropriate language about this in your separation agreement.

PLANS DIVISIBLE BY QDRO

A 1986 amendment to the Retirement Equity Act, a federal statute, gives domestic relations courts the power to order the division of certain pension and retirement plans. The divorce court signs a Qualified Domestic Relations Order (QDRO, pronounced "Q-dro" or "Quadro") that requires the plan administrator to divide the retirement account according to the to the terms stated in the order.

Defined Contribution Plan QDRO Decisions Checklist

1. Amount in the plan:

2. Amount to be transferred to the non-participating spouse:

OR

3. Percentage of balance on date of Decree to be transferred to the non-participating spouse:

Defined Benefit (Pensions) Plan QDRO Decisions Checklist

1. Fraction to be used to calculate receiving spouses share at time of participant's retirement.

2. Preretirement survival benefit for receiving spouse?

3. Retirement survival benefit for receiving spouse?

4. Other benefits extended to receiving spouse?

 Division of retirements between partners is not available, although you may agree that the participating partners will pay a certain amount or a percentage to the other upon receipt. The tax effect of such a transaction depends on its purpose. Be sure to consult a tax professional before you make any such agreement.

If your plan administrator provides a QDRO form for you, be sure to read it carefully. You must check that it does what you want it to do (transfers exactly what you want transferred to the person you want it transferred to), and that it does not add something that you do not want to do (pays out the money thus incurring 20% withholding, along with possible penalty).

The plans which are covered under this federal law are large public employers who are covered by Employee Retirement Income Security Act of 1974 (E.R.I.S.A.), and include both defined benefit and defined contribution plans.

Plans divisible by QDRO include defined benefit plan pensions (IBM, Lockheed Martin, Qwest, and many others); 401K's (thrift savings plans); some profit sharing and money purchase plans; Keogh plans; tax-sheltered annuities; ESOP's (Employee Stock Ownership Plans), and the old PAYSOP's and TRASOP's.

A QDRO for a defined contribution plan instructs the plan administrator to transfer a dollar amount or a percentage to the non-participating spouse. This can be done in several ways:

- pay out in cash, in which case the plan will withhold 20% of the amount in the QDRO and the receiving spouse will pay income tax on it.

- roll over into an IRA in the receiving spouse's name. No income tax is incurred when the transfer is directly from one account to the other, and doesn't go through your hands.

- open an account in the same plan for the receiving spouse. This option is not always provided, so ask your plan administrator is this is available.

- a combination of the above.

A QDRO for a defined benefit plan is more complex, and refers to future dollars and future payments. For many of these plans, you may create a formula that divides only the marital portion of the plan, and reserves any future contributions after the marriage for the participant spouse. The formula looks like this:

$$\frac{\text{\# years of marriage}}{\text{total \# years employed at retirement}} \times \text{50\%, (or other percentage you think is fair)}$$

 Since is it possible that the spouse who participates in the defined contribution plan could die before the QDRO benefits are paid out, many couples agree to keep the receiving spouse as beneficiary of the plan until the QDRO transfer is complete (usually about 6 weeks).

You may give the plan administrator this formula as part of your QDRO, after filling in all the numbers (except the number of years employed if the employee-spouse is still working there). But you may determine whatever portion you think is fair for the non-employee spouse to receive. Some plans (military and civil service) may require exact numbers instead of formulas.

The receiving spouse has no more rights to the retirement benefit than the participating spouse has. The QDRO for a defined benefit plan, a pension, usually divides the retirement payments at the source, so that the receiving spouse will receive her/his own check from the retirement plan, but not until the participating spouse retires and starts receiving his/her payments. Both payments will end when the participant spouse dies, unless you also provide for a survivor benefit. Thus your defined benefit plan QDRO may also need to address

 When you have completed your QDRO, be sure to send it to the plan administrator before you ask the court to sign it. Ask the plan administrator if he or she will carry it out as written. He or she must, by law, tell you specifically if there are any problems with it. You must be sure that you have time to correct any problems before giving it to the court for signature.

- Survival benefits

- Preretirement survival benefits

- Other benefits available throught the plan.

If you are dividing more than one plan, you will need a QDRO for each plan. If you want a retirement plan to remain entirely the asset of the participant spouse, you need to say that in your separation agreement, and you will not need a QDRO.

If you are dividing a defined contribution plan, ask your plan administrator if they provide a QDRO form, and use that. If not, you can draft your own QDRO using the sample that follows.

If you are dividing a defined benefit plan, you are in a more complex and specialized area of both law and accounting, and your QDRO needs to be coordinated with the wording in your separation agreement. Be sure to have your defined benefit plan QDRO drafted or reviewed by one of these specialists to be sure you obtain the outcome you both intend.

Sample Language for a Qualified Domestic Relations Order for Defined Contribution Plan Only

Directions: This sample order is provided for you to prepare well in advance of your final decree, so that you may submit it to the plan administrator for review before you send it to the court for signature, at the time of your final decree.

---

①

☐ District Court

_____ County, Colorado

Court Address:

③

☐ **In re the Marriage of:**

Petitioner:

v.

Respondent/Co-Petitioner:

▲ COURT USE ONLY ▲

Case Number:

②

Division: Courtroom:

QUALIFIED DOMESTIC RELATIONS ORDER

This matter comes before this Court, pursuant to Paragraph **④** of the parties' Separation Agreement, and pursuant to the Section 206(d)(3) of the Employee Retirement Income Security Act of 1974, as amended (ERISA), and Section 414(p) of the internal Revenue Code of 1986, as amended, for entry of a Qualified Domestic Relations Order ("QDRO"), the parties being in agreement and the court being fully advised in the premises.

A. On _____**⑤**_____(date), this Court entered a Decree of Dissolution of Marriage **⑥** (Legal Separation) which incorporates the parties' Separation Agreement (the "Agreement dated___**⑦**_____, resolving between them the matters of assets division and maintenance pursuant to The Colorado Dissolution of Marriage Act. The Agreement further allocates to _____**⑧**_____ , the Alternate Payee, benefits of his/her former spouse, which are carried out in this QDRO.

B. The name of the Plan to which this QDRO relates is _____

_____ ,

⑨ which is referred to herein as "The Plan." The address of the Plan (and of the Plan Administrator) is

_____

_____ .

C. The party entitled to benefits as a participant under the Plan, which benefits are subject to this QDRO, is referred to as the "Participant." The name, address, and Social Security number of the Participant is:

Name: _____

⑩ Address: _____

_____

Social Security No.: _____

D. The party who will receive a right, as a result of this QDRO, to receive all or a portion of the benefits under the Plan, is referred to as the "Alternate Payee." The name, address, Social Security number, and date of birth of the Alternate Payee is:

(11) Name: _____

Address: _____

_____

Social Security No.: _____

Date of birth: _____

E. No portion of any benefit of the Participant under the Plan is presently required to be paid to any other Alternate Payee under a QDRO, and no such order has ever been entered with respect to any benefits of the Participant under the Plan.

F. This QDRO is intended by the parties to constitute a Qualified Domestic Relations Order under Section 206(d)(3) of the Employee Retirement Income Security Act of 1974, as amended (ERISA), and Section 414(p) of the internal Revenue Code of 1986, as amended.

THIS COURT THEREFORE ORDERS AS FOLLOWS:

1. The Alternate Payee, as the former spouse of the Participant, is hereby assigned the right to receive from the accounts of the Participant under the Plan:

(12) a. _____% of the Participant's accounts, valued as of _____ (date), (Option 1). OR

   $ _____ to be charged against the Participant's accounts under the Plan (Option 2).

(13) b. Alternate Payee shall (shall not) be entitled to Alternate Payee's pro rata share of earnings or losses on the amount determined under paragraph (a) from the valuation date specified above to the date of distribution.

2. Distribution shall be made to the Alternate Payee according to Alternate Payee's election.

3. Benefits paid to the Alternate Payee from the Plan shall not exceed the benefits to which the Participant is entitled under the Plan.

4. In the event of the Alternate Payee's death prior to receipt of all of the benefits hereunder, any remaining payments shall be distributed to the beneficiary of the Alternate Payee designated in writing to the Administrator of the Plan. If no such designation has been filed, or the designated beneficiary has predeceased the Alternate Payee, such payments shall be distributed to the Alternate Payee's estate.

5. The Alternate Payee shall not be entitled to Plan benefits that are already required to be paid to another Alternate Payee under another order previously determined to be a Qualified Domestic Relations Order (QDRO).

6. This QDRO shall remain qualified with respect to any successor plans to the Plans identified in this QDRO.

7. In case of conflict between the terms of the QDRO and the terms of a Plan, the terms of the Plan shall prevail. For example, if a Plan is terminated and all benefits are distributed, amounts due under this QDRO from that Plan shall be immediately distributable.

8. The court retains jurisdiction to amend this QDRO for the purpose of establishing or maintaining this Order as a Qualified Domestic Relations Order and/or to effectuate the parties' intention.

9. The Alternate Payee shall keep the Plan Administrator informed of his/her current address and telephone number until all transfers under this QDRO are complete. Notice of change of address or telephone number shall be made in writing to the Plan Administrator at the address given above in Paragraph B.

10. The Alternate Payee shall promptly serve a copy of this QDRO upon the Plan Administrator of the Plan.

SO STIPULATED:

(14)

_____   _____   _____   _____
Alternate Payee   Date   Participant   Date

(15)

Approved_____ (date)   By _____
                                                                              Plan Administrator

SO ORDERED this _____ day of _____ , ____ .

BY THE COURT:

(16) _____
District Court Judge/Magistrate

INSTRUCTIONS FOR FILLING OUT THE QDRO

1, 2, and 3. Fill out the same as on the petition.

4. Type the number or letter of the paragraph in your separation agreement which states your agreement regarding the QDRO.

5. Type the date of the decree, or the date of your final hearing, or leave blank if you are obtaining your decree by affidavit and you intend for the QDRO to be signed at the same time as the decree.

6. Delete "Dissolution of Marriage" or "Legal Separation" as appropriate.

7. Type the date you signed your separation agreement.

8. Type the name of the spouse who is to receive a benefit from this QDRO.

9. Type the full name and address of the plan.

10. Type the name, address, and Social Security number of the spouse whose name is on the plan.

11. Type the name, address, Social Security number, and date of birth of the spouse who is receiving a portion of the plan.

12. If you have agreed on a percentage of the current balance to be transferred to the receiving spouse, write that percentage in Option 1 and delete Option 2. Enter the date of the decree or date you sign this or any date you choose for your final valuation. If you have agreed on a dollar amount to be transferred to the receiving spouse, write that amount in Option 2 and delete Option 1.

13. The receiving spouse's share may grow or shrink with the market it is in between the time of the valuation date or the date of your Decree and the time it is paid out. If you want that amount to adjust up or down accordingly, delete "shall not". If you don't want it to adjust, delete "shall".

14. Each of you must sign and date your signature.

15. Leave blank – this is for the Plan Administrator to date and sign.

16. Leave blank – this is for the court to sign.

If you are dividing a retirement plan by written agreement, you must give the plan administrator plenty of time to review and approve the plan before your court date. Without this approval, you would not be able to divide the this asset.

Future Income Stream as an Asset

If you treat a future income stream as an asset, the employee pays the tax on it when he/she gets it at retirement, and the payment from the retiring spouse to the former spouse is tax-free (in after tax dollars). These payments would not necessarily cease at either remarriage or death of the recipient.

Future Income Stream as Maintenance

On the other hand, if you treat a future income stream as income, rather than an asset, the employee spouse may be able to deduct the payments to the ex-spouse. They then become maintenance payments, deductible by the employee spouse and taxable to the former spouse. Such maintenance payments are presumed to terminate on the former spouse's remarriage unless you state specifically that they are to continue beyond that event. In any event, such payments terminate at the receiving spouse's death.

PLANS DIVISIBLE BY WRITTEN AGREEMENT "THE COLORADO QDRO"

The retirement plans of certain Colorado public employees can be divided in a divorce action. These plans include P.E.R.A. and group funds such as police, fire, city and state employees who are not presently subject to E.R.I.S.A. (i.e., can not do a QDRO). BOTH spouses MUST agree to the division of the plan, in writing. The Courts have no jurisdiction to order the division or modify the terms of the agreement if the couple does not agree.

If you are considering dividing one of these plans, obtain any relevant forms and instructions from your plan administrator and then consult an attorney who specializes in retirement plans at divorce. (If you are not dividing your benefits under the plan, you may still need your spouse's signature on some official form.) Usually you will need a written agreement to submit to the plan administrator for approval, include language in your separation agreement, and then have a separate document, like a QDRO, for the court to sign. Be sure to allow enough time for all of these steps. Then take the agreement, signed by both of you, to the final hearing. Once it is approved by the court—which makes it an order—you usually have 90 days to submit the certified order to the retirement plan administrator.

PLANS NOT DIVISIBLE AT ALL

These include some plans of small employers not covered by E.R.I.S.A. or the "Colorado QDRO" above. For these plans, the best you can do in your negotiations is to balance them with other assets or income. If you can find a current value for the plan or a portion of it (for example, employee contribution to date), then you can set this aside for that spouse and offset it with other assets for the other spouse (after discounting it for a Social Security equivalent if you decide that is fair).

You can set up a future payment in a lump sum, or as periodic payments, such as monthly or quarterly, by the retiring spouse to the non-employee spouse and call it a division of assets. You can set up a future payment in a lump sum, or as periodic payments, such as monthly or quarterly, and call it maintenance.

If the plan is a pension, or contains the employer's promise to match it at a future date, then you may wish to treat that future portion as income rather than an asset, as you may do with Social Security. This means that when the benefit starts to pay, you can include in your separation agreement a promise that the retiree will pay to the former spouse a percentage of the amount received. You might consider using the formula shown earlier to determine what this percentage should be. Most people define such payments as maintenance, and therefore not payable if the recipient spouse remarries or dies.

If you are treating the payout of retirement as maintenance and this is the first time since your divorce that maintenance is being paid, then you MUST say in your separation agreement that this maintenance arises from the marriage and is part of the divorce agreement **and** the recipient must not waive his/her right to maintenance altogether in the separation agreement. If you are trying a late payout, you will do well to have your agreements double-checked by an accountant or attorney who specializes in this kind of long term financial planning.

If you have now agreed on how you are going to divide your retirements, you may enter the appropriate information on the Division of Marital Assets and Debts Chart at the end of this chapter. If you have decided to divide some or all of your retirements according to some value other than monetary, you do not need to make an entry on the chart. If you have not yet reached agreement, just read on.

Business Interests Checklist

Directions: Complete the following information for each business interest either one of you has.

☐ Corporation (majority or controlling interest): _____ (spouse) owns _____ shares of common/preferred/ other stock in _____ corporation, at _____
_____ (address) constituting ____% majority or controlling interest. Shares are held by
_____ (broker or agent).

☐ Corporation (minority interest): We have listed these shares in our Stocks and Bonds Checklist.

☐ Limited Liability Company (LLC):
_____ (spouse) is a member with ____% ownership inter- est in_____ LLC at_____ (address),with the right to_____% of the profits.

☐ Partnership: _____ (spouse) is a ____% partner in _____
_____ business, at _____
_____ (address) . Managing partner is _____
_____ at
_____ (address).

☐ Limited Partnership.
_____ (spouse) is a ____% limited partner in _____
_____ (business) which we have listed in our Stocks and Bonds Checklist.

☐ Joint Venture.
_____ (spouse) is in a joint venture: _____
_____ (name of business) at
_____
_____ (address) with _____ (other persons), whose names are:

☐ Sole Proprietorship: _____ (spouse) is the sole proprietor of _____
_____ business at
_____
_____ (address)

BUSINESS INTERESTS

This section is about interests in business in which you play an active role. It could be a professional practice like dentistry, psychotherapy, massage, medicine, law, or accounting; the majority shares in a closely held corporation or family business; an active partnership or joint venture. For example, you might be an independent contractor or sole proprietor in a real estate business who pays rent and other fees to a broker with the franchise name. You might be a cosmetologist or stylist in a beauty salon. You and your brother might be running an old and very successful clothing store that has been in your family for three generations, owned by the two of you and your mother. One of you might sell Amway or Mary Kay products, either as supplemental or primary income. You might have a cottage industry, a small manufacturing or repair business in your home, or in a workshop, or be an artist, writer, or desk-top publisher.

Active businesses come in many forms:

- If your business is a *corporation*, your interest is a percentage of stock. In this case your actual assets is stock, and not the assets owned by the corporation itself—although the value of those assets is part of the value of the stock. If your shares constitute a *majority or controlling interest*, then your actions directly affect the conduct of business, and therefore the business is an asset to be considered in your settlement.

    If you are a *minority shareholder*, the business is not directly affected by your actions. In this case, value your shares as stock—see "Stocks, Bonds, and other Securities."

- If your business is a *subchapter S corporation* it is a special kind of corporation in which the profits and losses of the corporation are attributed directly to the shareholder(s) as income.

- If your business is a *limited liability company*, you are a member with a certain percentage ownership interest in the business and entitled to a certain percentage (usually the same) of the profits.

- If your business is a *partnership*, your interest is your agreed percentage of that business. For example, if there are two of you, you may have agreed to be 50%-50% partners, 60%-40% partners, or some other proportion. You then own that agreed percentage of each of the assets of the business, and are responsible for that same agreed percentage of each of the partnership debts and obligations.

- If you are a *limited partner,* by definition you do not have any control over the operation of the business. In this case, value your limited partnership interest as stock—see "Stocks and Bonds."

- If your business is a *joint venture,* then each of those in the venture is a sole proprietor.

- If your business is a *sole proprietorship,* you personally own all the assets and are personally responsible for all the debts of the business.

Valuing a Business

There are appraisers who value businesses as a specialty. (See "Divorce Services and Consultants" in Chapter 2.) However, agree on a single appraiser who will be working for both of you, and be sure you tell him/her that this is a friendly divorce and you will not be asking for legal testimony as an expert witness. You should be prepared to put that in writing. You may be surprised how much it will reduce the price of the appraisal or valuation. If you wish to try to find a value acceptable to both of you on your own, begin by gathering all the fiscal year-end accounting and balance sheets, as well as tax reports, such as the corporate tax return, partnership K-1 tax forms, or Schedule C's.

There are some simple concepts which may make it possible for you to come to agreement about the value of your business. All businesses can be valued, at least in part, by adding up the business assets and subtracting the business debts. Business assets include: commercial real estate, unsold inventory, accounts receivable (money others owe the business for services rendered or goods purchased) which you may want to discount if they are old or you know the person or company that owes the money is having financial troubles; business equipment (copier, fax, car), furniture (desks, chairs), and supplies (paper, stamps, etc.). It is customary to use the fair market value of assets such as furniture, equipment and car—rather than what you paid for them, or what it would cost to replace them.

Business debts (liabilities) include: loan balances, the balance on leases (building, car), and bills not yet paid this month or quarter. The result, when you subtract the liabilities from the assets, will give you the minimal value of the business.

The difficult part of valuing a business is that the more established it is, the more likely that someone will buy it for more than the minimal value. The buyer is then paying for something called *good will* or blue sky. Good will is what makes the business

---

Business Valuation Checklist

Directions: Complete the following information for each business interest either one of you has.

☐ We will hire _____
(name of appraiser) to value our business

_____
(name of business).

☐ We will try to value our business

_____
(name of business) and will therefore need to gather the following:

Who will gather	Date Done	
_____	_____	P & L statement for
		_____
		(date/period of time) prepared by
		_____
		(accountant, if any)
_____	_____	Balance sheets for
		_____
		(dates) prepared by
		_____
		(accountant)
_____	_____	K-1 tax return for _____ years.
_____	_____	Income tax Schedule C for ____ years.

As a result of the above information gathered, we believe the following is true about _____ (business):

Assets are worth $ _____

Liabilities are worth $ _____

Value of business $ _____ (assets minus liabilities)

In addition, we agree this business has (does not have) a good will value of $_____, figured using the following formula:

desirable because it already has loyal customers, a good reputation, a known name, or those other qualities which make the consumer come to this business rather than any other offering the same service or selling the same goods. If your business is very new or very small or very shaky, you may agree that it has no, or very little good will, and therefore you will value it at assets minus liabilities.

If you think your business has good will, see some of the excellent books on the subject of valuing (usually for purposes of sale) a small or family business. These books are available both at local bookstores and at libraries. Several are listed in the bibliography. These books describe a variety of formulas for valuing businesses based on: personal income of the owner, how much more than the average business of this kind the particular enterprise earns, or the gross income stream of the business. There are many other formulas, and each industry lends itself to different ones. Trade magazines and journals will contain articles about buying and selling business in that particular field. This can be a good place to look for valuation formulas and how to use them for your particular business.

Don't kill the goose that lays the golden eggs.

Dividing a Business

If you are dealing with a very small family business, or a business which has been in one of your families for some time, you may feel like you are getting two divorces at once. If the business in question is also the primary support for the two of you, then it can be deeply threatening both emotionally and financially. A helpful technique might be to think of the business as a child of your marriage who must be shielded from your hostilities. Your business, like your child, must survive the divorce of its parents and must be given the opportunity to grow and flourish. Here are some suggestions for how to do this:

- Evaluate each possible way of allocating or dividing the business between you in light of which is most likely to enhance the business itself.

- Avoid any way of allocating or dividing the business which will or is likely to destroy it.

- Remember that you each have much more than money invested in this business.

Some Possible Ways to Divide Your Business

Following are some options for you to consider for dividing your business:

1. *Don't divide it.* Plan to both be active in the business in either the short or long run. If you choose this, here are some things to remember:

   - *Protect the baby.* Don't allow your personal animosities or antipathy to overflow into your conduct of the business. If that keeps happening, despite your best efforts, then this is probably not a viable option for you in the long run.

   - *Try a plan* which allows you to re-evaluate at the end of 6 months or a year. This may be enough time for you both to go through the changes in yourselves which happen at the time of separation. You can then look at your changed relationship with each other and evaluate whether it will support your being business partners for the long term.

   - *Separate your roles* within the business as much as possible. Have separate offices or different hours. Share the necessary business travel, so one of you is always there, but there are times when each of you is alone with the business. Be responsible for different departments or different functions. Try to be independent in your authority and responsibility within the business.

   - *One of you takes an active role* (managing partner, runs the store) and the other keeps only a passive role (limited partner). The difficulty with this model is the possibility that the passive partner feels frustrated or is tempted to be critical of the active partner. Another consideration in this mode is whether the active partner should be paid the same in profits, and/or should be paid a salary or profit-based incentive or bonus if in fact he or she is doing all the work.

2. *Sell the business.*

   - If you have a *friendly buyer,* you can often keep control or feel as though you have. This is a viable option for some people, but it is very important to be clear about your on-going role in the business so that you do not "stick your nose in where it is not wanted." The friendly buyer, however, can enhance the likelihood of your being paid, since the buyer cares about you. The friendly buyer may

---

Your Business Is Your Baby

If your business was created by both of you, it may feel as though it were your child. If you cut it in half, as Solomon threatened, it won't survive. Better to work out for one or the other of you to have it, and then compensate the other in some way, or apply some of the ideas about joint custody, so that you both continue to own it.

"Divorced people can't possibly go on sharing a business."
This is not necessarily true. It can be done successfully. The key is to differentiate between your relationship as spouses and your relationship as business partners.

"But screw your courage to the sticking place, and we'll not fail." Macbeth I, vii, 59

Don't Pay More Tax Than You Need To

Ted and Betty, husband and wife, and their friend Arthur founded Friendly Corporation, Inc., "FCI." After a few years Arthur wanted out, so their corporate attorney arranged for the corporation to redeem (purchase) Arthur's stock, resulting in Ted and Betty each owning 50% of the outstanding stock. This corporate redemption is taxed as a capital gain to Arthur.

When Ted and Betty divorced, they agreed that Betty would keep the corporation and Ted would start up his own company with the funds he would receive for his half of FCI. To save attorney fees, they followed the same paperwork their attorney had prepared when Arthur left. Ted paid capital gains tax on the increase in value of the shares he sold back.

If they had, instead, arranged for Betty to purchase Ted's shares directly from Ted, it would have been a transaction between husband and wife, "incident to divorce," and not taxable at all. Betty would keep all the shares at their original basis.

also ease the transition for the clients and customers of the business, so that there is less danger of loss of business in the transfer.

- If the *buyer is a stranger,* the transaction and the transition may feel like a terrible loss to you. However, this is often the surest way to solve the issue of valuation. If you cannot agree on a value between yourselves, despite your best efforts, you may need to sell in order to get on with your separate lives.

3. *One of you keeps the business.*

- *Buy the other out* with cash or off-set with other assets, or a mix of cash and assets.

- *Trade stock* in the business for other stock or assets.

- *Do a long term buy-out.* You may do a long term buy-out as a straight assets settlement, or structure it like maintenance to provide some real tax advantages (see Chapter 11).

OTHER ASSETS

Other assets include intellectual property such as a patent or a copyright; Broncos, Rockies, and symphony tickets and ticket priorities; frequent flyer miles; hunting rights; club memberships; debts which people owe you. These may all be mentioned in your separation agreement, even if you choose not to place a monetary value on them. Whether or not you mention them in your agreement, you must be clear about these items between the two of you.

If one of you has composed a song, authored a book or screenplay, written a software program, or painted a picture, then the rights to that creation have value. How can these rights be divided in a divorce? You can transfer ownership of patents and copyrights, and you can assign a certain portion of income from them, even a certain percentage of future income.

If you have rights to season tickets to the Broncos, the symphony, or hunting areas, you can alternate the use of these ("I'll take them this year, you take them next year,") or, divide the season or time they cover or trade them between you (I'll take the Bronco tickets, you take the rights to the duck blind.

If you belong to a private membership club, such as a country club, you may find these permit only one member of a divorced couple to continue the membership. You will have to reach agreement on this one. Trade for some other right or assets, or flip a coin if you have to.

Frequent flyer miles have value, but often cannot be transferred. A clever way to divide them is to use them for the benefit of both of you. Use them for your children's travel, for instance, or limit their use to the family business.

Suppose you loaned your best friend $1,000 when his car broke down. This is an informal but real loan, and his obligation to pay it back to you is an asset, as is a more formal loan with a signed promise to pay. Your friend's obligation to pay can be allocated to either one of you, or the payments may be divided between you when they are received, or used to pay one of your marital bills.

Kinds of Debts

Debts can be organized into four major categories:

1. debts which go with the assets—"secured" debts which are tied to an asset, like your mortgage to your house, or your car loan to the car;

2. freestanding or "unsecured" debts—not tied to any asset, like most credit cards;

3. tax debt;

4. divorce expenses.

SECURED DEBTS

The best examples of secured debts are the mortgage(s) on your home or other real estate, and loans on cars and trucks. For a loan to be secured, one of you must have signed a document that says that if you default on your loan payments the lender can take the asset. It's called foreclosure of a house, and repossession of a car.

Usually in divorce the person who gets the asset also gets the responsibility for the loan. Be sure in your negotiations you bear in mind that the value you place on any asset should take into account any outstanding loan balance on it. Keep in mind also any negative cash flow that goes with these assets. One way of managing both debt re-payment and negative cash flow is through maintenance (see Chapter 11).

In practice, only secured debt must be included in the division of assets. You may choose to deal with the following three types of

---

Other Assets Checklist

Directions: Complete the following information for each additional asset either one of you has.

We have the following additional assets to be divided in our agreement:

☐ Intellectual assets:
  ☐ Patent #_____ for
  _____ in the name of
  _____ (spouse).
  ☐ Copyrighted (book, song, poem, art work, name, software, other)
  _____
  _____ (describe) in the name of
  _____ (spouse).

☐ Priority rights:
  ☐ Season tickets: _____
  _____ (describe).
  ☐ Fishing/hunting rights: _____
  _____ (describe).
  ☐ Frequent flyer miles:
  _____ (# of miles) in name of
  _____
  _____ (# of miles) in name of
  _____

☐ Membership in _____
  _____ (club, organization).

☐ Accounts receivable
  $_____ owed to _____
  (spouse) by _____
  (name of debtor) under the following terms:

☐ Other: Describe:

Debts Checklist

Directions: Provide the following information for each secured or unsecured or tax debt either or both of you owes.

Creditor	Amount	Payment Terms

Uneasiness About Tax Returns

You are both legally responsible for any tax return you sign. Physical separation, when emotions are running high and expenses running even higher, is a time when people are tempted to be unwise on their tax returns (by exaggerating deductible expenses, claiming doubtful deductions, or "forgetting" to list income). If either of you is likely to be less forthcoming than the other, consider filing married/separately, so you are not legally bound by a tax return you are uncomfortable with. You may pay more tax this way, but the peace of mind may be worth it.

debt as assets, or as a budgeting issue. If you chose to consider this a budgeting question, then hold your discussion of these debts until your discussion of support, maintenance and taxes, Chapters 9, 10, and 11.

UNSECURED DEBTS

Unsecured debts are those obligations which are not tied to an asset. They are "freestanding." Examples are most credit cards, personal bank loans, some lines of credit, and most loans from parents and friends.

TAX DEBT

Taxes rate their own category because Uncle Sam and the Colorado Department of Revenue are the most difficult creditors of all. One of your largest joint obligations may be your joint tax returns. The IRS can do random audits for 3 years after the filing, can question your return for good cause for 7 years, and forever for fraud. Therefore, your agreement should have some provision for what you will do about any additional taxes, penalties or interest, as well as the cost of a possible audit.

Your separation agreement should state clearly your plan for filing your taxes for the last full year of your marriage or before being legally separated. Your separation agreement should also state how you will deal with any audits or questions raised about tax returns which you filed together. See Chapter 11 Taxes. Sample clauses about taxes are included in Chapter 12.

DIVORCE EXPENSES

When you're focused on the marital debts, it's easy to forget that the expenses of the divorce must be negotiated as well. Be certain that your separation agreement contains your promises about which of you will be responsible for paying the direct and indirect costs of becoming separate. The most obvious ones are usually the court filing fee, appraisals, mediation, and attorneys. Some not so obvious divorce expenses are joint or individual accounting, financial planning, and counseling. To avoid having this become "the straw that broke the camel's back," try to treat these like any unsecured marital debt, regardless of whose lawyer's bill it is, or who ordered the appraisal.

Some of the divorce expenses may have been paid by one or both of you before you began bargaining together. You may want to remember these in your agreement by giving credit to the person who paid them (setting aside assets in that amount to the payor).

Some of the divorce expenses may take place after the decree. Examples of these are attorney fees for doing QDRO's and title transfers, tax preparation for the final joint return, mediation fees, and long-term divorce counseling for you or your children. You will need to be clear about these in your budgets and in your bargaining. You may wish to write these arrangements into your separation agreement.

Dealing with Debt

Talk about debts early on, since most must be paid regularly, or you risk a credit problem. It's very easy in a separation to have your debts fall through the cracks by assuming that your spouse is paying them all.

GATHER THE DATA

To avoid lots of heartbreak, expense, and recriminations later, begin by gathering all the information either of you has about your current and recently-paid debts, as delineated in Chapter 5. You must know whether bills such as the car insurance have been paid. If you are having any trouble agreeing about whether a certain purchase or expense was for the family, gather all the statements and/or charge slips which relate to that expense. Collect all this data before you begin talking about that debt.

Once you have collected all the data about the debts, agree which part of each debt is marital. For example, you may want to say that the expenses or charges incurred since your separation, or your charges for your own business, are your own and not marital. Remember, the presumption is that all charges during your marriage are marital. If you are agreeing to anything else, be very clear.

DEBT STRATEGIES

Try to pay off as many debts as possible before or at the time of the final decree. Consider using liquid assets (bank accounts, stocks, bonds) or other saleable assets (the extra car, the time-share condo, non-essential furniture) in order to do this.

If it is not possible to pay off your debts right away, then you must be clear about who will pay which debt and within what period of time. Debts are a good place to consider putting "teeth" in your agreement. If you fail to make a payment on a debt that is secured by an asset, you lose that asset to the other spouse. For example, if one of you fails to pay the loan on the washer and dryer, then the other spouse may have the washer and dryer and pay off the remaining debt.

Divorce Expenses Checklist

Directions: Provide the following information for each divorce expense owed by either or both of you, or expected to be incurred by either or both of you.

Divorce Expense	Amount	Payment Terms

"I'm not responsible for paying that VISA bill, my ex-husband/wife promised to pay it in our divorce agreement, and the judge approved it."

Any agreement you two make about who is going to pay this debt does not affect the creditor, because the person or company you owe a debt to is not a "party" to your divorce negotiation or agreement. If one of you defaults, the lender will attempt to collect from the other, and the default will be reported (to credit reporting agencies) in both your names.

Hold Each Other Harmless

Here is a typical hold harmless clause: Wife will be solely responsible for paying the loan at ABC Credit Union, holding Husband harmless therefrom.

To back-up your agreement about who will pay your unsecured debts, include a hold harmless clause in your agreement. This will *indemnify* the non-paying spouse. This means that the paying spouse gives the non-paying spouse the right to collect not only all missed payments, but also damages, interest and attorneys fees resulting from the failure to make the payment. Without a hold harmless clause, the non-paying spouse has only the right to collect the missed payments. With a hold harmless clause, the non-paying spouse has the additional rights.

Once you have divided the responsibility for paying the debts, examine the effect on your respective budgets. Some tax planning through maintenance may be very helpful here to generate some cash with which to pay bills (see Chapters 9 and 10).

Failure to allocate all your debts between you and to give teeth to this part of your agreement may come back to haunt you years later.

BANKRUPTCY AT THE TIME OF YOUR DIVORCE

In the frustration over money issues, the threat of one spouse declaring bankruptcy may come up. Try approaching the discussion of possible bankruptcy as an "Oh my god!"—the kind of thing which might happen in spite of both of your best efforts—like being laid off at work, or becoming seriously ill.

There are two basic kinds of bankruptcy for individuals. Chapter 7 bankruptcy provides complete discharge of all (unsecured) debts, and the forfeiture of all assets over certain minimum protected amounts. Chapter 13 bankruptcy is the "Wage Earner Plan" which may preserve the assets and allow the debtor to pay off all the secured and priority debts (mortgages, car loans and taxes, usually) as well as a portion of the unsecured debts, and discharge the rest of the unsecured debts.

Several things about bankruptcy, either kind, should be taken into account in any settlement in divorce:

- If either spouse files for bankruptcy before, during, or after the divorce, the creditors will absolutely look to the other spouse to pay any of the originally joint debts, regardless of what you decided about them in your separation agreement. If the possibility of bankruptcy is immediate, it is better to do a joint filing than risk undoing your settlement by sabotage.

- Once a bankruptcy petition is filed, all other legal actions are automatically *stayed* (halted). First, this means creditors can't sue the person who filed for bankruptcy (remember, they can still sue the other spouse). Second, it means that if you have filed for divorce but the final decree has not been entered, the divorce court must obtain written permission from the bankruptcy judge to rule or act on any matters which are also in the bankruptcy. Clearly, this will create chaos in your divorce negotiations if you don't know it is coming.

- When you file a petition in bankruptcy, the law imposes an *automatic stay* on all the creditors listed in the petition, as discussed above. This means that they are prohibited from attempting in any way to collect the debt from the petitioner as long as the stay is in effect, usually around three months. The automatic stay in bankruptcy can be a good planning tool. By filing a joint bankruptcy, you could use it to stop aggressive creditors and give yourselves time to reach agreement.

Filing the bankruptcy and the divorce at the same time can be very beneficial, especially if there is a possibility of using a Chapter 13 plan to pay off your marital debts. It may take three lawyers to make this plan work smoothly – one for each of you in the divorce and one for you both in the joint bankruptcy filing. Don't discard this option just because it is initially expensive or distasteful.

Bankruptcy declared after your divorce does discharge (erase) unsecured assets settlement payments, but does not discharge maintenance or child support payments, either current or arrearages. You can anticipate a possible bankruptcy by saying in your separation agreement that if either declares bankruptcy within a certain period of time, you will agree to re-negotiate part or all of the separation agreement. See sample wording in Chapter 12.

Dividing Marital Assets and Debts

Many people try to divide each asset as they discuss it ("Your half the house is $4,000, my half of the house is $4,000"). Since you will rarely divide the house like this, this may not be the most useful way to go about it. It may be more practical, to begin with, to list each asset as a whole under the name of the person who will keep it. For example, in wife's column list the marital equity in the house if she is thinking of continuing to live there. List the entire value of the husband's retirement in his column, if that is your initial inclination. An advantage to this method is that it allows you to see the balance, or lack of it, of your initial plan as you develop it.

Defining Our Sense of Fairness

A. We agree our marital assets should be divided 50/50% because:

or

B. We agree that the first $_____ in value of assets should go to _____ because:

or

C. We agree _____ should get all the _____ because:

and _____ should get all the _____ because:

or

D.

If you want to know dollar values, you may need a third party, such as an appraiser, to help you determine them. In order to avoid expensive competing professional opinions, as discussed earlier, agree on who you will hire as your appraiser and how you will pay for it. Agree further how conclusive the appraised value will be for you.

As you divide the marital assets between you, remember that the value may be a range, or other than monetary. It is okay to bargain without fixed numbers for value.

This is the time for a real heart to heart about the range of your sense of fairness. Is the only possibility for you 50-50 division of things by value? By number? Are you more interested in cash than in things? Will you take less than 50% if your share is all cash? Are you more interested in future security than in present assets? If you are willing to wait for a buy-out of your share, such as house or retirement, are you looking for more than 50% to compensate you for waiting? Are you interested in a "lopsided" agreement (more to one than the other) to compensate for the larger earnings of one of you now? Do you want to be "made whole"—end up where you were at the beginning of the relationship? Do you need to be compensated "off the top" for some contribution you made to the acquisition of assets? If you can agree on a generic plan which meets each of your ideas of fairness, you will find you have an agreement which practically writes itself.

As you divide marital assets, write down on the Division of Marital Assets and Debts Chart which follows, the costs involved in maintaining each asset, the debt which comes with it, and the potential for growth or income. This will help you make a more balanced settlement.

As you allocate your other debts, decide first whether they are marital, separate, or a mix. Then agree who will pay off the balance of each. Remember that the problem of unsecured debts may be more easily handled as budget than division of assets. If you find yourselves getting stuck on the division of unsecured debts, including tax debt and divorce expenses, consider setting aside this issue for now. Look at these debts again in the context of maintenance and tax planning after reading Chapters 10 and 11.

Think beyond the short term to the long term effect of the division of assets and debts you are considering. For example, suppose one spouse gets all assets which appreciate slowly or depreciate, and which take money to maintain (home, car, furniture). Then suppose the other spouse takes all assets which increase in value or produce income (stock, retirement, rental home). In such a case, even a few years after the divorce, what in the short term appeared to be a "fair" or "equal" division will look quite different. The net worth of the second spouse will far exceed the net worth of the first – and the gap will just continue to widen. Be sure to consider this information before you decide what is really "fair" or "equal" in your situation.

 Partners can define their sense of fairness by thinking along the same lines of those who are married.

DIRECTIONS FOR COMPLETING THE DIVISION OF MARITAL ASSETS AND DEBT CHARTS

Make several photocopies of each chart. Do your first drafts, preliminary bargaining, in pencil as you may want to try different possibilities.

Use the Marital Assets and Debts Chart to remind you of which assets and debts you have already agreed are separate, and list them in the appropriate column.

Now begin dividing the items you have agreed are marital. Use the checklists from throughout this chapter (a complete list of checklists and page numbers may be found at the end of the book) for the values and balances, to help you decide who gets the asset and the value of it, or the debt and its balance. Those checklists are:

> Calculation of Your Value of Real Estate
>
> Personal Assets Checklist
>
> Motor Vehicle Checklist
>
> Liquid Assets Checklist
>
> Stocks Checklist
>
> Bonds Checklist
>
> Life Insurance Checklist
>
> Retirements Checklist
>
> Business Interests Checklist
>
> Business Valuation Checklist
>
> Other Assets Checklist
>
> Debts Checklist
>
> Divorce Expenses Checklist

List under husband or wife, each marital asset and marital debt which that spouse will keep. Put debt balances in brackets < >.

For each asset or debt, whether marital or separate, anticipate and calculate the expected earnings or cost and increase or decrease in value in the cash flow/growth columns. Put decreases in brackets.

For example, if wife will be retaining the family home, all the costs of maintaining the home should be written in the cash flow column of the chart, along with the probable rate of increase in value (est. x % per year). You may wish to include the increase in equity as the mortgage is paid as part of the growth of that asset. If husband will retain his automobile, then the car payment, insurance, and costs of operating the car go in his cash flow column, as may also the rate of decrease in value of a depreciating asset, if you wish to include it. List debt balances in either the husband or wife column, as appropriate, and the monthly payment in the cash flow column. Remember to list any debts secured by an asset along with the asset.

When you have entered all your marital assets and debts, total the husband's marital assets minus husband's marital debts, and do the same for the wife. Then, for each spouse, total the cash flow column. These four totals will summarize your preliminary division of assets. Refer now to your answers to Defining Our Sense of Fairness. Review your division with this in mind, and make changes as you need to.

DIVISION OF MARITAL ASSETS AND DEBTS CHART
HUSBAND

ASSETS/DEBT	SEPARATE	MARITAL SHARE	CASH FLOW/GROWTH

DIVISION OF MARITAL ASSETS AND DEBTS CHART
WIFE

ASSETS/DEBT	SEPARATE	MARITAL SHARE	CASH FLOW/GROWTH

Finalizing Your Division

Use the Final Division Calculation to test whether the division of marital assets and debts which you have indicated on the Division of Marital Assets and Debts Chart is what you want to do.

Suppose your definition of a fair division of marital assets is 50-50. Add up the proposed assets and debts for each of you, in your separate columns, and compare these totals. If one of these totals is larger than the other, you will need to transfer one-half the difference to the spouse with the lower total. This can be done in a variety of ways. You can transfer an asset to effect this balancing, or actually pay it. This equalizing amount does not have to be cash. It could be a promissory note, amortized over time, or with a balloon payment when the home sells.

Whether you decide that your fair division is 60-40 or 70-30, the method is the same, only the arithmetic changes. For example, if you have agreed to a 60%-40% division, multiply the Net Marital Estate from the Marital and Separate Assets and Debts Chart times .6 to determine how many assets equals 60%. Then adjust the total for the spouse who is to receive 60% until you reach that number. This adjustment may be made by transferring assets, cash, or future payments, as discussed above.

Making Things Happen: Enforcement

There are two ways to enforce your agreements about assets and debt division—voluntary and involuntary. The first we call teeth, which is voluntary but effective. The second is enforcement by the court.

VOLUNTARY ENFORCEMENT

Some people worry, from time to time, that they might not completely fulfill their end of the bargain they are negotiating. If your ex gets a new lover, will you be less likely to pay the old marital debts? If you lose your job or the bonus does not come through, will you look for a way out of your agreement? Most people would have to answer yes to at least one of these—or, at least admit that the possibility exists they could be tempted.

If you have any doubts about yourself, or some secret doubts about your soon-to-be-ex, then try putting in some creative incentives to do what you say you're going to do. These incentives to

Final Division Calculation

Directions: Enter the appropriate numbers from the Marital Assets and Debts Chart

	Wife	Husband
Total Marital Assets	_____	_____
Less Total Marital Debt	_____	_____
Total Net Marital:	_____	_____
Difference (Subtract the lower from the higher)	_____	_____
1/2 the Difference (to effect a 50/50 division)	_____	

right behavior are called teeth and are limited only by your imagination. Try having the person against whom the penalty would act set the penalty. You may be surprised to learn what motivates each of you.

For example, pay the spouse-moving-out's equity in the home as described in a promissory note only if that person has paid all the marital obligations he or she agreed to pay. You can design baby teeth for minor misses. For example, the person who does not make a required mortgage payment on time owes the other spouse double the late fee if the other spouse "fronts" the payment. There are sample clauses about internal or voluntary enforcement included in Chapter 12. You may wish to review them after reading this chapter.

INVOLUNTARY ENFORCEMENT

The second kind of enforcement is the power of the court, or some other agency, to take remedial action if the promises you make are not kept. These are summarized in Chapter 13.

Conclusion

You have now finished your first rough look at your division of marital assets and debts. It will probably not be your final version. Go on to the next four chapters about the other essential components of your separation agreement. The agreements you reach as a result of each of those chapters may necessitate changes in the assets division you have worked out so far.

Take heart. Doing your own separation agreement is hard work. Don't expect to get it all done in one sitting. Don't even expect to complete the work of one of the separation agreement chapters in one sitting. Give yourself and each other the time you deserve to make the best decisions for both of you.

CHAPTER 8

CHILDREN
SEPARATION AGREEMENT – PART II

CHILDREN
SEPARATION AGREEMENT – PART II

Before the court can give you a final decree of dissolution of marriage or legal separation, you must resolve and write out all the financial and parental issues remaining from your marriage. This written summary is called the separation agreement whether you are obtaining a divorce or a legal separation. It must be read and approved by the court.

Your separation agreement must do the following:

1. All property you have accumulated must be accounted for and divided (Chapter 7, Assets and Debts).

2. All debts must be acknowledged and paid or the responsibility for paying them allocated between you (Chapter 7, Assets and Debts, and Chapter 11, Taxes).

3. You must establish a parenting plan for your children—decision-making and parenting time—and make commitments about their support (this chapter, Chapter 9, Child Support, and Chapter 11, Taxes).

4. If either spouse is to assist in supporting the other—spousal support or maintenance—the amounts and duration must be set (Chapter 10, Maintenance, and 11, Taxes).

5. You must arrange to pay any costs of the divorce itself: the court filing fee, mediators, lawyers, accountants, recording fees, and the like, if any (Chapter 7, Assets and Debts).

6. You must agree when and under what circumstances any of your agreements change or terminate (Chapters 7-10 and 13).

The five separation agreement chapters (7-10 and 13), designed to help you write your separation agreement, are full of technical terms and legal requirements. The information you will need for your separation agreement is listed in the Great Hairy Checklist, Chapter 5. Gathering this information now will make all your bargaining more effective and more complete. Using the Great Hairy Checklist will ensure that you don't omit anything vital to a comprehensive agreement.

Chapter 12 contains sample wording for a wide variety of options in a separation agreement, drawn from the topics discussed throughout this Guidebook. As you complete your agreement

"Divorce always hurts children." "You just can't possibly be a responsible parent and get a divorce."

The truth, shown by extensive research, is that divorce does not necessarily hurt children. What does hurt them is on-going hostilities between their parents, whether or not there is a divorce. Research shows that children of divorcing parents who stopped fighting were as well adjusted as those raised in successful marriages. The same research also shows that children of parents who stayed together, but who continued to fight, had as much trouble adjusting as children of the continually hostile divorce. So it's not the divorce that hurts the children, it's the ongoing anger and hostility that are harmful.

Emancipation: When your child is no longer your legal or financial responsibility.

"The age of emancipation in Colorado just changed to 19."

Not true. The age of presumed emancipation is still 21. Only the age for which a parent can stop paying child spport changed to 19.

Dates We Expect Our Children to Emancipate

We expect each of our children to emancipate on approximately the following dates, for the following reasons:

Name	Date of Birth	Expected Date and Circumstance of Emancipation

about each topic, you might wish to read the relevant sample wording in Chapter 12 for ideas about writing your own agreement. If you choose, you may use a separation agreement form, JDF 1115, instead of writing your own, but still incorporating the information you gather working through these topics. If you use JDF 1115 you will need to complete the parenting plan form, JDF 1113, and file both with the court before you can obtain your decree. The sample separation agreement provisions concerning children in Chapter 12, accomplish the same thing. You decide how creative or detailed you wish to be.

Who Is a Child?

For purposes of your divorce petition, a child is any person born to, conceived by, or adopted by both of you during your marriage, which is why you list all your children, whether or not emancipated.

The word *child* in Colorado law means anyone under the age of 21, with some exceptions. This is different from most other states, where the age of emancipation for all purposes is 18. Until your child reaches 21 in Colorado, you, the parents, may be liable for the child's financial needs, emotional welfare and perhaps for his or her actions. There are some circumstances in which a child never emancipates, such as severe disability.

At age 18 children can do many things without their parents' consent, some of which emancipate them. For example, they can go into the military or marry, either of which emancipates them. If the marriage is annulled, or if they leave the service before age 21, they may become unemancipated again. At age 18 anyone can sign a contract—to buy a car, for example—and be bound by their signature (they can be sued on the debt). They can make a will and inherit. The jurisdiction of the juvenile court ends at age 18, so anyone over 18 is treated like an adult in court. The terms *delinquency and dependency and neglect* do not apply to anyone over age 18.

At age 19 the duty of child support as calculated by the Colorado Child Support Guideline ends. Divorcing people cannot be made to pay each other money to support a child over the age of 19, unless the child is mentally or physically disabled or still enrolled in high school or an equivalent program. The duty to pay child support may end before age 19 if the child emancipates.

People sometimes use the terms *"emancipated minor,"* and *"emancipated in fact."* An emancipated minor is someone whom an institution (usually a school) has decided to treat as an adult, so they can live independently of their parents and/or sign their own permissions for absences and trips, etc. Usually, this is an arrangement between the institution and the child, and does not emancipate the child for any other purpose. Emancipation in fact is a determination by a court for a specific case or set of circumstances. For example, if a person under 21 causes an automobile accident and is uninsured, the injured party is likely to seek damages from both the child and his or her parents—on the so-called deep pocket theory that the parents are more likely to have money. The judge in this case might determine that the child was "emancipated in fact," if he or she lived away from home, was totally self-supporting and had no ties of any kind to the parents, and that therefore the parents are not liable. This emancipates that child for that case only.

As you can see, the age of emancipation in Colorado is far from a fixed point in time. Watch for this to change (probably to 19 or even 18 for all purposes) in the near future.

How to Be a Good Parent Through the Divorce Process

The time when parents begin living apart is one of the most stressful for children. Their worst fear is of losing a parent. They need both of you at this time. Each of you has a clear and distinct role to play. Children really can adjust to the separations and transitions involved in two-household parenting. They adjust best when you work together to support each other's relationship with them.

Children feel more secure when they are confident that their parents can take care of themselves. If they feel you are not doing that, they will try to take care of you, and the parent-child relationship becomes reversed. Therefore taking care of yourself at this difficult time is not only good for you, it is in the best interests of your children.

Critical to good parenting throughout the divorce process is insulating the children from any hostilities between the parents. This means managing your own conflict well. Work toward strengthening your children's sense of security while they navigate their own choppy waters as you separate and divorce. It's a time to be very careful what you say, and to whom you say it. Think your conduct through carefully. It's definitely not a time to introduce a new significant other.

Emancipated minor: Special status of a child with an institution, such as a school, which allows that child to be responsible for him or herself in matters of permission to attend certain events, participate in sports, absences. Juvenile court can also recognize this status.

Parenting-After-Divorce Classes

Most Colorado courts now require divorcing parents to attend a class about the impact of divorce. The class is a one-evening meeting usually lasting three hours, which costs $35-50 in most jurisdictions. You may apply to have the fee waived if you cannot afford it. You will receive a written order from the court when you file your case if the class is mandatory, and, if so, how to apply to attend without cost, and who is in charge of filing the certificate of attendance—you or the instructor. If the class is required, the certificate must be in your file before the court will issue a final decree.

Parental Responsibility Law

Colorado has a better way of talking about what used to be called "custody" of minor children. It was clear to a great many people for a long time that using the word custody to refer to children implied what lawyers call "possession and control" (as in, "You take custody of the airplane tickets, Dear, I'm afraid I might lose them"). For a long time in this country and in Colorado the legal system did, indeed, use very odd words about where children would live and how they would be cared for after their parents' divorce. The court was said to "award" the children to one or the other parent. One parent would have "legal custody" or the power to make all the major decisions. Or, the parents could elect to share legal custody which meant they were yoked in a double harness on all major decisions: pull together, or pull against each other until everything was at a dead stop and no decisions got made until a mediator, arbitrator or court stepped in. There were no other choices about the power to make decisions.

The law now uses the phrase "allocation of parental responsibilities" to mean the manner in which the court or the parents determine how the children should be raised. Strongly implied in this choice of wording is the idea that the worthy upbringing of children is a responsibility of the parents to the children—a responsibility that the state, in the person of the court, has the mandate to enforce. This is a far cry from the idea that children are a prize to be won by the parents. Most people welcome this change.

"Allocation of decision-making responsibilities" refers to your agreement or the court's order about who decides such things as education, health and religion for minor children. "Determination of parenting time" refers to where minor children will live. When the statute refers to child support, the phrase becomes "residential care." You will need to cover both decision-making and residence of your children in your agreements. The next section concerns decision-making, the following section covers the topic of where the children will live. You will present these agreements to the court at the final decree hearing in the form of a Parenting Plan or Separation Agreement or both. The appropriate forms are referred to in this chapter as each topic is discussed.

Who Will Make the Decisions Regarding Issues that Affect the Children?

This section of this chapter concerns the "allocation of decision-making responsibilities."

Allocation of Parental Responsibilities: This term means the manner in which parents agree or courts order that children shall be cared for following a divorce. Correlates to the former term custody.

Partners who are parents may go through the court for orders regarding parental responsibilities if you wish. When it comes to their children, many partners want to have the formality and official nature of court orders, as well as the opportunity for enforcement if needed. But you may also create your parenting plan and child support arrangements by private agreement. If you go through the court, the Colorado Parental Responsibility law and the Colorado Child Spport Guideline will apply. You can go through the Court and still do it all by agreement.

It is a generally accepted rule that when the child is with one parent, that parent will make any day to day decisions about the child. Some examples of this would be bedtimes, school vs. sack lunch, dress, hygiene, manners and discipline. Activities which take place only during one parent's time with the child would also be assumed to be the decision of that parent.

What the court concerns itself with are the so-called major decisions affecting the children. The previous law defined these as "major decisions affecting the health, education and general welfare." The new law simply refers to "each issue affecting the child."

You or the court may list the important decisions you anticipate making about your children and then decide if you will make these decisions together (the law uses the term "mutual"), or if one or the other of you will make them (the law uses the term "individual"). You can mix and match. You may agree to make some decisions together, and turn some decisions over to one or the other of you. An example would be that you decide you will be mutual decision-makers regarding discipline and after-school sports, but that the mother will be the individual decision-maker about health matters and the father about education matters.

The law says that the court should take into account, when considering mutual decision-making, the present ability of the parties to share decision-making about their children and the history of same, and whether such sharing might enhance the contact between the child and both parents. If there is proven child abuse or neglect or spousal abuse then the court is not encouraged to order mutual decision-making unless both parties want to try it.

A provision in the law states that conduct by a parent that does not relate to a child is not germane to a determination of decision-making ability. As with much of family law in Colorado, you are not bound by the considerations the court must take into account, but knowing what might be in the judge's mind is useful as you try to put together a parenting plan that will be approved.

You are not limited strictly to the exact terms used by the statute. If you have an agreement that says you will share certain decisions, or that the wife will make all the major decisions, the court will get the idea.

Allocation of decision-making responsibilities:

This term refers to how parents will make the major decisions about their children. Correlates to the former term Legal Custody. Choices include: one parent makes all these decisions, the parents make them all together, or each major decision-making area or category may be decided differently.

If both partners are already on the child's birth certificate, and you want to put your parenting plan and child support arrangement through the court, you would file a Petition for Allocation of Parental Responsibilities. You can do this in full agreement, or have the court decide things for you. To do it yourselves, you will need a parenting plan, as explained in this chapter, as well as child support worksheets as explained in Chapter 9. If one of the partners is the natural father but is not listed on the child's birth certificate, you will need to file a Petition in Paternity along with a Petition for Allocation of Parental Responsibilities. All of these forms are available at Bradford Publishing.

HOW DO WE DECIDE?

The following questionnaire may help you decide whether you are good candidates to make mutual decisions about your children. Select the six (or more, if you wish to expand the graph) important decisions you believe will have to be made regarding your children—for example, which schools to attend, which doctors to see, which activities and lessons, drivers license, car insurance, birth control.

a.

b.

c.

d.

e.

f.

In the table below, each of you, using different colored pens, answer "Yes" or "No" for each question in the left column regarding each anticipated decision you have listed above.

Parental Decision-Making Questionnaire

Decisions:	a	b	c	d	e	f
1. Can I bear to be left out of this decision?						
2. Must I have veto power over this decision (if I don't agree, it does not happen)?						
3. Is it sufficient that I am consulted about my opinion?						
4. Is it sufficient that I be informed of the decision before the fact?						
5. Do I have to be part of the fact-gathering (interviewing day care providers, pediatricians, checking out ballet school or karate class, visiting colleges, etc.)?						
6. If I'm not part of the decision, am I willing to pay my fair share of the cost?						

Interpreting the Parental Decision-Making Questionnaire

- For any decision about which you both answered "no" to 1 and "yes" to 5, you are probably good candiates to make that decision mutually.

- For any decision about which either of you answered "yes" to 3, 4, and 5, this probably indicates it is acceptable to that parent that the other parent may make that decision individually.

- For any decision about which either of you answered "no" to 1 and "yes" to 2, this probably indicates that the parent will wish to be in charge of that decision individually.

CAN WE DO MUTUAL DECISION-MAKING?

Can parents who could not get along during their marriage really make mutual decisions? The answer to this question depends on whether the mutual decision-making becomes a vehicle for continuing the marital hostilities. In fact, making mutual decisions does not require that you get along, or even that you like each other. It requires respect for each other and maturity—the ability to trust and to cooperate. Ask yourselves whether you can discuss and negotiate fairly with each other, keeping your children's interest utmost.

Research has shown there are some qualities which enable parents to overcome their hostilities and to work together as mutual decision-makers.

Notes:

Should We – Can We?

For most parents, the issue is not whether you should make mutual decisions about your children after your divorce, the issue is whether you can.

Who Is Not (Quite) Ready for Mutual Decison-Making?

Parents who have great difficulty making decisions together have many of these characteristics:

- They maintain intense, continuing conflict and hostility which they are unable to divert from the children.

- They exhibit overwhelming anger and the continuing need to punish the former spouse.

- There is a history of physical abuse.

- There is a history of substance abuse.

- One or both maintain a fixed belief that the other is a bad parent.

- One or both is unable to separate his or her own feelings and needs from those of the children.

If any of these apply to you or your spouse, doing mutual decision-making may still be a possibility for you if your determination is great enough, but you will probably require some professional help. There are therapists who specialize in teaching parenting skills. See "Divorce Services and Consultants" in Chapter 2.

Parenting Qualities Chart

Directions: Rate yourselves, and each other, individually and as a team, on a scale of one to ten, ten being excellent, on the following chart using different colored pens.

Mom	Dad	Team	Qualities of Parents who can make mutual decisions
			1. Makes clear to our children that he/she values their relationship and time with self and with other parent, despite all his/her anger and disappointment from the ending of our marriage.
			2. Maintains some objectivity throughout our divorce process, and insulates our children from our conflicts.
			3. Empathizes with our children's point of view, and with that of other parent.
			4. Successfully shifts his/her emotional expectations of the other from the role of mate to that of co-parent, and recognizes the boundaries of the new roles.
			5. Maintains high self-esteem, shows flexibility, and is open to both giving and receiving help from outside sources and especially from the other parent.

Interpreting the Parenting Qualtities Chart

- If your evaluations of yourselves and each other concide, and the estimate of your mutual functioning is 5 or better you are probably candidates for successful mutual decision-making.

- If your evaluation of yourselves and each other directly contradicts, and the estimate of your mutual functioning is 4 or less, then mutual decision-making might be difficult for you.

- If your answers are not consistent, and you still want to try major decisions together, then you've got your work cut out for you. The aspect of the new law that permits you to allocate certain decisions to one of you and other decisions to the other might be just right for you. You would then both stay involved in making decisions about your children, but you would not have to make any decisions together.

HOW TO MAKE MUTUAL DECISON-MAKING WORK

If you have agreed to be mutual decision-makers, it is crucial that you define the decisions which you will make together, and decide the process you will use if you do not initially agree.

Use the following shopping list together to write your Must-Share Decisions List.

Shopping List of Mutual Decisions

1. Any major expense (whether one-time or on-going) which you expect the other parent to share in. "We define a major expense as anything over $_____." For example: your child's teacher says you should enroll him or her in piano lessons and buy or rent a piano in each home.

2. Any activity which will or may take place on the other parent's time. For example: soccer league where the games are every Saturday and you plan on alternate weekends with each parent.

3. Any major change in your basic plan for time you each spend with the children and/or the basic support plan.

4. Choice of private or public schools, or which school.

5. Orthodontia.

6. Mental health counseling.

7. When do your children drive, whose car, and who pays for the extra insurance.

8. The birth control teaching and decisions of your children.

9. In-school electives and activities, whether or not they cost more money.

10. Parent-teacher conferences.

11. Results of medical/dental exams and recommended treatment.

12. **Elective** medical or dental treatment. Be sure you say that either parent is able to sign for **emergency** medical care when the other parent cannot be reached immediately. State that any follow-up care is a joint decision.

Mutual Decisions List

Our list of decisions which we both agree are to be made together.

1.

2.

3.

4.

5.

6.

7.

8.

Any decisions not on this list will be made by the parent who has the children at the time.

You may transfer this list to your Separation Agreement using the sample separation agreement provisions in Chapter 12, or to the Parenting Plan form, JDF 1113 (on the CD-ROM), if you are using the Separation Agreement form, JDF 1115.

AVOIDING DEADLOCK THROUGH GOOD COMMUNICATION

One key to making your mututal decision-making agreement work is to write out in detail your communication process.

This may sound too silly to work, but it usually does. Some couples find this very helpful at the beginning of their separation. It is up to you. It is also up to you whether you wish to include any of your agreements about process in your final separation agreement.

Communications Process Checklist

Directions: Discuss each of the following carefully, and decide which, if any, will work for you. Alter them as needed. Initial those statements below which you both agree will work for you.

Initial

1. We agree to meet at the same time, same place, for at least 15 minutes a week (every other week, month), whether we have anything earthshaking to report or not. (This will get you in the habit of talking face to face and listening carefully, before you have to do it "for real" when a problem comes up.)

2. We agree to share (or exchange) written agenda in advance of our meetings. (Big surprises are nearly always unpleasant and difficult.)

3. Each of us agrees to present the decision to be made without our own "pet" solution already in place. Instead, each of us will keep an open mind by suggesting a number of possible options.

4. If we really get stuck on something, we will each produce two alternate plans, solutions, or suggestions which each of us can live with, in the event one's favorite solution does not meet with the other's favor.

5. We agree to rank the three best solutions, any one of which is do-able by both of us, and let the children select.

6. If we agree, we may invite the child in question to the discussion.

7. We agree that unless there is real time urgency, we won't shake hands on the deal on the spot. We will write it up and exchange drafts the next day, then meet again.

8. We agree to suspend discussions until both of us have had time to cool off, if necessary, to gather more data, to get other input, to ask the children. In other words, we agree to force ourselves to look past our initial reaction and develop still more alternatives.

9. We agree to together seek the opinion of someone with special knowledge about the problem, such as a teacher, counselor, pediatrician, pastor.

10. We agree to initiate a short-term trial to gain more information and to check out our assumptions. For example: we agree to re-evaluate the school at the end of the semester, or re-evaluate after three sessions with the counselor.

LONG DISTANCE MUTUAL DECISION-MAKING

Can "long distance parents," parents too far apart geographically to meet face to face on a regular basis, be effective mututal decision-making parents? Yes, with great commitment by both parents. In fact, just as time heals much, so also may some significant mileage between the two of you greatly benefit your communication process. Distance may lend clarity and lessen pressure.

Following is some suggested language which you may wish to include in your agreement if you are considering becoming long distance mutual decision-makers. It's up to you whether to include any provisions about long distance communication in your agreement.

1. We will work together to make our list of must-share decisions as clear and well-defined as possible.

2. We agree to develop, at the outset, a communication process or sequence that will work for us, and to stick with it until and unless we both agree to change it. For example: "We will talk by phone until we disagree, then we will exchange our thinking in writing." OR, "We will never call each other on the phone (except in emergency). We will only communicate face to face three times a year."

3. Each of us agrees to present to the other, as early as possible, any question or future decision to be made—even if it might not occur.

4. Each of us agrees that if we get stuck on a particular mutual decision, we will first find a mediator who will work with us via conference call.

5. Each of us will develop a plan for exchanging news and information. Use the mail, e-mail, fax, audio and video tapes, as well as the telephone.

WHAT IF WE CAN'T AGREE ON A DECISION WE AGREED TO MAKE MUTUALLY?

Even in the best of communication processes, it is possible to get stuck. If you agree to mutual decision-making, consider including a paragraph in your agreement about what you will do if you really get stuck on one of your major decisions, after you've tried everything you can think of to get unstuck. The court will be reassured to know that you are not agreeing to mutual decision-making because you do not have the stomach to choose between your-

Communications With the Other Parent

Poor: "Jennifer got a scholarship to Europe, so she won't be coming to visit you."

Better: "Jennifer has a chance at a choir trip to Europe for June and July. Unfortunately, it is during your time with her. What do you think?"

Best: "Jennifer is getting so serious at her music, I wonder if we should explore, with her, options for camp, clinics, performance experience. For instance …."

What We Will Do if We Get Stuck:

Directions: Write here what you agree to do if and when you get stuck on a decision you agreed to mutually.

More Communications with the Other Parent

Poor: "Jennifer is going to Europe in June and July. I put down the first payment last night. It's not refundable."

Better: "Jennifer said she would like to consider the Europe trip for this summer, but she doesn't want to miss seeing you or hurting your feelings. Can you give her a call and discuss some alternatives with her?"

Best: "Here is Jennifer's vacation calendar with the dates of the possible Europe trip penciled in. I will see that she has no other activities scheduled for the summer. She also has nothing scheduled for spring break this year. (Spring break for her is _____ to _____.) By the way, parents are allowed to go on the Europe trip. Would you be able to go for all or some of it? I know Jennifer would be thrilled."

Our Information Exchange List

We agree to share with each other the following information about our children:

1.

2.

3.

4.

5.

6.

7.

8.

selves, and that you will not come back to court every time you cannot agree on a decision. The more confident your agreement sounds about how you are going to go about sharing your mutual decisions, the more likely the court is to approve it without question. If you find yourselves in a stuck place, there are some very workable ways to get past it—the following are some sample ideas.

- Assign a "sphere of influence" to each of you as individual decision-makers for times you cannot reach a decision mutually after trying all your agreed-upon deadlock-breaking techniques. For example, mother makes the medical decisions, father makes the educational decisions. This is the alternative specifically contemplated by the new law in permitting parents to select those decisions most important for them to be in charge of.

- Seek input from a person with special knowledge in the area of the decision you are stuck on. For example, ask the school counselor about whether your child should repeat kindergarten.

- Take the particular issue to mediation. A neutral third-party may help you find your solution.

- Choose a third party to make the decision for you. For example, let your priest or pastor decide a question about religion, your child's teacher make the decision about school.

- Take the particular issue to formal arbitration. You will each have the opportunity to argue for your position, and then the arbitrator decides.

INFORMATION EXCHANGE

Whatever mode of decision-making, in every parenting plan there are matters both parents must stay informed about. An Information Exchange List is very useful not only for mutual decision-making plans, but also for keeping peace within individual decision-making plans. The new law specifically protects the rights of any parent who has been allocated parental responsibility, to information about, but not limited to, medical, dental and school records. Following are some suggestions for your consideration.

- If you cannot arrange for the school, pediatrician or dentist to send a copy of everything concerning your children to both of you, then make arrangements for doing this yourselves. Be very specific about who will copy and send what to whom.

- The parent who first learns of an up-coming activity of a child must agree to notify the other parent (by making and sending a photocopy, by leaving a message on the other parent's answering machine, by putting a note in an agreed upon pocket in the children's backpacks).

- Any minor injury or illness which occurs on your time with the children. This is sometimes hard because you worry that it will reflect badly on your parenting. Sometimes having a promise in your parenting plan will make these most difficult phone calls happen.

- Any change in the normal behavior, sleep, eating pattern of a child. These are also often hard calls to make for fear the other parent will take the opportunity to criticize or worse.

- Let the other parent know about any special award, or accomplishment of a child. Sometimes having the child make this call or write this note is a very positive way of reinforcing your commitment to the importance of the other parent to your children.

- If any child repeatedly complains about something in the other home and/or tells of something you consider dangerous or probably untrue you will then immediately call the other parent to verify (with the child in earshot if appropriate).

INDIVIDUAL DECISION-MAKING RESPONSIBILITIES

The parent who has individual decision-making responsibilities makes decisions without having to consult with the other parent or having to reach agreement. Individual decision-making is appropriate when parents cannot or will not work together. Sometimes individual decision-making is a continuation of the way things were during the marriage in that one parent has historically been the decision-maker. Things may change, however, after you get beyond your initial fear, hurt, and anger. Be open to the possibility of wanting to share decisions about your children at a later date.

As individual decison-maker, you may never get a break. You will never be able to say, "Go ask your father/mother." Some people say single parenting is burdensome and lonely—the hardest job on earth. Even mutual decision-makers have feelings of loneliness and being burdened when they realize their former means of

Single Parent Overload?

Family counsellors, therapists, and parenting consultants and centers can provide counsel and assistance for single parents. Many of them sponsor groups for single parents to provide insight and mutual support, and even family activities. These resources can be helpful to the individual decision-maker who needs psychological and moral support, as well as to the mutual or joint decision-maker who finds the going rough.

communication and decision-making have to change so radically. The individual decision-maker may have to do without any communication at all with the other parent.

The ability to agree to different modes of decision-making for different decisions in the new law should help parents feel less trapped in an all-or-nothing situation. The combination of individual decision-making is a welcome solution for many parents. For example, when Johnny drives and whose car, or what college and who pays can be designated either individual or mutual decisions. Having some shared decisions can be both an act of self-preservation for the would-be individual decision-maker, and an opportunity for the other parent to be involved in shaping the child's life.

One decision that you might want to consider making mutual, even if no other, is the Big Ticket Item. Some examples might be the school band trip, summer camp, first real bicycle. Most parents can't handle this kind of expense alone, but it is often overlooked in the discussion of more obvious future expenses such as orthodontia or medical crises. Agreeing to discuss any elective major expense ahead of time will go a long way toward making the cost a shared expense. You may include this in either the sample separation agreement in Chapter 12 or in JDF 1113.

Where Will the Children Live?

The question of where your children live is now referred to as the determination of parenting time. The number of overnights the children spend with each of you will affect child support by a) determining which worksheet you will use, and b) becoming a direct calculation if it is over 25 percent per year with both parents. A parent who has the majority of overnights per year with a child has some tax advantages. These are discussed in the next chapter and in Chapter 10. Since most parenting is done while the children are awake, you should probably begin with your day-to-day schedules as they are now.

Parenting time, where your children live and when they will live there, can feel like the most important part of your agreement and you can get hopelessly mired in counting overnights. If you find yourselves getting stuck and angry about this issue, then consider the following information:

- Children change as they grow. The agreement you agonize over today may not work a year from now. One of the most important things that changes is how long a child can be away from the primary parent, or from either parent if you have both been active. Small children have an extremely short separation tolerance, sometimes a matter of less than a day for infants.

- Frequent transfers between parents may become stressful once a child is no longer so much in need of frequent contact.

PARENTING TIME AND THE DEVELOPMENTAL STAGES OF YOUR CHILD

Children have different needs at different stages in their growth and development, meaning that they should learn certain things at certain expected ages. It's vitally important in putting together your parenting plan that the developmental needs of your children be met.

Bear in mind that there is no single right way to allocate parenting time. What's right is what works best for all of you. Every family that succeeds in parenting from two households works out a unique schedule that makes sense for both the children and the parents.

Following is a summary of those stages taken largely from *Sharing the Children* by Robert E. Adler, Ph.D which is out of print and diffucult to find. See also *Children of Divorce* by Mitchell Baris, Ph.D., and Carla Garrity, Ph.D, a book that is widely used in this state and may well be the text for the parenting class you are required by the court to take.

Early Infancy – Birth to 6 Months:

The developmental tasks at this earliest of stages are physiological stabilization and bonding to one or more parental figures. The baby needs consistent care and nurturing, which includes feeding, diapering, being talked to, played with, held, and cuddled. This care must be consistent and continuous, with responsive caretakers. The number of caretakers should be small, settings stable, and routines smooth and predictable.

Most workable is that the majority of parenting time is spent with one parent and that parenting time with the other parent is frequent and fairly short (rather than longer contacts farther apart). Overnight visits are probably not in the baby's best interests, and separation from either parent should not be longer than a few days.

Determination of Parenting Time: The term for where children will live between divorcing parents. Correlates to a former term Physical or Residential Custody.

Visitation: Former word for parenting time of the "non-custodial parent."

Our Infant

Our child _____ (name) is in the birth to 6 months age range. He/she fits the description given here in the following ways:

He/she does not fit the description given here in the following ways:

"Children, especially very young ones, must be with their mothers."

This stereotyping is not borne out by the facts. Children need to be wanted. Research shows that single parents of both sexes struggle with the same problems, and young children fare equally well with parents of either gender.

Our 6-18 Month Old Child

Our child _____ (name) is in the 6 to 18 months age range. He/she fits the description given here in the following ways:

He/she does not fit the description given here in the following ways:

"Children need one home. They can't handle the constant back-and-forth of shared parenting time – young children especially."

The facts indicate otherwise. Long-term research shows that most children desperately want loving relationships with two parents, not just one. Be careful of a parenting time arrangement that views parenting time with the one parent as a disruption of the other household.

Some possible parenting time plans for this age:

- One main home. The other parent spends two or three hours, two or three times per week with the child; becomes primary caretaker one day per week.

- One main home supplemented by high quality day care (no more than four infants per adult). Other parent spends two or three hours, two or three times each week with the child.

Later Infancy – 6 to 18 Months

The developmental tasks of this age are the deepening of loving attachments to caretakers, development of basic trust and security, and exploring the environment from a secure base. The baby continues to have the same needs as the previous stage, with emphasis on the addition of predictability, familiarity, and a safe environment to explore.

If the infant is well attached to both parents, then contacts can be longer, spaced no farther than two or three days apart. If the infant is not familiar with one parent, caretaking periods by that parent should be short and frequent, as with a younger infant.

Try to match schedules to the child's temperament. An easy child can handle longer times away from each parent and a more flexible schedule; a slow-to-warm-up child may need to stay with frequent, short contacts until older; a difficult child may require even shorter visits on a very predictable schedule. Overnight stays are still likely to be stressful to the child. An easy and adaptable child with motivated and cooperative parents may handle them well, but other infants in less ideal circumstances will probably do better if overnights are not started this early.

Some possible parenting time plans for this age:

- One primary home. The other parent spends from two hours to a day, two to three times per week with the child.

- One primary home. The other parent has the child as above, but with one overnight per week.

- One primary home plus high quality day care. Schedule as in the first example above.

- Two homes, although the child spends significantly more time at one of them and no more than two overnights per week at the other. This arrangement should be considered only for mature, adjustable children and very cooperative parents.

Toddlers – 18 Months to 3 years

The developmental tasks at this age are becoming an individual, autonomy, and safe separation from parents.

The child needs firm support, meaning that the parents, secure and patient, need to set firm limits while allowing the freedom to explore. During the "terrible two's," parents need to allow the child to resist on unimportant issues, but must stand firm when it comes to safety, self-control, and interacting with others. The parents must be attentive monitors at this time. They must have the patience to provide verbal explanations and reassurance, repeated over and over.

The child needs close, consistent, frequent contact with both parents. Longer stays, entire days or overnights, spaced up to three or even four days apart, can be handled by secure, well-adjusted children towards the end of this age range. Entire weekends away from home base may still be too much for children this age. Less adaptable children, or those still not familiar with a parent, may still need shorter, more frequent contacts.

Some possible parenting time plans for this age:

- One primary home. The other parent has the child during the days up to three times per week, on a predictable schedule.

- One primary home. The other parent has the child as above, but with one overnight per week.

- One primary home plus good day care. Schedule as in either of the two previous examples.

- Two homes, with the child spending somewhat more time in one than the other. Two or three overnights spaced regularly throughout the week.

Preschoolers – 3 through 5 Years

The developmental tasks at this age are development of initiative, impulse management, sex role identification, and peer relationships.

At this age the child needs clear parental roles and values, parental cooperation. Children of this age react strongly to parental conflict. They need frequent and continuing contact with the same-sex parent. A child this age should not be encouraged to feel that he or she has driven away the same-sex parent, and that he or she now has a unique relationship with the opposite-sex parent.

Our 18 Month to 3 Year Old Child

Our child _____ (name) is in the 18 months to 3 years age range. He/she fits the description given here in the following ways:

He/she does not fit the description given here in the following ways:

Our 3-5 Year Old Child

Our child _____ (name) is in the 3 to 5 years age range. He/she fits the description given here in the following ways:

He/she does not fit the description given here in the following ways:

Our 6-12 Year Old Child

Or child _____ (name) is in the 6 to 12 years age range. He/she fits the description given here in the following ways:

He/she does not fit the description given here in the following ways:

The child needs frequent and predictable contacts with plenty of reassurance, love, and support. Predictability of schedules is at least as important as frequency or duration. Children this age need to know that the divorce is not their fault, and that they don't have the power to undo it.

The pre-school child needs access to nursery school or other settings for stimulation and socialization.

Even during holiday periods, children this age should not go longer than one week without contact with a parent. Longer separations should be supplemented with phone calls.

Some possible parenting time plans for this age:

- Two or three nights at one home, spaced throughout the week, the remaining time at the other home.

- Same as above, but supplemented by good day care.

- Three consecutive days and nights with one parent, four with the other.

- One week with one parent, the next with the other.

School-age Children – 6 to 12 Years

The developmental tasks at this age are to free energy from family concerns in order to focus on friends, school, learning, self-discipline, and cooperative play; to gain a sense of personal competence and self-esteem; to develop logical thought applied to concrete objects; to develop a sense of fairness.

The school-age child needs enough stability and security at home to allow full involvement outside the home, a reasonably well-structured schedule with some flexibility, exclusion from parents' conflicts, and insulation from their negative views of each other.

These children, especially the older ones, suffer when they feel they have to choose between their parents. They may respond with intense anger or by rejecting one parent completely. They need lots of explanation, discussion, being talked to and listened to. They need geographical proximity to and continuity of school and friends. Both parents continuing to live in the same area is an ideal arrangement for this child.

The child this age also needs flexibility. This becomes important as these children develop strong friendships and activities outside the home. Parental insistence on a planned contact at the expense of a much-desired activity can generate resentment.

Contacts with parents can be spontaneous. A parent dropping in on the child, or the child initiating a contact with a parent, can be valuable as long as such contacts do not stir up parental conflict. Particularly for younger school-age children, two weeks without contact with a parent is too long. Longer separations should be supplemented by brief contacts, spontaneous visits, and phone calls.

If parental conflict is low, school-age children can do well with many different parenting time plans, as long as they provide for relatively frequent and adequate contact with both parents.

Some possible parenting time plans for this age:

- Friday after school through Sunday evening or Monday morning, every other week, plus one or two overnights during the two-week stay with the other parent.

- Three days with one parent, four days with the other.

- Alternating weeks with each parent.

- Alternate weekends with each parent, two or three days at each home during the week.

- Three and a half days with each parent; weekends are also split.

- Two weeks with each parent, with one or two midweek overnights with the other.

- Older children may be able to handle even longer stays, if these are supplemented by phone calls and some contact with the other parent.

- Some parents find it manageable to have the child spend the school year at one home, and the bulk of vacation time at the other. Supplement contact with frequent and regular calls and visits.

"When children reach a certain age, they get to choose which parent they want to live with."

There is no age at which the law in Colorado shifts this decision to the child.

Our Teenager

Our child _____ (name) is in the 13 to 18 years age range. He/she fits the description given here in the following ways:

He/she does not fit the description given here in the following ways:

"**Kids can't make it if they go back and forth between very different parents.**"

Studies show that children can make these transitions with support and preparation from both parents for every transition.

Some experts say that for two households to work well together, they shouldn't be too terribly far apart in value systems. For example, if one parent lives a "laid-back" hippie lifestyle and the other household uses linen napkins, the child may begin to wonder whether to be like Mom and her household, or Dad and his.

Teenagers – 13 to 18 Years

The developmental tasks of teenagers include separation, peer involvement, development of own identity, sexual identity, and independence.

The teenager needs emotional stability and maturity on the part of both parents. He or she needs adequate, but flexible and age-appropriate parental controls, and continuing, meaningful contact with both parents.

Schedules must be flexible enough to respect the teenager's need for involvement with peers and independent activities. The level of parent-parent conflict about scheduling should be low.

Parents should be sensitive to a teenager's need to be consulted, informed, and listened to without giving up the adult/child relationship. The teenager needs to be treated as an individual. Teenagers do not need the same extended time with either parent that they once required.

Some possible parenting time plans for this age:

- Home base with one parent, a mixture of scheduled and spontaneous overnights, shorter visits, and outings with the other parent.

- Children spend school year as above; during summer vacation and other long holidays, the situation is reversed.

- For some teenagers, the more structured plans discussed for younger age groups may continue to work, particularly if the parents are geographically close.

- Some families work out year-by-year arrangements with older children. These plans need to respect the teenager's needs for continuity in friendships and school placement, and should always be supplemented with telephone and other contacts as frequently as possible.

MORE THAN ONE CHILD

Although it usually makes sense for all the children to share the same schedule, be open to the needs of each of your children, even to making different arrangements for each child. Infants have special needs for feeding and holding, teenagers for peer involvement and controlling their own lives. The needs of children of these two ages are significantly different from those from 3 to 12 years of age.

Having an older brother or sister along can be important support for a younger child. Nevertheless, the children don't always have to be together for time with parents. One-on-one time with a parent is terribly important to all children. Sometimes it's best for one child to live primarily with the mother and the other to live primarily with the father. If the children are split, then the schedule should also allow for times for the children to be together.

TIME SHARING

Some parents want equal time sharing when it may or may not be in the children's best interests. For example, infants and very young children may not be developmentally ready for two homes on a 50-50 basis. Small children may be better served by gradually expanding the overnights with the other parent, with a goal of reaching 50-50, or roughly equal time-sharing by a certain age, such as 5, or 6, or 7. However, a younger child may do quite well in equal time-sharing if his or her connections have been strong with both parents, and/or if there is an older sibling making the same transitions on the same schedule. Teenagers, who can do well with equal time sharing, need to have input about where and how they spend their time.

Developing Your Parenting Time Schedule

Don't expect to know right away what arrangements are going to be best for your children in the long term. Your first plan may not be your final agreement. If you are just starting to work out your parenting plan, you may want to review Chapter 4 about planning your separation.

BASIC SCHEDULE

Most parents begin a discussion of basic schedules by talking about whether it is in their children's best interest, at the present time, to have one home or two. To some parents this means dividing the children's time between Mom's house and Dad's house nearly equally, and having close to a complete set of clothes, toys, and equipment at each home. To others it means the child's bedroom set, bicycle, and computer are located with one parent, and the child carries a backpack with clothes to the other parent's home, and sleeps on a day bed or in a sleeping bag. For most parents, the distinction between having one home or two for the children is not so cut and dried. To decide this for yourselves, consider your children's developmental ages, the geographic distance you will be from each other, and your respective parenting styles. Remember that things change. What works today for your family will, in all probability, not work at some later time, perhaps sooner than you expect.

4-3-3-4 and Alternating Weeks

Florence and Fred separated, within the same neighborhood, when their two children were in first and third grade. They began with a 4-3-3-4 schedule, splitting the children's time equally between them over a two-week period. After 3 months of this schedule, the children asked if they could alternate weeks, rather than splitting each week. The parents made the change.

One Home or Two?

We believe our children would (would not) benefit from having two homes at the present time because:

☐ All our children look to both of us for day to day parenting.

☐ We will live too far apart to make frequent transportation between two households possible.

☐ One or more of our children is/are at a stage which makes frequent shifts from one home to another troublesome for them.

☐ Two homes are not possible now, because:

but we anticipate that it will be appropriate for

_____ (name)
by _____
(date/age/stage/circumstance).

Sometimes, at divorce, one parent has clearly been the major care-giver for the children, and the other has been more distant. Sometimes divorce brings the more distant parent "out of the woodwork" to become a more interested and active parent. Sometimes the less involved parent just wants to fade away. Sometimes the historical major care-giver resents that the other parent wants now, at the end of the marriage, to become a more active parent. If a parent has been distant from the children, it may be in the children's best interests to phase in the changes gradually. Parenting plans do not need to blindly perpetuate the status quo. Divorce is a time of great change for everyone. Getting away from a difficult or destructive marriage often enables people to become better parents.

Realistically, equal or substantial time sharing usually requires that the parents live near each other, optimally within the same school district. In that situation the children really can enjoy having two homes. This is feasible, usually, if the parents live close together—a few minutes driving or access by bicycle or walking.

Parents who live at least a significant distance apart, but still within driving distance, usually look for a weekend arrangement (every weekend, alternating, one or two a month), during the school year, complemented by some other arrangement during the summer. If you don't live in the same area—a judgment call of the parents who must do the traveling—you will need to look at an arrangement that is more appropriate for a long distance. These ideas reflect what appears to work for most people, not hard and fast rules. You must develop what will work for you, your spouse, and your children.

The two-home concept requires a plan for those times when you will transfer the children between you. Following are some of the questions you will need to consider and discuss. Remember, you may have different responses for each of your children. You may want to photocopy this page so that each of you can make notes.

- Is it important for your children to be in the same house on all school nights?

- How important is it that your children settle in on Sunday night before school?

- Is it important for your children to go to the same church with the same parent every week?

- Can either parent take your child to any given recurring activity (soccer practice, Scouts, doctor's appointment)?

- Can your children go to the same school from either home, and return home from their school to either home?

- Is there a maximum amount of time that any of your children can tolerate being away from either of you?

- How frequently do any of your children need to see each of you?

- Do you live so far apart geographically that your children will probably stay with one parent during school sessions and with the other during non-school time?

- Is this the time to change the day care schedule or provider for one or more of the children?

- Is it important to keep your children's day care schedule the same for the time being, in the face of other changes in their lives right now?

Notes:

Our Basic Schedule

Our initial basic time-sharing plan for our children will be:

☐ Alternating weeks

☐ Alternating two-week periods

☐ Alternating months

☐ Alternating semesters

☐ 4-3-3-4 every two-week period

☐ 5-2-4-3 every two-week period

☐ 6-1 each week

☐ 5-2 each week

☐ 4-3 each week

☐ One of us works a variable shift. We will arrange the children's schedule around this work schedule as follows:

☐ One of us works 24 hours on, 48 hours off. That parent will have all days off with the children, or:

☐ School sessions with one parent, school breaks with the other.

☐ Other:

SIX-WEEK CALENDAR

Fill in your basic schedule for six weeks. This may be any six weeks, or the next six weeks, whichever is more useful to you. On the following page are questions and suggestions.

This calendar ends the week with Saturday and Sunday together, unlike most published calendars which divide the weekend, a picture which is generally confusing for divorcing parents.

Mon.	Tues.	Wed.	Thurs.	Fri.	Sat.	Sun.

Directions for Six-Week Calendar

Fill in the following information on the calendar on the previous page. Make several photocopies first for your rough drafts. Sometimes it is useful to use different colored pens for each parent, or each member of the family.

1. Parents' fixed schedules. For example: work hours, fixed meetings and appointments.

2. Children's fixed schedules, such as school hours, day care, and planned regular activities such as soccer practice, piano lesson, Scouts, doctor's appointments.

3. If you are planning a specific six weeks, fill in the dates you are planning for, and any holidays or other special days, such as a child's birthday.

4. Sketch in your agreement from "Our Basic Schedule." For example, school nights with one parent, vacation nights with the other, alternating weeks with each parent, etc., dove-tailing with the information in 1-3 above.

5. Indicate on the calendar who will provide the transportation each time. The farther apart you live, the more important the transportation issue will become. If you each agree to bring the children to their other parent, you demonstrate your support and willingness for your children to leave you and relate to the other parent.

7. Make a note about any items which must move back and forth with the children, such as clothing, boots, homework, and musical instruments.

Our Important Days

Directions: Circle any of the following which are important to you, using different colored pens for each parent and each child. Be sure to add to this list any other days or events which are important to you to share with the children, such as Bolder Boulder, Russian Easter, St. Lucy's Day, Ramadan, County Fair, or Stock Show.

New Year's	July 4th
Martin Luther King Day	Labor Day
Super Bowl	Columbus Day
Valentine's Day	Rosh Hashana
Presidents Weekend	Yom Kippur`
St. Patrick's Day	World Series
Passover	Halloween
Easter	Thanksgiving
Mother's Day	Hanukkah
Cinco de Mayo	Christmas
Memorial Day	Kwanzaa
Fathers Day	Mother's Birthday
Children's Birthdays	Father's Birthday
Other	

Does the "Year" Start in January or September?

Your list of days might begin with Labor Day and the start of school, rather than New Year's Day and the start of the calendar year. Experience has shown that most parents and children plan in terms of the school year rather than the calendar year.

HOLIDAYS AND OTHER SPECIAL DAYS

Many parents begin by listing all the holidays recognized by their school, church, or wall calendar. They then alternate each of these by odd-or even-numbered years, or some other mathematical formula. When it comes to writing down your shared holidays, it may be easier to say that Mom will have the children for such-and-such holidays in even-numbered years, and Dad in odd-numbered years.

Typically, arrangements for holidays and special days pre-empt the regular schedule. Your parenting time plan must include agreement about how and when this happens. You may alternate the days themselves as discussed above, or consider one of the following.

Consider merging federal, state, or school holidays including teacher in-service days, which fall on a Monday or Friday with the weekend next to it. If you are doing an alternating weekend parenting plan, these three-day weekends will even out between you over a period of two or three years. If you can tolerate your sharing of holiday time not being equal within a single year, this can work out well in the long run.

Be sure to include on your list those **days which are special to your children.** For example, children typically care much more about Halloween than they do about New Years. Not all children or families feel the same way about the same holidays. These may change as the make-up of your new families changes. If you have any hesitation about where holidays fit on your children's list, ask them. Be prepared for some surprises. It is possible they will list Mother's and Father's Day or your birthdays, but don't be disappointed if they don't.

Most parents alternate the days special to their children year to year. Others agree that one parent has the children on the day itself, and the other parent celebrates the occasion on their next regular time with the children. If your children are small, and/or your relationship easy, you might consider spending these important days together with your children. For example, give a joint birthday party. If sharing the event is not possible, and if your children are old enough, you might try alternating portions of these days—Christmas morning at Mom's, Christmas afternoon at Dad's. For all but the most stable of children, however, this usually results in emotional overload, an exhausted child trying to be cheerful.

Make a parenting time plan for the **long school breaks,** usually summer, winter, and spring, and sometimes Thanksgiving. Many parents try to equalize the time contained in these school breaks over a calendar year. If you have a long distance parenting time arrangement in which the children spend the school year primarily with one parent, these breaks will constitute the other parent's time.

Summer vacation in most of Colorado starts during the first week in June and ends around the last week in August. Most parents agree that the children need to be where they are going to go to school for a few days to two weeks before school starts.

Some parents reverse primary physical care for the summer. In some long distance situations, the children simply travel to the other home and spend the entire summer there. Others continue their regular pattern (alternating weeks, alternating weekends). Some continue their regular pattern, but agree that either parent has the right to take the children on a 2-week vacation during that time, with a certain amount of notice to the other parent. Some parents agree to meet every April or so to make their summer plans.

Where the children will spend the **winter break** and holiday is of great importance in most families, partly because it contains important holidays, and partly because it is a two to six week period in which the children are out of school. Here are some ideas. For short-distance parenting time, some parents remain with their regular weekly schedule.

If the winter break contains an important holiday to you (Christmas, Hanukkah, Kwanzaa) then your planning will probably focus on that holiday. You may specify that the holiday will be spent with Mother in even-numbered years, with Father in odd-numbered years. You may wish to divide the holiday between the parents. For example, Christmas Eve with mother, Christmas Day with father; first half of Hanukkah or Kwanzaa with father, second half with mother. You can then alternate each year if you wish, but you will have to decide at what time the children travel from one home to the other, and who will provide the transportation.

You may divide the entire break into two parts: one parent for the first half, the other for the second, to be reversed for the next year. The two-week break will usually divide December 26th or 27th.

Three-day Weekends

The holidays which we agree to add to or include in the previous or following weekend, including teacher in-service days, are:

Special Handling

We will handle the following holidays in the following special way:

Summer Vacation

Our plans for summer vacation are:

Winter Break

Our plans for winter break are:

Thanksgiving Break

Our plans for Thanksgiving break are:

Spring Break

Our plans for spring break are:

Transporting Our Children

Our agreement about transporting our children between us is:

Thanksgiving break is usually four days, Thursday through Sunday. **Spring break** is usually nine days, starting and ending with a weekend. Many parents just continue their usual schedule, focusing on the holiday itself (sometimes spring break includes Easter). Some parents take part of their vacation during the school break and travel with the children. This is especially true if that parent works in a field in which summer or Christmas is the busiest time of year. For long distance parents, these can be additional times for travel to the home of the other parent.

If you are long distance parents so that the children spend the school session with one of you and school breaks with the other, you may wish to discuss reserving either Thanksgiving or spring break or both for the school year parent.

TRANSPORTATION

If you are a short distance apart, consider the responsibility for driving to be a shared problem. It's usually difficult for one parent to have to provide it all the time, and can, in itself, put an unfair burden on that parent's relationship with the child. Find a way to divide the picking-up and the dropping-off that creates the maximum convenience—or minimum inconvenience—or each of you. Sharing the transportation is a good way to demonstrate that you support the children's relationships with the other parent. The transportation time can be well used to help the children in their transition to the other home.

If you live far apart, then your parenting plan will have to take into account longer travel time for both you and your children. Look at how much time (how many days) make a long distance visit worthwhile.

Pre-school children must have someone travel with them. Airlines do not allow children to travel alone until age 6. (At age 6 children can fly alone, but the parents must make special arrangements and pay a higher rate.) This means that for very young children the parent may do the traveling rather than the children. Some parents share the additional cost by each accompanying the child in the trips to and from the other parent.

Your parenting plan should be clear about who pays for the transportation of the children between you. Travel tickets are more expensive when purchased at the last minute. Be sure to discuss who will pay the cost if the flight is missed, or if plans have to be changed after tickets are purchased and cannot be modified.

How to Tell the Children

How do you tell your children about your separation and divorce? Have both parents there, if possible, and tell the children not only your decision to separate, but also your plan. Help them understand that you are not separating from or "divorcing" them. Tell them that you will always take care of them, no matter what. Tell them how important it is to both of you that you both stay active in their lives. Be concrete with them about your plans.

When appropriate, share your six-week calendar with your children and ask for their input. Listen to their concerns about the mechanics: "Where will my bicycle live?" "How will my ice skates get from one house to the other?" "I only have one computer, how will I do my homework?"

If you can, discuss in advance the physical plans for your separation with the children. Involve them in the doing—take them with you to see possible new apartments or homes so they can participate in the creation of their second home. They will have their own ideas about which toys and books should be at which place, and how they want their spaces to look. You may have to override some of their choices, but they should be allowed to participate and to express themselves, even to carry out some of their wishes in their own way. The older your children, the more likely they are to have their own ideas about what they want out of your divorce, and the more willing they are to let you know about it. Working toward agreement between the two of you without any input from the children sends them the clear message that you do not care what they think. On the other hand, having them part of the negotiations from the beginning is to give them far too much power over the outcome. They, after all, are the children and you are the adults—a fact which is not always evident when the adults are at their craziest.

So, how do you give your children the chance to tell you what they think will work without deferring decisions to them which you must make as parents? Following are some rules of thumb which may help:

- Do a rough cut of the parenting and support plans by yourselves. Discuss what you each think would be acceptable to the children, but do not ask them yet.

- Invite the children to sit with you and read through the rough cut and react to it. Do this with both of you present. You can do it with the children individually if you think they will speak

Our Agreement About Telling Our Children

Our agreement about telling our children

 There are some countries which will not admit children traveling with only one parent, without the signed permission of both parents. Likewise, there are some foreign-based airlines which will not allow children in this situation to board their aircraft. Regardless of the nature of your parenting plan or marital status, a notarized statement signed by both parents authorizing any trip is probably a very good idea. is:

 Parents are parents, whether partners or married. Partner parents need to be cautious and respectful of their children's needs at this difficult time, and find a responsible way to tell them that their parents are moving apart.

more freely when the other children are not there, but it is usually the reverse. Many mediators are willing to have you do the sharing of your rough cut in a regular mediation session or in a shorter session just for that purpose.

- Be certain when you share your ideas with the children that you promise to listen carefully to what they have to say, but that you do not promise to do exactly what they ask.

- If any child objects continuously to an aspect of your proposed plan, then you may want to consider having that child speak with a therapist, or even have an attorney or special advocate appointed for your child (see Chapter 2, Parenting Consultants). It is possible to listen to the children but not hear what they are saying due to your own need to have them endorse your options. It is possible for the children to not feel free to speak because they feel any request they might make would sound disloyal to one or both of you.

- If the children have chosen their own confidant who is not one of you (such as a grandparent or babysitter) then you may wish to get the children's permission to have their confidant come to a discussion or mediation session instead of them. Sometimes it is easier for children to express themselves second hand.

- If there is a person with a special relationship to the children in addition to yourselves, you may want that person to attend the session when you present the agreement to the children, or to sit in on your early sessions about parenting so that you can begin being mindful of the children's wishes.

Odds and Ends

As you get close to a working draft of your parenting plan, try to have discussions about the following, even if those discussions never find their way into your written agreement:

- Describe what each of you will do to keep and strengthen your children's connection with the departing parent in his or her new home, to minimize any sense of loss or abandonment they may feel.

- What is the role of grandparents and extended family? Should they have fixed parenting times with the children? Will you count it as part of either parent's time?

- What is the role of your own adult friends, especially a live-in relationship, "significant other," or stepparent. The concern here is to what extent this person may do parenting. May this person discipline your children? May this person transport your children between parents? May this person attend parent-teacher conferences, be Scout leader, coach the soccer team, or be a teacher's aide?

- Do you want to make special commitments about religious upbringing?

- Do you want to put in restrictions about not taking the children out of the state or country, for any reason, without written agreement?

- What happens if the children are too sick to change houses? Go to school? Go to day care? Which parent stays home with the sick child? More otherwise excellent parenting plans have been sunk by the omission of this provision than any other.

- How do you handle make up days? What is the procedure for making a one-time change in the time schedule with the children.

- How do you want the other parent to handle it if the children start complaining about something which is going on at your house.

- What do you do if any child shows consistent signs of changes in behavior, stress?

Teeth

Most people worry, from time to time, that they might not completely fulfill their end of the bargain they are negotiating. If your ex has a new lover, will you be less likely to deliver the children on time, or to tell your ex about the teacher's conference? If you re-marry, will conflict between your loyalties to your new spouse and your former spouse interfere with your parental communications with your ex, so that cooperation would begin to break down? In a money crunch, would you try to increase the children's time with you in order to increase child support? Most people would have to answer yes to at least one of these—or, at least admit that the possibility exists they could be tempted.

Signing for Emergency Medical Care for Your Children

There are still a few emergency care facilities which will require both parents' signatures in mutual decision-making situations, in order to admit children for care and treatment—unless there is a written court-ordered stipulation which says that either parent may sign. Not only should you have clear agreement about this, but you should carry a copy of this agreement with you and give one to your regular pediatrician, day care provider, and school.

Glad We Asked

Matt and Claire were successful in equally sharing their time with their daughter Bonnie for two years after their divorce. When Bonnie was in second grade, however, Claire remarried and moved about an hour away. The distance made the equal sharing unfeasible. They were stalemated until they asked their mediator to find out what Bonnie thought. Bonnie wanted most not to have to spend the summer in day care. That meant spending summers with her Mom, who was not employed outside the home, and the school year with her Dad who was.

Our Agreement About Anticipated Changes and When We Expect Them to Occur

Write here your agreement about when and under what circumstances you expect to discuss changing your parenting plan.

What happens if I want to move away?

A Colorado law passed in 2001, requires that if your child resides with you a majority of the time, and you want to relocate with the child to a "residence that substantially changes the geographic ties between the child and the other party", that you must give the other parent written notice and a proposed revised parenting plan as soon as possible. The notice must tell the other parent where you intend to reside and the reason for the move.

If you have any doubts about yourself, or some secret doubts about your soon-to-be-ex, then try putting in some creative incentives to follow through with all your agreements about your children. Some examples are: the parent who delays deciding about travel dates for the summer pays the additional cost for plane tickets purchased late. The parent who delivers the children late to the other parent becomes responsible for all transportation for the children for the next week, two weeks, or month. You can design baby teeth for minor misses, molars for larger defaults, and even fangs if you need them—but use these last carefully. Giving notice about problems, and flexibility in dealing with them are frequently the best solutions.

These incentives to right behavior are limited only by your imagination. Try having the person against whom the penalty would act set the penalty. You may be surprised to learn what your former partner fears.

Anticipating Changes

Change happens. Your children's needs and yours will change before your children emancipate. Write down the changes you anticipate in the foreseeable future, and commit to them now. Here are several samples, along with two extra spaces to write in your own:

- "We expect our basic time schedule to change for each child when they begin first grade/begin middle school/high school/reach puberty."

- "We expect to discuss changing physical care if one of us moves so far away that regular transportation is no longer possible."

- "We expect to discuss changing decision-making responsibilities if one of us moves back into close proximity to the other and wants to be included in the important parenting decisions."

-

-

You have now finished your first rough look at your parenting plan. It will probably not be your final version. Go on to the next three chapters about the other essential components of your separation agreement. The agreements you reach as a result of each of those chapters may necessitate changes in your parenting plan.

Take heart. Doing your own separation agreement is hard work. Don't expect to get it all done in one sitting. Don't even expect to complete the work of one of the separation agreement chapters in one sitting. Now might be a good time to take a break, relax, and reread Chapter 3, Taking Care of Yourself. Give yourself and each other the time you deserve to make the best decisions for both of you and your children.

You may wish to immediately transfer your agreements about parental responsibilities, as you agree to them to JDF 1113, or draft your own parenting plan using the checklists throughout this chapter and the sample separation agreement provisions concerning parenting in Chapter 12.

Parenting Plan Checklist

Directions: Use this outline to check off each element of your parenting plan as you complete it.

I. Decision Making

☐ A. List the mutual decisions.

☐ B. List the decisions each of you will make individually.

☐ C. Spell out areas for consultation before individual decision making, if any.

☐ D. Spell out areas for information exchange.

☐ E. Dispute Resolution

1. Spell out your agreements for communication and process.

2. Spell out your agreements about what to do to avoid and resolve deadlock, and what you will do when you find yourselves stuck.

3. State your more formal dispute resolution mechanism (if any) that you wish to have in place as a condition before either of you may take a matter to court.

II. Parenting Time

☐ A. State the pattern of parenting times you will start with.

☐ B. State your exceptions to A., if any, for holidays and vacations.

☐ C. State who will provide and pay for the transportation of the children between parents.

III. Odds and Ends
☐

IV. Teeth
☐

V. Anticipated Changes
State what, if anything, you will look at to determine whether that pattern needs to change in the future.
☐

CHAPTER **9**

CHILD SUPPORT
SEPARATION AGREEMENT – PART III

CHILD SUPPORT
SEPARATION AGREEMENT – PART III

Before the court can give you a final decree of dissolution of marriage or legal separation, you must resolve and write out all the financial and parental issues remaining from your marriage. This written summary is called the separation agreement, whether you are obtaining a divorce or a legal separation. It must be read and approved by the court.

The introduction to Chapter 7 lists the things you need to do to prepare your separation agreement and directs you to the chapters with information necessary to accomplish this. This chapter discusses child support and its part in your separation agreement.

Chapters 10 and 11 cover ways in which you can save tax dollars by using maintenance to pay some family expenses. Chapter 11 also discusses the tax consequences of a divorce with children. These are consequences which will result with or without your planning for them, so it is wise to understand how to make them work for you.

Chapter 13 covers ways to enforce your child support agreement after your decree, and how to modify or amend your agreement when circumstances of you or your children change, as they undoubtedly will.

The Colorado Child Support Guideline

Child support in Colorado is defined by the *Colorado Child Support Guideline*, an adaptation of the Shared Incomes Model, one of several models suggested by a federal child support task force in 1985. The *Colorado Child Support Guideline* presumes that divorcing parents will share the support of their children in the proportion of their individual gross (before tax) incomes to the family gross income. The Guideline then sets, and therefore presumes, a certain minimum dollar amount which the parents, together, are expected to spend on the basic needs of their children (housing, food, clothing—these are also a presumption). This minimum amount appears in a schedule which is part of the Guideline. All these presumptions are rebuttable, that is, they can be overcome by evidence to the court that the presumption should not apply in this particular family. In practice, however, the presumptions are adhered to in nearly every instance. This does not mean that divorcing parents should cease to bargain about how they will support their children. You will both have to

"Child support is cut and dried. You have to pay whatever the chart says."

Colorado does have a formula-based child support statute, which tells you how much must be paid by parents to cover certain expenses for their children. However, for most couples there is some latitude in how you apply your facts and circumstances to the Guideline as well as questions for some about additional expenses for the children that the Guideline doesn't cover.

Retroactive Child Support

While this chapter is about arriving at an agreement about child support to take you into the future, the law also provides that you can reach an agreement about what either of you may owe the other for past child support. You may, if you wish, determine an amount one of you owes the other for past child support, going back to the date of your physical separation or the date of the filing of the petition or service upon the respondent, "whichever is latest," says the statute. You do not need to prepare a child support worksheet for this. Once you have a total for retroactive support that you both agree on, you can pay it now, put it in with all the other items in your property settlement, or decide on an interest rate and an amount for monthly payments. In this last case, it will be shown on the Support Order which accompanies your Decree.

Partners who put their parenting plan and child support arrangements through the court will need all the information in this chapter. If you have decided not to put the matter through the court, this chapter will help you to discuss and outline the present and future financial needs of your children.

 If there is a significant difference between your incomes now, and especially if there will be in the foreseeable future, you should read Chapter 10, Maintenance, and Chapter 11, Taxes before proceeding, to save money as a family with tax planning through maintenance.

 "We'll just plug our incomes into the Guideline, and it will tell us what we should do for our children."

You can do it this way if you wish, but the result may be neither payable by one or both of you, nor sufficient for your children's needs. In addition, you are far more likely to carry out a support agreement which you have carefully evolved yourselves, rather than simply obeying a number from a schedule.

 Potential Income: An amount of income attributed to a voluntarily unemployed or underemployed parent for purposes of calculating child support. You can estimate it by "determining that parent's employment potential and probable earnings level based on his or her recent work history, occupational qualifications, and prevailing job opportunities and earnings levels in the community." In other words, what has the parent earned, doing what, can he or she earn it now, here?

live with the decisions you make here for a long time. The more the decisions are truly yours, the more likely they are to work for you and your children.

This chapter does the following:

- helps you sort your children's expenses into basic, regular additional, and unpredictable additional expenses.

- helps you sort your respective incomes, actual and potential, regular and irregular.

- invites you to make your own agreements about how you want to support your children, both in dollar amounts and in terms of process between you.

- works through the *Colorado Child Support Guideline* showing you how to implement your own plan for supporting your children within the framework and spirit of the law.

- helps you deal with the problem if the Guideline results are too different from your own sense of fairness to your children and yourselves.

- suggests some built-in enforcement techniques to make sure your plan is followed, and discusses the enforcement techniques required by the guideline.

Children's Expenses

In Colorado, divorcing parents are directed by the Guideline to divide between them all the expenses of their children in proportion to their incomes. For example, the parent who has 60% of the family income is to pay 60% of all the costs of rearing the children—regardless of how you have allocated decision-making or parenting time (number of overnights).

There are two categories of expenses of rearing children to which this proportion applies: basic expenses and extraordinary ones. **Basic expenses** include housing, basic food, basic clothing, and may include regular transportation, school lunches, ordinary medical and dental expenses, allowances, and other customary expenses which the parents expressly include. The *Colorado Child Support Guideline* does not leave you any room for choices about the amount you both, together, are presumed to spend on the basic expenses of your children. The Schedule of Basic Child Support Obligations sets this amount. Your choice is how many of your children's expenses you believe are included.

The cost of raising children is not limited to those items usually presumed to be covered by the basic child support obligation. **Extraordinary expenses** are those beyond the basic. They are set by the parents, and will vary with each family.

Some typical expenses beyond basic needs are:

• For infants: special clothing, diapers and perhaps diaper service, special foods, well-baby medical visits, and certainly more expensive day care or babysitting as very few services will take infants, and many will not take children who are not yet toilet trained.

• For toddlers and pre-school children: usually full-time day care, immunizations.

• For school-age children: school supplies, school trips and activities, additional school clothing, lessons, activity fees, special clothing and equipment, organization fees and costs.

• For teenagers: car and car insurance, birth control, advanced lessons and clinics, more expensive activity fees, special clothing including shoes and equipment, and graduation expenses.

Gifted and talented children create additional costs. Special-needs children (handicapped, developmentally or educationally delayed, ill, injured, or emotionally troubled) are more expensive still.

Now you are ready to make some decisions for yourselves about how you want to support your children.

You may handle the additional expenses of your children in one of two ways. You may deal with each one as it comes up, or you may estimate them now, arrive at a monthly average, and add this average monthly amount to the basic support. You may choose a different method for different expenses. If you choose to make them part of the regular monthly support payment, you will list them on the appropriate child support worksheet.

The worksheets specifically include four "extraordinary" expenses: work-related child care, education-related child care, health insurance premiums, and extraordinary medical expenses. A space is also provided or additional expenses agreed to by the parents or by court order. Listing an additional expense on the worksheet has three results:

 Basic expenses: Those costs of rearing children which the State of Colorado includes in the Basic Support Obligation which it sets for divorcing parents. Usually assumed to include: housing, food, most clothing, and perhaps ordinary medical and other day to day costs.

Our Children's Basic Expenses

Directions: Complete the following sentence using the name of each expense, not the amount.

We agree that the basic expenses for our children are housing, basic food, basic clothing, and:

 Extraordinary expenses: Any costs of rearing children which the parents do not define as being included in the Basic Support Obligation from the Schedule. The worksheets name four, and the Guideline lists several more. Parents need to evolve their own list of these to be sure everything is covered.

 Expensive Money

Child support is paid in after-tax dollars. This is expensive money. It can be unnecessarily costly. It is possible to pay some of your children's expenses, especially the extraordinary ones, with pre-tax dollars by having the higher income spouse include these amounts in maintenance (alimony, spousal support, section 71 payments) to the lower income spouse. Therefore, if you are or might be considering maintenance in your separation agreement, read Chapters 10, Maintenance and 11, Taxes before proceeding further with child support.

Our Children's Regular Additional Expenses

We agree that the following expenses for our children are not included in the basic amount on the schedule, are foreseeable and can be quantified monthly:

☐ School expenses $_____

☐ Private school tuition $_____

☐ Religious training $_____

☐ Transportation between parents (especially long distance) $_____

☐ Gifts to and from the children $_____

☐ Sports: including fees, special clothing, equipment $_____

☐ Music and art: including lessons and equipment $_____

☐ Clubs $_____

☐ Scouts $_____

☐ Travel $_____

☐ Tutoring $_____

☐ Special education $_____

☐ Automobile: payments, insurance, fuel and maintenance $_____

☐ Camping $_____

☐ Family activities $_____

☐ Summer camp, activities and programs $_____

☐ Regular babysitting, other than work-related (parent at school, meetings, etc.) $_____

☐ Chronic medical, dental, mental health (insulin, medication, braces, counseling) $_____

☐ Infant expenses (shots, well-baby checkup, equipment) $_____

☐ Other $_____

- it fixes that expense, usually an average of this cost over a year or half year. If the expense varies greatly, you will sometimes have too much money and sometimes too little to pay the expense that month. Day care, for instance, varies greatly between school year and summer.

- it requires you to share it proportional to your incomes. There is no opportunity on the worksheet to share something 50/50 even if you believe that is fair, if that is not the proportion of your incomes.

- it makes enforcement easier. The final amount of child support becomes a support order (see Chapter 12) which streamlines collection procedures.

Any extra expense for your children which you do not list on the worksheet:

- can be shared in any proportion you choose;

- can be shared between you as it is incurred instead of estimating it ahead of time, allowing you to adjust for the unexpected and the irregular (such as a broken leg, or summer band camp);

- requires more communication between you on an on-going basis;

- is not as readily enforceable (see Chapter 13).

Sometimes an extra expense is not known at the time of the divorce and can not be included on the child support worksheet. It is therefore a good idea to make some agreement about these future unknown expenses. Most people make an agreement that any extraordinary expense for their children which is not on the worksheet must be agreed to by both parents ahead of time (except emergencies), and paid in a certain percentage. Sometimes parents agree that a certain category of expenses will be paid in one percentage and another category in another percentage. For example, medical expenses may be paid in proportion to the parents' income, but special activities may be paid 50/50.

Joe and Sandy

Joe earns a salary plus commission, plus a performance bonus. Sandy earns a salary plus interest from an investment. The children live with Sandy most of the time. They agree to base their basic support on their salaries, and their regular additional expenses on 70% of Joe's average commissions and 70% of Sandy's interest income. Joe may pay the additional expense amount quarterly in advance, to allow for the fluctuation in his commissions. They agree to put an agreed upon percentage of his remaining bonus and her interest income, when received, into a college and emergency fund for their children. Joe and Sandy are basing regular monthly payments on regular monthly income. They are paying periodic expenses with periodic income, and extraordinary expenses with extraordinary income.

Extraordinary Expenses of Your Children

The Colorado Child Support Guideline specifically anticipates four categories of additional expenses for your children: work-related child care, education-related child care, health insurance premiums, and extraordinary medical expenses. They are referred to as "Adjustments" on the worksheet forms.

WORK/EDUCATION RELATED CHILD CARE

Work/education related child care is defined as care for children which is necessary to enable a parent to go to work, search for a job or (in Colorado) obtain an education. It does not apply to babysitting for a parent's social life or other activities. It does include before and after school care if the parent's work or school day extends beyond the child's school day. Education-related child care is a Colorado tax credit only, is not subject to a Federal tax credit, and is shown separately on the worksheet.

The Child Support Guideline recognizes that the expense of work-related child care is mitigated somewhat by a Federal tax credit which refunds to the "custodial" parent from 20% to 35% of the amount paid, for work-related *(but not education-related)* care of the first two children. It is the after-credit amount of this child care cost which is shared between the parents in proportion to their incomes. The amount which goes on the child support worksheet is the net amount (the amount you actually spend minus the credit). Be sure you read Chapter 11 Taxes, to learn how either of you can qualify for this credit.

There is no child care credit if you pay your children's work-related child care through a "cafeteria plan" at your work. A Cafeteria or Flex Plan allows the employee to pay child care and family medical expenses with pre-tax dollars that are withheld by the employer and escrowed or held in trust for the benefit and use of the employee and his or her family. The child care credit effectively does the same thing, by returning the tax money already paid on dollars used to pay for work-related child care. You can use one or the other.

Federal Child Care Credit Table

Adjusted Gross Income	Appropriate Percentage	Maximum Allowed Credit for	
		One Child	Two or More Children
Up to $15,000	35%	$1050	$2100
15,001-17,000	34%	1020	2040
17,001-19,000	33%	990	1980
19,001-21,000	32%	960	1920
21,001-23,000	31%	930	1860
23,001-25,000	30%	900	1800
25,001-27,000	29%	870	1740
27,001-29,000	28%	840	1680
29,001-31,000	27%	810	1620
31,001-33,000	26%	780	1560
33,001-35,000	25%	750	1500
35,001-37,000	24%	720	1440
37,001-39,000	23%	690	1380
39,001-41,000	22%	660	1320
41,001-43,000	21%	630	1260
Over, 43,001	20%	600	1200

Directions for calculating your child care credit: Locate your income bracket in the first column. Multiply the percentage next to it times the amount you actually paid for work-related child care. If your result is less than or equal to the amount in the third or fourth column (depending on the number of children you have in child care), then your result is the amount of your credit. If your result is greater than the number in the table, then the number in the table is the amount of your tax credit. IRS Form 2441, which you must include with your tax return in order to take the credit, can also help you calculate the amount of your credit.

Example: Vanessa, whose adjusted gross income is $9,500, has two children in work-related child care, for which she pays $550 per month. $550 × 12 = $6,600 per year. 35% × $6,600 = $2,310 which is more than the maximum allowed at her income level for more than one child. The amount of Vanessa's tax credit is therefore $2,100.

Remember that the Automatic Temporary Restraining Order that went into effect when you filed your case forbids either of you to cancel the existing insurance for your children.

Our Children's Irregular Expenses

We anticipate the following irregular expenses may occur for our children.(List average monthly amount at right.)

One-time major purchases (full-size bed, bicycle, skis,):

Description $

Special events (birth, graduation)

Description $

Other

Description $

HEALTH INSURANCE COVERAGE FOR YOUR CHILDREN

The divorce statute requires you to maintain health insurance for your children, and to bring proof of coverage to your final hearing. You will each list the amount, if any, you pay as premium for the children on the worksheet. On Worksheet A, if the parent who pays child support also pays the insurance premium, his or her child support payment will be reduced by the amount of the premium. If the parent who pays child support is not the parent who also pays the insurance premium, the child support amount will be reduced by his or her percentage share of the premium. Worksheet B proportions the insurance premium between you, regardless of who makes the payment.

Colorado statutes are clear about the importance of health insurance for children. Any company which is covered by E.R.I.S.A. (Employment Retirement Income Security Act of 1974), the same group covered by QDRO'S and COBRA, **must** extend insurance coverage to the child of an insured employee **even** if a) the child does not live with the insured employee, b) the insured does not claim the child as a dependent exemption, or c) a request for payment is made by the other parent (who is not insured). This amendment also requires increased notice and information be provided to the parent who provides physical care, if not the insured, and extends coverage to adopted children, or children placed for adoption, under 18 years of age.

EXTRAORDINARY MEDICAL EXPENSES

The Colorado Child Support Guideline defines "extraordinary medical expenses" as "uninsured expenses, including copayments and deductible amounts, in excess of $250 per child per year." These include, but are not limited to, "such reasonable costs as are reasonably necessary for orthodontia, dental treatment, asthma treatments, physical therapy, vision care, and any uninsured chronic health problem." It may also include "professional counseling or psychiatric therapy for diagnosed mental disorders." You may want to re-define for yourself the meaning of extraordinary medical expenses to include some or all of the following:

- Your insurance deductible—the amount you pay out each fiscal year per person or per family before the insurance starts paying.

- Copayment – the amount you pay up-front on HMO (health maintenance organization) type plans and/or the amount you pay after the insurance has paid for medical expenses—80/20% on many plans—usually 50/50% on mental health and dental, if covered.

- Payment for injuries or illnesses not covered by the insurance or over the limit for that particular kind of illness/injury.

- Well-child care, inoculations, preventive care—unless you included this in your definition of basic expenses.

- Alternative treatments and healing such as chiropractic, acupuncture, massage, holistic healing.

- Ordinary dental expenses including cleaning—unless you included this in your definition of basic expenses.

- Eye exams and glasses.

- Counseling.

OTHER EXTRAORDINARY EXPENSES

Because the guideline specifically lists only four extraordinary expenses, this suggests to some people that there aren't any additional expenses beyond those named. For most parents, however, there are many others, as you will discover working through this chapter. The worksheets provide a place for you to include other, regular extraordinary expenses for your children. If you have agreed to include additional expenses for your children in the monthly support amount, you will list them on your worksheet.

Your children probably will have extraordinary expenses which are neither regular nor predictable enough to put on a worksheet. You will need your own agreement about how you will pay these. The Child Support Plan Questionnaire on the following page will help you do this.

Organizing Parents' Income and Children's Expenses

Dividing your income and children's expenses into the categories on the following Child Support Plan Questionnaire will help you decide which income will be used to pay which expenses. Being clear about this will help you remember expenses you are apt to forget, and not count on income you may never see.

Colorado Child Care Tax Credit

Colorado has a tax credit for work-related child care, which is a percentage of the amount of your federal tax credit.

Federal Adjusted Gross Income	Appropriate Percentage Of Your Federal Child Care Credit
Up to and including $25,000	50%
$25,001-$35,000	30%
$35,001-$60,000	10%
$60,001 and over	0%

As of this writing, this state income tax credit does not affect the calculation of child support under the Colorado Child Support Guideline.

These percentages may be adjusted if the State has surplus unallocated revenues from the previous year. Watch for the instruction book with your State tax forms to tell you that year's percentages. Or, you can ask your tax preparer.

See Chapter 11, Taxes, for who may claim the child care credit. You may not both claim this credit for the same child.

Maintenance Changes Child Support

Maintenance shifts before-tax (gross) income from one spouse to the other, therefore altering each parent's percentage share of child support. The result is that as you phase in maintenance the child support goes down, and a larger portion of the money being paid between spouses is labeled maintenance. This can be helpful, because paying maintenance instead of child support, where feasible, can reduce your total taxes.

Child Support Plan Questionnaire

Directions: Discuss the numbers/amounts you gathered and summarized on your Income Charts and IF Budgets in Chapter 5, and the lists of your children's basic and extraordinary expenses in this chapter. Then write down the answers to the following questions:

1. What income for each of you do you want to use in determining the amount of basic child support? All your income from every source (total income on Income Chart)? Only income each receives regularly (#1 on Income Chart)? Additional income (#2 on Income Chart)? Occasional income (#7 on Income Chart)? You may also want to read the definition of income and potential income from the *Colorado Child Support Guideline* near the end of this chapter. You do not need to include income from additional jobs that result in employment more than 40 hours per week or more than what would otherwise be considered full time employment. Describe the source of these incomes for each of you and estimated amounts:

    The more income you put on the guideline worksheets, the higher your support order for basic expenses.

2. Do you want to estimate all the foreseeable additional expenses for your children, average them monthly, and then apply the guideline formula so that they are pre-paid monthly between you? Which expenses would you include? List those expenses, averaged monthly, which you agree to pay or pre-pay monthly between you, and their estimated amount:

    The more additional expenses you put on the guideline worksheet, the more money is paid by one of you to the other under the support order.

3. Are there any expenses for your children which you cannot estimate monthly, or which you do not want to pre-pay between you monthly?

    a. If so, what are these expenses? List them, and the estimated amounts:

    Any expense you do not list on the worksheets, but which you identify and agree to, may be shared as it arises, in any proportion you feel is fair. It is not included in the support order.

    b. How are you going to handle the occasional expenses in #a (example: proportional to income, 50-50, 60-40, one of you pays all)?

4. Have you set aside some occasional or irregular income sources with which to pay these occasional expenses? (Example: annual performance bonus, sale of stock). If you have an agreement about this, write that agreement here.

Schedule of Basic Child Support Obligations

Having examined together what income you will use to pay which of your children's expenses, you may now use this information to figure your child support arrangement using the Colorado Child Support Guideline.

The centerpiece of the Colorado Child Support Guideline is the Schedule of Basic Child Support Obligations which is printed at the end of this chapter. The schedule contains the percentage of parents' combined gross incomes which the guideline expects them to pay for their children's basic needs.

The amounts in this schedule vary from about 9% to about 22% for one child, and from about 13% to about 32% for two children, in a curve, with the highest percentages reached before $1000 per month combined incomes and decreasing to the highest income. These percentages are based on actual cost-of-living studies of Colorado families.

The studies found that lower income families spend a higher percentage of their family income on the basic expenses of their children than higher income families. In addition, a parent whose income is below a certain level, but does not have primary physical care, has expenses for basic living like housing and food that requires more of that parent's income to be retained and less paid in child support. To address this, the Colorado legislature enacted a low-income adjustment for a paying parent with a monthly adjusted gross income between $850 and $1850.

The basic support amount fixed by the schedule increases with the number of children, but not in strict arithmetical increments. The schedule recognizes that the second child does not cost as much as the first—that there are some basic expenses incurred with one child which are not incurred again with additional children. Therefore, although the amount on the schedule increases with each additional child, it does not double for the second, or triple for the third, etc. This is an important concept to remember as you bargain about changes in support as each child goes to college or emancipates.

If the parents each have the children with them more than 92 overnights per year, the amount on the schedule is multiplied by 1.5, since the same studies show that children are 50% more expensive to maintain in two full homes (in contrast with one primary home and a place to visit).

Incomes Above the Guideline Levels

If your combined monthly adjusted gross income is greater than $20,000 ($240,000 per year), the highest level given in the Guideline, work through this chapter and complete the checklists to assist you in defining the actual costs of your children, as well as your incomes and IF Budgets (Chapter 5), as foundation for coming to agreement about child support. You can skip the sections that relate directly to the Guideline Schedule and the worksheets, because you will not have to prepare a worksheet. Many in this situation do prepare a worksheet, however, by extrapolating (using percentages) from the $20,000 level of the Guideline, to get their child support number. Some then reduce that somewhat, since the cost of rearing children does not necessarily increase at the same rate as the parents' incomes.

When the court decides these cases, the law presumes that the children cannot cost less than the Basic Child Support Obligation given in the Guideline for a combined $20,000 monthly income.

Adjustment for Incomes Under $1850 Per Month

If the parent with the lesser number of overnights per year has a monthly adjusted gross income between $850 and $1850, he or she may be eligible for a Low-income Adjustment on Worksheet A. See the second page of that worksheet to calculate whether this applies to you.

Incomes of $850 or Less

In circumstances where the parents' combined monthly adjusted gross income is $850 or less, the Guideline requires a minimum of $50 in child support from the paying parent, regardless of the number of children. And, if the paying parent's monthly adjusted gross income, by itself, is less than $850, the Guideline will require a $50 monthly child support payment, again regardless of the number of children. One's earnings may be in this range for any number of reasons, including working part time for minimum wage, and going to school.

BUNKY

"The child support schedule will tell us how much we have to spend on our kids."

Not quite. The schedule estimates your children's basic minimal monthly expenses: housing, ordinary clothing, ordinary food, and ordinary medical. As you know, your children cost more than this. You must decide which expenses are not included in the amount on the schedule and how you will share them.

Worksheets A and B will do four things:

a. Establish the Basic Support Obligation from the schedule based on your combined gross incomes. Income may be "potential" as discussed in this chapter.

b. Allocate the duty to pay the Basic Support Obligation between you in proportion to your gross incomes. Worksheet B also takes into account the number of overnights being spent with each parent.

c. Allocate between you, in proportion to your gross incomes, any "extra-ordinary" (additional) expenses which you choose to list on the worksheet. These are not affected by the number of overnights.

d. Provide a recommended child support amount which will be approved by the court unless you ask for and receive a deviation from that amount.

The Guideline expects parents to be responsible for the amount on the schedule in proportion to their gross incomes. For example, if the father's income is 60% of the family income, and the mother's is 40%, then the father pays 60% of the basic costs of the children, and the mother pays 40%. The Guideline helps you determine potential income if one or both of you is unemployed or underemployed. There are almost no circumstances under which a parent would have no financial responsibility for his or her children.

The guideline requires you to prepare and file at least one worksheet with your separation agreement if you have a minor child, or an unemancipated child. There are two worksheets:

- Worksheet A – Used when one parent has the children livingwith him or her more than 273 overnights per year.

- Worksheet B – Used when both parents have the children living with them more than 92 overnights per year. The statute refers to this as shared physical care.

When there are different children in different parenting plans, then you may be using more than one worksheet. The statute refers to this situation as split physical care. Here are several illustrations of which worksheet to use for a family with four children.

1. One parent has all the children more than 273 overnights per year. Use one Worksheet A.

2. All the children spend the same amount of parenting time with both parents, which is more than 92 overnights per year with each. Use one Worksheet B.

3. Each parent has more than 273 overnights per year with one or more children. Do two Worksheets A.

4. Each parent has more than 273 overnights per year with one child, and they have shared physical care of the other two. Use two Worksheets A, and one Worksheet B.

5. One parent has two children for more than 273 overnights per year, and they have shared physical care of the other two. Use one Worksheet A and one Worksheet B.

If you are using more than one worksheet because your children are in different parenting arrangements, remember that the Schedule of Basic Child Support Obligations is weighted for the first child in each home, while the increments between the first and second child and on up are all the same.

The following outline frames the approach to support of children taken in this chapter. Read this as a summary, a map, and come back to it if you get lost.

HOW TO MAKE THE *COLORADO CHILD SUPPORT GUIDELINE* WORK FOR YOU

The underlying presumption of the *Colorado Child Support Guideline* is this: divorcing parents should support their children in the proportion each parent's income is to the family income.

A. Determine the gross (before tax) incomes of each parent. See Definition of Income in this chapter.

　1.　Use potential income if either parent is unemployed or underemployed, with some exceptions.

　2.　Use business gross income minus necessary business expenses for the self-employed.

　3.　Decide how you are going to treat irregular or uncertain income.

B. If you pay or receive maintenance for a previous marriage, or have agreed to maintenance for this marriage, you can add/subtract that amount from your gross incomes. If you pay support for a child from another marriage or relationship, you can subtract this from your gross income. See the instructions for the worksheet for restrictions to these adjustments. Adding or subtracting these to your incomes in A will result in an adjusted monthly gross income.   *22,700*

C. If your monthly adjusted gross income is between $850 and $1850, and you have fewer overnights, you may qualify for a low-income adjustment on Worksheet A. Use the Low-income Adjustment worksheet on page 2 of the form to see if this applies.

D. Decide for this family which expenses will be included in the basic support (all clothing? all food? basic medical? transportation? etc.).

　1.　If the children live with one parent for 273 overnights or more per year, then assume these expenses are being incurred in that home.

　2.　If the parents both have parenting time of more than 93 overnights per year, then assume these expenses are being incurred by both parents in proportion to their time with the child. Verify that this is so. If not, note where this is not true for you for a later discussion of possible deviations from the Guideline. See "Brenda and Bob" example, later in this chapter, for how this works.

E. Agree which expenses for the children in this family are not covered by the basic support obligation from the schedule. Include all such expenses presently incurred by either parent.

　1.　Find and write down those expenses which are predictable and regular.

　2.　Discuss those expenses which are neither predictable nor regular.

F. Decide how many of the predictable and regular expenses for the children are to be shared between the parents in proportion to their incomes. Average these per month.

G. Decide which, if any, of the predictable and regular expenses for the children are to be shared between the parents in some other proportion. (This is counter to the presumption on which the Guideline is based, so be prepared to explain your reasons.)

H. Discuss how unpredictable and irregular expenses are to be handled and paid. (The presumption is that you will share them in proportion to income at the time of the expense.)

Once your agreements about the items on this page are clearly spelled out between you, the arithmetic on the worksheets will make sense.

District Court, _____ County, Colorado
Court Address:

In re _____ :
Petitioner:

v.

Respondent/Co-Petitioner:

Attorney or Party Without Attorney (Name and Address):

▲ COURT USE ONLY ▲

Case Number:

Phone Number: E-mail:
FAX Number: Atty. Reg. #:   Division: Courtroom:

WORKSHEET A—CHILD SUPPORT OBLIGATION: SOLE PHYSICAL CARE

Children	Date of Birth	Children	Date of Birth

Check box of parent with 273 or more overnights per year*	Mother	Father	Combined
1. MONTHLY GROSS INCOME	$	$	
a. Plus maintenance received	+	+	
b. Minus maintenance paid	–	–	
c. Minus ordered child support payments for other children [§14-10-115(7)(d), C.R.S.]	–	–	
d. Minus legal responsibility for prior born children not of this marriage/relationship [§14-10-115(7)(d.5), C.R.S.]	–	–	
e. Minus ordered post-secondary education contributions**	–	–	
2. MONTHLY ADJUSTED GROSS INCOME (If either the paying parent's income or Combined Income is less than $850, enter $50 on line 11 for paying parent.)	$	$	$
3. PERCENTAGE SHARE OF INCOME (Each parent's income from line 2 divided by Combined Income)		%	
4. a. **BASIC COMBINED OBLIGATION** (Apply line 2 Combined column to Child Support Schedule)			$
b. Each parent's share of basic support obligation (Each parent's percentage from line 3 times Combined obligation in 4a)	$	$	
5. LOW-INCOME ADJUSTMENT (If paying parent's income in line 2 is less than $1850, see Low-income Worksheet on page 2)	$	$	
6. ADJUSTMENTS (Expenses paid directly by each parent)			
a. Work-related Child Care Costs [Actual costs minus Federal Tax Credit. §14-10-115(11), C.R.S.]	$	$	
b. Education-related Child Care Costs [§14-10-115(11), C.R.S.]	$	$	
c. Health Insurance premium costs—Children's portion only [§14-10-115(13.5), C.R.S.] (See page 2 for calculation worksheet)	$	$	
d. Extraordinary Medical Expenses [Uninsured only. §14-10-115(13.5), C.R.S.]	$	$	
e. Extraordinary Expenses [Agreed to by parents or by order of the court. §14-10-115(13), C.R.S.]	$	$	
f. Minus Extraordinary Adjustments [§14-10-115(13)(b), C.R.S.]	$	$	
7. TOTAL ADJUSTMENTS (For each column, add 6a, 6b, 6c, 6d and 6e. Subtract line 6f. Add two totals for Combined column amount)	$	$	$

(18)	**8. EACH PARENT'S SHARE OF ADJUSTMENTS** (Line 7 Combined column times line 3 for each parent)	$	$
(19)	**9. EACH PARENT'S SHARE OF TOTAL CHILD SUPPORT OBLIGATION** (Add lines 4b (or line 5 if less) and line 8 for each parent)	$	$
(20)	**10. PAYING PARENT'S ADJUSTMENT** (Enter line 7 for parent with less parenting time only)	$	$
(21)	**11. RECOMMENDED CHILD SUPPORT ORDER** (Subtract line 10 from line 9 for the paying parent only. Leave receiving parent column blank)	$	$

(22)
COMMENTS:

* The children reside with one parent for 273 or more overnights per year. If this is not the case, use Worksheet B.
** This adjustment applies only to modification of child support orders entered between 7/1/91 and 7/1/97 that provide for post-secondary education expenses pursuant to §14-10-115(1.5)(b)(1), C.R.S.

(23)
PREPARED BY: DATE:

(24)
LOW-INCOME ADJUSTMENT WORKSHEET
If the parents' combined monthly adjusted gross income is more than $850 and the monthly adjusted gross income of the parent with fewer overnights per year is less than $1850, use this calculation worksheet to determine the adjustment allowed for that parent.

Low-income adjustment calculation
Adjusted monthly gross income of parent with fewer overnights (paying parent) from line 2
$ _____   minus $900 = $ _____   times 40% (.40)   = $ _____

Plus one of the following, according to number of children
1 child = $75   2 children = $150   3 children = $225
4 children = $275   5 children = $325   6 or more children = $350   + $ _____

Low-income adjustment amount $ _____

If this amount is less than the amount on line 4b (on page 1) for the parent with fewer overnights per year, this parent qualifies for the Low-income Adjustment. Enter this amount on line 5 in that parent's column on page 1. If this number is a negative or zero, enter zero.

(25)
HEALTH INSURANCE PREMIUM CALCULATION

   If the actual amount of the health insurance premium that is attributable to the child(ren) who are the subject of this order is not available or cannot be verified, the total cost of the premium should be divided by the number of persons covered by the policy to determine a per person cost. This amount is then multiplied by the number of children who are the subject of this order and are covered by the policy. This amount is then entered on line 6c on page 1 of this form.

$ _____ ÷ _____ = $ _____ x _____ = $ _____

| Total Premium | Number of Persons Covered by the Policy | Per Person Cost | Number of Children Who are the Subject of this Order | Children's Portion of Cost of Health Insurance Premium (Enter on line 6c) |

Worksheet A – One parent has more than 273 overnights per year.

Complete Worksheet A when one or more of your children spends 75% or more overnights with one parent. A parenting plan which provides for alternate one-overnight weekends, plus half of the holidays and major school vacations with the non-residential parent will usually total less than 25%. Just because you go over 25% of the overnights does not mean that you should use Worksheet B. It is used only if there are two homes for the children, rather than a primary home and a place to visit the other parent.

INSTRUCTIONS FOR FILLING OUT WORKSHEET A

1. Enter the same information here that you entered in these blanks on the petition.

2. List the names and birth dates of only those children for whom you are calculating child support on this worksheet. Check the box of the parent with 273 or more overnights per year.

3. Fill in the Gross Monthly Income (before deductions or taxes) for each of you from your income chart or as you have agreed to use in your Child Support Plan Questionnaire, under the appropriate columns. The definition of income in the Guideline (see excerpt near the end of this chapter) includes not only your regular employment, but any other income as well, such as bonuses, capital gains, severance pay, and monetary gifts. You do not need to include income from additional jobs that result in employment more than 40 hours per week or more than what would otherwise be considered full time employment. In practice, you do not have to include your occasional income on this line of your worksheet if you agree not to do so. The decision of what income to include on this worksheet will affect the amount of money one of you pays to the other. If you used the Child Support Plan Questionnaire earlier in this chapter you have already made this decision.

4. Write any amounts either of you is actually receiving in line 1a, or paying in line 1b for court-ordered maintenance for another marriage or have agreed to for this marriage.

 If one of you is paying or planning to pay maintenance (spousal support, alimony) to the other, deduct it from the income of the spouse who will pay it, and add it to the income of the spouse who receives it. Do not include it in the gross income of that spouse on line 1. See Chapter 9 Maintenance for more about why you might want to do this.

5. Write any amounts either you or your spouse are actually paying for court-ordered child support for other children not of this marriage.

6. Write any amounts which either of you is legally obligated to pay for children other than of this marriage or relationship, who are born prior to the children of this marriage. The parent wishing to use this adjustment to income must prove that the children in question are living with him or her, or that he or she is actually making such payments. The amount of the adjustment may not exceed the amount of support for that number of children calculated from the Schedule of Basic Support at that parent's income alone. Nor may this adjustment be used to reduce a previously-set child support amount for the children of this marriage.

7. Write any amount either of you is ordered to pay for post-secondary education for another child of this marriage, from an order entered in Colorado between 1/1/91 and 7/1/97. This adjustment is limited to the amount of child support on the Schedule of Basic Support, for that child, based on the paying parent's income.

8. Add lines 1 and 1a and subtract lines 1c, 1d and 1e, for each of you. Then add these two adjusted totals and put that amount under the combined column. If either the paying parent's income or the coambined income in line 2 is less than $850, the minimum support for the paying parent is $50. Enter this amount

on line 11 for that parent. If your combined monthly adjusted gross income is more than $20,000, then you may not use the Schedule of Basic Support, but must agree on a fair amount based on the actual cost of rearing your children as set forth in your parenting plan. This amount may not be less than the amount shown in the schedule for $20,000.

9. Divide each of your individual totals by the combined total to get the percentage of the total family income each of you earns. These two percentages should total 100%.

10a. Find the Schedule of Basic Child Support Obligations on the CDROM (Form 1173) and find your combined monthly gross income in the left-hand column. Read across columns to the number of children you have listed on this worksheet.

If your combined monthly adjusted gross income falls between numbers on the schedule, then you will need to interpolate between the two closest amounts to find the support figure. For example, if you have a combined monthly adjusted gross income of $1960.00 and have three children, on the schedule your income falls between $1950.00 and $2,000.00, and your support obligation falls between $648.00 and $661.00. Your combined monthly adjusted gross income is 1/5 of the way between $1950.00 and $2,000.

$$\frac{\$1960.00}{-1950.00} \qquad \frac{\$2000.00}{-1950.00} \qquad \frac{10.00}{50.00} \quad = \quad \frac{1}{5}$$
$$ 10.00 \qquad 50.00$$

The difference between $661.00 and $648.00 is $13.00. To calculate the additional amount, find 1/5 of $13.00 and add that to $648.00

$$\frac{1}{5} \quad \times \quad \frac{13.00}{1} \quad = \quad \frac{13.00}{5} \quad = \quad \$2.60 \qquad \$648 \quad + \quad \$2.60 \quad = \quad \$650.60$$

10b. For each of you, multiply the combined basic obligation in line 4a times your percentage share of income in line 3 and enter that amount in your respective columns.

11. If the amount on line 2 of combined income is more than $850, and the income on line 2 for the parent with less overnights per year is between $850 and $1850, that parent may be eligible for an adjustment to support. To calculate this amount, go to instruction number 24.

12a. Write the amount each of you pays for work-related child care for the children who are listed on this worksheet. The child care to be included on this line refers only to work-related child care, meaning that care necessary for either of you to go to work or search for a job. If that child is your dependent for the purpose of Head of Household tax filing status (see IRS form 2441, and Chapter 10) and if the child care is not paid through a cafeteria or flex plan, then subtract the amount of the child care credit taken from the child care credit table in this supplement (for 2003) from the amount you pay out. If you do not qualify for the child care credit, use the amount you actually spend.

12b. Write the amount each of you pays for education-related child care (while you are in school) for the children who are listed on this worksheet.

You must decide whether child care or babysitting for reasons other than education or work is included in your basic child support obligation from the schedule. If not, and you wish to include it on this form, include that amount in your total for line 6e.

13. Write the actual cost paid by either of you for health insurance premiums for the children listed on this worksheet. In practice, many people also include the premium paid for dental and vision insurance. If your employer does not separate the amount for the employee and the amount for additional persons or family, then use the formula in instruction 25 to calculate the amount for the children on this worksheet.

14. Write any amount in excess of $250 per child, per year, either of you makes for medical expenses (including dental, optical, mental health or copays), for the children listed on this worksheet, which are not paid by insurance, and which you have agreed to include in your child support calculation—unless they are paid by cafeteria or flex plan. If your children's out of pocket medical and dental expenses exceed the deductible on your insurance, you may want to include that amount of that monthly deductible here.

15. Write any additional regular expenses, for the children listed on this worksheet, paid by either of you, which you both agree to include in your child support calculation or which have been ordered by the court.

16. Write any amounts either of you receive or the child receives, as income of, or on behalf of, the children listed on this worksheet, which you agree should offset the children's need for support. Some common examples are child's regular earnings, SSI paid for the child, adoption subsidy for child, income from child's trust. List the amount in the column for the parent in whose home the money is received. Most people do not include on this line occasional income earned by a child that is not being used to defray his or her necessary expenses (money from a weekend job that is being used for dates, gifts, incidental food, entertainment, for instance).

17. Add together any amounts on lines 6a, 6b, 6c, 6d and 6e, and then subtract any amount on line 6f for each of you. Then add the totals for each of you to obtain the combined extraordinary adjustments being paid out by you both and put that amount in the Combined column.

18. Multiply the amount in the combined column in line 7 by the amount in line 3 for each of you and put that amount in your respective columns. This is each parent's share of the adjustments.

19. For each of you, add the amounts in your columns on lines 4b (or line 5 if one parent qualifies for the low-income adjustment) and 8. This is the basic support and adjustments for each parent.

20. Write, in the paying parent's column only, that parent's number from line 7. This number represents those extraordinary expenses which the paying parent disburses directly to third parties for the children.

21. Subtract line 10 from line 9 for the paying parent only and put the result on Line 11, under that column. The recommended child support amount resulting from the use of this worksheet and the guideline should be an amount that makes sense for both of you—meaning that it is payable by the parent who will pay it, and sufficient for the parent who receives it. If this is not so, then read the "What if . . ." section of this chapter following the material on Worksheet

22. If you wish to ask the court to deviate from the amount on line 11, state your reason here.

23. Whoever prepares this worksheet should sign and date it. If you both prepared it, then you should both sign it. If the preparer is not a parent, that person should also indicate his or her status (CPA, lawyer or one or both, mediator, etc.)

24. Use this worksheet only if the amount on line 2 of combined income is more than $850, and the income on line 2 for the parent with less overnights per year is between $850 and $1850. For example, if the parent who has less overnights has a monthly adjusted gross income of $1600 and 3 children:

$1600.00 - $900 = $700 x .40 = $280.00.

$280.00 + $225.00 = $505.00

If this is less than the amount on line 4b for that parent, this parent qualifies for the low-income adjustment and would write $505.00 on line 5 in that parent's column. If the amount from this worksheet results in a negative or zero number, zero would be entered on line 5.

25. Use this to determine the children's share of the health insurance premium if your policy does not state a particular amount. Enter the total premium, divide it by the total number of persons on the policy, and multiply that amount by the number of children who are covered. Write the result on line 6c.

WORKSHEET B

Use Worksheet B when any of your children spends more than 92 overnights per year with each of you, and you both provide a home for them. Based on the concept of two homes, Worksheet B increases the amount you are jointly expected to spend for the basic expenses of your children by 50%. If your parenting plan is more like one primary home and the other more a place to visit (children do not have their own bedrooms, toys and clothes don't stay there), then you may wish to use Worksheet A even if the children spend more than 92 overnights per year with both parents.

Worksheet B factors the basic child support obligation twice: first by percentage of income, and second by percentage of time the children spend with each parent. It should not be too surprising that when one takes a percentage (ratio of income) of a percentage (ratio of time), the figure one is working with reduces very fast. It is important to remember, therefore, the silent presumption in this worksheet.

Worksheet B contains the silent presumption that parents who share physical care disburse payment for the basic expenses of their children in proportion to parenting time. For example, if the father has 60% of the time and the mother 40%, he is assumed to be disbursing payments for 60% of the cost of shoes, clothing, food, and all other basic expenses. If the parents have 50-50 time, they are each assumed to be disbursing payment for half these costs. If you are developing a parenting plan with shared physical care, it may be wise to begin disbursing payment for these expenses in the ratio of your time, right from the beginning. If you do not, you may find that the child support which results from this worksheet will not be adequate, because it is based on an assumption which is not being met.

You can also resolve the problem by adjusting the recommended support amount for the basic expenses which are in fact being paid by the "wrong" parent. See the later section of this chapter, "Deviations," especially "Brenda and Bob," if the amounts you get when you work through Worksheet B seem to be "off." Especially if they do not match up with the agreements you reached in the Child Support Plan Questionnaire earlier in this chapter.

"If you get more than 92 overnights with your kids, your child support will go down."

This is a widely-held misconception. The payments between the parents may go down, but each parent is still expected to carry his or her income percentage share of the cost of rearing their children. The presumption shifts from expecting only one parent to be disbursing all the children's basic expenses, to expecting the parents to be disbursing them in proportion to their parenting time.

The parent receiving a child support payment shall be presumed to spend his or her total child support obligation directly on the children." Colorado Revised Statutes 14-10-115 (14)(a).

District Court, _____ County, Colorado
Court Address:

In re _____ :
Petitioner:

v.

Respondent/Co-Petitioner:

Attorney or Party Without Attorney (Name and Address):

▲ COURT USE ONLY ▲

Case Number:

Phone Number: E-mail:
FAX Number: Atty. Reg. #:   Division: Courtroom:

WORKSHEET B—CHILD SUPPORT OBLIGATION: SHARED PHYSICAL CARE

Children	Date of Birth	Children	Date of Birth

		Mother	Father	Combined
1. MONTHLY GROSS INCOME		$	$	
a. Plus maintenance received		+	+	
b. Minus maintenance paid		–	–	
c. Minus ordered child support payments for other children [§14-10-115(7)(d), C.R.S.]		–	–	
d. Minus legal responsibility for prior born children not of this marriage/relationship [§14-10-115(7)(d.5), C.R.S.]		–	–	
e. Minus ordered post-secondary education contributions*		–	–	
2. MONTHLY ADJUSTED GROSS INCOME		$	$	$
3. PERCENTAGE SHARE OF INCOME (Each parent's income from line 2 divided by Combined Income)		%	%	
4. BASIC COMBINED OBLIGATION (Apply line 2 Combined column to Child Support Schedule)				
5. SHARED PHYSICAL CARE SUPPORT OBLIGATION (Line 4 times 1.5)				
6. EACH PARENT'S PORTION OF SHARED PHYSICAL CARE SUPPORT OBLIGATION (Line 3 times line 5 for each parent)		$	$	
7. OVERNIGHTS WITH EACH PARENT (Must total 365)				= 365
STOP HERE IF LINE 7 IS LESS THAN 93 FOR EITHER PARENT. IF SO, USE WORKSHEET A.				
8. PERCENTAGE TIME WITH EACH PARENT (Line 7 ÷ 365)		%	%	
9. SUPPORT OBLIGATION FOR TIME WITH OTHER PARENT (Line 6 times other parent's line 8)		$	$	
10. ADJUSTMENTS (Expenses paid directly by each parent)				
a. Work-related Child Care Costs [Actual costs minus Federal Tax Credit. §14-10-115(11), C.R.S.]		$	$	
b. Education-related Child Care Costs [§14-10-115(11), C.R.S.]		$	$	
c. Health Insurance premium costs—Children's portion only [§14-10-115(13.5), C.R.S.] (See page 2 for calculation worksheet)		$	$	
d. Extraordinary Medical Expenses [Uninsured only. §14-10-115(13.5), C.R.S.]		$	$	

20	e. Extraordinary Expenses [Agreed to by parents or by order of the court. §14-10-115(13.5), C.R.S.]	$	$	
21	f. Minus Extraordinary Adjustments [§14-10-115(13)(b), C.R.S.]	$	$	
22	**11. TOTAL ADJUSTMENTS** (For each column, add 10a, 10b, 10c, 10d and 10e. Subtract line 10f. Add two totals for Combined Column amount)	$	$	$
23	**12. EACH PARENT'S SHARE OF ADJUSTMENTS** (Line 11 Combined column times line 3 for each parent)	$	$	
24	**13. ADJUSTMENTS PAID IN EXCESS OF SHARE** (Line 11 minus line 12. If negative number, enter zero.)	$	$	
25	**14. EACH PARENT'S ADJUSTED SUPPORT OBLIGATION** (Line 9 minus line 13)	$	$	
26	**15. RECOMMENDED CHILD SUPPORT ORDER**** (Subtract lesser amount from greater amount in line 14 and enter result under greater amount)	$	$	

27 COMMENTS:

 *This adjustment applies only to modification of child support orders entered between 7/1/91 and 7/1/97 that provide for post-secondary education expenses pursuant to §14-10-115(1.5)(b)(I), C.R.S.
**If either the paying parent's monthly adjusted gross income or the combined monthly adjusted gross income is less than $850, see §14-10-115(10)(a)(II)(B) and (C), C.R.S.

28 PREPARED BY: DATE:

The amount of child support ordered for shared physical care should not be more than an order for sole physical care. Complete a Worksheet A for comparison.

29 **HEALTH INSURANCE PREMIUM CALCULATION**

 If the actual amount of the health insurance premium that is attributable to the children who are the subject of this order is not available or cannot be verified, the total cost of the premium should be divided by the number of persons covered by the policy to determine a per person cost. This amount is then multiplied by the number of children who are the subject of this order and are covered by the policy. This amount is then entered on line 10c on page 1 of this form.

$ _____ ÷ _____ = $ _____ x _____ = $ _____

| Total Premium | Number of Persons Covered by the Policy | Per Person Cost | Number of Children Who are the Subject of this Order | Children's Portion of Cost of Health Insurance Premium (Enter on line 10c) |

Worksheet B

Use this form if both parents have more than 92 overnights per year with the children and both provide a home for them.

INSTRUCTIONS FOR FILLING OUT WORKSHEET B

1. Enter the same information here that you entered in these blanks on the petition.

2. List the names and birth dates of those children who spend at least 93 overnights with each of you.

Steps 3 through 10a are the same as Worksheet A.

11. Multiply the amount on line 4 on the form by 1.5 (150%) and place on line 5.

12. Multiply the Shared Care Support Obligation from line 5 by the percentage of incomes on line 3 for each of you.

13. Write the number of overnights with each of you. If you have 50/50% shared time parenting of more than one child and each wants to be head of household (see "Tax Filing Status," Chapter 11), you might want to fill in this line with the overnights for each child individually, like this:

	Mother	**Father**
Overnights with children	183/182	182/183

This would indicate that Mother has Child A for 183 overnights and child B for 182; Father has child A for 182 overnights and Child B for 183. Mother will have head of household for child A and Father will have head of household for Child B.

14. Divide the number of overnights with each of you by 365. This will result in a percentage (60/40, 57/43, 50/50, etc.).

15. Multiply the amount in the Mother's column on line 6 by the percentage on line 8 in the Father's column and place the result under the Mother's column on line 9. Then multiply the Father's amount on line 6 by the percentage on line 8 in the Mother's column and place the result in the Father's column on line 9. By doing this calculation, each of you is "paying" the other parent your proportional (income-based) share of the basic support obligation for the time the children are with the other parent.

16. Write the amount each of you pays for work-related child care when the children who are listed on this worksheet are with you. The child care to be included on this line refers only to work-related child care, meaning that care necessary for either of you to go to work while the children are with you. If that child is your dependent for the purpose of Head of Household tax filing status (see IRS form 2441, and Chapter 11) and if the child care is not paid through a cafeteria or flex plan, then subtract the amount of the child care credit taken from the Child Care Credit Table on page 219 from the amount you pay out. If you do not qualify for the child care credit, use the amount you actually spend.

You must decide whether other child care or babysitting is covered in the basic child support obligation from the schedule. If not, and you wish to include it on this form, include that amount in your total for line 10e.

17. Write the amount each of you pays for education-related child care (while you are in school) when the children who are listed on this worksheet. Do not include work-related child care in this total.

18. Write the actual cost paid by either of you for health insurance premiums for the children listed on this worksheet. In practice, many people also include the premium paid for dental and vision insurance. If your employer does not separate the amount for the employee and the amount for additional persons or family, then use the formula on the back of this worksheet to calculate the amount for the children on this worksheet.

19. Write any amount in excess of $250 per child, per year, either of you makes for medical expenses (including dental, optical, mental health or copays), for the children listed on this worksheet, which are not paid by insurance, and which you have agreed to include in your child support calculation—unless they are paid by cafeteria or flex plan. If your children's medical and dental expenses always exceed the deductible on your insurance, you may want to include the amount of that monthly deductible here.

20. Write any additional regular expenses, for the children listed on this worksheet, paid by either of you, which you both agree to include in your child support calculation or which has been ordered by the court.

21. Write any amounts either of you receive or the child receives, as income of, or on behalf of, the children listed on this worksheet, which you agree should offset the children's need for support. Some common examples are child's earnings, SSI paid for the child, adoption subsidy for child, income from child's trust. List the amount in the column for the parent in whose home the money is received. Most people do not include on this line occasional income earned by a child that is not being used to defray his or her necessary expenses (money from a weekend job that is being used for dates, gifts, incidental food, entertainment, for instance).

22. Add any amounts on lines 10a, 10b, 10c, 10d, and 10e then subtract any amount on line 10f for each of you. Add the totals for each of you to obtain the combined extraordinary expenses being paid out by you both and put that amount in the Combined column.

23. For each of you, multiply your total adjustment, line 11, times your percentage share of income, line 3. Place the total in your respective columns. This is your share of the extraordinary expenses for your children based on your relative incomes. These expenses are not factored by your time with your children.

24. For each of you, subtract line 12 from line 11 to find out how much more or less than your income share of extraordinary expenses you are each paying. The differential will be the same—one parent will be underpaying the same amount the other is overpaying—so don't record the underpayment (the minus number).

25. Subtract the overpayment on line 13 from the support obligation, line 10. This number may be a negative for one of you if either of you is overpaying extraordinary expenses by more than your share of the basic support. (Example: Low income parent who is paying large amounts of day care or medical insurance.)

26. Subtract the lower amount of support owing from the higher amount. The difference is the recommended amount of support to be paid. If the lower amount is a negative number, you will ADD it to the higher amount to find the correct amount of support to be paid.

27. If you wish to ask the court to deviate from the amount on line 15, state your reasons here.

28. Whoever prepares this worksheet should sign and date it. That may be both or only one of the parents. If it is neither parent, that person should also indicate his or her status (CPA, lawyer for one or both, mediator, etc.)

29. Use this section to calculate the children's share of your health insurance premium.

"Deviate Circumstances"

The statute lists factors for which the court may consider deviating from the recommended support amount on your worksheet:

These reasons may include, but are not limited to:

"where its application would be inequitable, unjust, or inappropriate,"
"the extraordinary medical expenses incurred for treatment of either parent or a current spouse,
"extraordinary costs associated with parenting time,
"the gross disparity in income between the parents,
"the ownership by a parent of a substantial non-income producing asset,
"consistent overtime not considered in gross income . . .
"income from employment that is in addition to a full-time job or that results in the employment of the obligor more than forty hours per week or more than what would otherwise be considered to be full-time employment.
"The existence of a factor enumerated in this section does not require the court to deviate from the guidelines, but is a factor to be considered in the decision to deviate".
"The court may deviate from the guidelines even if no factor enumerated in this section exists."

Deviations: What if the Recommended Support Is Too High or Too Low for You?

The Child Support Guideline creates a *rebuttable presumption* – something which will happen unless you can convince the court that it should not. This means that the court will expect your agreement to require the payment of the recommended child support amount from your worksheet. In practice, most courts will readily approve a child support amount which is higher than the recommended amount, but deviation is more difficult to obtain when the amount you wish is lower than the recommended support.

Before you consider asking the court to approve a support amount that deviates from the recommended amount on the worksheet, go back to the amounts you agreed to for gross income and your decisions about which extra expenses to include in monthly support on the worksheet as shown on your Child Support Plan Questionnaire earlier in this chapter. See if by changing your agreements about these numbers, you can adjust the recommended amount on the worksheet to a number which will work for you. For example, agree not to use any income except base salary. This may change the shared basic obligation from the schedule, and therefore the support to be paid by support order. Or, agree to not list some or all of the extraordinary or additional expenses on the worksheet. This may also considerably reduce the amount on the support order. You may instead agree to pay these additional expenses as they occur, from irregular or additional income or from a "kitty" account you both contribute to periodically.

You can always pay more money to each other for your children. The issue here is what amounts you wish to make binding on you and enforceable by the court as regular monthly court-ordered child support reflected on the support order and paid automatically.

The Guideline may allow you to deviate from the recommended support amount under some circumstances. If you fit any of the circumstances in the statute, you may be able to convince the court that the recommended child support amount should not apply to you. You must present to the court not only your own suggested amount for support and your reasons for asking for a deviation, but also the appropriate worksheet(s) showing your calculations of the recommended support amount so the court can compare them.

One of the most frequently encountered situations in which the recommended child support payment may not seem fair occurs when the parents are not spending money on their children in the way the Guideline assumes. Read the following story to see if it explains a difficulty you may have been experiencing.

BRENDA AND BOB

Brenda and Bob have one child, Billy, age 14. Billy is growing four inches a year and is "eating both parents out of house and home." Bob earns $2,000 per month and Brenda earns $1000 per month. The basic child support obligation for them is $540. This means the State of Colorado expects Billy to cost that much per month for housing, food, clothing, probably daily transportation to school, and possibly ordinary medical expenses like school checkups.

The ratio between Brenda and Bob's incomes is 33%/67%. If Billy lives with Brenda, Bob would pay $540 × .67 = $361.80. If Billy lives with Bob, Brenda would contribute $540 × .33 = $178.20.

Bob has been paying for all of Billy's clothing while they have been living together, and he thinks the clothes alone have been running $150 per month. Billy has been coming to Brenda's home every day after school until Bob picks him up after work. Billy eats a minimum of two peanut butter and jelly sandwiches and drinks a quart of milk every day which Brenda budgets at $50 per month. Both Bob and Brenda think Billy costs more than $540 per month for his basic expenses.

If Brenda and Bob agree that Billy could live most of the time with either of them, they might agree to adjust the amount of support to allow for the parent paying a larger share of one of the basic expenses that the other parent is presumed to cover. In this case, Bob buys all the clothes —if Billy does not live with him he would be presumed to buy none. Brenda buys more groceries than she would be presumed to be buying if Billy lived with Bob.

If Brenda and Bob agree to shared physical care, the problem is more dramatic. If they have 50/50 time with Billy the numbers for child support will look like this.

The basic amount becomes $540 × 1.5 = $810. Brenda's share is $810 × .33 (income %) × .50 (time share) = 133.65. Bob's share is $810 × .67 (income share) × .50 (time share) = 271.35. Bob would pay Brenda the difference, $137.70 in support each month.

But, wait a minute, $133.65 (Brenda's share) + $271.35 (Bob's share) equals $405. That is only half the $651 Billy is supposed to cost for basic support. (Remember, Brenda and Bob think he costs even more than that.) What happened to the other half of Billy's basic support? The answer is that the Guideline assumes the parents are disbursing the cost of Billy in proportion to their time with him. Brenda and Bob are assumed to be spending half of $810 or $405 per month each on housing, food, clothing, daily transportation to school and possibly ordinary medical costs, such as school checkups, and such, in their individual homes.

The purpose of the shared physical care child support paid by Bob to Brenda is to bring Bob's share of Billy's overall expenses back to 67% (his income share). The $405 Bob is assumed to be spending on Billy plus the $137.70 he gives Brenda is indeed 67% of $810. (810 × .67 = $542.70. $405.00 + 137.70 = 542.70. The $405 Brenda is assumed to be spending on Billy minus the $137.70 from Bob equals her 33% share (810 × .33 = 267.30. $405 - 137.70 = 267.30).

As you can see, if Brenda and Bob are not each disbursing half of Billy's expenses then the support paid between them will not be their fair (income) share of Billy's expenses. In this case, Bob is paying for all of Billy's clothes, so Brenda is paying less than half of that component of the basic support amount. Brenda is paying more than half the food cost, since she is feeding Billy all of his after-school "snacks".

Brenda and Bob can figure out the actual cost of the snacks and the clothing and adjust their support accordingly, or they can increase the support overall on the general principle that Billy costs more than what the State thinks. Or they can leave the support amount alone and assume the amount Brenda spends on extra food is equal to her share of the clothing which Bob is paying for.

In many cases no adjustment needs to be made, but the discussion about how the parents are paying out their children's expenses does need to be examined in light of the presumptions the Guideline is making.

Once you have agreed to an amount of child support and how you will pay the extraordinary expenses and health insurance, you may write these provisions into your separation agreement draft, using the sample language at the end of Chapter 12 or JDF 1115.

Post-Secondary Education

The present Colorado law no longer permits the court to consider whether divorcing parents should be required to make provision for higher education expenses for their children. However, if you both agree about these expenses you may ask the court to approve that agreement as part of your settlement. Once the court has done so, it will be a court order and enforceable like any other.

If you want to think about making some provision about college or other education or training after high school, even if your children are very young, then the following suggestions might be useful.

- Consider stating that you acknowledge that your child or children will probably attend higher education, and that you will share this expense when the time comes.

- Consider reserving the choice of school and setting of costs (what you will and will not pay for) as a must-share decision between you regardless of the kind of parental decision-making you have agreed to.

- Consider determining the percentage in which you will carry these expenses, or say it will be according to your incomes at the time.

- Consider setting a ceiling on the amount, either in dollars per year or for the whole cost, or by setting a standard such as in-state costs for the state university that year, as assessed by that college at the time.

- Consider actually starting a fund for your children to be used for higher education or any other purpose you agree on now. You could base the goal for this account on your estimate of the future college costs for which you wish to be responsible, then set a monthly savings amount which you will share in proportion to income. For example, if you feel $40,000 is what you together wish to pledge for a child's higher education, and that child is now two, you would have that amount in savings if you shared an investment of $200 per month beginning now. If the ratio of your incomes were 60/40% now you would put aside $120 and $80, respectively—adjusting these amounts if the ratio of your income changes.

Once you have entered into an agreement about post-secondary expenses, you may include it in your separation agreement draft using the sample provisions at the end of Chapter 12 or using JDF 1115.

Life Insurance and Other Security for Child Support

Both parents may secure the support of their children with insurance on their lives. Even though only one parent may have a monthly child support payment to make, both parents are contributing to the support of the children, as you can see from reading Line 7 of Worksheet A and Line 13 of Worksheet B. Think about whether, if either of you died, your children would be adequately supported without life insurance.

One way to calculate what your anticipated contribution is worth is to take the worksheet lines mentioned above, and multiply.

Post-Secondary Education Checklist

Directions: Complete the following statements:

1. We agree that we want _____ _____ (child's name) to attend _____ (college or other post-secondary institution). (Repeat for each child.)

2. We agree to be responsible for paying all of the following expenses for post-secondary education for _____ _____ (name of child):

   We agree that the upper limit on these expenses is:

   We agree that we will pay these expenses in the following proportion:

3. We agree that we will share the following post-secondary education expenses with the child:

   We agree that we will share these expenses with the child in the following proportion:

4. We agree that we will establish (have established) a bank account at _____ (bank) by_____ (date) to pay the following post secondary education expenses for _____ _____ (name of child):

   We agree to contribute to this amount in the following amounts or proportions:

5. We agree that _____ (name of child) shall be responsible for paying the following post-secondary education expenses himself/herself:

Vanishing Refund

Failure to pay court-ordered child support can result in an interception of any refund on an income tax return for the delinquent parent. At the moment, this can only be done if enforcement is being done through a Child Support Eforcement Unit. See Chapter 13.

Winner is Loser

A parent who fails to pay child support asordered should be prepared to share any large windfall such as lottery winnings or a large court settlement as soon as it becomes public.The Child Support Enfrcement unit can see to it that his or her children are the big winners.

them times 12, for the annual contribution, times the number of years until your child reaches age 19. If you have more than one child, decrease the amount slightly as each child reaches 19, then add your best guess as to your likely share of unexpected estraordinary expenses which you did not put on the worksheet, and your share of post-secondary expenses if you think this is likely.

Agree on the total amount of life insurance you each should carry. You may wish to name each other as trustee for the benefit of the children so long as the children are minors. This can be decreasing term insurance, i.e., the death benefit decreases each year over a certain term—usually the number of years until your last child emancipates or finishes college (age 22 is a good guess). Decreasing term is usually the least expensive life insurance available and is the most common insurance available as a benefit through your employer. Some parents prefer, however, to purchase an annuity which will pay out as life insurance in the event of death, or, be available as a lump sum in time to pay for higher education.

Teeth for Your Child Support Agreement

If your ex gets a new lover, will you be less likely to pay the child support, or make the payments on time? If you lose your job or the bonus does not come through, will you look for a way out of your agreement? Most people would have to answer yes to at least one of these—or, at least admit that the possibility exists they could be tempted.

There are several kinds of internal enforcement which can be used in agreements about child support. What we call "teeth" are voluntary, private, and effective ways of penalizing yourselves with more or less costly consequences if you don't do what you say you will do. What does each of you need to put into your agreement to make sure you keep the promises you make to each other with regard to supporting your children? These incentives to right behavior are limited only by your imagination. Try having the person against whom the penalty would act set the penalty. You may be surprised to learn what motivates each of you.

Here are some examples of teeth in a child support agreement. You can state that the parent who has the tax exemption for the child loses it automatically to the other parent if his or her part of the child support agreement is not kept, or not current as of December 31, or some other date. You can state that if either parent does not disburse his or her share of the expenses included in the basic support obligation as you have agreed, then that parent carries 100% of the extraordinary expenses for the next month.

See the example of "Brenda and Bob." There are sample clauses about internal enforcement included in Chapter 12. You may wish to review them after reading this chapter.

Read Chapter 13 for information about modification of child support.

Conclusion

You have now finished your first rough look at your child support plan. It will probably not be your final version. Go on to the next two chapters about the other essential components of your separation agreement. The agreements you reach as a result of each of those chapters may necessitate changes in your child support.

Take heart. Doing your own separation agreement is hard work. Don't expect to get it all done in one sitting. Don't even expect to complete the work of one of the separation agreement chapters in one sitting. Give yourself and each other the time you deserve to make the best decisions for both of you and your children.

 Under Colorado law, failure to pay child support ordered by the court can result in the following enforcement remedies being brought against the non-paying parent:

1. Suspension of driver's license;
2. Denial, suspension or revocation of an occupational or professional license;
3. Income tax refund intercept;
4. Lottery winnings intercept;
5. Liens against real or personal property;
6. Denial or freezing of a passport.

Contact your local child support enforcement office for a list of current remedies, and for more specific information about how each remedy is being used in your county. To find the agency located in your district look in the blue pages under the county department of human services or social services. This works for all counties except Arapahoe, where the Child Support Enforcement unit is part of the District Attorney's office.

III. DETERMINATION OF CHILD SUPPORT AOUNT

To calculate child support fo children who are under 19 or still in high school, or disabled, use: Worksheet A when physical care is for 273 or more overnights per year; Worksheet B if shared physical care [see (4)(J) below].

(A) Income

(1) Definition. For purposes of this Guideline, "income" is defined as actual gross income of the parent, if employed to full capacity, or potential income if unemployed or underemployed. Gross income of each parent should be determined as specified below and entered on Line 1 of the appropriate worksheet.

(2) Gross income. Gross income includes income from any source and includes, but is not limited to, income from salaries; wages, including tips declared by the individual for purposes of reporting to the federal internal revenue service or tips imputed to bring the employee's gross earnings to the minimum wage for the number of hours worked, whichever is greater; commissions; payments received as an independent contractor for labor or services; bonuses; dividends; severance pay; pensions and retirement benefits; royalties; rents; interest; trust income; annuities; capital gains; and moneys drawn by a self-employed individual for personal use; social security benefits, including social security benefits actually received by a parent as a result of the disability of that parent or as the result of the death of the minor child's stepparent; workers' compensation benefits; unemployment insurance benefits; disability insurance benefits; funds held in or payable from any health, accident, disability, or casualty insurance to the extent that such insurance replaces wages or provides income in lieu of wages; monetary gifts; monetary prizes, excluding lottery winnings not required by the rules of the Colorado Lottery Commission to be paid only at the lottery office; taxable distributions from general partnerships, limited partnerships, closely held corporations, or limited liability companies; alimony or maintenance received; and overtime pay only if the overtime is required by the employer as a condition of the employment.

For income from self-employment, rents, royalties, proprietorship of a business, or joint ownership of a partnership or closely held corporation, gross income is defined as gross receipts minus ordinary and necessary expenses required to produce such income. "Ordinary and necessary expenses" does not include amounts allowable by the Internal Revenue Service for the accelerated component of depreciation expenses or investment tax credits or any other business expenses determined by the court to be inappropriate for determining gross income for purposes of calculating child support. Ingeneral, income and expenses from self-employment or operation of a business should be carefully reviewed to determine an appropriate level of gross income available to the parent to satisfy a child support obliation. In most cases, this amount will differ from a determination of business income for tax purposes. Expense reimbursements or in-kind payments received by a parent in the course of employment, self employment, or operation of a business shall be counted as income if they are significant and reduce personal living expenses.

Gross income does not include benefits received from means-tested public assistance programs, including but not limited to assistance provided under the Colorado Works Program, Supplemental Security Income (SSI), Food Stamps, and General Assistance. Gross income does not include child support paymets received; social security benefits received by a minor child or on behalf of a minor child as a result of the death or disability of a stepparent of the child; income from additional jobs that result in the employment of the obligor more than forty hours per week or more than what would otherwise be considered to be full-time employment.

(3) Potential income. If a parent is voluntarily unemployed or underemployed, child support shall e calculated based on a determination of potential income, except that a determination of potential income should *not* be made for a parent who is physically or mentally incapacitated or is caring for a child under the age of 30 months for whom the parents owe a joint legal responsibility.

Determination of potential income shall be made by determining employment potential and probable earnings level based on the obligor's recent work history, occupational qualifications, and prevailing job opportunities and earnings levels in the community. If there is no recent work history and no higher education or vocational training, it is suggested that income be set at least at the minimum wage level. Income shall not be imputed if actual income is less due to a good faith career choice or if under-employment is temporary and is reasonably intended to result in higher income within the foreseeable future.

(4) Income verification. Income statements of the parents should be verified with documentation of both current and past income. Suitable documentation of current earnings (at least three full months) includes pay stubs, employer statements, or receipts and expenses if self-employed. Documentation of current income must be supplemented with copies of the most recent tax return to provide verification of earnings over a longer period.

SCHEDULE OF BASIC CHILD SUPPORT OBLIGATIONS

COMBINED MONTHLY ADJUSTED GROSS INCOME	ONE CHILD	TWO CHILDREN	THREE CHILDREN	FOUR CHILDREN	FIVE CHILDREN	SIX OR MORE CHILDREN
$ 100	ORDER OF $50 PER MONTH					
200						
300						
400						
500						
600						
700						
800						
850	$ 184	$ 269	$ 319	$ 352	$ 382	$ 409
900	193	282	334	369	400	428
950	202	294	349	386	418	447
1000	211	307	364	402	436	467
1050	220	320	379	419	455	486
1100	228	333	395	436	473	506
1150	237	346	410	453	491	525
1200	246	359	425	470	509	545
1250	255	372	440	487	528	565
1300	264	385	456	504	546	584
1350	273	397	471	520	564	603
1400	281	410	486	537	582	622
1450	290	422	500	553	599	641
1500	298	435	515	569	617	660
1550	307	447	530	586	635	679
1600	315	460	545	602	652	698
1650	324	472	559	618	670	717
1700	333	485	574	634	688	736
1750	341	497	589	651	705	755
1800	350	510	604	667	723	774
1850	358	522	619	683	741	793
1900	367	535	633	700	759	812
1950	375	547	648	716	776	830
2000	383	558	661	730	792	847
2050	391	570	674	745	807	864
2100	399	581	687	759	823	881
2150	407	592	700	774	839	898
2200	415	604	714	789	855	915
2250	423	615	727	803	871	931
2300	431	626	740	818	886	948
2350	439	638	753	832	902	965
2400	447	649	766	847	918	982
2450	455	660	779	861	934	999
2500	462	672	793	876	949	1016
2550	470	683	806	890	965	1033
2600	479	694	819	905	981	1050
2650	487	706	833	920	997	1067
2700	495	718	846	935	1013	1084
2750	503	729	859	950	1029	1101
2800	511	741	873	964	1045	1119
2850	519	752	886	979	1061	1136
2900	527	763	898	993	1076	1151
2950	533	772	910	1005	1089	1166
3000	540	782	921	1017	1103	1180
3050	547	792	932	1030	1116	1194
3100	554	801	943	1042	1130	1209
3150	560	811	954	1054	1143	1223
3200	567	821	965	1067	1156	1237
3250	574	831	977	1080	1171	1253
3300	581	841	989	1093	1185	1268
3350	589	851	1002	1107	1200	1284
3400	596	862	1014	1120	1214	1299
3450	603	872	1026	1133	1229	1315
3500	610	882	1038	1147	1243	1330
3550	617	892	1050	1160	1258	1346
3600	624	903	1062	1173	1272	1361
3650	631	913	1074	1187	1287	1377
3700	638	923	1086	1200	1301	1392

COMBINED MONTHLY ADJUSTED GROSS INCOME	ONE CHILD	TWO CHILDREN	THREE CHILDREN	FOUR CHILDREN	FIVE CHILDREN	SIX OR MORE CHILDREN
3750	645	934	1098	1214	1315	1408
3800	652	944	1110	1227	1330	1423
3850	660	954	1122	1240	1344	1439
3900	667	964	1135	1254	1359	1454
3950	673	973	1145	1266	1372	1468
4000	677	980	1153	1274	1381	1478
4050	682	987	1161	1283	1391	1488
4100	686	993	1169	1292	1400	1498
4150	691	1000	1177	1301	1410	1509
4200	695	1006	1185	1310	1420	1519
4250	700	1013	1193	1318	1429	1529
4300	704	1020	1201	1327	1439	1539
4350	708	1026	1209	1336	1448	1550
4400	713	1033	1217	1345	1458	1560
4450	717	1039	1225	1354	1467	1570
4500	722	1046	1233	1362	1477	1580
4550	726	1053	1241	1371	1486	1590
4600	731	1059	1249	1380	1496	1601
4650	735	1066	1257	1389	1505	1611
4700	739	1071	1262	1395	1512	1618
4750	742	1075	1267	1400	1517	1623
4800	745	1079	1271	1405	1523	1629
4850	748	1083	1276	1410	1528	1635
4900	751	1088	1280	1415	1533	1641
4950	755	1092	1285	1420	1539	1647
5000	758	1096	1289	1425	1544	1652
5050	761	1100	1294	1430	1550	1658
5100	764	1105	1298	1435	1555	1664
5150	768	1109	1303	1440	1560	1670
5200	771	1113	1307	1445	1566	1676
5250	774	1117	1312	1450	1571	1681
5300	777	1122	1316	1455	1577	1687
5350	781	1126	1321	1460	1582	1693
5400	784	1130	1326	1465	1588	1699
5450	787	1135	1331	1470	1594	1705
5500	790	1139	1336	1476	1600	1712
5550	792	1143	1341	1482	1606	1718
5600	795	1147	1346	1487	1612	1725
5650	798	1152	1351	1493	1618	1731
5700	801	1156	1356	1498	1624	1738
5750	804	1160	1361	1504	1630	1744
5800	807	1164	1365	1509	1636	1750
5850	809	1168	1370	1514	1641	1756
5900	812	1172	1375	1520	1647	1762
5950	815	1176	1380	1525	1653	1769
6000	818	1180	1385	1530	1659	1775
6050	820	1184	1390	1536	1664	1781
6100	823	1188	1394	1541	1670	1787
6150	826	1193	1400	1547	1677	1794
6200	831	1199	1407	1555	1686	1804
6250	836	1206	1415	1563	1695	1813
6300	840	1212	1422	1572	1704	1823
6350	845	1219	1430	1580	1713	1833
6400	849	1225	1437	1588	1722	1842
6450	854	1232	1445	1597	1731	1852
6500	858	1238	1452	1605	1740	1861
6550	863	1245	1460	1613	1749	1871
6600	868	1251	1467	1621	1758	1881
6650	872	1258	1475	1630	1767	1890
6700	877	1264	1482	1638	1775	1900
6750	882	1271	1491	1647	1785	1910
6800	887	1278	1499	1656	1795	1921
6850	892	1285	1507	1665	1805	1932
6900	897	1293	1515	1675	1815	1942
6950	902	1300	1524	1684	1825	1953
7000	907	1307	1532	1693	1835	1963
7050	912	1314	1540	1702	1845	1974
7100	917	1321	1549	1711	1855	1985
7150	922	1328	1557	1720	1865	1995
7200	927	1336	1565	1729	1875	2006
7250	932	1343	1573	1738	1884	2016
7300	937	1349	1581	1747	1893	2026

COMBINED MONTHLY ADJUSTED GROSS INCOME	ONE CHILD	TWO CHILDREN	THREE CHILDREN	FOUR CHILDREN	FIVE CHILDREN	SIX OR MORE CHILDREN
7350	942	1356	1588	1755	1902	2036
7400	946	1362	1596	1763	1912	2045
7450	951	1369	1603	1772	1921	2055
7500	955	1375	1611	1780	1930	2065
7550	960	1382	1619	1789	1939	2075
7600	965	1389	1626	1797	1948	2084
7650	969	1395	1634	1805	1957	2094
7700	974	1402	1641	1814	1966	2104
7750	979	1408	1649	1822	1975	2113
7800	983	1415	1657	1830	1984	2123
7850	988	1422	1664	1839	1993	2133
7900	993	1428	1672	1847	2002	2143
7950	997	1435	1679	1856	2011	2152
8000	1002	1441	1687	1864	2021	2162
8050	1006	1448	1694	1872	2030	2172
8100	1011	1454	1702	1881	2039	2181
8150	1016	1461	1710	1889	2048	2191
8200	1020	1468	1717	1898	2057	2201
8250	1025	1474	1725	1906	2066	2211
8300	1030	1481	1732	1914	2075	2220
8350	1034	1487	1740	1923	2084	2230
8400	1039	1494	1748	1931	2093	2240
8450	1043	1501	1755	1939	2102	2250
8500	1048	1507	1763	1948	2111	2259
8550	1053	1514	1770	1956	2121	2269
8600	1057	1520	1778	1965	2130	2279
8650	1062	1527	1785	1973	2139	2288
8700	1066	1533	1793	1981	2148	2298
8750	1070	1539	1800	1989	2157	2308
8800	1075	1546	1808	1998	2166	2317
8850	1079	1552	1815	2006	2175	2327
8900	1083	1558	1823	2014	2184	2336
8950	1088	1565	1830	2023	2193	2346
9000	1092	1571	1838	2031	2202	2356
9050	1096	1577	1845	2039	2211	2365
9100	1101	1583	1853	2048	2220	2375
9150	1105	1590	1860	2056	2228	2384
9200	1110	1596	1868	2064	2237	2394
9250	1114	1602	1875	2072	2246	2404
9300	1118	1609	1883	2081	2255	2413
9350	1123	1615	1890	2089	2264	2423
9400	1127	1621	1898	2097	2273	2433
9450	1131	1628	1905	2106	2282	2442
9500	1136	1634	1913	2114	2291	2452
9550	1140	1640	1920	2122	2300	2461
9600	1144	1647	1928	2130	2309	2471
9650	1149	1653	1935	2139	2318	2481
9700	1153	1659	1943	2147	2327	2490
9750	1157	1666	1950	2155	2336	2500
9800	1162	1672	1958	2164	2345	2510
9850	1166	1678	1965	2172	2354	2519
9900	1170	1685	1973	2180	2363	2529
9950	1175	1691	1981	2188	2372	2538
10000	1179	1697	1988	2197	2381	2548
10050	1183	1703	1995	2204	2389	2557
10100	1187	1709	2002	2212	2398	2565
10150	1191	1715	2008	2219	2406	2574
10200	1195	1720	2015	2227	2414	2583
10250	1199	1726	2022	2234	2422	2592
10300	1203	1732	2029	2242	2430	2601
10350	1207	1738	2036	2250	2439	2609
10400	1211	1744	2043	2257	2447	2618
10450	1215	1749	2050	2265	2455	2627
10500	1219	1755	2056	2272	2463	2636
10550	1223	1761	2063	2280	2471	2644
10600	1227	1767	2070	2288	2480	2653
10650	1231	1773	2077	2295	2488	2662
10700	1235	1778	2084	2303	2496	2671
10750	1239	1784	2091	2310	2504	2680
10800	1243	1790	2098	2318	2513	2688
10850	1247	1796	2104	2325	2521	2697
10900	1251	1802	2111	2333	2529	2706

COMBINED MONTHLY ADJUSTED GROSS INCOME	ONE CHILD	TWO CHILDREN	THREE CHILDREN	FOUR CHILDREN	FIVE CHILDREN	SIX OR MORE CHILDREN
10950	1255	1808	2118	2341	2537	2715
11000	1259	1813	2125	2348	2545	2724
11050	1263	1819	2132	2356	2554	2732
11100	1267	1825	2139	2363	2562	2741
11150	1271	1831	2146	2371	2570	2750
11200	1275	1837	2152	2378	2578	2759
11250	1279	1842	2159	2386	2586	2768
11300	1283	1848	2166	2394	2595	2776
11350	1287	1854	2173	2401	2603	2785
11400	1291	1860	2180	2409	2611	2794
11450	1295	1866	2187	2417	2619	2803
11500	1299	1871	2194	2424	2628	2812
11550	1303	1877	2201	2432	2636	2821
11600	1307	1883	2208	2440	2644	2830
11650	1311	1889	2215	2447	2653	2838
11700	1315	1895	2222	2455	2661	2847
11750	1319	1900	2229	2463	2669	2856
11800	1322	1906	2235	2470	2678	2865
11850	1326	1912	2242	2478	2686	2874
11900	1330	1918	2249	2486	2694	2883
11950	1334	1923	2256	2493	2703	2892
12000	1338	1929	2263	2501	2711	2901
12050	1342	1935	2270	2508	2719	2909
12100	1346	1940	2276	2515	2726	2917
12150	1349	1945	2283	2522	2734	2925
12200	1353	1951	2289	2529	2742	2934
12250	1357	1956	2295	2536	2749	2942
12300	1360	1961	2302	2543	2757	2950
12350	1364	1967	2308	2551	2765	2958
12400	1367	1972	2315	2558	2772	2966
12450	1371	1977	2321	2565	2780	2975
12500	1375	1983	2327	2572	2788	2983
12550	1378	1988	2334	2579	2795	2991
12600	1382	1993	2340	2586	2803	2999
12650	1386	1998	2347	2593	2811	3007
12700	1389	2004	2353	2600	2818	3016
12750	1393	2009	2359	2607	2826	3024
12800	1397	2014	2366	2614	2834	3032
12850	1400	2020	2373	2622	2842	3041
12900	1405	2026	2380	2630	2851	3050
12950	1409	2032	2387	2638	2859	3059
13000	1413	2038	2394	2646	2868	3069
13050	1417	2044	2402	2654	2877	3078
13100	1421	2050	2409	2662	2885	3087
13150	1425	2056	2416	2670	2894	3096
13200	1429	2062	2423	2678	2902	3106
13250	1433	2068	2430	2685	2911	3115
13300	1437	2074	2437	2693	2920	3124
13350	1441	2080	2445	2701	2928	3133
13400	1445	2086	2452	2709	2937	3142
13450	1449	2092	2459	2717	2945	3152
13500	1453	2098	2466	2725	2954	3161
13550	1457	2104	2473	2733	2963	3170
13600	1461	2110	2481	2741	2971	3179
13650	1465	2116	2488	2749	2980	3189
13700	1469	2122	2495	2757	2989	3198
13750	1473	2128	2502	2765	2997	3207
13800	1477	2134	2509	2773	3006	3216
13850	1481	2140	2517	2781	3014	3225
13900	1485	2146	2524	2789	3023	3235
13950	1489	2152	2531	2797	3032	3244
14000	1493	2158	2538	2805	3040	3253
14050	1497	2164	2545	2813	3049	3262
14100	1501	2170	2553	2821	3058	3272
14150	1505	2176	2560	2829	3066	3281
14200	1509	2181	2567	2836	3075	3290
14250	1514	2187	2574	2844	3083	3299
14300	1518	2193	2581	2852	3092	3308
14350	1522	2199	2589	2860	3101	3318
14400	1526	2205	2596	2868	3109	3327

COMBINED MONTHLY ADJUSTED GROSS INCOME	ONE CHILD	TWO CHILDREN	THREE CHILDREN	FOUR CHILDREN	FIVE CHILDREN	SIX OR MORE CHILDREN
14450	1530	2211	2603	2876	3118	3336
14500	1534	2217	2610	2884	3126	3345
14550	1538	2223	2617	2892	3135	3354
14600	1542	2229	2624	2900	3144	3364
14650	1546	2235	2632	2908	3152	3373
14700	1550	2241	2639	2916	3161	3382
14750	1554	2247	2646	2924	3170	3391
14800	1558	2253	2653	2932	3178	3401
14850	1562	2259	2660	2940	3187	3410
14900	1566	2265	2668	2948	3195	3419
14950	1570	2271	2675	2956	3204	3428
15000	1574	2277	2682	2964	3213	3437
15050	1578	2283	2689	2972	3221	3447
15100	1582	2289	2696	2980	3230	3456
15150	1586	2295	2704	2987	3238	3465
15200	1590	2301	2711	2995	3247	3474
15250	1594	2307	2718	3003	3256	3484
15300	1598	2313	2725	3011	3264	3493
15350	1602	2319	2732	3019	3273	3502
15400	1606	2325	2740	3027	3282	3511
15450	1610	2330	2746	3034	3289	3519
15500	1613	2334	2750	3039	3294	3525
15550	1615	2338	2755	3044	3300	3531
15600	1618	2342	2759	3049	3305	3537
15650	1621	2346	2764	3054	3311	3542
15700	1624	2350	2768	3059	3316	3548
15750	1626	2353	2773	3064	3322	3554
15800	1629	2357	2778	3069	3327	3560
15850	1632	2361	2782	3074	3332	3566
15900	1634	2365	2787	3079	3338	3572
15950	1637	2369	2791	3084	3343	3577
16000	1640	2373	2796	3089	3349	3583
16050	1643	2377	2800	3094	3354	3589
16100	1645	2381	2805	3099	3360	3595
16150	1648	2385	2809	3104	3365	3601
16200	1651	2389	2814	3109	3371	3607
16250	1654	2392	2818	3114	3376	3612
16300	1656	2396	2823	3119	3381	3618
16350	1659	2400	2828	3124	3387	3624
16400	1662	2404	2832	3129	3392	3630
16450	1665	2408	2837	3134	3398	3636
16500	1667	2412	2841	3140	3403	3641
16550	1670	2416	2846	3145	3409	3647
16600	1673	2420	2850	3150	3414	3653
16650	1675	2424	2855	3155	3420	3659
16700	1678	2428	2859	3160	3425	3665
16750	1681	2431	2864	3165	3430	3671
16800	1684	2435	2868	3170	3436	3676
16850	1686	2439	2873	3175	3441	3682
16900	1689	2443	2878	3180	3447	3688
16950	1692	2447	2882	3185	3452	3694
17000	1695	2451	2887	3190	3458	3700
17050	1697	2455	2891	3195	3463	3706
17100	1700	2459	2896	3200	3469	3711
17150	1703	2463	2900	3205	3474	3717
17200	1705	2467	2905	3210	3479	3723
17250	1708	2471	2909	3215	3485	3729
17300	1711	2474	2914	3220	3490	3735
17350	1714	2478	2918	3225	3496	3740
17400	1716	2482	2923	3230	3501	3746
17450	1719	2486	2928	3235	3507	3752
17500	1722	2490	2932	3240	3512	3758
17550	1725	2494	2937	3245	3518	3764
17600	1727	2498	2941	3250	3523	3770
17650	1730	2502	2946	3255	3528	3775
17700	1733	2506	2950	3260	3534	3781
17750	1736	2510	2955	3265	3539	3787
17800	1738	2513	2959	3270	3545	3793
17850	1741	2517	2964	3275	3550	3799
17900	1744	2521	2968	3280	3556	3805

COMBINED MONTHLY ADJUSTED GROSS INCOME	ONE CHILD	TWO CHILDREN	THREE CHILDREN	FOUR CHILDREN	FIVE CHILDREN	SIX OR MORE CHILDREN
17950	1746	2525	2973	3285	3561	3810
18000	1749	2529	2978	3290	3567	3816
18050	1752	2533	2982	3295	3572	3822
18100	1755	2537	2987	3300	3577	3828
18150	1757	2541	2991	3305	3583	3834
18200	1760	2545	2996	3310	3588	3839
18250	1763	2549	3000	3315	3594	3845
18300	1766	2552	3005	3320	3599	3851
18350	1768	2556	3009	3325	3605	3857
18400	1771	2560	3014	3330	3610	3863
18450	1774	2564	3018	3335	3616	3869
18500	1776	2568	3023	3340	3621	3874
18550	1779	2572	3027	3345	3626	3880
18600	1782	2576	3032	3350	3632	3886
18650	1785	2580	3037	3355	3637	3892
18700	1787	2584	3041	3360	3643	3898
18750	1790	2588	3046	3365	3648	3904
18800	1793	2592	3050	3370	3654	3909
18850	1796	2595	3055	3376	3659	3915
18900	1798	2599	3059	3381	3664	3921
18950	1801	2603	3064	3386	3670	3927
19000	1804	2607	3068	3391	3675	3933
19050	1807	2611	3073	3396	3681	3938
19100	1809	2615	3077	3401	3686	3944
19150	1812	2619	3082	3406	3692	3950
19200	1815	2623	3087	3411	3697	3956
19250	1817	2627	3091	3416	3703	3962
19300	1820	2631	3096	3421	3708	3968
19350	1823	2634	3100	3426	3713	3973
19400	1826	2638	3105	3431	3719	3979
19450	1828	2642	3109	3436	3724	3985
19500	1831	2646	3114	3441	3730	3991
19550	1834	2650	3118	3446	3735	3997
19600	1837	2654	3123	3451	3741	4003
19650	1839	2658	3127	3456	3746	4008
19700	1842	2662	3132	3461	3752	4014
19750	1845	2666	3137	3466	3757	4020
19800	1847	2670	3141	3471	3762	4026
19850	1850	2674	3146	3476	3768	4032
19900	1853	2677	3150	3481	3773	4037
19950	1856	2681	3155	3486	3779	4043
20000	1858	2685	3159	3491	3784	4049

CHAPTER 10

MAINTENANCE
SEPARATION AGREEMENT – PART IV

MAINTENANCE
SEPARATION AGREEMENT – PART IV

Before the court can give you a final decree of dissolution of marriage or legal separation, you must resolve and write out all the financial and parental issues remaining from your marriage. This written summary is called the separation agreement, whether you are obtaining a divorce or a legal separation. It must be read and approved by the court.

The introduction to Chapter 7 lists the things you need to do to prepare your separation agreement and directs you to the chapters with information necessary to accomplish this. This chapter discusses maintenance and how it can be a part of your separation agreement.

Maintenance

Maintenance is a series of payments (or a lump sum payment or payments) made by one spouse to the other, or to some third party (such as the Credit Union for a car loan) on behalf of the receiving spouse. The IRS refers to maintenance as "alimony" or "Section 71 (of the Internal Revenue Code) payments."

Many spouses who would or could pay maintenance shy away from the idea because they don't want to be "on the hook," are angry at the thought of supporting an ex-spouse, or don't want to feel tied to their ex-spouses. Spouses who might receive maintenance may avoid the idea because they must pay tax on it, or because they don't want to be dependent on their ex-spouse through these kinds of payments, even for a short time. For many, if not most, maintenance is an emotional subject.

Allowing your feelings to take over on this issue may prevent you from saving a great deal of money. Maintenance saves money by means of smart tax planning, just at a time when you both need it. We recommend that you read the rest of this chapter so that you understand the potential value this tool has for you before deciding whether or not you wish to use it.

Hot Words

There are certain incendiary words which can turn a healthy discussion of maintenance into an inferno. Some of them are:

"I'm entitled…"

"You've got no right…"

"You owe me…"

"I owe you nothing…"

"It's my right…"

"You don't deserve…"

This Guidebook avoids these hot words by taking a problem-solving, tax-saving approach to the question of maintenance.

 Maintenance: Money paid by one separated spouse to or on behalf of the other, also referred to as spousal support. The IRS uses the term alimony.

 Tax Significance of Maintenance

The tax significance of a maintenance payment is that it is deductible from income by the person who pays it and taxable as income to the person who receives it.

 "If we don't say anything about maintenance in our agreement, then there won't ever be any."

Possibly, but don't count on it. Unless both of you waive (give up your rights to) maintenance, in so many words, in your agreement, the court can possibly re-open the question in the future if either of you asks. If you do not want the court ever to have the power to consider maintenance, then you both need to expressly waive it.

 Spousal support: In some jurisdictions this term means maintenance or alimony.

Maintenance as an income tax shifting device is not available to partners. You may agree to a series of payments similar to maintenance, as part of your agreement, but it will not be tax deductible for the paying partner, and it may be included in income for the receiving partner. Consult your accountant about this.

 Open ended maintenance: Maintenance without either an explicit termination or total amount.

 Fixed term maintenance; Maintenance in which the total amount is either stated or calculable from its terms.

Sometimes referred to as Contractual Maintenance or Maintenance in Gross.

No Formula for Maintenance

While Colorado now has a formula for calculating temporary maintenance (for the period before your decree) for couples whose combined income is less than $75,000 per year (Chapter 4), there is no such formula for maintenance after the decree, although you may use the same formula if you wish.

None of the following statements is true:

"Maintenance is always paid to the wife for life."

"Don't ever pay maintenance – you're just opening up the door to more."

"Don't ever accept maintenance, you have to pay taxes on it."

"Maintenance has to be paid monthly."

"You can't use maintenance to pay child support or property division."

"Once you open the door to maintenance, you can't ever close it again."

"The trouble with maintenance is it locks you into a certain payment for life."

None of the following statements is necessarily true:

"Why would I pay maintenance when she's just going to get re-married."

"He/she shouldn't get maintenance, he/she doesn't need it."

"Nobody in this family needs maintenance."

"Why should I pay for her/him to go to school when she/he can work and earn his/her own living?"

"If I agree to maintenance I have to keep paying even if I lose my job."

SMART MAINTENANCE

Making maintenance work for your unique circumstances is a smart way to save money for your family. There are many ways to do this, some of which are summarized here and discussed in detail in the text that follows. Alongside each discussion is a place for you to initial whether that particular use for maintenance might work for you.

Open-ended maintenance is of unlimited or undetermined duration. It may be used for a variety of purposes including the following:

- To balance income between spouses in two households;
- To provide long term full or supplemental income for a spouse, based on need;
- To meet on-going expenses with tax-deductible dollars;
- To pay spousal support with business income.

Fixed term maintenance is paid for a designated period of time or until a certain amount of money is paid. It is generally for a specific purpose and is often referred to as contractual or in gross. It may be used for a variety of purposes including the following:

- To pay specific marital debts;
- To pay specific expenses for children or spouse;
- To pay for training, education, or therapy of a spouse;
- To supplement while a spouse's income phases in or up;
- To balance property division.

1. OPEN-ENDED MAINTENANCE

Open-ended maintenance is a maintenance plan in which the total amount to be paid in the plan cannot be calculated. Payments of this type of maintenance are usually periodic, and presumed to be modifiable as circumstances change.

a. Maintenance to Balance Income Between Spouses in Two Households

If your goal after divorce is to be able to support your children equally and/or to pay off the remaining marital debt equally, then you may accomplish this with maintenance paid by the higher income spouse to the lower income spouse. In some cases separation will cause a drastic change in lifestyle for one spouse unless some income is shifted. When both spouses are employed full time or have careers, but there is a significant difference in incomes, this kind of "income balancing" can create a foundation for an equal sharing of child support and debt payment after divorce.

Fred and Linda

Fred and Linda are the parents of two children ages 7 and 12. Fred has 70% of the family income, Linda has 30%, and this percentage is likely to continue into the foreseeable future. They have marital debts, freestanding debts not related to any piece of property, which will take three years to pay off if they make minimum payments.

If Fred pays maintenance to Linda of 20% of his gross income, Linda and Fred will then each have 50% of the family gross income. They would continue the income leveling for three years, and each contribute equally to the debt payments during that time.

If they share equal physical care of their children, there will be no child support—each of them is presumed to be paying out 50% of the children's expenses due to the 50/50 time, and that is the same as the ratio of their incomes after maintenance. See Chapter 9, Worksheet B, for how this works. They can each file head of household by agreeing to one more overnight per year of one child to each. See Chapters 9 and 11 for how this works. They can share the dependency exemptions, thus equalizing the tax effects (see Chapter 11).

If you are considering paying substantial maintenance right from the beginning ($1250 per month or $15,000 per year or more) and if you are planning to have it decrease significantly within the first three years, read Chapter 11, Taxes.

Maintenance Checklist 1b

We agree that _____ needs long term full or supplemental income because:

_____   _____
      Initials   Initials

"If we agree to monthly maintenance, nobody can change it in the future, even the court."

Not true. If maintenance is open ended, then it is presumed to be modifiable by the court on a "showing of a change of circumstances so substantial and continuing" as to render the original order unfair.

An income-leveling maintenance plan can serve to make ex-spouses literally equal partners in supporting their children and paying off the debts remaining from their marriage.

b. Maintenance to Provide Long Term Full or Supplemental Income for a Spouse, Based on Need

Long term spousal support was the original concept of alimony. The divorcing wife in a long marriage, who had dedicated her life to making a home and thus had never worked outside the home, had need of ongoing support for life or until remarriage. The value of the homemaker to the acquisition of property is also affirmed in the current statute. Maintenance of this kind often relates to the length of the marriage and the standard of living established.

Central to planning for long term maintenance is the concept of need, which is reflected in the current statute. Typically, plans of this type begin with the projected living expenses of the spouse who will receive the maintenance. If your circumstances are like any of the following examples, long term spousal support may be an appropriate solution for you.

- One of you has not worked outside the home, or not substantially so, and for reasons of age or mental and/or physical health, cannot look forward to adequate employment. This situation may call for lifetime spousal support.

- One of you is taking care of a child or other dependent whose needs require that you be constantly available, making employment outside the home inappropriate. Perhaps you have an infant you both agree should not yet be in day care, or a disabled or ill child, or an ailing parent. Your individual feelings about this situation may be very different, especially if the dependent is not a child of this marriage.

- One of you is in a line of work that pays significantly less than the other spouse's line of work, sometimes not enough to live on. One of you may be an artist, musician, small rancher or farmer, day-care provider, piece worker, or work in other in-home or "cottage" industries. Even if you both endorsed this career choice while you were together, your feelings about it at this time may be very changed. One of you may feel you are having to pay forever for someone else's career choices. The other of you may be threatened or angry at the difficulties that surround your career choice. It may feel like everyone is saying that you are less valuable or less worthy. Be certain your negotiations around the question of maintenance allow plenty of time to air these feelings and to insure that the career choices of each of you are supported by the other.

If lifetime spousal support is payable until the death of the recipient, it may be adjusted upon the retirement of the paying spouse, or when Social Security or other retirement benefits begin for either spouse, so that both parties share in the usual reduction of income experienced at retirement.

If either of you is now struggling with feelings of righteousness, distrust, anger, helplessness, being trapped, dependence, guilt, panic—you are not unusual. Most people feel some of these emotions at different times during this type of long term arrangement. It may be that this is the time for you both to seek professional help—therapists, financial counsel, mediator, medical evaluator, employment evaluator—rather than being weighed down by this emotional baggage long after the divorce is over. See "Divorce and the Legal System," Chapter 2, for resources.

c. Maintenance to Meet Ongoing Expenses
    With Tax-Deductible Dollars

Maintenance can be used to pay such on-going expenses as a spouse's (or ex-spouse's) life insurance, medical insurance, medical expenses, or to pay all or a part of a mortgage. Some of these costs may be deductible, in whole or in part, by the person who pays them, which can make this alternative particularly attractive. Medical insurance and medical expenses become deductible only after they exceed 7.5% of your adjusted gross income. The interest portion of a home mortgage payment is deductible, but only if the person paying it uses this property as a personal residence.

To investigate the possibility of paying these through maintenance, do the calculations in the following example.

Charlie and Pearl

Charlie and Pearl pay $800 per month in mortgage payments on the family home where Pearl will continue to live. $650 of the $800 is deductible interest and taxes. Pearl's life insurance premium will be $25 per month, and her health insurance premium will be $175 per month after the divorce. The money Charlie could use to pay maintenance would be taxed to him at 25% Federal, 4.63% Colorado totaling 29.63%. Pearl's maintenance income will be taxed at 15% Federal (her earned income will fill the 10% bracket), 4.63% Colorado totaling 19.63%. See Taxes, Chapter 11.

Maintenance Checklist 1c:

We are interested in using maintenance to pay the following expenses:

Expense:_____   Amount:_____

Expense:_____   Amount:_____

Expense:_____   Amount:_____

Expense:_____   Amount:_____

Expense:_____   Amount:_____

_____   _____
      Initials   Initials

Sometimes It's Maintenance Whether You Like It or Not

The IRS may treat as maintenance any payment made on behalf of a spouse which qualifies as alimony under their definition. Some examples of what you might say in your separation agreement that the husband may pay after the divorce, but that the IRS may treat as maintenance ("alimony"), even if you did not call these maintenance payments are:

• wife's health or life insurance

• wife's mortgage

• upkeep or payments on property that the wife uses but the husband still owns

This would give the husband an after-the-fact tax windfall, and the wife unexpected taxes to pay. Be clear in your agreement whether a payment is or is not taxable maintenance.

Paying Spouse Pays F.I.C.A. First

The spouse paying maintenance does not save F.I.C.A. (Social Security or Self Employment Tax) on the maintenance amount, only the Federal and State taxes. The recipient does not pay F.I.C.A. on this money.

Step 1: Add up the amount of the payments which you are considering paying as maintenance. Charlie and Pearl's total is $800 + $25 + $175 = $1,000

Step 2: Subtract Pearl's tax deductions for these payments.

$1,000 – 650 = $350. (If Pearl's medical insurance premium and medical expenses total more than 7.5% of her taxable income, she may be able to deduct some or all of the medical insurance premium. These are not large enough to be deductible in our example.)

Step 3: Subtract Pearl's tax rate from 100% (100% – 19.63% = 80.37%)

Step 4: Calculate Pearl's likely income tax on the remaining maintenance: $350 ÷ 80.37% = $435.49

$435.49 – $350 = $85.49

Step 5: Add together the payments and the remaining tax, to figure the amount to be paid as maintenance. $1,000 + $85.49 = $1085.49.

Step 6: Charlie deducts the full amount as maintenance. Charlie saves the following in taxes: $1085.49 × 29.63% = $321.63

Step 7: Calculate their overall tax savings. $321.63 - $85.49 = $236.14. Charlie and Pearl save $236.14 every month this maintenance agreement is in effect. This total monthly tax savings is money saved from the IRS. The greater the spread between your tax rates, the more you can save in taxes.

The more the amount of maintenance paid exceeds the amount the recipient pays for taxes on the maintenance, the more that spouse shares in the overall savings.

Step 8: Consider increasing the amount of maintenance in order to share the tax savings each month. For example, if Charlie paid $1125 in maintenance, his tax savings would be $333.34. Pearl would pay $93.24 in tax. Their overall savings would be $240.10 per month, of which Pearl would receive $125 and Charlie would keep $115.10.

 If Charlie and Pearl continued to own the home together, and Charlie paid the entire mortgage payment directly, the IRS might well assume that half the mortgage payment was on Pearl's behalf and therefore maintenance, and unexpectedly deduct it from Charlie's taxable income and tax Pearl on it. Charlie might not be able to deduct all or even half of the mortgage interest and property taxes because the home is no longer his principal residence.

Work with your numbers and these steps until you arrive at an arrangement which is satisfactory to both of you.

d. Maintenance Paid From Business Income

You may define your maintenance amount as a percentage of income from the paying spouse's business. This may feel exactly right if the receiving spouse has been part of the business and its development—it satisfies the feeling of getting your share of the family business. This way of defining the amount has a unique tax advantage in that it is not subject to the *recapture* rules (see

Maintenance Checklist 1d:

We are interested in exploring paying maintenance through _____ business:

_____   _____
   Initials   Initials

Chapter 11 Taxes). Although this isn't a property settlement, it can feel like one, and thereby help with accomplishing what feels like a fair division of your assets.

Since this use of maintenance is unusual, it is wise to utilize the services of an attorney and/or accountant familiar with divorce taxation and this particular use of maintenance before you enter into an agreement of this type.

2. FIXED TERM MAINTENANCE

Fixed term maintenance is a maintenance plan in which the total amount to be paid can be calculated precisely. Payments of this type of maintenance are often short term or lump sum, contractual (sometimes called "in gross"), for a specific purpose, and are presumed to be not modifiable.

a. Maintenance to Pay Specific Marital Debts

If there is a difference in your incomes—or a significant difference in the tax treatment at the same income level—then you can do some money-saving tax planning as you pay off your marital debts. Have the higher taxed spouse pay to the lower taxed spouse the amount of the debt payments plus the receiving spouse's tax on the payments. Then the lower taxed spouse makes the debt payments. You will save, outright, the difference between the paying spouse's federal income tax rate and the receiving spouse's federal income tax rate. The greater the difference in your tax rates, the larger the savings—often $.13 or more on every dollar.

Sid and Sue

Sid and Sue have some free-standing bills—not tied to, or secured by a piece of property—which will be paid in full over two and a half years if they continue to make the minimum payments. The initial total of these payments is $300 per month.

Assume Sid is in the 28% Federal tax bracket for much of his income, and Sue can absorb a good deal of income before leaving the 15% Federal tax bracket. See Chapter 11, Taxes.

If Sid initially pays $375 in maintenance (including Sue's tax burden), and Sue makes the minimum bill payments, Sid will initially deduct $375 from taxable income instead of paying the debt payment in after-tax dollars. The extra $75 paid for Sue's taxes is less than the savings on Sid's taxes through having $375 per month less in taxable income. The calculations which illustrate are as follows.

To calculate Sue's tax needs if she receives the $300 as income, divide the initial amount of maintenance by the 80.37% (which is the same as diving by .8037).

Maintenance Checklist 2a:

We are interested in using maintenance to pay the following specific debts:

Creditor	Balance	Mo. Pmts.
_____	_____	_____
_____	_____	_____
_____	_____	_____
_____	_____	_____
_____	_____	_____

_____   _____
Initials   Initials

If your maintenance, including the lump sum options, will total more than $15,000 in the first post-separation tax year, you may be running into the recapture rules. A solution might be to pay the bulk of the maintenance before your final decree, since temporary maintenance can be exempt from the recapture rules. See Chapter 10, Taxes.

(100% – [15% Fed + 4.63% State]) = 80.37%   If Sid pays $375 (slightly rounded up), he saves:

$$\frac{300}{.8037} = \$373.27$$

(28% Fed + 4.63% State) = 32.63%

$375 × .3263 = $122.36

Sid paid $75 per month more than the debt payments, but saved $47.36 per month beyond that ($122.36 – $75 = 47.36).

If the amount paid to Sue is more than $375, for example $415, then Sue has an extra $25.49, and Sid saves $27.15 overall, thereby sharing the tax savings through doing maintenance between them.

- Maintenance to pay off marital debts can stair-step down as the total of the debt payments goes down. Following the example above, the payments could be $375 at first, then $300, then $200, paralleling the total of the minimum payments plus Sue's tax needs, phasing out at the end of the two and a half years when the debts are paid in full.

- Maintenance to pay off marital debts can be paid in a steady amount for a fixed period of time—paying less than the total minimum payments in the first years, and more than the debt payment in the later years. A flat payment plan such as this has the advantage of looking more like traditional alimony to the IRS, as well as being predictable. In the above example, maintenance payments could be $200 per month for 2.5 years, if $200 were the average of debt payments plus Sue's tax needs.

- Maintenance to pay marital debts can also be paid in a lump sum, or several lump sums. In the above example, figure the total amount of debt, add to it the receiving spouse's tax on that amount, and pay it as a lump sum. The receiving spouse then pays off the debts in total. In the above example:

    12 months × 2.5 years = 30 months

    30 months × $150 = $4,500 (assuming the debt payments begin at $300 and decrease steadily to zero over the 2.5 years).

    The lower income spouse's taxes 15% + 4.63% = 19.63%. $4,500 ÷ .8037 = $5,599. (Be sure that such a large amount will not move the lower income spouse from the 15% bracket—see Chapter 11, Taxes for tables which will help you do this).

- Some marital debts are single payment debts—such as joint taxes owing for the last year of the marriage, or from an audit, or a balloon payment on a mortgage, signature loans, short-term loans from friends and family. You can use the same type of planning as on the lump sum example above.

b. Maintenance to Pay Specific Expenses
    for Children or Spouse

Maintenance can be used to indirectly pay child care. Suppose only one of you qualifies as head of household for tax purposes and therefore is the only one who can use the Child Care Credit— but you both want to share responsibility for paying for work-related child care. In order to maximize the credit, the non-head-of-household parent pays the head-of-household parent his/her portion of the child care as maintenance, and the head-of-household parent pays the child care provider. This enables the head-of-household parent to take the full amount into the formula to figure the credit, while the non-head-of-household parent deducts his/her share of the day care as maintenance. Be sure to add the receiving spouse's tax need on the maintenance to the amount of the payment if the tax rate is larger than the child care credit. See Taxes, Chapter 11, for a complete discussion of head of household status and the child care credit.

If you agree to a fixed amount for a certain number of years for this purpose, then this is contractual or fixed term maintenance, and will be presumed not to change. If your purpose is to lock it in, safe from any change, then this is the way to do it. A different result comes about if you allow the maintenance amount to fluctuate with the costs of child care. An agreement to that affect would be open-ended maintenance, preserving your ability to modify the amount as needed. However, paying child care through maintenance might look to the IRS like child support. See the next section of this chapter, and Chapter 11, Taxes. In practice, whichever kind of maintenance you are designing, don't link the provisions in your agreement about maintenance with the provisions about who pays the child care. These should be in separate sections of your written agreement.

The same kind of planning can be done around medical and dental expenses for a child which are expected to be significant (chronic asthma, braces). These expenses can't be deducted until they reach 7.5% of adjusted gross income. Since the lower income spouse is likely to reach 7.5% sooner than the higher income spouse, have the lower income parent pay the bills and the higher income parent pay his/her share as maintenance. This kind of agreement might also look to the IRS like child support (see the next section of this chapter) and could also fall under the related contingency rule if the children are approaching

Maintenance Checklist 2b:

We are interested in paying the following expenses with maintenance:

Expense:_____   Amount:_____

Expense:_____   Amount:_____

Expense:_____   Amount:_____

Expense:_____   Amount:_____

Expense:_____   Amount:_____

_____   _____
       Initials   Initials

If your plan calls for a reduction in maintenance when any child reaches the age of majority (see Chapter 8, Children for why this is a unique problem in Colorado) and/or you plan reductions in maintenance during the time any two or more of your children are between 18 and 24, see Chapter 11, Taxes about the *related contingency* rule. This rule could undo all your good planning if you do not check.

Maintenance Checklist 2c: We are interested in maintenance to pay for
_____'s training, education, or therapy as follows:

Item:_____   Cost: $_____

Item:_____   Cost: $_____

Item:_____   Cost: $_____

Item:_____   Cost: $_____

Item:_____   Cost: $_____

_____   _____
Initials   Initials

State Income Tax on Maintenance Too

Remember in your budget to add in the cost of State income tax on maintenance. The Colorado income tax rate is 4.63% for everybody— there are no tax brackets to play with here.

Maintenance Checklist 2d:

We are interested in using maintenance to supplement _____'s income as follows:

_____   _____
Initials   Initials

emancipation. See Chapter 11, Taxes. Be sure both your maintenance and child support agreements will stand on their own.

Whatever your maintenance provision, whether to pay spouse's or children's expenses, you must be absolutely clear in writing about when and under what circumstances you expect it to be modifiable, and when if ever it ends. See Chapter 13, Finishing Up.

c. Maintenance to Pay for a Spouse's Training, Education, or Therapy

Maintenance can be used to provide an opportunity to renew or rejuvenate a career, to obtain the education or training necessary to become self-supporting, or to supplement the new income as it phases in and up. If you are considering maintenance for any of these purposes, the spouse seeking maintenance should gather the following data:

• What will your training or education cost? Direct costs: tuition, books, parking?
• What are the indirect costs: babysitting, loss of income?
• What, if anything, can you earn during your training?
• How long will it take?
• What can you expect to earn once you have completed your plan?

Gathering this information can help assuage some of the feelings which often accompany this situation: anger at paying for someone else's choices; anger at needing someone else to pay for your choices; guilt; fear of poverty, failure, the unknown; concern that your children lose something during this time, and worry about not being able to make ends meet.

Tie the maintenance in your agreement directly to your purpose. For example, maintenance is payable only so long as the spouse is in school, in good standing and working toward a degree or certificate. Sometimes it is easier on the family budget if some of this is paid in a lump sum or several lump sums—from a year end bonus or other occasional or irregular income of the paying spouse. Once the recipient spouse's training is completed, the maintenance can stair-step down as the recipient's income increases.

d. Maintenance to Supplement While a Spouse's Income Phases In Or Up

If one spouse has recently re-entered the job market or changed careers, that spouse is probably earning entry-level or probationary pay, which is probably less than that person's earning potential. It may take a while for the income to build. This is such a common occurrence that it is even acknowledged in the Child Support Guideline where it says that a parent shall not be treated as under-employed if: "The employment is temporary and is reasonably intended to result in higher income within the foreseeable future;" or "The employment is a good faith career choice...."

Maintenance that stair-steps down can complement nicely a spouse's income that is stair-stepping up. Many people want to make the steps a dollar for dollar reduction: every time the receiving spouse earns a $100 a month more, the maintenance reduces by $100 the next month. Correlating the two this closely, however, can become a disincentive to the lower income spouse (and also makes it open-ended maintenance). Often it is better to agree in advance to regular decreases in maintenance over a fixed period of time, based on your best estimates of the timing of the receiving spouse's future earnings. This way everyone knows what to expect, and not expect.

e.   Maintenance to Balance a Property Division

Occasionally spouses will agree to a division of their property which makes sense to them, but which places a larger amount of property with one spouse. If that property does not include liquid assets which can be transferred readily, a compensating amount may need to be paid periodically to make the division feel fair.

Donald and Roxanne

Donald and Roxanne have divided their marital property in a manner which places $20,000 more in value on Roxanne's side of the balance sheet due to a large retirement fund which she cannot touch now. Roxanne can pay $12,000 in maintenance ($10,000 to equalize the property, plus $2,000 to pay Donald's tax on this amount). It can be a lump sum, or periodic (quarterly, monthly), depending on how Roxanne receives income. If she gets quarterly income from stock, or a twice-yealy company performance bonus, these can be a dandy source of funding for this kind of maintenance.

Be sure to disconnect this maintenance provision from the section in your agreement about division of property, since the IRS has historically frowned on paying for property with alimony. Recite in the property division section of your agreement that your division is "fair," even though it is not 50-50. Then put your maintenance agreement in another section. You may wish to state that the receiving spouse needs maintenance so that the maintenance provision stands on its own.

Maintenance Changes Child Support

Maintenance shifts before-tax (gross) income from one spouse to the other, therefore altering each parent's percentage share of child support. The result is that the child support goes down, and a larger portion of the money being paid between spouses is labeled maintenance.

Maintenance Checklist 2e:

There is an imbalance in our property division of $_____ which we are considering using maintenance to offset as follows:

_____   _____
Initials   Initials

Maintenance must not survive the death of the receiving spouse. If it does, it is deemed to be a property payment, and therefore included in the taxable income of the payor. Similarly, maintenance is presumed to end on the re-marriage of the receiving spouse. You can agree that it will not do so—but this might suggest to the IRS that it is actually part of your property division.

Purpose, Amount Needed, and Duration of Our Maintenance Plan

Directions: Fill in any of the following (1-3) uses of maintenance to which you have agreed.

1. (For maintenance use 2a through 2e above.) We will use lump sum maintenance for these specific purposes:

   in this (these) needed amount(s):

   to be paid as follows (dates):

2. (For any use of maintenance.) We will use monthly or periodic maintenance for a specific period of time for the following purposes:

   In this (these) needed amount(s):

   To be paid monthly (or other frequency):

   For the following time frame:

3. (For maintenance use 1a through 1d above.) We will use maintenance with no built-in time limit (lifetime maintenance) for the following purpose:

   In the beginning needed amount of:

IRS MAINTENANCE RULES

Since 1986, the rules about what is and is not permanent maintenance (alimony in IRS language) have simplified. In order to qualify as maintenance which will be deductible by the payor and taxable to the payee, a payment must meet the following requirements:

1. It must be in cash or cash equivalent, like a check, not property (i.e., not in-kind, like a car or horse).

2. It must be received by a spouse or former spouse, or by a third party on behalf of a spouse or former spouse, of the payor.

3. The payments must be made according to a divorce or legal separation instrument (a decree or written separation agreement).

4. You cannot be members of the same household at the time any payments are made after the final decree (see Chapter 4 for pre-decree temporary maintenance payments).

5. The obligation to make the payment cannot continue after the receiving-spouse's death.

6. The payment is not "fixed as child support." See also the related contingency rule in Chapter 11, Taxes.

7. You have not said anywhere in your agreement (see 3. above) that these payments are not to receive maintenance tax treatment.

Before you finish your maintenance agreement, be certain it meets all these criteria.

ORGANIZING YOUR INCOME AND EXPENSES

Since many kinds of maintenance are based on the ability of the paying spouse to pay, as well as on the needs of the receiving spouse, you must be knowledgeable of your incomes and expenses in order to develop a sound maintenance plan. Review the Income Charts and IF Budgets you prepared for Chapter 5, and update them as needed. If you prepared IF Budgets while designing a temporary agreement (Chapter 4), review and update them now.

PUTTING YOUR MAINTENANCE PLAN TOGETHER

Putting together a smart maintenance plan for your unique circumstances requires that you consider carefully each of the following:

- purpose
- amount needed
- duration
- stair-step, if any;
- circumstances under which it is modifiable, if any;
- tax consequences and amount to be paid;
- circumstances under which it terminates, if any;
- security or teeth.

Following is a discussion of each of these, with examples. Write the elements of your own plan in the sidebar.

Purpose, Amount, and Duration

Review any of the ways to use maintenance at the beginning of this chapter in which either of you indicated interest. How many ways to use maintenance are still of interest to you both? Review and discuss these. Write in detail each purpose for which you both agree to use maintenance. For each purpose, calculate the amount needed based on your Income Charts and IF Budgets in Chapter 5.

- If one of your purposes for maintenance is to level incomes or supplement income to the lower income spouse, then use the Budget Analysis Chart in Chapter 4. This chart will compare the incomes and budgets in your two homes.

- If your purpose for maintenance is to supplement income to the lower income spouse for a specific purpose, you will base your analysis on that spouse's IF Budget. For example, write down the amount for tuition, books, transportation, parking, and children's day care for a spouse entering college. Estimate the budget needs for the lower income spouse for the immediate future.

- If another purpose for maintenance is to pay specific expenses, be sure you look on both IF Budgets. It is possible that a certain expense is now being paid by the "wrong" spouse. Perhaps this expense might be better paid by the other spouse with money received as maintenance.

Stair Steps and Modification

The next step after determining the purpose, amount and duration of your maintenance, is to decide if and under what circum-

Our Stair Steps

Directions: Complete the following statement as needed to reflect your unique circumstances.

We foresee predictable changes (for example, completion of degree, quitting school, payoff of a debt, child no longer needs day care, receiving spouse's income increases in a predictable amount, specific length of time from decree) in the amount of our maintenance as follows:

Future Changes

Directions: Complete the following statement as needed to reflect your unique circumstances.

We agree that the amount of our maintenance may be re-examined and adjusted by us if the following (for example, unforeseen changes in either income or expenses) happens:

Calculating The Amount To Be Paid

We make the following calculations to determine the tax as well as the amount to be paid for our proposed maintenance:

Therefore our initial maintenance amount to be paid is:

stances the amount should change. You can agree ahead of time to change the amount on the occurrence of a certain event, or after certain periods of time, or when your incomes change in certain ways, or some other circumstance.

You may want the amount to change when the purpose is satisfied, in whole or in part. You may set the modification amounts now, not to be changed regardless of future occurrences for either spouse. For example, you anticipate that the receiving spouse's income will increase in fairly predictable increments, so you plan for maintenance to phase down at a certain amount per month each year, whether or not either spouse actually earns according to the plan. This is a clear stair-step plan.

If you anticipate future changes for either spouse, instead of stair-stepping the amount as above, you can plan your future changes based on a formula. For example, maintenance will decrease by a percentage of the amount of increase in the receiving spouse's income.

Lastly, you can agree now to review and adjust your maintenance plan in the event circumstances arise later which you cannot foresee now. For example, the paying spouse loses his or her job, illness changes the earning capacity of either of you, or one or several of the assumptions on which you based your maintenance agreement do not prove true, such as your career choices do not produce the income you anticipated.

For more on the question of modifying maintenance after the final decree, see Chapter 13.

Tax Consequences and Amount to be Paid

Now that you know how much maintenance needs to be received, for how long and under what circumstances, you need to calculate how much needs to be paid. To do that you must look at the projected tax status of each of you and the tax effect of your proposed maintenance plan.

Once you have reached agreement about Maintenance you may want to include this agreement in your draft separation agreement using the sample provisions in Chapter 12. The remaining sections of this chapter discuss some important elements of fine tuning.

Termination of Maintenance

Maintenance is presumed to end on the death or re-marriage of the recipient. You are required to state this in your agreement if your state law does not also presume this. Colorado does, but it is good practice to include it anyway.

Can maintenance survive the death of the payor? There is no presumption about this. Many people secure a maintenance obligation with life insurance on the life of the payor. Some people create an annuity tied to the life of the payor, payable to the recipient.

If your agreement to pay maintenance arises from your division of property, you might wish the payments to continue beyond the re-marriage of the recipient. In this case, you must say so in your agreement. It is also possible to agree that maintenance is to be neither deductible to the payor nor taxable to the payee. In circumstances where the spouses are in the same tax brackets there are circumstances under which you might not want the presumed tax treatment to happen.

Long term maintenance frequently terminates at the retirement of the paying spouse, especially if the division of property included divisions of retirement or pension monies via QDRO, or if the receiving spouse has sufficient Social Security. See Chapter 7.

Some couples prefer to define their goals for maintenance and set an amount for the first year only. They then meet toward the end of that year to adjust the amount according to their pre-defined criteria.

Life Insurance as Security for Maintenance

You may secure the payment of maintenance with insurance on the life of the paying spouse. To figure the amount of insurance to get, take the amount of the payments times the maximum number of months it could be paid. The maximum total amount which could be paid is probably the initial amount of the death benefit. This can be decreasing term insurance, i.e., the death benefit decreases each year over the term of the maintenance.

Cohabitation

When divorcing couples are putting together an agreement about maintenance (spousal support) which will last for some time after the final decree, they usually end up in a discussion of cohabitation sooner or later. As with many things divorcing couples argue about, the word doesn't convey the real issue. The paying spouse wants the maintenance to end when the receiving spouse is married or living in a marriage-like arrangement. The thinking being that he or she should not pay for a former spouse if that spouse is living in an arrangement which implies that someone else is

Our Plan for Terminating Maintenance

Directions: Complete the following statement as needed to reflect your unique circumstances.

We agree that our maintenance will end under the following circumstances:

Former Spouse's Medical Insurance – COBRA

Since 1986, every employer of more than 25 employees who is subject to the Federal law called "E.R.I.S.A", (The Employee Retirement Income Security Act of 1974), has been required to allow divorced spouses of their employees to continued coverage under the same health insurance policy by which they have been covered as the spouse of an employee. The non-employee spouse pays the premium, which may not be more than 105% of the full premium (including the amount the employer may have been paying on behalf of an employee as a benefit). Employers are now required to tell any employee what the cost of this "COBRA" (The Consolidated Omnibus Budget Reconciliation Act of 1985), option would be for their ex-spouse after a divorce. This option is available for thirty-six months from the date of the final decree. Since the ex-spouse does not have to qualify for this insurance, no "pre-existing" conditions will prevent him/her from being insured. Remember, you may use maintenance to pay the premiums.There is usually a time limit within which to activate the COBRA insurance provision for a former spouse. Missing the deadline can be fatal to your agreement. So, be certain to check with the employer and insurer long before you put pen to paper.

Social Security Eligibility in 10-Year Marriage

Once you have been married for 10 years or more, both spouses have the option of having their Social Security benefit at retirement calculated on either their own earnings or on those of their former spouse. If you choose the latter, the benefit is half of that of the former spouse. It is an independent entitlement and does not reduce the benefit to the former spouse. To collect this benefit you must apply for it and be at least 62, and divorced for at least two years and not have remarried before age 60 (or have terminated that second marriage).

taking care of or sharing expenses with the former spouse. From the receiving spouse's point of view, a co-habitation provision may feel like the former spouse is trying to tell him or her how to live —or at least trying to dictate the seriousness of his or her new sexual relationship.

The cohabitation label arose in states which do not recognize common law marriage. Therefore, a former spouse could, and did, go on receiving maintenance while in a new relationship which was a marriage in all but the name. Colorado recognizes common law marriage, so many former spouses who live with someone of the opposite sex whom they treat as a spouse may be married by their actions. You could agree that maintenance ceases if the receiving spouse remarries, whether ceremonial or common law.

The real issue is one of economic self-sufficiency, not of sex. For example, you might say that maintenance would cease or decrease within a certain time after the receiving spouse shares the home with an able-bodied adult who is, or is capable of, contributing to basic expenses like housing, utilities, and food. It should not matter what sex this person is, or what the relationship is to the receiving spouse. Such a person could be a relative or a paying boarder. Try to find language for your agreement about when maintenance ceases which focuses on money and not behavior.

TEETH TO MAINTAIN YOUR MAINTENANCE AGREEMENT

If your ex has a new lover, will you be less likely to pay the maintenance? Will you be less likely to pay the debts you agreed to pay through maintenance? If you lose your job, or the bonus does not come through, will you look for a way out of your agreement to pay maintenance? Would any of these be tempting for you?

There are several kinds of internal enforcement which can be used in maintenance agreements. What we call "teeth" are voluntary, private, and effective ways of penalizing yourselves with more or less costly consequences if you don't do what you say you will do. What does each of you need to put into your agreement to make sure you keep the promises you make to each other with regard to maintenance? These incentives to right behavior are limited only by your imagination. Try having the person against whom the penalty would act set the penalty. You may be surprised to learn what motivates each of you.

Agreements you might try: if the maintenance payment is not made on time, the paying spouse loses the tax deduction, and the recipient does not have to declare it as income. Or, if the maintenance is not used for the agreed-upon purpose (paying the house payment), the maintenance will cease, or reduce, and the spouse who was paying maintenance has first option to assume the obligation and receive the property.

It may or may not be appropriate for you to put such strict punishments in your own agreement. That's your decision. But, if you begin right away treating your agreement as a very serious bargain between the two of you, there will be less chance that you will be tempted to take it lightly later on.

Conclusion

You have now finished your first rough look at your maintenance plan. It will probably not be your final version. Go on to the next chapter about taxes if you have not already read it. The agreements you reach as a result of the tax chapter may necessitate changes in your maintenance plan.

Take heart. Doing your own separation agreement is hard work. Don't expect to get it all done in one sitting. Don't even expect to complete the work of one of the separation agreement chapters in one sitting. Give yourself and each other the time you deserve to make the best decisions for your family.

TAXES
SEPARATION AGREEMENT – PART V

Reading this chapter is 90% likely to save you money; not reading it is 100% likely to cost you money.

"The art of taxation consists in so plucking the goose as to obtain the largest possible amount of feathers with the smallest possible amount of hissing." Attributed to Jean Baptiste Colbert. (c. 1665).

"The wisdom of man never yet contrived a system of taxation that would operate with perfect equality." Andrew Jackson, Proclamation to the People of South Carolina, Dec. 10, 1832.

"Taxes, after all, are the dues that we pay for the privilege of membership in an organized society." Franklin D. Roosevelt, Worcester, Mass., Oct. 21, 1936.

 A partner's tax filing status is either single, or head of household if you have a dependent living with you. That doesn't change when partners move apart. Partners in Colorado who file married filing jointly (or married filing separately) are probably common law married (see Chapter 1).

TAXES
SEPARATION AGREEMENT – PART V

Before the court can give you a final decree of dissolution of marriage or legal separation, you must resolve and write out all the financial and parental issues remaining from your marriage. This written summary is called the separation agreement, whether you are obtaining a divorce or a legal separation. It must be read and approved by the court.

The introduction to Chapter 7 lists the things you need to do to prepare your separation agreement and directs you to the chapters with information necessary to accomplish this. This chapter discusses taxes and tax planning as a part of your separation agreement.

The Tax Effects of Divorce

There are many tax effects of divorce which will happen whether or not you plan for them. There may be a profound change in your incomes; there certainly will be a profound change in their taxability. Dollars which are exempted or deducted from taxable income will change, as will your tax filing status and the tax credits for which you are eligible. Unique to divorce is the concept of maintenance (alimony), the tax rules for which are discussed in this chapter. Property that is transferred between spouses as part of a divorce is not taxed as though it were sold, but any built-in capital gain is a factor to be considered in your bargaining about that property, as you can see in Chapter 7.

The four aspects of your taxes which are impacted by your divorce are:
- filing status
- exemptions
- deductions
- credits

Following is a brief discussion of each.

Tax Filing Status

The IRS taxes income in percentages: the first and lowest portion of your income is taxed at 10%; the second and higher portion, over a certain threshold, at 15%; and above that at 25%, then 28%, then 33%, and then at 35%. Your tax filing status determines how much of your income is taxed at each of these percentages.

There are four statuses: *married filing jointly, married filing separate, single,* and *head of household*. Married filing jointly permits the largest amount of income to be taxed at 10% and 15%. In married filing separately, the smallest amount of income is taxed at 10% and 15% before the percentage changes to 25%. You have probably been filing in one of these statuses. Your current withholding rate at work is probably based on the assumption that you will continue to file in that status, so it is important to begin your tax planning early in your negotiations.

Table of Tax Brackets for 2003*

Tax Rate	Single Over — But not over	Head of Household Over — But not over
10%	0-$7,000	0-$10,000
15%	$7,000-28,400	$10,000-38,050
25%	$28,400-68,800	$38,050-98,250
28%	$68,800-143,500	$98,250-159,100
33%	$143,500-311,950	$159,100-311,950
35%	$311,950	$311,950
Standard Deduction*	$4,750	$7,000

Tax Rate	Married Filing Joint Over — But not over	Married Filing Separate Over — But not over
10%	0-$14,000	0-$7,000
15%	$14,000-56,800	$7,000-28,400
25%	$56,800-114,650	$28,400-57,325
28%	$114,650-174,700	$57,325-87,350
33%	$174,700-311,950	$87,350-155,975
35%	$311,950	$155,975
Standard Deduction*	$9,500	$4,750

*Revised after passage of the 2003 tax cut bill.

Initially, your choices for tax filing status are determined by your marital status on December 31st. If your final decree of dissolution (divorce) was signed on or before December 31, then you are single for that tax year, and must file as single or head of household. You no longer have a choice of filing married.

If you remain married through December 31, you may file married filing jointly or married filing separately. If you were still married on December 31st, but you have been separated for more than six months, you have the additional option of filing as head of household if you qualify.

Tax filing status: Category in which your taxes are figured which determines how much of your income is taxed at what percentage. For example: married filing jointly.

"If we were married for most of the year, then we have to file our taxes as married."

No. You file your tax returns according to your marital status on December 31st. If your divorce was final that day you may not file as married. There may be some tax advantages for you in filing separately because only then can you do planning through maintenance. See Chapter 10.

Uneasiness About Tax Returns

You are both legally responsible for any tax return you sign. Separation, when emotions are running high and expenses running even higher, is a time when people are tempted to be unwise on their tax returns (by exaggerating deductible expenses, claiming doubtful deductions, or "forgetting" to list income). If either of you is likely to be less forthcoming than the other, consider filing Married Separate, so you are not legally bound by a tax return you are uncomfortable with. This might cost you some additional tax, but the peace of mind may be worth it.

Finalizing your divorce before or after December 31st may have enormous consequences for this tax year. You can put off finalizing your divorce until after the first of the year if you will save money by filing jointly. You might choose to finalize your divorce before the end of the year if at least one of you will save money by filing as head of household.

Head of household status is the most favorable way to file for divorced or separated persons because it results in the least amount of tax. The head of household income brackets are higher for every tax rate below 35% as compared to those for single filers; so more earnings are allowed to be taxed at the lower rate. The standard deduction is also higher for head of household than for single.

A single taxpayer may file as head of household if he or she provides a household for more than half the year for any legal dependant. Still-married persons who have been separated for more than six months may file as head of household if they provide a household for a dependent child.

Tax Exemptions

A tax exemption is an opportunity to take out, or exempt, a certain amount from your taxable income. The exemption commonly discussed in divorce cases is the *dependent exemption*. This is a fixed amount per person, one for each parent, one for each child. The exemption for any given child cannot be split—one parent gets it for a full tax year. If you have one child you may alternate years, but you must each adjust your withholding every year. If you have more than one child, you may allocate the exemptions between you. The amount of the personal or dependent exemption varies annually and is available by calling the IRS ($3,050 in 2003 and $3,100 in 2004).

The IRS will presume that the parent who has more overnights with a child gets the dependency exemption for that child. But the exemption can be allocated to the other parent, and can be bargained for. Consider whether it will help the family budget or ease a significant tax burden for the non-residential parent to have the exemption this time.

The dependency exemption and the head of household filing status are not the same thing. They are two separate lines on your tax return. To declare head of household status, you must list at least one qualifying person as your dependent, which means that your home was that person's principal place of abode for that tax year. The qualifying person is often a child. You are NOT required to

---

"Filing head of household means that I get the tax exemptions for our children."

This is a frequent misunderstanding. Your filing status and dependent exemptions are different. The dependent exemptions may be taken by either parent, if you agree. The IRS will presume they go to the head of household parent unless you agree otherwise.

Tax exemption: Category of income on which you are not taxed. For example, the personal exemption for yourself and members of your family.

If You Don't Do This, It Won't Happen

Judges do not have to take into account the anticipated tax consequences when they decide divorce cases. Many lawyer-negotiated settlements do not consider this, either. Working together, you have the advantage of being able to do tax planning.

also list that child as your tax exemption. See form 1040 on the next page. Note the difference between line 4 and lines 6 c and d.

If you wish the dependency exemption to be claimed by the parent who does not name that child as the basis for his or her head of household filing status, the head of household parent for that child must sign IRS form 8332. Both parents must file a copy with their tax return. See form 8332 on the next page.

Note that IRS form 8332, shown on the following page, allows you to select whether the exemption will be claimed for one year, or for future years. Since things change, expecially where children are concerned, doing this release one year at a time probably makes sense.

Both parents taking the same child as either a dependent or basis for head of household status will absolutely cause an audit by the IRS and may trigger a penalty. Be very clear about these arrangements in your agreement.

Begin with the assumption that the parent who has a child for more than half the overnights per year will file as head of household, claim the child care credit, and have the dependent exemption for that child. If you want to reverse the last of these—to balance the tax benefits of having children, or as part of your overall bargaining—you may do so by using IRS Form 8332.

Tax Deductions

A deduction is an amount you are allowed to subtract from your taxable income before you figure your tax. Some common examples are: interest you paid on your home mortgage, certain taxes and a certain percent of medical and dental costs beyond insurance coverage and medical and dental insurance premiums. These deductions are shown on Schedule A—Form 1040 if you itemize your deductions. Follow Schedule A to estimate your itemized deductions, compare this to the standard deduction in your tax filing status. You will probably want to use the higher of these.

Certain additional expenses, such as tax preparation, tax advice, and certain accounting and other fees, are deductible to the extent they exceed 2% of your adjusted gross income. Some portions of your divorce expenses—for attorney, accountant, mediator—may be deductible in this category. Be sure you seek expert advice on this point as these deductions are not clearly defined in the tax code.

If you have few deductions and choose not to itemize, or are filing the short form tax return (1040 EZ), you may take a "standard deduction." The amount of the standard deduction changes annually and varies with your tax status, the highest one being for head of household. You can learn the amount of the current standard deduction for each filing status by requesting this information from IRS or your payroll department. 2003 amounts are on the Table of Tax Brackets earlier in this chapter.

Tax Credits

A tax credit is just what the name implies. You subtract it (give yourself credit) from the amount of tax you would otherwise pay (bottom line on your income tax return). The child care credit is the most significant one for divorcing or separated parents of young children.

The child care credit is a fixed percentage (varying from 20-35% for up to two children) of the day care amount paid out by single parents while they are at work or seeking work. For divorcing couples the credit is linked to having head of household tax filing status. The qualifying "dependent (child)" is defined the same way. Therefore, even in your very early tax planning you must be careful that the parent who would benefit most from the credit will be able to file as head of household for that child. The parent with head of household filing status for a child must

Tax deduction: Specific expenditures which may be deducted from your income before figuring your tax. For example, the interest portion of your home mortgage is a deduction.

A tax deduction is not the same as a tax exemption.

IRS requires that when one married spouse, filing separately, itemizes his/her deductions, so must the other spouse.

"If I pay the mortgage, I get the deduction."

It's not that simple. In addition to actually making the payments, the home must be your primary residence, and your name must be on the mortgage.

Tax credit: A percentage of certain expenditures which may be subtracted from your tax. For example, a percentage of what one pays for work-related child care is a credit against income tax.

The tax reduction act of 2003 overlaps with those of 2001 and 2002, so that some reductions and increases phase in and then phase out. The child tax credit, for example, was increased to $1,000 for 2003 and 2004, then falls to $700 in 2005, to gradually increase to $1,000 in 2010. "The result is a roller coaster of rate and other changes between now and 2010." CCH Incorporated, 2003.

be the one to pay for child care of that child. You can't take credit for something you didn't pay.

There is no child care credit if you have a "cafeteria plan." See Chapter 9.

You can use either the child care credit or a cafeteria (flex) plan, but not both. A cafeteria or flex plan allows the employee to pay for child care and family medical expenses from pre-tax dollars which are withheld by the employer and escrowed or held in trust for the benefit and use of the employee and his or her family. The child care credit effectively does the same thing, by returning to you the tax money already paid on dollars used to pay for work-related child care. A cafeteria plan can, like maintenance, shift the tax benefits of child care to the non-head-of-household parent.

"If I pay the day care, I get the child care credit."

It's not that simple. For divorcing couples, in addition to making the payment to the care giver, you must also qualify and file as head of household—using the same child for whom you are paying the day care as the basis for your head of household filing status.

You will use IRS form 2441 to claim the child care credit. You can calculate the amount of your credit by using the Child Care Credit Table in Chapter 9.

There are other fairly new credits in additon to the child care credit. The child tax credit for 2003 and 2004 of $1,000 per child under 17 goes to the parent who claims the child as a dependent exemption. It "phases out", disappears slowly, at higher incomes. In 2005, the child tax credit is scheduled to fall back to $700, but increases to $1000 by 2010.

There are two education credits. For students in their first and second year of college, graduate school, or vocational training, the Hope scholarship credit refunds to the paying parent up to $1500 per year for college expenses (tuition, fees, books, but not room and board or transportation).

You can estimate the amount of your child care credit by using the child care credit table in Chapter 9.

The Lifetime Learning credit rebates up to 20 percent of the first $10,000 of qualified tuition expenses for 2003 and thereafter, for college, graduate school, and job training for children and adults. It goes to the person who pays the expense.

Both education credits phase out for persons earning between $41,000 to $51,000 or households in the $83,000 to $103,000 range.

Estimate Your Taxes

Unless you have agreed to 50/50 physical care of more than one child, or you have physical care of at least one child each, only one of you will qualify for the child care credit—the one with more overnights for that child.

Taking into account the tax consequences of your proposed plan is essential to a workable final agreement. As you have seen from the previous sections of this chapter, the tax consequences happen whether you plan for them or not. Misunderstanding or ignoring the tax consequences of your plan can unravel it altogether.

Pre-test your divorce plan to be sure you know your tax result for the next year, or to be sure you have the best overall tax result. Use a current federal income tax form 1040 to estimate taxes for each of you, and be sure you have budgeted for how you will pay them. You may need to revise the W-4 instructions to the employer about witholding from your paycheck or adjust the amounts of your estimated tax payments if you are self-employed. If you can't figure out how to do it yourself, most tax accountants will do an estimated tax calculation for you if you give them your agreement draft and ask them to check for glaring errors or unforseen traps.

Maintenance Recapture

Your maintenance agreement must meet the IRS rules for what is "alimony". See Chapter 10.

There are some circumstances under which the IRS may void your maintenance arrangement and *recapture* the payments into the income of the paying spouse. This not only voids the tax savings back to the beginning, but, since it is usually discovered later (often in an audit), may incur interest and penalties as well. These circumstances are contained in two *recapture rules:*

1. Maintenance must not decrease more than the rules allow in the first three years if paid from an income source within payor's control; this can be referred to as the "Steep Stair-Step" rule;

2. Maintenance must not reduce on the "happening of a contingency relating to a child" or a "time which can clearly be associated with [such] a contingency;" this can be referred to as the "Related Contingency" rule.

THE STEEP STAIR-STEP RULE

This rule applies to all cases where maintenance is being paid, whether or not there are children. The "steep stair-step" rule was designed to prevent "front-end loading"—a large amount of maintenance being paid in the first year of the divorce, and then reduced rapidly within the first 3 years. Its purpose is to catch divorcing taxpayers who are trying to transfer their property settlement as maintenance in order to gain a tax deduction. Since this is some of the tax planning smart couples need do at this time, this is an important rule to be mindful of.

The Internal Revenue Code says that $15,000 per year is the cut-off point, so if you plan to pay less than this amount in maintenance you are in the "safe harbor," as accountants frequently call it. The IRS will examine alimony plans for "front-loading" for three years. So, if you plan maintenance payments over $15,000

Alimony: The name the IRS uses for maintenance.

If you are considering maintenance of $15,000 or more to be paid before December 31st of the year of your separation, **you must read this section**.

Separate Households Required for Maintenance After the Decree

You must actually live in separate households before or within 30 days of your first permanent maintenance payment.

If you are considering paying substantial maintenance— $1250 per month or $15,000 per year or more—and you are planning to have it decrease significantly during the first 3 years, **you must read this section**.

"First post-separation year:" defined by the IRS as the first calendar year in which payments which the IRS will recognize as "alimony" are paid. This means the first year in which payments are made which fit the rules in Chapter 10. Note the different rules regarding pre-decree temporary maintenance, depending on whether it is part of a court order. See Chapters 4 and 10.

CONFUSED YET?

Payments made BEFORE divorce, by a written separation agreement which is NOT made into a court order DO count in the maintenance considered in this recapture rule. BEFORE-divorce-maintenance paid by a written agreement which IS made into a court order does NOT count.

IRS publishes lots of pamphlets about all aspects of tax law and practice. Two particularly useful publications for separating couples are: *Divorced or Separated Individuals,* Publication 504 and *Selling Your Home,* Publication 523, which contains details on capital gains calculations for many situations too detailed to cover here: Armed Forces personnel, recapture of Federal subsidies, etc.

"We have to write up our temporary agreement and take it to the court in order for the IRS to honor our temporary maintenance."

Not quite. The law does not require that you have your temporary agreement made into a court order. You may do so if you wish. To be maintenance, for IRS purposes, it must be by court order or by written agreement.

a year which will decrease, don't decrease them more than the rules allow during the first three years.

According to this rule, maintenance payments in the first year cannot exceed the average payments for the second and third years by more than $15,000. And payments in the second year cannot exceed payments in the third year by more than $15,000. This rule essentially applies to planned excess payments, but paying late (for whatever reason) can trigger a recapture if the payment is made in the next calendar year.

There is no recapture because of:
>   death;
>   remarriage;
>   temporary payments;
>   or because the payment is based on a percent payment from income or business profits for at least three years.

If there's any chance your maintenance plan might violate this rule, complete the following worksheet. This is the official form from the IRS's own publication *Divorced or Separated Individuals,* Publication 504.

Worksheet for Recapture of Alimony

Note: Do not enter less than zero on any line.

1. Alimony paid in **2nd year** ...... _____

2. Alimony paid in **3rd year** .... _____

3. Floor $15,000

4. Add lines 2 and 3.................... _____

5. Subtract line 4 from line 1 .... _____

6. Alimony paid in **1st year** .... _____

7. Adjusted alimony paid in **2nd year** (line 1 less line 5) ... _____

8. Alimony paid in **3rd year** .... _____

9. Add lines 7 and 8 .... _____

10. Divide line 9 by 2 .... _____

11. Floor $15,000

12. Add lines 10 and 11 .... _____

13. Subtract line 12 from line 6 .... _____

14. **Recaptured alimony.** Add lines 5 and 13 .... _____

Your result on Line 14 is the amount to be recaptured—taxed to the person who paid it and deducted from the income of the person who received it. Perform this test on your maintenance plan. If your result on Line 14 is zero or negative, there will be no recapture under this rule. If your result is positive, adjust the amounts to be paid under your agreement to avoid recapture.

Any amount paid as temporary maintenance before the decree, so long as it is by court order, does *not* have to be counted in this rule. A solution to the problem of high up-front maintenance is to pay as much as you can before the decree, where there is no recapture. If you want to start the 3-year clock running, begin the payments before the decree, by written agreement, and do not have that agreement made into a court order.

THE RELATED CONTINGENCY RULE

This rule applies to cases with minor children, in which there is a blurring of the distinction between maintenance and child support.

If your plan calls for a reduction in maintenance when any child reaches the age of majority and/or you plan reductions in maintenance within one year of when your children reach the same age between 18 and 24, **you must read this section**.

The IRS restricts child-support-as-maintenance by applying two rules to any **reductions** in maintenance which are measured by events that may be tied to your children. (See "Who is a Child?" in Chapter 8 for a discussion of the presumed age of emancipation in Colorado.) The first circumstance under which the IRS will *presume* a relationship between the reduction in maintenance and children is if the reduction occurs when a child reaches a certain income level, leaves the household, becomes employed, dies, marries, or leaves school. Second is if the reduction occurs within six months on either side of the date any child reaches 18 or 21, or if there are two or more children and two or more reductions in maintenance occur when two children reach the same chronological age between 18-24 (or within a year of the same age).

Example: Mary and Tom have two daughters, Sarah (12) and Michele (18). Mary and Tom must make sure that if they reduce maintenance one year either side of when Michele turns 20, that they do not also reduce maintenance one year either side of when Sarah turns 20.

In either of these circumstances the IRS will presume the reductions were contingent on a child reaching a certain age and will disallow the amounts of all reductions as maintenance and treat them, retroactively, as child support. IRS will recapture the amount of all such reductions—all the way back to the beginning. Even including a separate amount of child support is not enough to stop these rules.

Maintenance Changes Child Support

Maintenance shifts before-tax (gross) income from one spouse to the other, therefore altering each parent's percentage share of child support. The result is that the child support goes down, and a larger portion of the money being paid between spouses is labeled maintenance. This can be helpful, because paying maintenance is tax deductible, and child support is not.

Before you throw your hands in the air and give up any hope of an agreement for reducing maintenance when your children are leaving the nest, try making the reductions clearly contingent on something which has nothing whatsoever to do with your children. For example: Make the reductions occur regularly over a long period of time, beginning before any child reaches the "dangerous" age range, and continue the payments past the time the last child could possibly have emancipated. Or, make the contingency which triggers the reduction something related to one of you (for example, 2, 4, 6, 8, and 10 years from the date of the decree, when the recipient remarries, when the paying spouse retires, or when there is a change in income for either of you).

Another way is to state specific dates for reduction of maintenance which are not within 6 months (before or after) of any child's 18th, 19th, or 21st birthday.

But note the downside: if your child or children are emancipated at any unexpectedly early date, the maintenance payments will continue until the date you specify. Decide whether this is too high a price to pay for the tax savings.

It is possible to *rebut* the IRS presumption of relatedness of the reductions in maintenance with a solid, independent reason for the reductions occurring when you agreed to. Then, if the reductions just happen to fall in the danger zone, you can plead coincidence, that you did not plan it that way, and weren't even thinking about how old your children would be and whether they were nearing emancipation. Remember, the IRS will presume the *relatedness* of your planned maintenance reductions and your children's emancipation, if the dates of the reduction(s) fall within a corresponding time. Overcoming any IRS presumption is very hard to do.

Conclusion

You have now finished your first rough look at your tax plan. It will probably not be your final version. Review now Chapters 7-10, the other four separation agreement chapters, and revise or adjust your tentative agreements according to your tax plan, moving toward reaching your final agreement. The sample clauses in Chapter 12 should help you with drafting.

Take heart. Doing your own separation agreement is hard work. Don't expect to get it all done in one sitting. Don't even expect to complete the work of one of the separation agreement chapters in one sitting. Give yourself and each other the time you deserve to make the best decisions for your family.

CHAPTER 12

THE FINAL COURT PAPERS

Decree:
Final order signed by the court granting your dissolution of marriage or legal separation.

Checklist of Our Final Court Papers

Directions: Initial each document you agree to be responsible for preparing, and write in the date you will have it ready.

Person responsible	Date promised	Document
_____	_____	Husband's Financial Affidavit
_____	_____	Wife's Financial Affidavit
_____	_____	Separation Agreement and / or including a Parenting Plan
_____	_____	Affidavit for Decree Without Appearance
_____	_____	Support Order
_____	_____	Decree
_____	_____	Written Agreement to Divide Retirement
_____	_____	QDRO
_____	_____	Child Support Worksheet ___
_____	_____	Child Support Worksheet ___
_____	_____	Notice to Withhold Income for Support
_____	_____	Certificate of Attendance from parenting-after-divorce class (if ordered)

The Final Court Papers

When you ask the court to sign your final decree of dissolution of marriage or legal separation, you must provide the court with some or all of the forms in this chapter.

Everyone, with or without children, needs the following:

- **Proof of Service,** if the case is not a co-petitioner filing. This will be either a signed Waiver or Certificate of Service from the back of the Summons, or it will be a copy of the Order permitting service by certified mail or publication with proof of certified mail or a copy of the publication with the last date published. See Chapter 6 if any of this is a surprise.

- An **Affidavit with Respect to Financial Affairs (No. 253)** from each of you, signed and notarized. You may use the **Financial Affidavit—Simplified Version (JDF 1112)** for couples with no children or maintenance.

- A typed **Separation Agreement**, double-spaced, on 8 ½ x 11" paper, with both of your notarized signatures. Chapters 7-11 of this Guidebook show you how to develop this and this chapter contains sample clauses to write your own. Or, you may use forms JDF 1115 or JDF 1215 on the CD.

- A **Decree (No. 251)** for the court to sign. See this chapter.

- A **QDRO**, if applicable, to transfer retirement assets. See Chapter 7.

- **Notice to Set (No. 1195)** Used in most courts to set a time for the hearing date. This is not needed under the Simplified Domestic Relations Procedure or if you are filling a Decree Without Appearance of Parties.

- **Notice of Hearing Date (JDF 1108)** You will need this to notify the other party of the date of any hearing. Under the Simplified procedure, this may be a separate form supplied by the court.

If you have minor children of this marriage, you will need most of these forms.

- **Written Parenting Plan.** You may include the parenting plan in your separation agreement—merely labeling a section "Parentng Plan", do a separate document for this, or use JDF 1113 on the CD. See Chapter 8.

- The correct **Child Support Worksheet(s) (Nos. 1170 or 1171)** depending on the mode of physical care you have agreed to for your children. See Chapter 9.

- **Certificate of Attendance** by each of you for any court-ordered parenting-after-divorce class. See Chapter 8.

- **Notice to Employer to Deduct for Health Insurance (No. 1162).** If the court orders payment of health insurance for the children, this notifies the employer to withhold and pay the amount ordered to the insurance company.

If one of you will be are paying child support and/or maintenance to the other you may need:

- **Support Order (No. 251A).** You will need this if one of you is paying either child support or maintenance to the other. When signed by the Court, it then becomes an order.

- **Notice to Withhold Income for Support (No. 1155),** if one of you will be paying child support and/or maintenance to the other and want to have it paid by an income assignment.

If you have hired a mediator, or have worked with some other third party to reach all or some of your agreement, then that person will probably write up the agreements you reached there. If there are still some issues you worked out by yourselves, you will need to write them up. Mediators or other facilitators may title their summary of your agreement(s), "Memorandum of Agreement," or "Memorandum of Understanding." You don't need to re-title it if you are using it as all or part of your separation agreement.

If you have hired attorneys to do the basic paperwork, they will prepare all these papers for you—including the separation agreement. This is true whether they negotiate all the terms of the agreement for you, or you negotiate by yourselves and describe the terms to your attorney.

SEPARATION AGREEMENT

Once your separation agreement is complete, label it "Exhibit A" and reference it as such in number 5 of the decree. The decree summarizes the terms from your agreement which have the greatest legal consequences (such as marital status and parenting plan).

The court will read your separation agreement as you present it to be sure it contains certain minimal provisions (support if there are children, division of property and debts, etc.) and to be certain it is not so bizarre as to be "unconscionable" (i.e. a person of conscience would not have done it). The court will not help you negotiate your agreement. Chapters 7-11 of this Guidebook are

Caption:

The top portion of forms filed in court which contains specific information that is mandatory according to Colorado Court Rules. This incudes the name and location of the court, the case number, the names of the parties filing the case and the form name.

See page 297 for a sample caption that you can copy onto the top of any forms you create for the court.

Partners don't need any of the papers in this chapter in order to legally *conclude* their relationship. You may need to reach many agreements about your financial separation. Some of the sample wording for a separation agreement in this chapter may be helpful as a checklist of items to talk about, although the wording will probably need to change to reflect a dissolving partnership rather than a marriage.

If you have children of this relationship and wish to have child support ordered through the court, you will need a child support order, worksheets, financial affidavits, and possibly an income assignment. Additional forms for parental responsibility, a parenting plan, and notice forms can be found at Bradford Publishing Company.

Divorce by affidavit: Also called Decree Without Appearance of Parties; procedure which permits certain parties to a divorce to mail their papers to the court instead of having a hearing.

Sample Cover Letter to the Clerk of the Court for Divorce by Affidavit

Date

Clerk of the _____ District Court
Address

Re: marriage of _____
Case # _____

Dear Clerk,

Enclosed please find the final documents for our Dissolution of Marriage. Please return a copy of the conformed decree in (each of) the enclosed stamped self-addressed envelope(s).

Thank you for your assistance.

Sincerely,

_____

Enclosures: List all your final documents here, as you have indicated on your Checklists. Send originals with original signatures. Include a photocpy of the decree and a self-addressed, stamped envelope for yourself. Your spouse may do the same.

designed to help you work out an agreement of which you will both be proud.

If you have only constructive service on your spouse (see Chapter 6), or your spouse has elected not to take part in the divorce, you will not have a written separation agreement. Instead, you will give testimony in court regarding your requests for child support, parenting plan, and property. See the sample testimony on page 339 to help you write down what you will say. You may also fill out JDF 1115 to use as "Information for the Court."

DECREE

The Decree is the final *order* of the court which grants you a dissolution of marriage or legal separation. Although this is an order to be signed by the court, you fill out the form the way you want it to be signed. If the court is satisfied that your agreement is fair and that you have met all the other requirements for a Decree, then the court will sign it. If you are ever called upon to prove that you are single, this is the one piece of paper you will need. Similarly, if you are ever asked to prove what kind of parental responsibilites you have after the divorce, this piece of paper may be enough.

DECREE WITHOUT A HEARING

If you *do not* have minor children (under 21), then you may avoid a hearing entirely by mailing in an affidavit for decree without appearance of parties, your separation agreement, proposed decree, affidavits with respect to financial affairs, and any other order(s) you have agreed the court should sign. Send these near the end of, or some time after, your 90 day waiting period.

If you *do* have minor children, you may also avoid a hearing if EACH of you has a lawyer and they sign your separation agreement, proposed decree, and support order.

The procedure is:

a) Complete and have notarized the Affidavit for Decree Without Appearance of Parties. Both sign it (and both lawyers sign it if there are minor children).

b) If only you are signing the affidavit, send a copy to your spouse by certified mail—using the best address you have for your spouse if his or her whereabouts are presently unknown. Attach the certified mail receipt to the original Affidavit when you send it to the court. Note: Remember to jot down your case number on the green return card, when you get it back with your spouse's signature, so the court will know what file to put it in when you send it to the court to prove your spouse received the Affidavit.

Once you have provided the Affidavit for Decree Without Appearance and other papers, the court, frequently a magistrate or commissioner assigned to non-contested divorces, will read your agreement and affidavits at his or her convenience—sometimes on set days of the week.

If you have left something out or done something inadequately (in terms of filling out a form or following a procedure), the court will send you a form telling you what you did not do correctly and offer you a chance to straighten it out. Once you amend your papers to the court's satisfaction, and return them, the court will sign your decree and you will be divorced.

DECREE WITH A NON-CONTESTED HEARING

In most courts the hearings for non-contested divorces are very low key and short (10-15 minutes). The magistrates who conduct these hearings know you are nervous and usually sad and will try to help you present your documents clearly and with a minimum of discomfort. There is a script for a hearing later in this chapter that you can use to get started.

DECREE WITH A PARTIALLY-CONTESTED HEARING OR AN ABSENT SPOUSE

Many courts will allow a person filing his or her own divorce action to have a short hearing in front of the magistrate instead of the judge, even if there isn't a complete signed separation agreement, if: a) the spouse is absent and the case was served by constructive service (see Chapter 6), or b) the case was personally served but the spouse has never filed a response or taken part in the case in any way. Lawyers call this a "default". If you are doing such a hearing, you will need to be particularly careful about the Notice to Set and the Notice of Hearing forms.

AFFIDAVITS WITH RESPECT TO FINANCIAL AFFAIRS

The purpose of the "financial affidavits" is to tell the court enough about your individual financial situations to allow the court to determine if your written agreement is fair. The court will read the three documents (two financial affidavits, one separation agreement) side by side to see if you can each pay the debts you say you will be responsible for, or the support and maintenance you have agreed to pay, and that you each can live on the income you show yourself receiving—including any maintenance or support you have agreed to. If you do not have children and are not agreeing to maintenance, you may use the simplified version.

"The Judge will order all the things we want at the final hearing."
It's not that simple.

If you and your spouse have worked out a settlement, then you will appear for a short, non-contested hearing. The court will order exactly what is in your separation agreement, nothing more. The court will make no decisions, just approve or disapprove your settlement.

If you and your spouse have not worked out a complete settlement, you will set your case for a contested hearing concerning anything you have not agreed on. This is a real trial, at which you will each ask for what you want and give your reasons. **No one can guarantee the outcome.**

Only if your spouse can not be personally served, has not been a part of the case and will not appear at the final hearing, will you probably get pretty much what you ask for. Under these circumstances, however, the court may lack jurisdiction to order some of the things which are most important to you. See Chapter 6 about the problem of jurisdiction.

Notice: If the support of children is an issue in this case, you must:
1. List all sources of gross income and potential income pursuant to § 14-10-115(7), C.R.S.
2. Attach copies of recent pay stubs or employer statements from **ALL** employers, and your most recent tax return.
3. If self-employed, attach copies of receipts and expenses.
4. If child support is ordered, the obligor must execute an income assignment pursuant to §14-14-111.5, C.R.S.

District Court, _____ County, Colorado
Court Address:

In re the Marriage of:
Petitioner:

v.

Respondent:

Attorney or Party Without Attorney (Name and Address):

▲ COURT USE ONLY ▲

Case Number:

Phone Number: E-mail:
FAX Number: Atty. Reg. #:   Division: Courtroom:

AFFIDAVIT WITH RESPECT TO FINANCIAL AFFAIRS

I, _____, Social Security No. _____ declare under oath that:

1. My occupation is: _____

.2. I am employed _____ hours per week at (company name and address) _____
_____

3. I am paid ☐ weekly ☐ every other week ☐ twice each month ☐ monthly on (pay dates) _____
Each paycheck amounts to (gross) $

4. My **MONTHLY GROSS** income from my primary employment is $_____

5. My **MONTHLY** payroll deductions from my primary employment are:
(Number of exemptions being claimed: _____)

Federal Withholding Tax	$_____
Social Security Tax	$_____
Colorado Tax	$_____
Medical Insurance	$_____
Life Insurance	$_____
Dues	$_____
Bonds	$_____
Credit Union	$_____
Other	$_____

TOTAL deductions from primary employer $_____

6. My **NET MONTHLY TAKE HOME** pay from my primary employment (4-5) $_____

7. List all other sources and amounts of gross income, including expense account allowances.

SOURCE	AMOUNT
_____	$_____
_____	$_____
_____	$_____

TOTAL $_____

8. List all other deductions from the income sources listed in part 7.

TYPE OF DEDUCTION	AMOUNT
_____	$_____
_____	$_____
_____	$_____

TOTAL $_____

9. My **NET MONTHLY INCOME** from income sources in part 7 is (7-8). $_____

10. My **NET MONTHLY INCOME** from **ALL** sources is (6+9). $_____

11. My dependent children have a monthly income of $_____

12. My total income reported on my last Federal tax return was $_____
My occupation then was _____

13. I believe the monthly gross income of the other party to be $_____
I believe the monthly net income of the other party to be (Attach all information available.) $_____

Bradford Publishing, 1743 Wazee St., Denver, CO 80202 — 303-292-2500 — www.bradfordpublishing.com

Affidavit With Respect to Financial Affairs

Each spouse, unless served by constructive service, must complete this form. Otherwise, the court will not consider your agreement or enter your decree. The first page describes your income. The second page shows your respective monthly expenses and your debts. The third page lists all your assets, marital and separate. You may use a simplified form if you do not have minor children of this marriage and there is no maintenance agreed to. Reading these instructions will also help you fill out the simplified version.

INSTRUCTIONS FOR FILLING OUT PAGE 1 OF THE FINANCIAL AFFIDAVIT

See Chapter 5 for a complete discussion of income, **especially** the Income Chart.

1. Fill out these lines the same as you did on your petition and all previous forms. Be sure to include the case number and the division or courtroom number.

2. Write the full name of the person filing this affidavit, and his or her social security number.

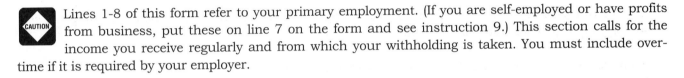 Lines 1-8 of this form refer to your primary employment. (If you are self-employed or have profits from business, put these on line 7 on the form and see instruction 9.) This section calls for the income you receive regularly and from which your withholding is taken. You must include over-time if it is required by your employer.

If you rarely earn a bonus, overtime or commissions, then you may wish to discuss these amounts as additional income beginning at line 7. Income-in-kind, such as expense advances, reimbursements, or a car allowance, should also be reserved for the additional income on line 7. "Cafeteria plan" (or "Flex" dollars) pre-paid expenses may be included in income in which case the expenses these pay for will be either treated as a deduction on line 5 below, or as an expense on D or I on page 2. (See instructions for page 2 of this affidavit.)

3. Write your job title or description of your employment.

4. Write the number of hours you actually work each week (if it varies, write the average) and name and address of your employer.

5. Check the box next to the term for which you are regularly paid. If you are paid on the same dates each month write those dates; or "every two weeks," or "every Friday," for example. Write the amount of your paycheck *before* any taxes or other deductions.

6. Write the total of your before-tax *monthly* income from your primary employment. Be careful here. Twice monthly is not the same as every other week. For the latter, take each paycheck amount times 26, then divide by 12. If you are paid weekly, multiply the amount by 52, then divide by 12.

7. Your deductions can usually be determined by looking at your paycheck stub. The number of exemptions comes from the W-4 form you filed with your payroll office. Be sure to indicate if your W-4 shows you as married or single. If you have a deduction that is not listed, write the amount on an unused line and change the name for that line to explain the deduction. Then add all the deductions you have listed and write the total on the line provided.

8. Your net monthly take home pay is the amount remaining after subtracting all the listed deductions from your gross monthly income (Step 6 minus Step 7). Do not list here expenses which are not paid through deductions from your paycheck —these will be listed on page 2 of this affidavit.

9. List income from other sources averaged monthly. This includes income or profits from self-employment or your own business, dividends and interest, profits from rental property, maintenance (including any received from this marriage) and child support, expense advances or car allowances, non-required or occasional overtime, bonus or commission, second job. Add these up and write the total on the line provided.

10. List any deductions from the income listed in Step 9 averaged monthly. Most people don't actually have any deductions from additional income, but instead pay estimated taxes. Be sure to list your estimated federal and state tax on all this income including any self-employment tax. Remember that child support is not taxable. Deduct F.I.C.A. and medicare (totaling 7.65%) from any *earned* income covered by F.I.C.A. (but not from disability, alimony, dividends or interest, or expense or car allowances). Refer to current tax tables, to accurately calculate your federal tax rate.

11. This is your monthly net income from sources other than your primary employment including any self-employment tax (step 9 minus step 10).

12. Add step 8 to step 11. This is your monthly net income from all sources combined.

13. Write the monthly income of your children whom you claim as dependents. Such income would be part-time jobs, babysitting, paper route, trust, or investment income.

14. This is your total gross taxable income as reported on Form 1040 of your last federal income tax return, before any adjustments or deductions. Be sure to give your occupation as you reported it on your last tax return. If the income you list *here* is very different from the amount you are showing *now* for gross income ([step 6 plus step 9] x 12), especially if now it is much lower, it is a good idea to explain it somewhere on this page or refer the court to an explanation in your separation agreement.

15. Write your spouse's monthly gross and net income from all sources. The amount you write here should agree with your spouse's financial affidavit, and vice versa. If these numbers don't agree the court may wonder if you actually worked together on your divorce.

16 14. My **MONTHLY EXPENSES** for a household consisting of _____ adults and _____ children are as follows:

			TOTAL	Of Total, Amount For Children Of This Marriage **19**

17 A. HOUSING (1) Rent/1st Mortgage $_____

B.   (2) 2nd Mortgage $_____

             (3) Maintenance Fee $_____ $_____ $_____

B. UTILITIES (1) Gas/Electric $_____

            (2) Phone/Long Distance $_____

            (3) Water/Sewer $_____

            (4) Trash Removal $_____ $_____ $_____

C. FOOD (1) Groceries $_____

            (2) Eating Out $_____ $_____ $_____

D. MEDICAL (1) Doctor $_____

(Do not duplicate paragraph 5.) (2) Dentist $_____

            (3) Medicine/RX Drugs $_____

            (4) Other _____ $_____ $_____ $_____

E. INSURANCE (1) Life $_____

(Do not duplicate paragraph 5.) (2) Health/Hospital $_____

            (3) Homeowners $_____ $_____ $_____

F. TRANSPORTATION (1) Vehicle Payment(s) $_____

Vehicle Description(s) (make, model, year) (2) Fuel $_____

            (3) Maintenance $_____

_____ (4) Insurance $_____

_____ (5) Parking/Bus $_____ $_____ $_____

_____

G. CLOTHING $_____ $_____

H. LAUNDRY & CLEANING $_____ $_____

I. CHILD CARE

    (1) Work related (after tax credit) $_____ $_____

    (2) Other babysitting $_____ $_____

J. EDUCATION (1) Tuition, Books,

☐ Self   Supplies $_____

☐ Children (2) Lunches $_____ $_____ $_____

K. CHILD SUPPORT/ ☐ This Family

   MAINTENANCE ☐ Other Family $_____ $_____

L. RECREATION, CONSISTING OF_____

_____ $_____ $_____

M. MISCELLANEOUS, CONSISTING OF _____

_____

_____ $_____ $_____

N. TOTAL REQUIRED MONTHLY EXPENSES (1) $_____ (2) $_____

18 15. My DEBTS are:

Creditor	Item	Unpaid Balance	Monthly Payment
A. _____		$_____	$_____
B. _____		$_____	$_____
C. _____		$_____	$_____
D. _____		$_____	$_____
E. _____		$_____	$_____
F. _____		$_____	$_____
G. _____		$_____	$_____
H. TOTAL MONTHLY DEBT PAYMENT(S)		$_____	$_____

I. TOTAL MONTHLY EXPENSES PLUS DEBTS (14N(1) + 15H) $_____

INSTRUCTIONS FOR FILLING OUT PAGE 2 OF THE FINANCIAL AFFIDAVIT

See the Informational Family "IF" Budget in Chapter 5. See also the discussion of children's expenses in Chapter 9.

 If you pay day care or medical expenses through "cafeteria plan" pre-tax estimated payments then you may either:

- list the total monthly amount withheld by your employer on Page 1 of this Affidavit, line 5, "other deductions," and do NOT list it as an expense here. Write the words "pre-paid through cafeteria/flex plan, see page 1." OR

- list the amount on this page on lines D or I. If you do this, be sure to write in "paid through cafeteria plan" (or "Flex dollars") so the court knows that these are paid in pre-tax dollars.

16. Write the number of adults and children in your household. Include the children of this marriage if they are in your home at least part of the time.

17. Write your monthly expenses for these items. If you do not know the exact amounts, estimate them. If you have already separated from your spouse, list your current expenses. A good way to calculate these expenses is to take the total you have paid for each item over the last six months (or the length of time you have been separated) and divide by the number of months. See the IF Budget in Chapter 5 for a complete discussion of this.

18. List the debts for which you are currently personally liable. If you include the marital debts your spouse is paying, do not include the monthly payment, but indicate "spouse paying" instead. See complete discussion of debts in Chapters 7 and 9, and refer to information you gathered in Chapter 5.

19. In practice, many people ignore this column. You may wish to complete it in case it is required by your particular court. To figure the children's portion, many people take the whole of a monthly expense, such as rent or food and divide by the number of persons in the home, times the number of children. This is probably not very useful or accurate. For example, a teenage boy eats more than his pro rata share, while a nursing infant uses less. Small children sharing a bedroom, especially if they are there part time, use less of the home than an adult. For more accurate figures for children's expenses, see discussion in Chapter 9.

16. The ASSETS of the parties of this action are as follows:

Husband's/Wife's: Acquired before this marriage, or by gift, or by inheritance, only.

Joint: Acquired during the marriage, other than by gift or inheritance.

Does not refer to how titled or how possessed.

	(20) HUSBAND'S	**WIFE'S**	**JOINT**
A. REAL ESTATE (Attach schedule giving location, market value, encumbrances, and how titled.)	$_____	$_____	$_____
B. FURNITURE AND HOUSEHOLD GOODS (Attach schedule showing location value, and encumbrances.)	$_____	$_____	$_____
C. MOTOR VEHICLES (Attach schedule showing make, year, value, and encumbrances.)	$_____	$_____	$_____
D. CASH ON HAND	$_____	$_____	$_____
E. BANK ACCOUNTS (Attach schedule specifying for each account, the name and location of bank.)			
(1) Savings	$_____	$_____	$_____
(2) Checking	$_____	$_____	$_____
(3) Certificate/Deposit	$_____	$_____	$_____
F. STOCKS AND BONDS (Attach schedule describing holdings, including company name, number of shares, names in which held, market values and date of.)	$_____	$_____	$_____
G. LIFE INSURANCE (Attach schedule showing company name, policy number, beneficiary, and cash surrender value.)	$_____	$_____	$_____
H. PENSION, PROFIT SHARING, OR RETIREMENT FUNDS (Attach schedule naming source and location of funds.)	$_____	$_____	$_____
I. MISCELLANEOUS			
(1) _____	$_____	$_____	$_____
(2) _____	$_____	$_____	$_____
(3) _____	$_____	$_____	$_____
(4) _____	$_____	$_____	$_____
(5) _____	$_____	$_____	$_____
17. TOTAL ASSETS **(21)**	$_____	$_____	$_____

(22) 18. The assets of the children of this marriage are valued at $_____

I declare under penalty of perjury that I have read this affidavit and the statements contained in it are true and correct.

(23)

Dated: _____   _____
                                                                  Signature

Subscribed under oath before me on _____
                                                   Date

My commission expires:_____   _____
                                   Date   Notary Public/Address

_____

_____

INSTRUCTIONS FOR FILLING OUT PAGE 3 OF THE FINANCIAL AFFIDAVIT

For a complete discussion of marital and separate property see Chapter 7, especially the Marital and Separate Property and Debts Charts.

The definitions of "Assets," "Husband's," "Wife's," "Joint," at the top of this form reflect the statutory definitions of marital and separate property at the time of filing. You are free to define marital and separate property in your own way and tell the court what that definition is. If you use another definition, cross off the one printed on the form and substitute your own definition.

You may want to use this page to show the court how your property balances out after the division you have agreed to. In this case, you will cross off the definitions of Husband's/Wife's/Joint at the top of the page and write: "This page shows our division of property as agreed to in our separation agreement."

If there is some separate property or if some of the value of some of the marital property is separate, you can indicate this by noting the separate property and writing "separate" or "sep." next to it. For example, if the wife receives the home, valued at $100,000 of which $20,000 is separate, you would write $80,000 in the Joint column and $20,000 in Wife's separate column. (See Chapter 7 for a complete discussion of how to do this.)

20. List the value of your assets using net fair market value (FMV minus any balance owing on that property). See Chapter 7 for how to value different classes of assets.

   If your separation agreement clearly identifies assets with values and balances due, you may not need to attach schedules to this affidavit. The court needs to see enough detail to help it determine if your agreement is fair. If you have any doubts, bring the data concerning asset values, etc., to the hearing in case the court asks to see supporting documents or information.

   If you have reached agreement about the division of a class of assets without setting specific values, then ignore the "$" signs on the form and describe what you have agreed to in words. For example, "furniture divided agreeably between us without placing a value on it."

   Cash on hand is a category without much in it for most people in this age of plastic money. If this or any category is not significant for you, simply write "not applicable" or "n/a" in the spaces next to it.

21. Write the total for each column.

22. List the total value of any assets owned by your minor children, such as furniture, pedigreed animals, stocks, bank accounts, etc.

23. Sign and date your financial affidavit in the presence of a notary. Make sure the notary then completes the section immediately below the space for your signature.

 What if my finances change *after* I do my Financial Affidavit but before the final hearing? Financial circumstances often change during the divorce process. If they do, draft a new one and provide a copy to your spouse and the court.

District Court, _____ County, Colorado

Court Address:

In re _____ :

Petitioner:

v.

Respondent/Co-Petitioner:

Attorney or Party Without Attorney (Name and Address):

▲ COURT USE ONLY ▲

Case Number:

Phone Number: E-mail:

FAX Number: Atty. Reg. #:

Division: Courtroom:

FINANCIAL AFFIDAVIT— SIMPLIFIED VERSION

THIS FORM MAY BE USED ONLY FOR CASES WITHOUT CHILDREN OR SPOUSAL SUPPORT
(USE THE STANDARD AFFIDAVIT WITH RESPECT TO FINANCIAL AFFAIRS FOR ALL OTHER CASES)

Name: _____

Social Security Number: _____

Home Telephone: _____ Work Telephone: _____

I declare under oath that the following is true:

1. I am employed as: _____

2. Employer's name, address and phone number: _____
    _____
    _____

3. I am employed _____ hours per week. I am paid ☐ weekly ☐ twice a month ☐ monthly.

4. The amount of each paycheck is $ _____. **(Attach your last pay stub and last income tax return.)**

5. My monthly income is: $ _____ (To figure this out, take each paycheck amount times number of pay periods per year divided by 12.)

6. The following amounts are taken out of each paycheck **monthly:**

Federal Withholding Tax:	$ _____	PERA:	$ _____
Social Security:	$ _____	Union Dues:	$ _____
Medicare:	$ _____	Charity:	$ _____
Colorado State Tax:	$ _____	Stock Purchase:	$ _____
Life Insurance:	$ _____	Cafeteria Plan:	$ _____
Health Insurance:	$ _____	Credit Union:	$ _____
401K Plan:	$ _____	Other: _____	$ _____
Other: _____	$ _____		

7. I get income from other sources, in addition to my main employment. The amount per month is: $ _____ and is from:

☐ Another Job:	($ _____)	☐ Unemployment Compensation:	($ _____)
☐ SSI:	($ _____)	☐ Worker's Compensation:	($ _____)
☐ SSDI:	($ _____)	☐ Interest:	($ _____)
☐ Pension/Retirement:	($ _____)	☐ Maintenance:	($ _____)
☐ Child Support:	($ _____)	☐ Dividends:	($ _____)
☐ Other federal or state benefits:	($ _____)		

8. My deductions from sources in (7) are (type of deduction and amount):

_____

_____

_____

_____

9. The monthly debts that I am paying are as follows:

Creditor	Unpaid Balance	Monthly Payment

10. The debts acquired during the marriage that I owe but am not paying on are:

Creditor	Unpaid Balance	Monthly Payment

11. I own the following property:

ASSET DESCRIPTION (Include VIN #s or any ID#s)	FAIR MARKET VALUE	LOAN BALANCE	EQUITY	PURCHASE DATE	NAME TITLED

I declare under penalty of perjury that I have read this affidavit, and the statements contained in it are true and correct.

Date: _____   __ _____
                                                              Signature

STATE OF COLORADO

_____ COUNTY }

Signed before me under oath on this date: _____

My commission expires: _____

_____
Notary Public

[Seal]

District Court, _____ County, Colorado Court Address:	
In re _____ **:** **Petitioner:** v. **Respondent/Co-Petitioner:**	
Attorney or Party Without Attorney (Name and Address): Phone Number: FAX Number: E-mail: Atty. Reg. #:	▲ COURT USE ONLY ▲ Case Number: Div.: Ctrm.:

The Caption

The top portion of any form that gets filed in court is called the "Caption". It includes the information that the court needs to keep track of your case — the name and location of the court, the case number, the names of the parties who are filing and the title of the form.

The book contains most of the forms you will need, but if you decide to create your own Separation Agreement and/or Parenting Plan, you may copy the caption shown above onto the top of a blank sheet of paper, block out this instruction before you make your copy, and leave a top margin of 1 1/2" and a left margin of 1". Fill in the title of the form in the blank box across the bottom of the caption, and add your own document below it. Fill out the caption just like you did in the petition.

Sample Wording for Writing Your Separation Agreement

The following sample wording is drawn from the material throughout this Guidebook. You may use it as the basis for writing up your own separation agreement. If you want to use a ready-made agreement, you may use JDF 1115 plus the Parenting Plan, JDF 1113. If your spouse has not participated in the case, is not signing a complete separation agreement, or if you served by constructive service, then you may wish to use the JDF forms above as your written requests to the court. To determine if a form is best for you, this might be a good time to go back and read the caution on page 15.

If you and your spouse have been working through this book, you will already have written drafts of most of this material, perhaps even already on these sample paragraphs. If not, gather your notes and all the partial agreements you have made and assemble them, using these paragraphs as a guide to wording and arrangement. The order of topics follows the chapters in this book, and the language is the same as the partial agareements within each chapter. You are referred back to the appropriate chapters so if you have forgotten a topic or agreement you can go back and retrieve it.

It is a good idea to write in these pages in pencil, adding extra paragraphs on a separate piece of paper. When you have finished your first draft, you may wish to flip through the book to be sure your have picked up every agreement and question. Then sit down at your home computer or a friend's and write it up. Copy the caption from the previous page onto the top of your agreement and fill in the information from the caption like all your other papers. Put the document title SEPARATION AGREEMENT in all capital letters and then, using double spacing, start putting in the agreements you have made, as you have written them.

A. GENERAL INFORMATION

We, _____ *(full name, how you will be referred to in this agreement)*, and

_____ *(full name, how you will be referred to in this agreement)*, agree to the following:

We were married on _____ *(date)* and separated on _____ *(date)*. Our current addresses are *(as stated in your petition)* _____ , and

_____ , respectively. Our children are:

_____ *(name)*, _____ *(age)*, _____ , _____ , and

_____ , _____ . They have special needs of _____

_____

_____ *(See Chapter 8)*.

_____ is employed at _____ and earns _____ per month before taxes. _____ is employed at _____ and earns _____ per month before taxes. *(See Chapter 9)*

OR: We agree that _____ need not seek employment outside the home at this time (in order to be at home with our children) (in order to complete school or training at _____) (due to _____ [illness]) (or _____). *(See Chapter 9)*

We agree our marriage is irretrievably broken, and agree to obtain a decree of dissolution of marriage (legal separation). (*See Chapter 1 and this chapter.*)

We state that we have each provided the other with complete copies of all required disclosures and have each filed a Certificate of Compliance. (See Chapter 6).

We agree that this separation agreement is fair to both of us (and is in the best interest of our children).

We mediated (portions of) this separation agreement with _____ , (during the months of _____ , _____ , and _____) (over a period of _____ hours).

_____ *(one spouse)* consulted with _____ *(attorney/accountant/financial planner/therapist)* concerning the terms of this agreement as to him/herself. *(See Chapter 2.)* _____ *(other spouse)* consulted with _____ *(attorney/accountant/financial planner/therapist)* concerning the terms of this agreement as to him/herself.

Should either or both of us decide to convert our decree of legal separation to a decree of dissolution of marriage, we agree that the terms of our separation agreement are acceptable as is and should not be modified.

OR

Should either or both of us decide to convert our decree of legal separation to a Decree of Dissolution of Marriage, we agree to re-negotiate the following portions of our separation agreement:_____ _____ _____ .

B. PROPERTY AND DEBTS *(See Chapter 7)*

1. Family Home or Other Real Estate

We estimate the fair market value our home to be: $ _____

Balance on first mortgage $_____

Balance on second mortgage or lien $_____

We calculate the capital gain for the present as being $_____ . We estimate the costs of sale to be $_____ . _____ _____ shall retain the family home located at _____ and shall receive a Quitclaim Deed to that home not later than the date of the final decree of _____ . _____ *(person getting the home)* shall pay the mortgage(s), taxes, insurance, upkeep from the date of the decree. _____ will be solely responsible for any tax on capital gain on the home. _____ will hold _____ *(other spouse)* harmless on any indebtedness or expenses related to the home after the date of transfer of title.

_____ will pay to _____ $_____ in payment of _____ (his or her) interest in the home OR to balance the division of property. This amount will be paid when the home is sold, within _____ days of when _____ remarries, when _____ occupies the home with an adult (for longer than _____), on or before _____ *(date)*, whichever comes first. _____ will execute a Promissory Note and a Deed of Trust for this amount to _____ *(other spouse)*.

OR

We will retain title to the family home together—converting title to a Tenancy in Common on or before the date of the final decree of _____ into a _____% / _____% division, _____ having a _____% share and _____ having a _____% share. We will share all expenses for this home in the ratio of our ownership. AND/OR _____ will live in the home and will be solely responsible for payment of: _____and, we will share the expenses for: _____.

OR

We will sell the family home located at _____ and will share the proceeds, after payment of all mortgages, and expenses of sale as follows: _____% to _____ , and _____% to _____. We will share the responsibility for any capital gain and/or benefit of any depreciation in the ratio of our share of the profits, OR _____% to _____, and _____% to _____ .

OR

We will rent out the home and will split the proceeds, after payment of _____, in the ratio of _____% to _____, and _____% to _____ . We will share the responsibility for any capital gain in the ratio of our share of proceeds, OR _____% to _____, and _____% to _____, We will share the cost of any capital improvements or repairs not covered by the rent, or the mortgage, utilities and upkeep whenever it is empty. _____ (one spouse) will be responsible for keeping it rented and for minor repairs. We will pay for _____ (utilities) _____ (repairs).

2.   Personal Property.

_____ will keep the following items of furniture, household goods, and other personal property: _____ _____ , with a total value of $_____ .

_____ will be responsible for payment to _____ of $_____ for purchase of _____ or which is secured by _____ .

(Repeat for other spouse.)

OR

We have already divided our personal property to our satisfaction. We both agree that this division is fair. We agree that our personal property shall become the separate property of the party who now possesses it. We choose not to place a value on this personal property in our settlement.

OR

_____ will keep the following items of personal property for _____ until _____ *(date, has own house, etc.)*. All other items of personal property have been divided to our satisfaction.

3. Cars and Other Motor Vehicles

_____ will retain the _____ *(year and make)* automobile and will be solely responsible for all costs related to it, including loan payments, taxes, insurance, license, upkeep, and will hold _____ *(other spouse)* harmless on these payments.

We value this vehicle at $_____ . There is a loan balance on this vehicle of $_____ .

(Repeat for each vehicle. Be sure to include docking and storage fees for boats, aircraft, trailers, etc.)

4. Liquid Assets: Cash and Bank Accounts.

_____ will retain his or her checking account at _____ , balance of $_____ ;
savings account at _____ , balance of $_____ ;
credit union account at _____ , balance of $_____ ;
and other account at _____ , balance of $_____ .

(Repeat for other spouse.)

We will continue to operate the home out of the joint account at _____ , AND/OR we will use the joint account at _____ *(for the expenses of this separation and divorce) (until the final decree)* OR *(all the expenses for the home or divorce are paid)* OR the home is sold and the expenses of sale are paid. OR, We will contribute $ _____ per _____ *(week, month, etc.)* each, OR _____ will contribute $ _____ and _____ will contribute $_____ , per _____ *(week, month, etc.)*, until it is closed by us.

5. Stocks, Bonds, and Options

_____ will retain the following stocks OR stock accounts OR investment accounts:

Account at/stock in _____
_____ present value of $_____ presently in _____ name(s).
We believe there is/is not a capital gain on this stock/account (of $_____) at the present time.

(Repeat for all stocks and investment accounts and for both spouses.)

_____ will retain the following bonds:

_____
with a face value of $_____ , and a maturity date of _____ , presently in _____ name(s). *(Repeat for each bond for both spouses.)*

We own in_____'s name, by grant dated _____ , the option to purchase_____shares of_____ stock at $_____. These options are _____% vested. The pre-tax fair market value of these options, after paying the purchase price, is $_____ *(state an amount,or 'current zero')*. The expiration date of this grant is _____.

We agree that all of the options in this grant, (vested and unvested), shall be _____'s *(The named spouse)* sole and separate property

OR

(For transferable options) We agree that we shall transfer _____ of these options to _____ *(other spouse)* to be his/her sole and separate property. The options remaining in _____'s *(named spouse)* name shall be his/her sole and separate property.

OR

(For options that are not transferable) We agree that _____ *(named spouse)* shall maintain _____ of these options for _____'s *(other spouse)* benefit, and upon exercise shall pay the net proceeds after taxes to _____ *(other spouse)* to be his/her sole and separate property. The remaining options after those held for _____ *(other spouse)* shall be _____'s *(named spouse)* sole and separate property. *(Consult counsel for further wording about who decides to exercise the options, and when, how to calculate the taxes, and other complexities.)*

6.   Life Insurance.

Be certain that these provisions are consistent with Section D of this Agreement, about security for child support and maintenance, see Chapter 9.

_____ will retain his or her whole life insurance policy with _____ company, including the cash value of $_____ OR as shown on the division of marital property in this Agreement AND is free to name any beneficiary of this policy OR must name our children as the irrevocable beneficiaries of not less than $_____ in benefits, so long as they are minors, to secure the child support we have agreed to AND/OR must name _____ *(other spouse)* as the beneficiary of the first $_____ so long as he/she is paying maintenance as we have agreed.
(Repeat for other spouse.)

_____ will retain his or her term life insurance policy with _____ Company on which there is no cash value, AND is free to name any beneficiary of this policy OR must name our children as the irrevocable beneficiaries of not less than $_____ in benefits, so long as they are minors, to secure the child support we have agreed to AND/OR must name _____ *(other spouse)* as the beneficiary of the first $_____ so long as he/she is paying maintenance as we have agreed. *(See Chapters 8 and 9.)*
(Repeat for other spouse.)

Annuities are included in Retirement.

7.   Retirement, Pensions, and Profit Sharing.

IRA's and SEP's

The IRA (SEP) in _____ 's name, balance of $_____ as of _____ *(date)*, shall be his/her sole and separate property.

OR

The _____ IRA (SEP) account in _____ 's name has a balance of $_____ as of _____ *(date)*. We agree to transfer $_____ (or _____%) from this account into an IRA in _____ 's *(the receiving spouse)* name to be _____ 's *(receiving spouse)* sole and separate property, the balance remaining to be _____ 's *(paying spouse)* sole and separate property.

For a defined benefit plan under ERISA, whether you are dividing it or not, obtain the wording you need from your attorney or CPA.

For a defined contribution plan qualified under ERISA

The_____ Plan account in _____ 's name, balance of $_____ as of

_____ (date), shall be his/her sole and separate property.

OR

We agree that $_____ (or _____% of the balance as of the date of our Decree) in the _____ Plan account in _____'s name shall be transfered to _____ *(receiving spouse)* by means of a Qualified Domestic Relations Order to be presented to the Court for signature at the time of our Decree, to be _____'s *(receiving spouse)* sole and separate property, the balance remaining in the account to be _____'s *(paying spouse)* sole and separate property. *For all other retirements, obtain the wording you need from your attorney or CPA.*

8. Business Interests.

_____ will retain all rights to the business _____ ,
including all stock, membership rights, and/or assets, specifically including: _____
_____ *(car, computer, any other property which may have been stored at the home and/or used by family member other than the business owner).*

As between_____*(spouse)* and_____*(other spouse),*_____ will be solely responsible for all liabilities and debts incurred in the name of the business or in _____ name for the benefit of the business, including: _____
_____ *(list any debts which the spouse may have signed, or the proceeds of which may have gone into a joint account or have been used for the family home, car, etc.)*

We believe the present net value of this business to be $ _____ , which includes $ _____ which we agree is the value of goodwill of this business.

9. Dividing the Debts

_____ will pay the following and hold _____ *(other spouse)* harmless:

Loan or credit card	Name on the account	Balance
_____	_____	_____
_____	_____	_____

(Repeat for other spouse.)

10. Enforcement *(See Chapter 13)*

If _____ does not transfer the _____ *(property)* as agreed by us, then the court may issue a Commissioner's Deed, and order of transfer of property under Rule 70 of the Colorado Rules of Civil Procedure, for that property on _____ days notice to the court of the failure to transfer.

AND/OR

If _____ does not pay the $ _____ *(debt)* to _____ as promised, then he/she will not receive the following property as agreed _____
_____ *(will not get share of home per promissory note, for example, or won't get title to car, boat, stock, etc.).*
(Repeat for other spouse.)

If either of us should file Chapter 7 or 13 bankruptcy on any debt included in this agreement, then we agree that the entire division of property and debts must be re-worked by us. We agree now that if we are unable to work out a new division, and/or if one of us is unwilling to do so, that the court retains jurisdiction over the matter of property and debt division, and may order a different division to compensate for the additional debt for which the spouse not filing bankruptcy is now liable. *(See Chapters 7 and 13.)*

C. ALLOCATION OF PARENTAL RESPONSIBLILTIES: PARENTING PLAN *(See Chapter 8)*

1. Allocation of Decision-Making Responsibilities: Who Will Make the Major Decisions Regarding Our Children

a. We agree to make the following major decisions about our children together;

_____
_____
_____
_____.

b. _____ (one parent) will make the following major decisions about our children:

_____
_____
_____

c. _____ (other parent) will make the following major decisions abut our children:

_____
_____
_____

d. Communication

In order to effect the kind of parental decision-making to which we have agreed and also to facilitate communication between us, we agree to meet _____ *(times weekly, monthly, annually),* AND/OR telephone _____ *(times weekly, monthly, annually)* AND/OR write _____ *(times weekly, monthly, annually)* concerning our children. We agree that we will forewarn the other parent of any major decisions which we wish to discuss at the next regular _____ *(meeting, phone call, communications).*

AND *(optional):* We agree to write down all agreements, "sleep on it" for at least 24 hours before signing them, then sign and date them.

e. Information Exchange

Regardless of the form of parental decision-making we have agreed to, we agree that there are certain facts, events, and other matters about which we must exchange information. Therefore, we agree to keep one another continually informed about:

_____
_____
_____

f.   Emergency Medical Care

We each hereby agree and consent to any emergency care for our children which the other consents to. Any follow-up care, however, will be determined according to our decision-making responsibilities agreement.

g.   Day-to-day Decisions

All day-to-day decisions will be made by the parent in whose physical care the child is at the time of the decision and whose exclusive physical care the decision will affect.

2.   Determination of Parenting Time

a.   Schedule

We agree to the following schedule of parenting time/physical care with our children *(copy or re-write the schedules, including holidays, which you agreed to in Chapter 8)*: _____

_____

_____

_____ .

OR

We agree to the following pattern of parenting time/physical care with our children: *(copy the calendar you have agreed to AND/OR describe this pattern in words).*

We agree to the following arrangements about holidays with our children: _____

_____

_____ .

AND: We agree to the following arrangements about our annual vacation times *(if this is not included in your arrangements about holidays)*: _____

_____

_____ .

The parenting time we have agreed to, described above, results in _____ overnights per calendar year with _____ *(parent) (This may be a percentage, a number, a range or a limitation—not less than _____ OR not more than _____).*

b.   Transportation of the Children

We agree to the following about transporting the children between us: _____

_____

_____

_____ .

c.   Additional Agreements About Children

We agree that on the occurrence of the following events we will adjust our short-term time schedule with the children: _____

_____

_____

We agree to notify each other of the following concerning our children: *(medical and dental exam results, significant events, minor injury or illness, teachers conferences, PTA meetings, recitals, homework or project deadlines)*: _____ _____ _____ .

We agree that if either of us becomes involved in a new "significant" relationship, then _____ _____ _____ .

We agree to the following arrangements about parenting time between our children and *(their grandparents) (other relatives)*: _____ _____ .

d. Modification

We will discuss changes in the decision-making responsibilities of _____ from _____ to _____ if_____ _____ .

We will change decision-making responsibilities at the point in time when_____ _____ ..

We will change our long-term time arrangements *(parenting time/physical care)* from_____ _____ when: _____ if: _____ , as follows: _____ .

(Repeat each for other children or circumstances.)

e. Enforcement *(See Chapter 13)*

Should the parent from whom the children are coming not have them ready on the date and times we have agreed to, then _____ _____ _____ .

Should the parent who is picking up the children not arrive on the date and time agreed to, then _____ _____ _____ .

f. Legal Residence

We agree that the legal residence of _____(child(ren)) will be with _____(parent) and the legal residence of_____child(ren)) will be with the _____(other parent) only for the purposes of IRS or interstate or international travel or other reasons why a designation of legal "custodian" or residence is necessary.

D.   CHILD SUPPORT *(See Chapter 9)*

We agree that the following sources of income have been and will be used for _____ *(parent)* in calculating support for our children:

Source   _____   Kind of income   _____

_____   _____

_____   _____

(Repeat for other parent.)

1.   Worksheet A

_____ *(paying parent)* shall pay to _____ *(other parent)* $_____ per month as child support, as shown on the attached Worksheet A, beginning _____ and continuing until _____ *(date, child's 19th birthday, emancipation, or high school graduation if child is already 19, or until changed by written agreement or court order).*

AND

We agree that the following expenses for our children are included in the basic support as calculated by us from the Schedule of Basic Child Support Obligations: _____

_____

(housing, food in the home, basic clothing, possibly medical and dental check-ups, immunizations, transportation, etc.). We acknowledge that these basic expenses are being paid by the parent with physical care.

AND

We agree that the following additional expenses for our children are known and/or can be estimated with accuracy and therefore have been included on the Worksheet A attached:

_____

_____

_____ *(work-related day care, orthodontia, insulin or other regular medication, lessons, summer camp, allowances, special clothing, sports, school supplies, fees, and one-time costs, if you wish to pre-calculate these).* We acknowledge that these are being paid out, and will continue to be paid by us as shown on the worksheet, until and unless amended by us in writing.

2.   Worksheet B

_____ *(paying parent)* will pay to _____ *(other parent)* $_____ per month as child support, as shown on the attached Worksheet B, beginning _____ and continuing until _____ *(date, child's 19th birthday, emancipation, high school graduation—if child is already 19, or until we otherwise agree in writing, or court order).*

AND

We agree that the following expenses for our children are included in the basic support as calculated by us from the Schedule of Basic Child Support Obligations as shown on the attached Worksheet B: _____

_____

_____ *(housing – both homes, food – both homes, basic clothing, possibly medical and dental check-ups, immunizations, transportation, etc.).* We acknowledge and agree that we will continue to pay out to third parties these basic expenses in proportion to our time with the children: _____%/_____%, as shown on the worksheet.

AND

We agree that the following additional expenses for our children are known and/or can be estimated with accuracy and therefore have been included in the Worksheet B attached: _____

_____

_____ *(work-related day care, orthodontia, insulin or other regular medication, lessons, summer camp, allowances, special clothing, sports, if you wish to pre-calculate these).* We acknowledge that these are being paid out, and will continue to be paid out to third parties, by us as shown on the Worksheet.

3. Other Agreements About Child Support

We agree that the following expenses for our children can not be pre-calculated, but will be shared between us as they are incurred in proportion to our incomes OR equally between us, OR 60-40%, etc., OR _____ will pay the first $_____ and we will share the rest.

We agree that any one-time expense for our children in excess of $_____ must be a shared decision.

We agree to pay the extraordinary expenses for our children which cannot be calculated now *(one-time expenses)* from (with) the following irregular sources of income: _____

_____

_____ *(bonus, commission, non-required overtime, dividend),* in the following way: We will set aside _____% of the income from these sources into an account to pay for the unforseen expenses for our children as incurred.

We agree that our combined incomes, as set forth in our financial affidavit, exceed $20,000 per month, and that the Child Support Guideline does not apply in our present circumstances. _____ will pay $ _____ per month to _____ , as child support beginning _____ , and continuing to _____ *(date, child's 19th birthday, emancipation, high school graduation—if child is already 19, or until we otherwise agree in writing, or court order). (Follow wording under worksheets about expenses and how you will divide them.)*

We agree that _____ (paying parent) owes _____ (other parent) retroactive child support of $ _____ total, to cover the period from _____ (date) to _____ (date). We agree this amount shall accrue at _____ % interest. _____ (paying spouse) will pay this in regular monthly payments of $ _____ until paid in full.

4. Health Insurance Coverage for the Children

_____ will maintain the existing health insurance coverage for our minor children until emancipation unless we agree otherwise in writing. Should our children's health insurance no longer be available as a benefit to _____ , then _____ *(the other parent)* will seek coverage for our children as a benefit. Should health insurance coverage for the children not be available to either of us as a benefit, we will cooperate in obtaining the best insurance available between us. *(If you include insurance premiums for your children on the child support worksheet, you will share the cost of this insurance proportional to income regardless of who initially pays the premium.)*

_____ *(parent paying child support and/or providing medical insurance coverage for the children)* will keep the other parent informed of his/her current employer, and provide information on any health insurance coverage for the children to which he/she may have access.

5. Tax Consequences About Children *(See Chapter 11)*

_____ *(parent)* will have _____ *(names of child or children)* as the basis for his or her Head of Household filing status. _____ *(other parent)* will have _____ *(child/children)* as the basis for his or her Head of Household filing status.

We acknowledge that because _____ *(parent)* has _____ *(child/children)* as the basis of his or her filing status as head of household, therefore _____ *(same parent)* will have the exclusive right to any Child Care Credit for work-related child care paid on behalf of _____ *(that child or children)* and will therefore make those payments directly to the care provider.

We acknowledge that because _____ *(other parent)* has _____ *(other child/children)* as the basis of his or her filing status as head of household, therefore _____ *(same parent)* will have the exclusive right to any child care credit for work-related child care paid on behalf of _____ *(this child/these children)* and therefore will make those payments directly to the care provider.

_____ *(parent)* will claim _____ *(child/ children)* as an Exemption for _____ years, OR until emancipation, so long as _____ he/she is current for the child support for this child OR the parenting time/physical care of the children remains as written in this agreement, etc.).

_____ *(other parent)* will claim _____ *(other child or children)* as an Exemption for _____ years OR until emancipation, so long as he/she is current for the child support for this child (these children), the parenting time/physical care of this child (these children) remains as written in this agreement, etc.).

We will prepare IRS form 8332 as required if we have agreed that the "non-custodial" parent may "claim" the child(ren).

We agree that whichever of us takes our child's personal exemption also will receive the child tax credit.

OR

We agree to split any child tax credit between us _____% to _____ and_____% to _____.

6. Post-Secondary Education Expenses (Optional) *(See Chapter 9)*

_____ *(paying parent)* will pay $_____ per _____*(month, quarter, semester, year)* to _____ *(other parent, child, institution)* for _____ *(tuition, books, fees, room and board on campus, other).*

_____ *(other paying parent)* will pay $_____ per _____ *(month, quarter, semester, year)* to _____ *(other parent, same child, same institution)* for _____ *(tuition, books, fees, room and board on campus, other).*

_____ *(paying parent)* will pay $ _____ per _____*(month, quarter, semester, year)* to _____ *(other parent, child)* for _____ *(off-campus housing, other).*

_____ *(other paying parent)* will pay $ _____ per _____ *(month, quarter, semester, year)* to _____ *(other parent, same child)* for _____ *(off-campus housing, other).*

_____ *(paying parent)* will pay to _____ *(other parent)* $ _____ *(per month for the months of _____),* on or before _____ *(date, annually, the occurrence of a particular event)* for board and room during breaks from post-secondary education while the child is residing with _____ *(other parent).*

We will pay the costs of transportation for _____ *(child/children),* to and from school, _____ times per year, in the following proportion: _____ .

We agree that we will (not) be responsible for re-payment of any student loans obtained by _____ (child/children) (in the following proportion _____.

We agree that our children are likely to wish to attend college. We agree now that we will share the parents' portion of the cost as determined by the institution (to the limit of $ _____ per child) to which we have agreed in the following way: _____.

We have estimated our portion of the cost of post-secondary education for each of our children to be $_____ . We will set aside the money for this at the rate of $ _____ per _____ (month, quarter, year, other) which we will share proportional to our incomes as determined on the child support guideline for each year. We will change this proportion if we change the child support due to a change in the percentages of our incomes.

OR

_____ (parent) will contribute $ _____ per _____ (month, quarter, year, other), and _____ (other parent) will contribute $ _____ per _____ (month, quarter, year, other).

We or _____ (other person) have/has established a college fund (trust) for our child (children) which we agree will be sufficient to cover the cost of post-secondary education OR is sufficient that we agree not to contribute further to post-secondary education.

7.   Life Insurance as Security for Child Support *(See Chapter 9)*

_____ (paying parent) will maintain not less than $_____ of *(decreasing term)* life insurance, for the benefit of the children with _____ *(other or both parent(s))* as trustee, as security for the obligation to our children until the last child emancipates or reaches age _____ , whichever comes last. *(To allow for college completion, termination time may be later, usually age 22-24.)*

8.   Modification of Child Support *(See Chapter 13)*

We agree that the following sources of income will be used for _____ (parent) in calculating future child support: _____ .

We agree that the following sources of income will be used for _____ (other parent) in calculating future child support: _____ .

AND

We agree to exchange income tax returns, including all schedules, evidence of current income and verification of medical insurance coverage for the children and its cost on or before April 15 of each year, beginning _____. Using the income sources as we defined them above, we will re-calculate the basic child support on the appropriate worksheet on or before May first of each year beginning _____. If the resulting child support is more than ten percent different from the existing child support amount, we will change to the new amount. We will agree to make this change in writing, sign it in front of a Notary, and send it to the Court (along with current financial affidavits) for placing in our file. *(Once either or both of you have remarried, you may wish to change this clause to provide for exchange of income tax information only, such as your W-2's, 1099's, or schedules which relate only to the two of you, in order to protect the privacy of your new spouses.)*

AND

Should either of us experience a major change of income (loss of job, retirement, promotion, raise, step-increase, any change greater than _____%, win the lottery, receive a large inheritance, Worker's Compensation, Unemployment Insurance, or other benefits), we will notify the other parent within thirty days, and will, within forty-five days, re-calculate the child support incorporating the change.

AND

We agree that as each of our children emancipates we will re-calculate child support for the remaining children on the appropriate worksheet using our then current incomes as defined by us in this agreement.

9. Enforcement of Child Support *(See Chapter 13)*

We agree that all child support (and maintenance) payments will be made by income assignment. _____ *(paying spouse)* will sign an Notice to Withhold Income for Support before/on the day of the entry of our decree and deliver it to his/her employer immediately.

OR

We agree that there is good cause not to require the immediate activation of an income assignment for child support (and maintenance) payments because _____ *(paying parent)* agrees to keep _____ *(receiving parent)* informed in writing of his/her employer and information on any health insurance coverage to which _____ *(paying parent)* has access.

If either of us fails to make any child support or any other payment on behalf of a child as agreed to here, the tax benefits related to that payment may be taken by the other parent. (Failure to pay day care will result in the other parent having the child care credit if they qualify; failure to pay basic child support loses the dependency exemption for that parent, etc.)

AND/OR

No money owing to _____ *(paying parent)* as written in this agreement (promissory note for division of property, repayment of any kind, etc.) will be paid unless all child support obligations have been paid in full at the time the money is due.

AND

Any missed child support payment is a judgment and may be collected by any means, including garnishment and levy on assets.

AND

_____ *(paying parent)* will immediately execute an income assignment for payment of the child support agreed to and will amend it each time we change the amount.

OR

If any payment for child support is more than twenty days late, the paying parent will immediately execute an income assignment or other direct transfer for all subsequent child support payments, including any arrears through the date of the first payment made by _____ *(income assignment/direct deposit/electronic transfer/other).* (Use this provision if the court has given you permission to opt out of an automatic income assignment at the time of your decree.

OR

_____ *(paying parent)* will arrange for the electronic transfer of each child support payment into _____'s *(receiving parent's)* checking account on the _____ day of each month.

E. MAINTENANCE *(See Chapter 10)*

1. Maintenance Provisions

Each of the following kinds of maintenance may have its own tax rules and consequences, its own rules for modification, and may tie to other parts of your agreement in different ways. The following clauses are suggested in the alternative, but some can be combined and some can be used sequentially. READ CHAPTERS 10 AND 11 BEFORE INCLUDING ANY MAINTENANCE IN YOUR AGREEMENT.

a. _____ will pay to _____ the sum of $_____ per month as maintenance, starting _____, 200____ (usually month of following your Decree, or whenever you started it), in order to equalize our gross incomes. This amount will be adjusted on an annual basis by subtracting the lower of our incomes from the higher of our incomes, and dividing this difference in half. This resulting figure is the new maintenance amount to which we will agree in writing, sign before a notary, and file with the Court, asking that it be made into an Order.

We will calculate maintenance this way (for not less than _____ years/months) (for not more than _____ years/months) (from _____ [date] through _____ [date]).

OR

b. _____ will pay to _____ as maintenance the sum of $_____ per _____ *(month, quarter, year)*, starting _____, 200____ (usually month of following your Decree, or whenever you started it). This amount will reduce to $_____ per _____ *(month, quarter, year)* OR an amount to be determined on each of the following occasions: the retirement of _____ *(the paying spouse)*; receipt by _____ *(the receiving spouse)* retirement or other income. *(You may wish to include here such windfalls as winning Lotto or inheriting a substantial sum.)*

OR

c. _____ will pay to _____ as maintenance $_____ per month, starting _____, 200____ (usually month of following your Decree, or whenever you started it), in order to assist _____ *(receiving spouse)* in the payment of housing. This amount will be adjusted as and when _____'s *(receiving spouse's)* mortgage payment changes. These payments will end entirely in the month in which _____'s *(the receiving spouse's)* mortgage is paid off OR when _____ sells or moves from the property OR when _____ *(receiving spouse)* no longer pays for his or her own housing OR if receiving spouse loses the house through non-payment.

OR

d. _____ will receive directly from _____ *(paying spouse's business)* as maintenance, per _____ *(month, quarter, year)*, ____% of the business net profits for that period of time as shown on profit and loss statement calculated monthly *(quarterly)* by _____ *(accounting service, bookkeeper, etc.—not the paying spouse's calculation).* *(This use of maintenance may be unfamiliar to your accountant or even your lawyer. Be certain you work with a CPA or attorney with special knowledge of this method. It is beyond the scope of this book.)*

OR

e. _____ *(paying spouse)* will pay to _____ *(receiving spouse)* the sum of $_____ per month for _____ months through _____ *(year) (the term remaining on a certain joint debt which the receiving spouse will make the payments on).* This amount will not be modifiable, and will terminate only on the death of either party or the sale or payoff of the _____ *(loan for item of property, or house second mortgage)*, except that the receiving spouse will re-finance, pay-off or sell the _____ *(property)* within 30 days of his or her re-marriage, and pay the remaining balance on this debt, at which time all maintenance will cease.

OR

f. _____ will pay to _____ as maintenance $_____ per month for a period of _____ years *(months)* unmodified. *(This goes with a clause agreeing to make equal payments on the marital debts.)*

For any kind of maintenance you need to say how long it will last. Maintenance shall continue until _____'s *(receiving spouse)* death or remarriage, or _____ *(date)*, whichever occurs first. *(Omit the date if you are doing lifetime maintenance.)*

For any kind of maintenance where you want to shift the income taxes, you must say so.

We intend for all maintenance payments to be included in income for _____ (receiving spouse), and to be deductible from income for _____ (paying spouse), for income tax purposes.

OR

If one or both of you is not receiving maintenance in your agreement, then you must have the waiver in writing in your separation agreement.

_____(one spouse) hereby waives, now and for all time, any right to ask for maintenance from _____(other spouse). He/She understands that if he/she does not provide for maintenance now, he/she can not ask for it in the future. *(Repeat for other spouse if both are waiving maintenance.)*

2. Life Insurance as Security for Maintenance

_____ shall continue to maintain _____ years decreasing term of life insurance in (initial) amount of $_____ , and with _____ *(receiving spouse)* as irrevocable beneficiary until all maintenance provided for in this agreement has been paid in full. *(This insurance policy can be the same as the policy securing child support, but be sure to add the amounts of coverage together.)*

3. Medical Insurance

_____ *(non-employee spouse)* will *(not)* exercise the COBRA option available through
_____'s *(employee spouse's)* place of employment. We understand the premium will initially be $_____ per _____ *(month, quarter, year)*. _____ *(non-employee spouse)* will be solely responsible for paying this premium, and will hold _____ *(employee spouse)* harmless.

OR

_____ *(employee spouse)* will pay this premium as maintenance on behalf of
_____ *(non-employee spouse)*.

4. Modification of Maintenance

Many of the sample clauses in this Guidebook have built-in modifications. You may use the following in addition, or instead. You MUST specify when and if your maintenance is to be modifiable or to cease.

a. We agree that our maintenance provision(s) is/are contractual and therefore not to be modified even if circumstances change, except for _____ *(termination on the death of the recipient, remarriage of the recipient, other)*.

We agree that our maintenance provision(s) is/are to be modifiable on the following occurrences: _____ months/years from the date the signing of our agreement *(from the date of our decree)*; major increase *(decrease)* in *(either of our) (paying spouse's) (recipient spouse's)* incomes; completion by recipient spouse of _____ degree/training; payment of $_____ ; _____ moving from _____ ; death or remarriage of recipient spouse in which case maintenance will cease (reduce to $_____); other.

5. Enforcement of Maintenance

We agree that all maintenance payments will be made by income assignment. _____ *(paying spouse)* will sign a Notice to Withhold Income for Support before/on the date of our Decree, and deliver it to his/her employer immediately.

OR

We agree that there is good cause not to require the immediate activation of an Income Assignment for maintenance because _____ *(paying spouse)* has previously made timely payments.

Any maintenance payment required in this agreement which is more than twenty days late will not be tax deductible by the paying spouse or taxable to the receiving spouse.

OR

The maintenance payments required in this agreement are to be secured by a promissory note and a deed of trust against the residence occupied by the paying spouse until the maintenance has been paid in full. *(This is useful only for fixed-term maintenance where the total amount can be calculated.)*

OR

(You may use the following if you are using maintenance to meet certain joint obligations such as mortgage payments on jointly titled property, or payments on marital debts or car loans.) Should _____ *(receiving spouse)* fall more than forty-five days behind on _____ *(joint mortgage payment, car or debt payment)* then _____ *(paying spouse)* is no longer responsible for paying maintenance, and/or has first option to assume the obligation and receive the property.

_____ *(paying spouse)* will establish a voluntary income assignment at his or her place of employment for the full amount of the maintenance beginning _____ *(month after the decree, or month after the agreement, whichever comes first).*

OR

_____ *(paying spouse)* will arrange for the electronic transfer of each maintenance payment into _____'s *(receiving spouse's)* account on the _____ day of each month.

① ☐ District Court   ☐ Denver Juvenile Court

_____ County, Colorado

Court Address:

② ☐ **In re the Parental Responsibilities concerning the children named herein:**
☐ **In re the Marriage of:**
Petitioner:

v.

Respondent/Co-Petitioner:

▲   COURT USE ONLY   ▲

Case Number:

Division: Courtroom:

SUPPORT ORDER

Petitioner:
Date of Birth: _____ Social Security No.: _____
Mailing Address: _____
Residential Address: _____
Name of Employer: _____
Address of Employer: _____

③ Respondent/Co-Petitioner:
Date of Birth: _____ Social Security No.: _____
Mailing Address: _____
Residential Address: _____
Name of Employer: _____
Address of Employer: _____

④ The Court orders the ☐ Petitioner ☐ Respondent/Co-Petitioner _____

⑤ (the Obligor), to pay ☐ Child Support ☐ Maintenance to _____

(the Obligee), commencing (date) _____ **⑥** _____. Payments are due on _____ **⑥** _____

_____, Total arrears owed as of (date) _____ **⑦** _____

for Child Support $_____ **⑧** _____, and/or Maintenance $_____ **⑨** _____.

The total monthly obligation is as follows: **⑩** $ _____ Current Child Support

      ⑪ $ _____ Current Maintenance

Total Retroactive Child Support $ _____ .... **⑫** $ _____ Retroactive Support

      ⑬ $ _____ Payment Toward Arrears (child support)

      ⑭ $ _____ Payment Toward Arrears (maintenance)

For a total monthly payment of .... **⑮** $ _____

⑯ ☐ Upon payment in full of the Retroactive Support, the monthly payment is reduced to $_____.

⑰ The children of this marriage for whom support is ordered are: (State name, sex, date of birth and Social Security number of each children):

Name of Children	Sex	Date of Birth	Social Security No.
_____	_____	_____	_____
_____	_____	_____	_____
_____	_____	_____	_____
_____	_____	_____	_____
_____	_____	_____	_____

Bradford Publishing, 1743 Wazee St., Denver, CO 80202 — 303-292-2500 — www.bradfordpublishing.com

18 ☐ The Court orders the immediate activation of an income assignment against the Obligor pursuant to Section 14-14-111.5, C.R.S.

    19 ☐ Income assignments must be paid through the Family Support Registry, pursuant to Section 26-13-114(6)(a), C.R.S.

    ☐ The income assignment shall be paid directly to the Obligee.

OR

20 ☐ This Order is not subject to the immediate activation of an income assignment because either:

    A ☐ Both parties have agreed in writing to an alternative arrangement.

    B ☐ The Court finds there is good cause not to require immediate deductions because:

_____

_____

_____

21 ☐ The Court orders the ☐ Petitioner ☐ Respondent/Co-Petitioner to provide medical insurance for the children through the employer. Insurer _____

Insurer Address _____ Policy No. _____

22 ☐ The Court orders the ☐ Petitioner ☐ Respondent/Co-Petitioner to provide dental insurance for the children through the employer. Insurer _____

Insurer Address _____ Policy No. _____

23 ☐ The Court finds that ☐ health ☐ dental insurance is not currently available to either party at a reasonable cost and does not order either party to provide coverage for the children at this time, but does order the parties to provide coverage when it becomes available at a reasonable cost.

24 Payments shall continue until further order of the Court or as otherwise set forth in the Decree or Support Order, which is dated _____. Payments shall be mailed to:

    25 ☐ Family Support Registry   OR   ☐ Directly to the Obligee
        P.O. Box 2171
        Denver, CO 80201-2171

26 Date: _____

                                  _____

                                  ☐ District Court Judge
                                  ☐ District Court Magistrate

Support Order

You will use this form if you have children and child support calculated on Worksheets A or B. (If you do not have children, skip this form.)   See Chapter 9 for how to develop a complete and workable child support agreement. You may also use this form for maintenance if there is no child support.

INSTRUCTIONS FOR FILLING OUT THE SUPPORT ORDER

1. Check the box for District Court in the first section and "In re the Marriage of" if you are using this form in a divorce or legal separation action. Check the box for Denver Juvenile Court and "In re the Parental Responsibilities etc., if you are not married and seeking support.

2. Fill in the names of each of you as you would on the Petition.

3. Complete the information about the Petitioner and the Respondent/Co-Petitioner, if either of you is self-employed, note that in the space for the name of employer.

4. Check the box for Petitioner or Co-Petitioner/Respondent according to who will pay support (called the Obligor) and fill in the name of that person.

5. Check one or both boxes according to whether this is child support, maintenance, or both, and the name of the party who will receive it. The person is called the Obligee.

6. Fill in the date the support will begin and when the payments will be paid, i.e. monthly on the first day of each month.

7. If there is any unpaid past due support or maintenance owing, fill in the probable date this order will be signed or the date on which you last calculated the arrears.

8. Fill in the total amount of unpaid past due child support as of the date of the hearing. If none, put "0" or "none".

9. Fill in the total amount of unpaid past due maintenance as of the date of the hearing. If none, put "0" .

10. Fill in the amount of current support you have agreed to.

11. Fill in the amount of current maintenance you have agreed to, if any. If none, put "0" or "none."

12. If you have agreed on an amount of retroactive support (from the date of your physical separation, filing the petition, or service upon the respondent) enter that total in the first blank and the monthly payment in the second blank

> **D** **Retroactive Child Support**
> **DEFINITION** You may, if you wish, determine an amount one of you owes the other for past child support, going back to the date of your physical separation or the date of the filing of the petition or service upon the respondent, "whichever is latest," says the statute. You do not need to prepare a child support worksheet for this. Once you have a total for retroactive support that you both agree on, you can pay it now, put it in with all the other items in your property settlement, or decide on an interest rate and an amount for monthly payments. In this last case, it will be shown on the Support Order which accompanies your Decree.

13. Fill in the monthly payment you have agreed to for unpaid past due support listed in step 8 above.

In practice, many people make this 1/24 of the whole, plus interest, so it is paid off in 2 years. However, you can also design the payments so that it will be paid off at the end of the tax year, or the annual date on which you have agreed to review the support amount, or any other date which you agree on.

14. Fill in the monthly payment you have agreed to for unpaid past due maintenance that you listed in step 9. (see Caution at step 13).

15. Fill in the total of steps 10 through 14.

16. If you filled in an amount in step 12 for retroactive support, check this box. Subtract the monthly payment that you entered on step 12 from the total in step 15 and enter that new payment in this blank.

17. List the name, sex, date of birth, and social security number of all children for whom this support is being paid.

18. Check this box if you have agreed to payment by income assignment. (For more information on income assignments see later in this chapter and Chapter 9.)

19. If you have agreed to pay support through the Family Support Registry, or the court has ordered you to do so, check the first box. If payment will be deducted by income assignment, but made directly to the parent receiving the payment, check the second box.

20. Check this box if you wish the court to permit you to do without an income assignment, and check A or B to indicate the reason. Check A if you have included a provision in your agreement which ensures the payments, such as a direct transfer (useful when self-employed) or payment by a third party such as a business or trust. Check B and write an explanation of why you expect the court to allow you to do without an income assignment, such as a proven record of direct, timely payments. There is no guarantee that the court will approve either exception. It may be wise to prepare an income assignment form just in case.

Check whichever of the boxes in steps 21 to 23 describes your agreement about health and dental insurance for the children:

21. If one of you will be paying for health insurance, check the first box and then the box for either the Petitioner or the Respondent/Co-Petitioner. Fill in the name and address of the insurance company and the policy number.

22. If one of you will be paying for dental insurance, check the first box and then the box for either the Petitioner or the Respondent/Co-Petitioner. Fill in the name and address of the insurance company and the policy number.

23 If either health or dental insurance is not available at this time at a reasonable cost, check the first box and the type of insurance that it applies to.

24. Write here the date you expect the decree to be signed (date of hearing) or leave blank if you are doing a divorce by affidavit.

25. Check the box for whether payments will be mailed to the Family Support Registry or directly to the Obligee.

26. Leave this blank. The court will sign and date this.

Income Withholding for Support and Insurance

Since January 1994, Colorado has required that child support and maintenance with child support, be paid by means of an income assignment, in most situations. This means that the court-ordered amount is withheld directly by the employer of the paying spouse and sent directly to the receiving spouse. In cases brought through the Child Support Enforcement Unit, the money is sent to the Colorado Family Support Registry in Denver and then forwarded to the receiving spouse. In some private cases, the money is sent directly to a bank account designated by the receiving spouse. The important aspect of this law is not where the money is sent but how it is obtained. With an income assignment, because the money never goes through the paying spouse's hands, he or she is never tempted to hang onto it or use it for other purposes.

The court will presume your support, or support plus maintenance, will be paid via income assignment unless: a) you have agreed in writing that it will be paid directly or in some other manner, or b) the paying spouse is self-employed or working for a number of employers so that an income assignment is not possible or is cumbersome.

In addition to an income assignment for support, a more recent amendment to the law permits an income assignment for health insurance premiums for minor children.

An even newer wrinkle permits the court to order the employer to cover the minor children, even if the paying spouse had failed or refused to do so. There has long been some question among employers and insurance companies whether they could or should insure children who do not live with their employee or, more often, when their employee did not, or could not, claim the child as a dependent exemption. Now it is clear that the employer and insurer can and should, and must if the company is covered by ERISA. See Chapter 7 about ERISA companies and Chapter 11 about dependency exemptions.

The forms include a lengthy advisement to the employer about how much he must withhold and how much income is protected as to his employee. This information makes collection that much more likely and hassle-free.

Select from these forms to fit your facts. Do use them if you can in order to protect your children from the all-too-human potential frailties and temptations of their parents. No receiving parent need feel they are being mean by asking that the payments for their children be paid in this reliable manner. No paying parent need feel punished by being asked to see that payments for the benefit of their children are secure.

"If the court orders a garnishment I'll get fired."

Your employer is not allowed to fire you because you have a garnishment for child support or maintenance—whether the garnishment is by court order or a voluntary wage assignment.

"I don't have to do a wage assignment if I don't want to."

This is true only if you and your soon-to-be-ex agree to an alternate method of payment. Otherwise, the law requires an income assignment where possible.

(1) District Court, _____ County, Colorado
Court Address:

In re: _____
Petitioner:

v.

Respondent/Co-Petitioner:

Attorney or Party Without Attorney (Name and Address):

▲ COURT USE ONLY ▲

Phone Number: E-mail:
FAX Number: Atty. Reg. #:

Case Number:

Division: Courtroom:

NOTICE TO WITHHOLD INCOME FOR SUPPORT

(2) Date of Notice: _____
To: (Employer, Trustee, or Other Payor of Funds)

(3) Re: Obligor:
Social Security No.:
(4) Family Support Registry (FSR) Account No.: _____
(5) Obligee:

CHILD(REN) INFORMATION

Name	DOB	Name	DOB

(6)

NOTICE INFORMATION: This is a Notice to Withhold Income for Support based upon an order for support from
_____**(7)**_____. By law, you are required to deduct these amounts from the
above-named employee's/obligor's income until you are notified in writing by the Obligee, Obligee's representative, the child
support enforcement unit or the Court, even if the Notice is not issued by your State.

(8) ☐ If checked, you are required to enroll the child(ren) identified above in any health insurance coverage available through the
employee's/obligor's employment.

$ ___**(9)**___ per month in current child support
$ ___**(10)** **(A)**___ per month in past due support at ___**(B)**___ % interest (1/24th of total)
$ ___**(11)**___ per month in current maintenance
$ ___**(12)** **(A)**___ per month in past due maintenance at ___**(B)**___ % interest (1/24th of total)
$ ___**(13)**___ per month in medical support
for a total of $ ___**(14)**___ per month to be forwarded to the payee below.

You do not have to vary your pay cycle to be in compliance with the support order. If your pay cycle does not match the ordered
support payment cycle, use the following to determine how much to withhold:

**Note: Colorado state law requires that you divide the withholding among the pay periods for the month, but the total
amount withheld in a month must equal the monthly amount due as specified on the income assignment.**

$ ___**(15)**___ per weekly pay period
$ ___**(16)**___ per biweekly pay period (every two weeks)
$ ___**(17)**___ per semimonthly pay period (twice a month)
$ ___**(18)**___ per monthly pay period

No. 1155. Rev. 7-00. NOTICE TO WITHHOLD INCOME FOR SUPPORT (JDF 1804) (Page 1)

Bradford Publishing, 1743 Wazee St., Denver, CO 80202 —303-292-2500 —www.bradfordpublishing.com

REMITTANCE INFORMATION

You must begin withholding no later than the first pay period occurring 14 working days after the date of this Notice. Send payment within 7 working days of the paydate/date of withholding. You are entitled to deduct a fee to defray the cost of withholding. Refer to the laws governing the work state of the employee for the allowable amount. The total withheld amount including your fee, cannot exceed 65% of the employee's/obligor's aggregate disposable weekly earnings, (see #9)

19 When remitting payment, provide the paydate/date of withholding and FSR Account Number _____.
Make it payable to:
Send check to:

ADDITIONAL INFORMATION TO EMPLOYERS AND OTHER WITHHOLDERS

20 ☐ **If checked you are required to provide a copy of this form to your employee.**

1. **Priority:** Withholding under this Notice has priority over any other legal process under State law against the same income. Federal tax levies in effect before receipt of this Notice have priority. If there are Federal tax levies in effect please contact the requesting agency.

2. **Combining Payments:** You can combine withheld amounts from more than one employee's/obligor's income in a single payment to each agency requesting withholding. You must, however, separately identify the portion of the single payment that is attributable to each employee/obligor.

3. ***Reporting the Paydate/Date of Withholding:** You must report the paydate/date of withholding when sending the payment. The paydate/date of withholding is the date on which the amount was withheld from the employee's wages. You must comply with the law of the state of employee's/obligor's principal place of employment with respect to the time periods within which you must implement the withholding order and forward the support payments.

4. ***Employee/Obligor with Multiple Support Withholdings:** If there is more than one Notice to Withhold Income for Support against this employee/obligor and you are unable to honor all support Notices due to Federal or State withholding limits, you must follow the law of the state of employee's/obligor's principal place of employment. You must honor all Notices to the greatest extent possible. (see #9)

5. **Termination Notification:** You must promptly notify, in writing, the payee or the FSR, if payments are made through the FSR, when the employee/obligor is no longer working for you. Please provide the information requested and return a copy of this Notice to the payee or the FSR, if applicable.

   Employee's/Obligor's Name: _____

21 Employee's Case Identifier: _____ Date of Separation: _____
   Last Known Home Address: _____
   New Employer's Name and Address: _____

6. **Lump Sum Payments: You may be required to report and withhold from lump sum payments such as bonuses, commissions, or severance pay.**

7. **Liability:** If you fail to withhold income as the Notice directs, you are liable for both the accumulated amount you should have withheld from the employee's/obligor's income and any other penalties set by State law.

8. **Anti-discrimination:** You are subject to a fine determined under State law for discharging an employee/obligor from employment, refusing to employ, or taking disciplinary action against any employee/obligor because of a support withholding.

9. ***Withholding Limits:** You may not withhold more than the lesser of: 1) the amounts allowed by the Federal Consumer Credit Protection Act (15 USC §1673(b); or 2) the amounts allowed by the State of the employee's/obligor's principal place of employment. The Federal limit applies to the aggregate disposable weekly earnings (ADWE). ADWE is the net income left after making mandatory deductions such as: State, Federal, local taxes; Social Security taxes; and Medicare taxes.

10. Colorado employers, trustees, or other payers of funds must comply with §14-14-111.5, Colorado Revised Statutes attached.

***NOTE:** If you or your agent are served with a copy of this Notice in the state that issued the Notice you are to follow the law of the state that issued this Notice with respect to these items.

NOTICE: A fraudulent submission of a Notice to Withhold Income for Support shall subject the person submitting the Notice to an employer, trustee, or other payor of funds to a fine of not less than one thousand dollars and court costs and attorney fees. (Section 14-14-111.5(4)(n), C.R.S.)

CERTIFICATE OF MAILING

I certify that a true and correct copy of this Notice to Withhold Income for Support and a certified copy of the Support order were placed in the United States Mail, postage prepaid, on (date) _____, addressed to the employer as follows:

_____
(Signature)

No. 1155. (JDF 1804) (Page 2)

Notice to Withhold Income for Support

This form is used to inform an employer or other withholder what amount is required to be withheld from the paying spouse's income for child support or maintenance. Self-employed persons, people doing sub-contracting for several companies, or others who do not have a steady paycheck from a single payroll office probably won't be able to do an income assignment. These persons can usually set up some kind of auto-matic transfer from an account of one spouse to an account of the other, or simply mail or deliver a perso-nal check on a regular and timely basis.

INSTRUCTIONS FOR FILLING OUT THE NOTICE TO WITHHOLD INCOME FOR SUPPORT

1. Check the box for District Court and fill in the county and case number as on your petition. After "In Re:" write "the marriage of:"

2. Fill in the date you are completing this form and the name and address of the employer, trustee, or other person or entity who pays your spouse.

3. Fill in the name, and social security number of the paying spouse.

4. Fill in the account number of the Family Support Registry, if you have one.

5. Fill in the name of the spouse to whom the support is to be paid.

6. Fill in the name and date of birth of each child for whom support has been ordered.

7. Fill in the name of the paying spouse.

8. Check this box if the paying spouse is required to provide health insurance coverage for the children.

9. Fill in the amount you wish to be deducted every month for current child support (the total amount on your child support worksheet).

10. Fill in here: (A) the amount toward child support owing from the past and (B) the interest rate. You may have agreed to a temporary settlement and the full amount may not have been paid in full by this date. If no amount is owing from the past, enter "0".

11. Fill in the amount you wish to be deducted every month for current maintenance.

12. Fill in (A) the monthly payment amount toward maintenance owing from the past, and (B) the interest rate. You may have agreed to a temporary settlement and the full amount may not have been paid in full by this date. If no amount is owing from the past, enter "0".

13. Fill in the amount you wish to be deducted every month for medical support.

14. Add steps 9 through 13.

15. Multiply the amount in 14 times 12, then divide the result by 52.

16. Multiply the amount in 14 times 12, then divide the result by 26.

17. Divide the amount in 14 by 2.

18. Same amount as in step 14.

19. Fill in the FSR account number and the name of the receiving spouse, and the address to which you want the payments sent.

20. Check this box if you want the employer to give a copy of this document to the paying spouse.

21. This section will be filled out by the employer if the paying spouse changes employers.

22. If you wish, you may prove that the paying spouse's employer received the Notice to Withhold Income for Support by filling in the date on which one of you sent it by certified mail or personally delivered it. If you wish to formally serve it, you may adapt the form for return of service (see the back of the summons in Chapter 6).

For most friendly divorces, the paying spouse will provide this form to his or her employer, and can fill in this section with a third option:

I handed a copy of this Notice to Withhold Income for Support to my employer or his agent _____ / the payroll office at my employment / or _____, on _____ (date).

_____
Signature

The original of this form goes to the court to be placed in your file. Make additional copies for the paying spouse's employer, for yourself, and for the receiving spouse.

Note: If you are the paying spouse, you must keep the receiving spouse informed of your current employer and any health insurance that you have access to.

①

District Court, _____ County, Colorado
Court Address:

In re:_____
Petitioner:

v.

Respondent/Co-Petitioner:

Attorney or Party Without Attorney (Name and Address):

▲ COURT USE ONLY ▲

Case Number:

Phone Number: E-mail:

FAX Number: Atty. Reg. #:   Division: Courtroom:

NOTICE TO EMPLOYER TO DEDUCT FOR HEALTH INSURANCE

② TO: Name of Employer _____

Address of Employer _____

Pursuant to §14-14-112, C.R.S., you are required to enroll the child, or children listed below, of the Obligor (and the Obligor, if required by the plan) in the health insurance plan offered by you for the Obligor's benefit.

③ Name of Obligor _____ Soc. Sec. No. _____

Address _____

Name of Child or Children   Birthdate   Soc. Sec. No.

④

You are required to deduct from the wages due the Obligor an amount sufficient to provide for premiums for health insurance for the Obligor and his/her child. **PREMIUM PAYMENTS ARE TO BE MADE DIRECTLY TO THE INSURANCE CARRIER.** Please deduct for health insurance premiums before you deduct any amounts for child support pursuant to §14-14-111.5, C.R.S.

If the Obligor is no longer employed by you, you shall promptly notify the Court in writing of the Obligor's last-known address, social security number, and the name of the Obligor's new employer, if known.

THE OBLIGOR'S CHILD SHALL BE ENROLLED IN THE HEALTH INSURANCE PLAN IN WHICH THE OBLIGOR IS ENROLLED IF THE CHILDREN CAN BE COVERED UNDER THE PLAN. If the Obligor is not enrolled in a plan, the child shall be enrolled in the least costly plan otherwise available to the child regardless of whether the child was born out of wedlock, is claimed as a dependent on the Obligor's federal or state income tax return, lives with the Obligor, or lives within the insurer's service area, notwithstanding any other provision of law restricting enrollment to persons who reside in an insurer's service area. Health insurance shall include medical insurance and dental insurance, if available.

This withholding shall take effect no later than the first pay period after 14 days from the date on which this Notice is mailed to you or from the date on which the Obligor submits an oral or written request to you, whichever occurs sooner. The deduction for health insurance is treated as a significant life change under open enrollment requirements.

IT IS YOUR RESPONSIBILITY to ensure the enrollment of the child of the Obligor in a health insurance plan and that premium payments are withheld and forwarded to the insurer. If you wrongfully fail to deduct health insurance premiums, you, the employer, may be liable for the amount of accumulated premiums that should have been withheld from the Obligor's wages. You shall not discharge, refuse to hire, or take disciplinary action against an employee because of the entry or service of this Notice. If you do, you may be found in contempt of court and the Obligor may bring a civil action against you for reinstatement, lost wages, costs, and attorney's fees. Compliance with this Notice shall not subject you to liability to the Obligor for wrongful withholding. As long as the Obligor is employed by you, this Notice shall not be terminated or modified, except as follows: (a) upon written notice by the Court, Obligee, or the Delegate Child Support Enforcement Unit; or (b) you determine (and the Obligor verifies in writing) that the child is enrolled in a comparable health insurance plan that takes effect no later than the effective date on which the child is no longer enrolled under your plan; or (c) you eliminate family health coverage for all employees. When enrollment is terminated for any of these reasons, within 14 days, you shall send, to the location described on the health insurance premium notice, a written notice of cancellation or a copy of the verification that the child is enrolled in a comparable health plan.

If the Obligor terminates employment, you must notify the Court, Obligee, or Delegate Child Support Enforcement Unit in writing within ten days after termination, and provide, if known, the name of the Obligor's new employer.

The Obligor may file an objection to this Notice with the Court if the premium amount does not meet the definition of reasonable cost as provided in §14-10-115(13.5)(g), C.R.S. A premium that results in a child support order of fifty dollars or less or that is 20 percent or more of the Obligor's gross income shall not be considered reasonable.

---

⑤   **CERTIFICATE OF MAILING**

I certify that on _____ (date), I filed a copy of this Notice with the Court, and sent the following by U.S. Mail, first class postage prepaid:

Original to Employer on _____.   Copy to Obligor on _____.

Name: _____   Name: _____

Address: _____   Address: _____

_____   _____

_____   _____

_____

Signature (Obligee or Obligee's Representative)

No. 1162. (Page 2 of 2)

Notice to Employer to Deduct for Health Insurance

You will use this form if you have children and child support and either parent has agreed or been ordered to provide health insurance for the children through his or her employment.

INSTRUCTIONS FOR FILLING OUR THE NOTICE TO DEDUCT FOR HEALTH INSURANCE

1. Fill out these lines the same as on the petition.

2. Fill in the name and address of the employer who provides the insurance for the children.

3. Fill in the name and address of the parent working for the employer in #2 who is providing insurance for the children, and that parent's social security number.

4. Fill in the name, birthdate, and social security number of each of the children who are to be covered by this insurance.

5. Fill out and sign the Certificate of Mailing showing that you sent the original Notice to the employer, one copy to the Obligor, and filed one copy with the court

NOTICE: If child support has been ordered in this case, an income assignment will be activated in the event of default in child support.

(1) District Court, _____ County, Colorado
Court Address:

In re the Marriage of:

Petitioner:

v.

Respondent/Co-Petitioner:

▲ COURT USE ONLY ▲

Case Number:

Division: Courtroom:

(2)   **DECREE OF**   ☐ **DISSOLUTION OF MARRIAGE**   ☐ **LEGAL SEPARATION**

This matter was reviewed by the court on _____**(3)**_____ (date).

Petitioner **(4)**
☐ Appeared in person
☐ Signed the non-appearance affidavit
☐ Was represented by _____

(5) ☐ Respondent   ☐ Co-petitioner
☐ Appeared in Person   ☐ Did not appear
☐ Signed the non-appearance affidavit
☐ Was represented by _____

(6) The court has examined the record,   ☐ heard the evidence and statements of _____
                 ☐ read the non-appearance affidavit of _____

and makes the following findings:

(7) 1. **(A)** ☐ The court has jurisdiction over both parties based upon:
     (B) ☐ The parties filing jointly on _____ (date)
     (C) ☐ Respondent signed waiver on _____ (date)
     (D) ☐ Service on _____ (person), on _____ (date)
         at _____ (place)
     (E) ☐ The court has jurisdiction over in-state property by *quasi in rem* publication.
     (F) ☐ The court has only subject matter jurisdiction by publication by consolidated notice, or certified mail.

(8) 2.   The _____ was domiciled in Colorado for ninety days before this case was filed.

3.   At least ninety days have passed since filing, service or completion of publication, whichever is later.

4.   The marriage between the parties is irretrievably broken.

(9) 5.   ☐ The separation agreement between the parties
       ☐ which is attached as Exhibit_____
       ☐ which has been read into the record and will be filed by the parties on or before _____
has been considered by the court and is found not to be unconscionable as to support, maintenance, and division of property.
(10) ☐ The court has entered permanent orders that will be filed by _____ (date).
☐ The court finds it is in the best interest of the parties that a decree be entered even though there is no permanent order on this date.

(11) 6.   ☐ All provisions of the parenting plan, including residence, parenting time, and decision-making, are in the best interests of the children.

(12) 7.   ☐ The name change request is not detrimental to the interest of any person.

(13) 8.   ☐ The attached support order becomes a part of this decree.

No. 251. Rev. 10-03. DECREE OF DISSOLUTION OF MARRIAGE OR LEGAL SEPARATION

Bradford Publishing 1743 Wazee St., Denver, CO 80202 — 303-292-2500—www.bradfordpublishing.com

14 The Court therefore ORDERS:

A ☐ The marriage is dissolved and a Decree of Dissolution of Marriage is entered.

B ☐ A Decree of Legal Separation is entered. The parties are advised that either may, six (6) months from this date, apply for entry of a Decree of Dissolution of Marriage, which will be granted upon proof of notice to the other party.

C ☐ Each parent shall perform the applicable provisions of the parenting plan.

D ☐ The _____ is granted a restoration of name to _____

Each party shall perform the applicable provisions of the separation agreement, permanent orders, or non-appearance affidavit.

THE COURT FURTHER ORDERS:

15

_____　　_____　　_____　　_____
Attorney for Petitioner　　　　　　　　　Date　　Attorney for Co-petitioner/Respondent　　　Date

16

_____　　_____　　_____　　_____
District Court Judge　　　　　　　　　　　Date　　District Court Magistrate　　　　　　　　　Date

Instructions For Decree of Dissolution of Marriage or Legal Separation

Although the decree reads as though the court wrote it, the court does not, in practice, fill it out. You must fill out the decree form as you wish the court to sign it.

1. Fill out these lines the same as you did on the petition. Be sure to include your case number and the division or court room number.

2. Check the appropriate box depending on whether you are asking for a dissolution of marriage or a legal separation.

   You may now be requesting something different from what you asked for in the petition. For example, you may have decided during the 90-day waiting period that you really do want to get divorced after all, even though your petition asks for a legal separation. Or, you might have asked for a dissolution in your petition and now prefer a legal separation in order to continue some benefit or to give yourselves a chance at preserving your relationship. (See Chapter 1 for a discussion of these considerations.)

   It is perfectly okay to "waffle" throughout the waiting period about whether you want a divorce or legal separation. Just be clear in your decree and separation agreement which marital status you both want now. If this is a change from what you asked for in your petition, it is a good idea, in either your separation agreement or your testimony at the final hearing—or both—to point out to the court that this is a change and why you want it. Once the decree is signed by the judge, you become that marital status, divorced or legally separated, so it is important to be certain you agree on which one you want in the final order of court.

3. If you are asking for a decree by affidavit (without hearing) leave this blank—the judge will write in this date. If you are expecting to have a hearing, fill in the date of the hearing.

4. As to the Petitioner: Check the box next to "Signed the non-appearance affidavit" if you are asking for a decree without a hearing. If you are going to the hearing, check the "Appeared in person" box.

5. As to the Co-Petitioner/Respondent: Check the same box you checked in step 3. In the boxes below, check the appropriate space for you, the Co-Petitioner, or your spouse, the Respondent, depending on whether he or she also signed the non-appearance affidavit, will personally appear in court, is represented by an attorney, or will not appear.

6. Check the box next to "heard the evidence and statements of" only if you or your spouse plan to appear in court. Indicate which of you will appear at the hearing by writing "Petitioner," "Respondent," or "Co-Petitioner,"—or "the parties" if you will both appear—in the space that follows. Check the box next to "read the affidavit of" if no one is appearing and you are filing the affidavit for decree without hearing. Indicate who signed that affidavit by writing "Petitioner," "Co-Petitioner," "Respondent," or "the parties" if you have both signed it.

7. Check the appropriate box according to whether you filed as co-petitioners, whether there was service, or waiver of service. (See Chapter 6 for a discussion of service of process.)
   - Check boxes A and B if you are co-petitioners. Show the date you filed the petition with the clerk of the district court and paid your filing fee.
   - Check boxes A and C if the respondent signed a waiver and acceptance of service. Show the date he or she signed the waiver.
   - Check boxes A and D if the respondent was personally served with a copy of the summons. Show the date, city and state where he/she was served.
   - Check box E only if the respondent was served by individual publication which included marital property specifically described in the summons.
   - Check box F if you published by consolidated notice or served by certified mail.

8. Indicate which or both of you was domiciled in Colorado for ninety days prior to filing your petition.

9. Check the appropriate box depending on whether:
   - You are making your separation agreement a part of your decree, in which case this will read, "attached as Exhibit A;" (Be sure to write "Exhibit A" on page 1 of your separation agreement.)
   - You have told the court the terms of your agreement and will write it up later (you run the risk of the court withholding approval of your decree until the written agreement is received).

10. Leave these boxes blank. These situations won't arise if you are doing your own divorce.

11. Check this box only if there are minor children.

12. Check this box only if either of you is asking for a former name back.

13. Check this box if you have completed a support order.

14. Check box A if you are asking for a dissolution of marriage.

   Check box B if you are asking for a legal separation.

   Check box C if you have completed a parenting plan.

   Check box D if you or your spouse are asking for a former name back, indicate this by writing whether the Petitioner or Co-Petitioner or Respondent—or both—wants the change, and then write in the complete new name(s). (Remember, you can only return to one of your names before the marriage through your divorce action, not change to a completely new name.)

15. You may both sign the Decree on the lines provided for attorneys. Delete "Attorney for" beneath both signature lines.

16. Leave these blank.

① District Court, _____ County, Colorado
Court Address:

In re the Marriage of:
Petitioner:

v.

Respondent:

Attorney or Party Without Attorney (Name and Address):

②

▲ COURT USE ONLY ▲

Case Number:

Phone Number: _____ E-mail: _____
FAX Number: _____ Atty. Reg. #: _____

Division: _____ Courtroom: _____

AFFIDAVIT FOR DECREE WITHOUT APPEARANCE OF PARTIES

③ The ☐ Petitioner ☐ Respondent/Co-petitioner files this affidavit in support of a request for issuance of a Decree of Dissolution of Marriage without appearance of parties.

④ 1. The petition was filed on _____. On that date, the _____⑤_____ had been domiciled in Colorado for more than ninety (90) days immediately before the petition was filed. The parties were

⑥ married on _____ at _____
and separated _____.

⑦ 2. The petition and summons were served on _____ (date) by:
    ☐ Personal Service ☐ Waiver of Service ☐ Publication/Certified Mail ☐ This is a co-petitioner filing.
    ☐ At least ninety (90) days have elapsed since that date.

⑧ 3. ☐ There are no minor children of the marriage and the wife is not pregnant. OR
    ☐ There are minor children, each party is represented by counsel, and the parties have entered into a separation agreement that provides for the allocation of parental responsibilities and child support for the child(ren) of this marriage.

⑨ 4. ☐ There is no marital property to be divided and there are no marital debts, OR
    ☐ The parties have filed a written separation agreement, supported by financial affidavits, that addresses
        ☐ maintenance, and provides for the division of marital property and debts.
        ☐ child support, the allocation of parental responsibilities and health insurance. A Parenting Plan has been completed that provides for the allocation of decision-making responsibilities and parenting time.

⑩ 5. ☐ Parties agree that the attached separation agreement is fair and not unconscionable ☐ that it is in the best interests of the child(ren).

6. There is no genuine issue of material fact, and the marriage is irretrievably broken.

⑪ 7. Restoration of the ☐ Petitioner's ☐ Respondent's/Co-petitioner's name to _____
will not defraud any creditors or injure any third party.

⑫ 8. Other: _____
_____
_____
_____
_____

13 The ☐ Petitioner ☐ Respondent/Co-petitioner requests that the attached Decree of Dissolution of Marriage be entered on or after _____ (date), without appearance of the parties.

14 _____

_____   _____   _____   _____
Petitioner Signature   Date   Respondent/Co-petitioner Signature   Date

_____   _____   _____   _____
Address   City/State/Zip   Address   City/State/Zip

(_____)_____   (_____)_____
Home Phone No.   Home Phone No.

(_____)_____   (_____)_____
Work Phone No.   Work Phone No.

15 State of Colorado   State of Colorado

County of _____ }   County of _____ }

Signed under oath before me on _____   Signed under oath before me on _____

My Commission expires _____   My Commission expires _____

_____   _____
Notary Public   Notary Public

16 _____   _____
Petitioner's Attorney   Respondent/Co-petitioner's Attorney

17 ═══

CERTIFICATE OF MAILING

(If Affidavit is signed by only one party, complete this Certificate of Mailing)

I certify that on _____ (date) I placed a copy of this *Affidavit for Decree Without Appearance of Parties* in the United States mail, postage pre-paid, addressed to the following:

TO: _____

_____

_____

_____
Signature

No. 252. (Page 2)

Divorce By Affidavit: Affidavit for Decree Without Appearance of Parties

If you have no minor children or you are both represented by different lawyers, and you are requesting a decree of dissolution of marriage, then you do not need to present your agreement at a hearing in order for the court to grant a final decree. You may mail in your final papers. If you have lawyers, they will probably prepare and mail the final papers for you.

If you are preparing your own papers and doing your divorce by affidavit, see the Checklist of Our Final Court Papers at the beginning of this chapter.

INSTRUCTIONS FOR FILLING OUT AFFIDAVIT FOR DECREE WITHOUT APPEARANCE OF PARTIES

1-2. Complete these lines the same as you did on your petition and all the other papers. Be sure to include the case number and the division or courtroom number.

3. Check the appropriate box or boxes to tell the court who is signing this affidavit, one of you or both of you.

     If only one of you signs this affidavit, you must prove that the other party received a copy. See step 17.

4. Write the date the petition was filed.

5. If you both were domiciled in Colorado for ninety (90) days prior to filing your petition, write "the parties" here. If only one of you was domiciled for 90 days, write "Petitioner," "Co-Petitioner," or "Respondent," whichever is true.

6. Write the date and place (city and state, or country if outside the U.S.) of your marriage. (See Chapter 1 for a discussion of common law marriage.) Write the date you physically separated.

7. If you are co-petitioners, this is the date you both signed the petition. Check the box for "A co-petitioner filing."

    If you are petitioner and respondent, this is the date on which the Respondent a) signed the Waiver and Acceptance of Service, or b) was personally served, or c) date received certified mailing, or d) last date of publication)." Check appropriate box in the second line depending on which of these kinds of service you used. (See Chapter 6 for definitions of these. This information is the same on the proposed Decree.)

8. Check the appropriate box.

9. Check either the first or second box. If you checked the second box, then check the third box if your agreement addresses maintenance and how you will divide your property and debts; and the fourth box if your agreement addresses child support, health insurance, and a parenting plan.

10. If you have property and minor children, be sure to check both boxes. If you have property but no minor children, check only the first box. If you have no property or children and you are not filing a separation agreement, do not check either box.

11. Cross out this line if neither party is asking the court to restore a prior name. If one or both of you plans to return to a former name, write "Petitioner," "Co-Petitioner," or "Respondent" here and fill in the name to be restored.

12. Add here any other requests you would like the court to order.

13. Check the appropriate boxes the same as you did for step 3. In the blank write the date of the day after the 90 day waiting period ends. This is 90 days from the date:

   a. You and your spouse signed your petition as petitioner and co-petitioner and filed it with the court; or
   b. your spouse signed a waiver and acceptance of service; or
   c. process was served on your spouse, or
   d. the last day of publication; AND
   e. the petition was filed within 10 days of b, c, or d.

 The date the 90 days began is the same as in Step 7.

14. One party must sign in the presence of a notary. If the other party is joining in this affidavit, he or she should also sign in front of a notary.

   NOTE: If you are not both signing this form, the signing spouse must notify the other (see step 17).

15. Leave these spaces blank.

16. If you are represented by attorneys, they will sign here. If you are doing this yourselves, write "none."

17. If only one of you signs this form, that person must send a copy by certified mail to the other spouse. Fill in the date you mail the copy, the name and address of the other spouse, and sign the certificate of mailing on the back of the affidavit. In practice, allow reasonable time for your spouse to object to not having a hearing, such as 20 or 30 days. You must allow for at least five working days from the date in this step to the date the court is likely to receive this affidavit. If the other spouse's address is not known, mail a copy of this form to his or her last known address. When you receive them back, file with the court the green receipt card from the Postal Service, or the entire envelope marked that delivery was not possible. In either case, be sure to put your case number on it.

Getting Your Case Set for a Hearing

The court may give you a date for a non-contested hearing either at the time you file, at the status conference (if you are under the simplified procedure), or afterward according to the procedures of your particular court. This is one of the areas in which the courts differ from one another. You will have to ask how they want the hearing set if they do not give you a sheet of instructions when you file. Some courts require an interim step called a Notice to Set—something you will not need if you are using the simplified procedure.

NOTICE TO SET

The purpose of a Notice to Set is to let the other party know that the case is being set for a hearing. You are telling your spouse that on a certain date and time you will call or drop by the court and ask them to find a date on the magistrate's calendar for hearing your case. The Notice to Set form follows this section and is on the CD-ROM.

Notice to Set
A form required by some courts that states the date and time you will contact the clerk of the court to set the date and time of your final hearing; not to be confused with Notice of Hearing Date or Setting Order.

Nowhere do courts differ as much as they do in how they want you to obain the date and time mentioned in this Notice. Some likely options are:

- The court may ask you to call the Setting Clerk when you are ready to set your case, and ask for a date to be put on the Notice to Set.

- The court may require that you send in the Notice of Hearing Date form—filled out except for the date. Then when you call, the clerk will fill in the date and mail it back.

- The court may ask that you bring or send in your final papers at which time they will give you a date for the Notice to Set.

- Some courts set certain kinds of cases on certain days and times—for example, all domestic cases do their settings on Thursday morning, all criminal cases on Friday—so you will just put down the next one of these days on your Notice to Set, once you learn from the clerk what that day is.

- Some courts always hear all non-contested divorces and/or all *pro se* divorces on the same day of the week or month, so you can simply pick one after the 90 days have passed and go directly to the Notice of Hearing Date and skip the Notice to Set.

Once you have ascertained that your court uses a Notice to Set and you have the correct date on it, send the original to the court.

If You Are Concerned About Privacy

In practice, the only document you are required to leave in your court file at the time of your final hearing is the decree, plus the child support worksheet(s) if you have children.

You must show your financial affidavits and your separation agreement to the judge at your hearing, in order for the judge to "find" your agreement to be "fair and not unconscionable" with regard to property, debts, and maintenance, and to be "in the best interest of the children" with regard to child support and your parenting plan. You may then ask that these documents be returned to you if you do not wish to have the separation agreement incorporated into the decree. Or, you may ask that all or some of your documentation be "sealed," which means that they may not be read without a judge's approval. See Chapter 2 for a more complete discussion of privacy in your divorce.

Most courts need at least three days before the date on which you will be calling to pull your file and make sure your case is ready to be set for hearing. For example: are there certificates of attendance for the parenting-after-divorce class, was there correct service of process, when will the 90 days be up?

Be sure that you send a copy of the Notice to Set to your spouse and fill in the Certificate of Service/Mailing on the original Notice to Set before you send it to the court. If there is the slightest chance that your spouse will want to come to court for the hearing, and/or if your spouse has a particularly rigid schedule (fireman, long distance truck driver) then it is best to send this form by certified mail. It shows the court that you did your best to be certain your spouse would be able to help find a date in order to attend the hearing.

District Court, _____ County, Colorado

Court address:

In re _____:

Petitioner:

v.

Respondent/Co-Petitioner:

Attorney or Party Without Attorney (Name and Address):

▲ COURT USE ONLY ▲

Case Number:

Phone Number: FAX Number:

E-mail: Atty. Reg. #:   Division: Courtroom:

NOTICE TO SET

You are hereby notified that the undersigned will contact the Clerk of the above-named Court at

_____ , on _____ , and set a date and time for hearing on:

Hour and AM/PM   Date

☐ Temporary Orders

☐ Final Hearing on Dissolution of Marriage

☐ Motion to Modify Child Support

The Court Clerk's phone number is _____ .

Date: _____

_____
Signature

_____
Name

_____
Address

_____

_____
Telephone Number

No. 1195. Rev. 2-03. NOTICE TO SET   Copyright 1997

Bradford Publishing, 1743 Wazee St., Denver, CO 80202 — (303) 292-2500 — www.bradfordpublishing.com

District Court, _____ County, Colorado

Court Address:

In re _____ :

Petitioner:

v.

Respondent:

Attorney or Party Without Attorney (Name and Address):

▲ COURT USE ONLY ▲

Phone Number: E-mail:

FAX Number: Atty. Reg. #:

Case Number:

Division: Courtroom:

NOTICE OF HEARING DATE

The ☐ Petitioner OR ☐ Respondent/Co-Petitioner confirms that a hearing date has been set in the following matter:

1. ☐ Permanent Orders for Dissolution of Marriage or Legal Separation.

2. ☐ The Motion for _____ filed by the ☐ Petitioner OR ☐ Respondent/Co-Petitioner.

3. The hearing will be held on _____ (date) at _____ (time)
   in Division/Courtroom _____. The hearing has been set for _____ hours/minutes.
   The address of the Courthouse is: _____

Date: _____

_____

☐ Petitioner OR ☐ Respondent/Co-Petitioner

_____
Address

_____
City, State, Zip Code

_____
(Area Code) Telephone Number (home and work)

CERTIFICATE OF SERVICE

I certify that on _____ (date) the original and one copy of this document were filed with the Court; and, a true and accurate copy of the *NOTICE OF HEARING DATE* was served on the other party by ☐ Hand Delivery OR ☐ Faxed to this number _____ OR ☐ by placing it in the United States mail, postage pre-paid, and addressed to the following:

TO: _____

_____

_____

_____
(Your Signature)

JDF 1108 R7/00 NOTICE OF HEARING DATE

Bradford Publishing, 1743 Wazee St., Denver, CO 80202 — 303-292-2500 — www.bradfordpublishing.com

NOTICE OF HEARING DATE (SETTING ORDER)

This is the form you will send your spouse that states the day and time of your final hearing. Fill in the top of this form, and the address for your spouse on the Certificate of Mailing. Send, or bring, the original to the court at the same time you send, or bring, the completed Notice to Set, if the court has a setting clerk. If your court skips the Notice to Set, then just fill out the Notice of Hearing Date with the date.

Once you have the Notice of Hearing Date all filled out, including the date and time of the hearing, mail a copy to your spouse by certified mail with sufficient time to allow the signed receipt or the whole envelope to come back to you before the hearing. You will take whichever it is to the hearing with you to show the court that you did, indeed, try to notify your spouse of the hearing date.

It is best if you both attend the hearing. This reassures the court that you do, indeed, agree. It also provides the court with a chance to ask any questions it might have of either of you.

APPEARANCE BY TELEPHONE

Some courts allow the appearance by telephone for one of the parties in non-contested hearings. This is especially useful when one spouse has already moved to another state. You must arrange the telephone call procedure in advance with the clerk of your particular courtroom. Most require a written request of the judge. Make clear arrangements including the exact time of the call, who will place the call, and of course the phone number. This information should be included on your Notice of Hearing Date.

WHAT TO BRING TO THE FINAL HEARING

Many courts require that all your final papers be filed with the court two or more weeks before your hearing date, while some courts ask you to *bring* them to the final hearing. Some require the originals plus one photocopy of every document. Be sure to keep copies of everything for each of you, not only for your own records, but to refer to at the hearing if there are questions. Make two copies of the Decree and clip them to the original, along with two stamped envelopes—one addressed to each of you.

AT THE HEARING

Make sure you are on time for your hearing. You should dress nicely, because it shows respect for yourself and for the legal process. Avoid jeans, shorts, undershirts or tank tops, halter tops, or play clothes.

Checklist of Our Papers Ready to Send to Court, or to Bring to Court for Our Final Hearing

Directions: Initial and date each item when it is ready for court.

Initials | Date Done

____ ____ Affidavit for Decree Without Appearance (if doing decree without a hearing, divorce by affidavit)
OR

____ ____ Notice of Hearing Date and Receipt (if only one of you is attending)

____ ____ Separation Agreement and / or including a Parenting Plan

____ ____ Wife's Financial Affidavit

____ ____ Husband's Financial Affidavit

____ ____ Decree

____ ____ QDRO (if applicable)

____ ____ Agreement to Divide Retirement Plan (if applicable)

If we have children:

____ ____ Child Suppor Worksheet(s) (usually attached to the separation agreement)

____ ____ Support Order

____ ____ Notice to Withhold Income for Support

Non-contested hearing: Appearance by one or both spouses before a magistrate to present their final separation agreement, and request that a final decree be signed by the court.

Unless you have previously filed all your final papers, hand them to the magistrate, clerk, or court reporter, as you are directed. In some counties, the clerk and court reporter are the same person. The magistrate, clerk, or court reporter will swear you in. Everything you say will be taken down either by a court reporter or tape recording.

Preparing your sample testimony ahead of time will help you stay organized during the hearing. Sometimes, the magistrate will ask you questions, usually the same ones that you have prepared, so you can look at your notes. The magistrate has the right to ask you what you are reading from and even to ask to see it. If the magistrate does not ask questions, he or she may tell you to "state your case." If this happens, begin reading your sample testimony out loud.

SAMPLE TESTIMONY

Most magistrates and other court officials who hear non-contested divorces are accustomed to working with laypersons. They will help you present your agreement or arguments and will direct how you are to file your papers. Just in case you encounter a magistrate who is as new at this as you are, here are the things you must not forget to say and do:

1.   State your name and address (both mailing and physical address if you have both).

2.   Tell the court whether you are the Petitioner, Co-Petitioner or Respondent in the case.

3.   Give the original of all your final papers to the magistrate, court clerk or reporter—whichever the court directs you to do. If you are not certain, ask.

4.   Read the statistical information in your Petition, pointing out any corrections which have come to light during your case. Have a copy of your Petition in front of you, so you can read down it in order. The magistrate will be following along on the court original.

You must state:
   a)   names of the parties; names and birth dates of the children, if any;
   b)   whether the wife is pregnant and, if so, if this is a child of the marriage;
   c)   date of the marriage and date of the separation;
   d)   date the case was filed, and which of you lived in the state for at least 90 days before that date.
   Point out if this is a Co-Petitioner filing.

5.   If your case is not a Co-Petitioner filing, turn to the back of the Summons and read the information there about the manner in which the case was served (waiver and acceptance of service or personal service) and, most important, the date of this service. Remember, this began your 90 days.

6.   If you served by certified mail or publication, draw the court's attention to the Order giving you permission to do so, and either the certified mail receipt or the proof of publication. These must have been completed at least 90 days before the hearing.

7.   State that you believe the marriage to be irretrievably broken, with no hope of a reconciliation. These are very precise phrases which enable the court to make the correct "finding" which in turn enables the court to issue the Decree, so be sure you state them exactly this way.

8.   Draw the court's attention to your separation agreement, partial agreement or written request for permanent orders. Tell the court the major points in this document, in the order they appear. Be certain you cover:

   a)   Parenting Plan for your children, if any, especially your decision-making and physical care provisions.
   b)   The amount of child support and maintenance, if any, and whether this is being paid by income assignment. Remember, if you are asking for a deviation from the recommended support or to pay directly instead of by assignment, you must have the court's permission. See Chapter 9 if this is news.
   c)   The way in which you are dividing your assets and paying your debts. Be certain to draw the court's attention to the fact that you made the mandatory exchange of documents and have each filed

financial affidavits so the court is reassured that you each had full knowledge of your assets and liabilities. Review Chapter 5 if you skipped this step.

If your spouse is not participating, then remind the court of this by way of explaining why there is only one financial affidavit and perhaps incomplete disclosure. If you served by publication, this is absolutely the time to tell the court that you want title to certain in-state assets and to point out that you specifically described these assets in the Summons which was published. This sets up the process for having the court clerk sign these assets over to you. See next chapter and review Chapter 6 if you missed out on this although you will almost certainly have to re-serve if you did.

d)   Any agreement about division of retirement accounts which requires the court to sign a separate document, such as a QDRO.

e)   Whether either of you wishes to be restored to a former name.

f)   Any other peculiarities of your agreement or requests which you think are important to place on the record.

g)   State that you believe the separation agreement is fair to you and your spouse, and that it is in the best interest of your children, if any. These are more of the phrases which you must say exactly this way so the court can make the correct findings and issue the orders you need.

9. Ask the court to approve your separation agreement, and to sign the Decree, Support Order, Notice of Income Withholding(s) and QDRO if any.

10. Introduce your spouse if he or she is present. The court will ask if your spouse wishes to testify also, and will almost certainly ask if he or she agrees the marriage is irretrievably broken with no hope of reconciliation and if he or she feels the separation agreement is fair and if the parenting plan is in the best interest of the children.

Once you have both given your testimony, the magistrate will spend a moment or so reviewing the papers you have filed, may ask another question or two to clarify things, and then will sign the Decree, Support Order, Notice of Income Withholding(s) and QDRO, if any. You are divorced the moment the magistrate signs the Decree, a fact which the court will undoubtedly announce as he or she does so.

You will probably not be able to go home with a signed copy of the Decree in your pocket, however. In most courts, the magistrate will return your court file to the clerk's office and they will "conform" the copy(s) of the Decree you left with the court and mail them to you in the self-addressed envelope(s) you provided. Some smaller jurisdictions do this for free without you having to supply either the Decree copy or the envelopes. You should ask in court if this is so, if the clerk of your court has not given you this information in writing or conversation.

What to Do if the Court Does Not Sign Your Decree

If the magistrate does not sign your decree, or another order you have asked for, he or she will tell you why, in person if you are there, or by mail if you apply for your decree by affidavit. It might be that you left out one of the necessary forms, or did not wait the full 90 days, or did not sign one of the papers. It may be that the court did not think some provision(s) of your separation agreement was fair or complete. You may:

- supply the missing form
- provide the missing signature
- wait the correct number of days
- amend or complete your separation agreement to conform to the court's questions

If the court is questioning your separation agreement and you are present in court, you may ask for a continuance to a later date to give you time to deal with the objection. If you applied for your decree by affidavit and your written response from the court does not tell you the reasons, you may request a hearing or a meeting with the judge or magistrate to discuss the problem.

If the court does not approve your agreement even after you have had a chance to explain, don't give up. This would be a good time to consult with a lawyer or lawyer-mediator, with expertise in family law, to find out either how to change your agreement to make it acceptable to the court, or how best to go about persuading the court to approve your agreement as is.

Copies of Your Decree

To prove you are divorced or legally separated, a copy of your final decree showing the court's signature and the date signed is usually sufficient. However, some insurance companies or other institutions may require a *certified copy*. Since the ORIGINAL which the court signs stays in the court file, you may ask the court clerk to certify your copies.

CERTIFIED COPIES

In some courts, the magistrate will sign the extra copies of your decree during your hearing or just afterwards. If this is done, you can take them to the clerk of the district court to be certified the same day. The clerk certifies that it is an accurate copy of the decree which the judge or magistrate signed that day, by signing and applying the court seal.

If the judge or magistrate does not sign the copies at the time of the hearing, then you may have all of your copies certified and returned to you by mail. You must give the court as many copies as you would like certified, a fee for each (usually $5.00), and stamped envelopes addressed to where you want them sent. Payment must be made by cash, cashier's check, or money order. The clerk will certify the copies by stamping them with a facsimile of the judge's signature, or a stamp that says "Original signed by _____ ," date it the day the original was signed, apply the court's seal, and mail it back to you in the envelope(s) you provide.

CONFORMED COPIES

If you do not need a certified copy, but just a copy showing the date the judge signed it, then follow the above procedure, but ask for *conformed* rather than certified copies, and omit the payment. This means the clerk uses the court's signature stamp and dates the copies to "conform" to the original decree, without the certification. If you supply the photocopies, this service is usually free.

SEND SPOUSE A COPY

If your spouse does not come to the hearing, you are responsible for sending him or her a signed copy of your final decree, and any other orders signed at the final hearing,. If you know where your spouse lives, it is good practice to send it by certified mail, with return receipt requested, and then send the returned receipt to the court to be put in your file. Be sure to put your case name and number on the receipt so it will find its way into the correct case file.

Certified copy: A copy of any order of court on which the clerk has signed under seal that it is a true copy of an actual order of court.

Conformed copy: a copy of any order signed by the court, showing the date signed by the judge or magistrate and his or her facsimile signature (sometimes a stamped statement saying, "Original signed by ….").

CHAPTER **13**

FINISHING UP

FINISHING UP

This chapter is about carrying out all the terms of your separation agreement, including transferring titles to real estate, motor vehicles, stocks, bank accounts, retirements, and other assets. Finishing up also requires paying debts as agreed, which may include a payment by one of you to the other, or signing a promissory note and deed of trust. Notices of changes in either names or addresses are a must.

Once your separation agreement has been incorporated into your decree, whether of dissolution of marriage or legal separation, it becomes an order of the court (in addition to being a contract). As a court order, certain enforcement measures are readily available. Since this guidebook is for the friendly divorce or legal separation, how to carry out enforcement measures is not discussed in detail.

Transfers of Title

Your agreement may have been silent about when certain transfers were to take place, or it may have specified that some transfers are to take place later. Now is the time to take care of all of these. Be certain every item which may have value is specifically transferred. For transfers which we have not described in this Guidebook, you may wish to ask the appropriate entity (the company in which you own stock, the breed organization in which your livestock or pet is registered), how to carry out the transfer.

For many items, such as household goods and furniture, transferring ownership is a matter of transferring possession. Information about simple transfers of real estate, and promissory notes secured by real estate is provided next, followed by information about how to transfer motor vehicles, stocks and stock accounts, insurance policies, and business interests.

REAL ESTATE

Quitclaim Deed

A quitclaim deed is used to transfer title to real estate from both spouses to one spouse. There is no warranty of title with this type of transfer—whatever interest is owned by one spouse is simply "quitted" to the other. For transferring real estate outside of Colorado, contact a real estate attorney in that state.

The signed, notarized, quitclaim deed is recorded, for a fee, by the clerk and recorder in the county where the real estate is located.

"We don't need to do all this paperwork about our house. We trust each other."

Trust is not enough to cover the possibilities your future may hold. Should either of you become disabled or die, or feel pressure from future relationships, things could get very difficult indeed without this paperwork.

This is an area partners frequently overlook, perhaps because of the rush to get away from a painful situation, as well as the absence of a court or other process that requires you to look at it all. Not taking timely action to wind things up can lead to much frustration later on, trying to find your ex to sign off on something. Be sure to make your own checklist of all items to be split or titles transferred, including joint obligations or debts, and then get it done. Consult an attorney or CPA about any tax effects you need to plan for.

Where to Find the Forms I Need

There are a number of forms mentioned in this chapter and throughout this book that you will need to accomplish your divorce or separation. Most of the forms in other chapters are found on the CD-ROM. The forms in this chapter that you need to transfer property, enforce your agreement if things don't go as expected, or modify your support in the future, can be found at Bradford Publishing Company, the publisher of this book. Bradford, where most attorneys go for their forms, has been the provider of Colorado legal forms since 1881. Printed forms are available from their Denver store below or can be filled out and printed from their website at www.bradfordpublishing.com.

Bradford Publishing
1743 Wazee Street
Denver, CO 80202
303-292-2590

Checklist of Titles We Need to Transfer

Directions: With your separation agreement in hand, review it paragraph by paragraph to check each item on the following list which has not yet been transferred according to your agreement. Once the transfer is completed, write the date on the line next to the item.

Real Estate

Check if needed   Date Done

_____ Quitclaim Deed _____

_____ Promissory Note _____

_____ Deed of Trust _____

Motor Vehicles

_____ Title _____

_____ Title _____

_____ Power of Attorney _____

_____ Power of Attorney _____

Other

_____ Stock _____

_____ Stock _____

_____ Bond _____

_____ Bond _____

_____ Bank account _____

_____ Bank account _____

_____ Investment account _____

_____ Investment account _____

_____ IRA _____

_____ IRA _____

_____ Registered/
       pedigreed pet _____

_____ Membership _____

_____ Ticket Priorities _____

_____ Other   _____

_____   _____

_____   _____

Promissory Notes

Use a promissory note to ensure any payment of money to each other that is part of your property settlement other than child support or maintenance. Payments may be regular and frequent, variable in amount, or in one lump sum. There are many different published forms for promissory notes.

When the promissory note is signed by the person promising to pay, the original should be kept by the person who will receive the payments. When the note is paid in full, the recipient should write "Paid in full" across the face of the original note, then sign it, and return the original to the person who paid it, keeping a photocopy for records. The Deed of Trust or other security should then be released.

Deed of Trust

A Deed of Trust is the document that spells out the terms of your mortgage and, when recorded, creates a lien against your real estate. The real estate thus becomes *security* for the payment. The real estate must be owned by the person who signs the promissory note. If there is already a mortgage on the real estate, the deed of trust becomes a second mortgage. If there is already a second mortgage on the property, the deed of trust becomes a third, etc.

There are many forms of Deed of Trust, each with different enforcement provisions. Whichever one you use, record it, along with the Quitclaim Deed, and ask that the Quitclaim Deed be recorded first. This insures that the person who signs the Deed of Trust has full power to *convey the security interest*. The recording fee is currently $6.00 for the first page and $5.00 for each additional page. Record it with the Public Trustee in the office of the Clerk and Recorder in the county where the real estate is located.

When the Promissory Note is paid in full, the person to whom the money is paid and who holds the Deed of Trust will fill out a Release of Deed of Trust and send it to the Clerk and Recorder.

PERSONAL PROPERTY

Items of personal property are not usually titled. Once your decree is entered, your separation agreement controls ownership. Your personal property should either be divided by the time of the decree, or at the time stated in your separation agreement. If one of you will care for some pieces of personal property for the other, that arrangement should be clearly stated in your separation agreement.

Art and other creative works can frequently prove a problem if they come into vogue and therefore increase in value after the divorce. If the item does not have a paper title now, you can create one by drafting a bill of sale which describes the item in detail. For example, "12 x 24 water color of boat and dock in shades of blue, with 6-line original poem in calligraphy on bottom right corner." Create a paper trail of the disposition of your important things now and you won't have to find one another later in order to sell or transfer them.

MOTOR VEHICLES

Titles to motor vehicles are easily transferred. The person who keeps the vehicle should obtain the spouse's signature on the title. You may then take the signed title to the motor vehicle registration office and request that a new title be issued in your name.

If there is a loan on the vehicle, the lender probably holds the title. Typically, lenders do not allow either party to sign off the title until the loan is paid in full. In this case, the releasing spouse signs a Motor Vehicle Power of Attorney. This is Form 910P, available at Bradford Publishing Company. Take the signed Power of Attorney to the motor vehicle registration office in your area. The registration will then be issued in your name.

LIQUID ASSETS: CASH AND BANK ACCOUNTS

Cash is, of course, easily divided. Just count it out. If you have significant amounts, prepare and sign a receipt.

Transferring ownership of bank accounts usually requires one or both of you to prepare a new signature card, or to sign other transfer documents provided by the bank. Be sure that the bank has the correct Social Security number on each account after the transfer.

Directions: Complete the following checklists as they relate to your situations. Do on separate piece of paper as necessary.

Personal Property Transfer Checklist: We have the following artworks, antiques and collectibles which have been transferred in writing and in fact as follows:

Item	To Whom	Date Transferred
_____	_____	_____
_____	_____	_____
_____	_____	_____

Motor Vehicle Transfer Checklist: Wife (or husband and wife) has/have transferred title or signed power of attorney to husband of:

Vehicle Descrption	Date Transferred
_____	_____

Husband (or husband and wife) has/have transferred title or signed power of attorney to wife of:

Vehicle Descrption	Date Transferred
_____	_____

Bank Account Transfer Checklist: Only husband's name appears on the following bank accounts:

Bank	Type of Account	Date Transferred
_____	_____	_____

Only wife's name appears on the following bank accounts:

Bank	Type of Account	Date Transferred
_____	_____	_____

Stocks, Bonds and Securities Transfer Checklist:

Stock/Bond	To Whom/Date
_____	_____
_____	_____
_____	_____
_____	_____
_____	_____

Insurance Transfer Checklist

Directions: Complete the following as you accomplish each one.

Husband has changed his insurance policies as follows:

Life insurance at _____ (company) now benefits _____.

Life insurance at _____ (company) now benefits _____.

Health insurance at _____ (company) now covers _____.

Car insurance on _____ (vehicles) is in his name only.

Wife has changed her insurance policies as follows:

Life insurance at _____ (company) now benefits _____.

Life insurance at _____ (company) now benefits _____.

Health insurance at _____ (company) now covers _____.

Car insurance on _____ (vehicles) is in her name only.

Non-employee spouse has elected _____ years of COBRA option through _____ and completed the paper work, so that coverage for _____ will begin on _____ date.

STOCKS, BONDS, AND OTHER SECURITIES

If your stocks and bonds are owned through a broker account, it is sufficient to simply change the name on the account, or, if you are dividing the contents of the account, to open a second account with the same broker and ask that shares be allocated between the two accounts. As long as you don't sell any of your securities, you will not incur any taxes transferring these securities between you. See section about capital gains in Chapter 7.

If you have the actual stock certificates, you will find a form on the back of the certificate for transferring ownership. Be sure, after you have filled it out, that you sign it in front of the proper authority indicated on the certificate. The new owner must present the signed certificate to the company so that a new certificate may be prepared by the company, and ownership of the shares transferred on the books of the company.

A bond should be transferred according to the procedures which accompanied the bond when you received it. If it is not being held for you as part of an investment account and you do not know how it should be transferred, contact the entity which issued the bond (U.S., municipality, Power Company, etc.).

LIFE INSURANCE

Transferring ownership of life insurance is handled by completing forms provided by the insurance company. Contact your agent or the company directly to obtain the appropriate forms.

Be sure to make any necessary changes in your beneficiary designation required by your agreement. Your designation must be absolutely accurate. You may obtain a copy of your existing beneficiary designation from the insurance company. If you have agreed to continue designating each other, for the benefit of the children, be sure your designation does not refer to the other as "wife" or "husband" or "spouse." This will create a serious ambiguity if you re-marry.

MEDICAL INSURANCE; COBRA

Make certain that if the non-employee spouse will take the COBRA option to continue his/her medical insurance you have prepared all the necessary paperwork before the final decree. Most insurance is paid to the end of the month or a month in advance, so there may be a grace period within which a former spouse is covered.

MOTOR VEHICLE INSURANCE

Contact your agent to separate your motor vehicle insurance. You will likely separate one of your cars from the family policy. Your agent will do this for you. If there are only two cars, you will both lose the multi-car discount and each pay more than half the previous joint premium. Be very clear about who will be insuring your children's cars.

RETIREMENT, PENSIONS, AND PROFIT SHARING

Tax deferred savings plans and IRA's may be divided by directly transferring all or some of the balance to a similar account in the name of the other spouse. As long as such a transfer is done by one trustee to another, and the money in no way comes directly into your hands, you will avoid withholding, tax, and penalty. See Chapter 7.

To transfer all or a part of a military retirement, contact the accounting office for the service in question for their forms and procedures. Similarly, for Civil Service Retirement System, Federal Employees Retirement System, and TIAA-CREF, contact the Plan Administrator for their forms and procedures for transfers. You must have all this lined up before you finalize your separation agreement because the terms you put in your agreement about these assets controls what you can do after your Decree.

For those plans which are covered by E.R.I.S.A. and are therefore divisible or transferable by Qualified Domestic Relations Order (QDRO), send a certified copy of the QDRO, previously signed by the judge, to the Plan Administrator who will carry out the transfer as described in the Order. For greater security, you can request a signed receipt for it, or send it by Certified Mail. However, NOTE that it is generally a good idea to have obtained the Plan Administrator's approval of the QDRO or agreement *before* giving it to the court to Order. In most cases, it will go to the Plan administrator twice, once to approve (or tell you why he or she won't so you can amend it and resubmit) and then again to carry out. See Chapter 7 for more on this.

For a defined contribution plan QDRO, the plan administrator will then contact the receiving spouse to determine how he/she wants the transfer to occur (rollover to an IRA, cash with withholding for income taxes, other, a combination of these). The actual transfer is usually completed within six weeks of the Decree. For a defined benefit plan QDRO, ask your attorney, CPA, or plan administrator for what to expect.

Retirement Transfer Checklist:

Directions: Complete the following as it relates to your situation. Do on separate piece of paper if necessary:

Retirement	To Whom/Date
_____	_____
_____	_____
_____	_____

 Have your QDRO, or other agreement that divides or transfers the retirement plan, approved by the Plan Administrator before the final decree.

Business Interests Transfer Checklist:

Directions: Complete the following as it relates to your situation. Do on separate piece of paper if necessary:

Business Interest	To Whom/Date
_____	_____
_____	_____
_____	_____

Notice of Change of Name Checklist

Check off each of the following, as you send or show them a conformed copy of your signed decree.

Husband Wife

_____ _____ Employers

_____ _____ Dept. of Motor Vehicles Drivers License Office

_____ _____ Social Security office (name on your Social Security card)

_____ _____ bank

_____ _____ credit union

_____ _____ life insurance

_____ _____ auto insurance

_____ _____ homeowner's insurance

_____ _____ other insurance

_____ _____ mortgage company

_____ _____ credit card companies

_____ _____ doctor

_____ _____ dentist

_____ _____ children's school

_____ _____ day care

_____ _____ pediatrician

The persons relating to your children are especially important if your last name will now be different from your children's.

_____ _____ other

_____ _____

You probably do not need to supply a copy of the signed decree to most of these, but do not forget to notify them.

_____ _____ newspaper and magazine subscriptions

_____ _____ membership organizations

_____ _____ personal correspondents

_____ _____ other

_____ _____

BUSINESS INTERESTS

If your business interest is a corporation, the transaction may be simply a transfer of stock from one spouse to the other, or from both spouses to one spouse.

For either a partnership or a sole proprietorship, usually no other transfer of ownership is necessary beyond the statement in your separation agreement. If the business has a trade name, however, notice of the change in ownership must be given to the office of the Secretary of State.

OTHER ASSETS

For other assets, contact the related institution or organization to find out what they require. For pedigreed animals, for example, contact the breed organization. For Avalanche or symphony ticket priorities contact the ticket office. For frequent flyer miles, contact the airline to see how and if they can be transferred.

DEBTS

As a rule, creditors don't need to be notified that you have divorced and that one of you is now responsible for paying the debt, rather than both of you. It's very important, however, to be sure each creditor has the address of the person responsible for paying. If it was a joint debt, you may ask the creditor to remove the non-paying spouse's name from the debt, but the remaining spouse must have sufficient income alone to manage the debt. Remember that the creditor has no obligation to do this. See "Dealing with Debt" in Chapter 7.

Changing Your Name

If one of you asked that a former name be restored as part of your divorce, you will need to follow up to make this a reality. Make many photocopies of your conformed final decree and give or send one to anyone who needs official notice of your new name. Be sure to change this name as a beneficiary on any life insurance or other assets.

Changing Your Address

You probably agreed fairly early in your separation how to divide the mail. You each did, or should now do, a change of address for any mail to each of you individually. But, what about mail, magazines, etc., which come addressed to Mr. and Mrs.? Holiday cards will prove particularly difficult if you are not clear about this.

Usually, it is best to agree that one of you will receive the joint mail, sort it, and promptly send or deliver it to the other spouse. If, and only if, it is ok with your children, you might consider sending mail with them. However, the most innocuous mail can sometimes prove explosive—the catalogue from which you disagreed about a large purchase, for example. If you have even the slightest doubt about the volatility of exchanging mail in person, don't. Send it in a large envelope—after leaving a telephone message telling the other spouse that it is coming.

Calendaring Later Events

You may have agreed to some transfers of title or payments, or changes and stair-steps in your parenting, support or maintenance plans, which are to take place on a date or event in the future. For example, you may have agreed to sell the home when the last child emancipates and pay the other spouse his or her interest in the home. You may have anticipated changes in your parenting plan, in the support of your children or each other. Be sure to calendar all of these now and have a system to remind you of the date. If the payout or transfer is tied to the sale of the home, put a note to yourself on the Deed, or Deed of Trust, in the house file or safety deposit box. If an event is tied to the tax year, put a note to yourself in your tax file. If an event is related to a child's age, put a note in that child's file.

Check Your Credit Ratings

Whether or not you requested your credit ratings during the early stages of your negotiations, you should do this now. Finishing your divorce with an adequate credit rating is a major step toward financial health in the years to come. Make certain that any corrections to your credit reports that you both agreed to have been made, and that your new names are reflected on your current rating along with your correct addresses. See Chapter 4 for more about credit.

Converting from Legal Separation to Dissolution of Marriage

Six months after the court has signed a Decree of Legal Separation, either spouse may ask that it be converted to a Decree of Dissolution of Marriage; or you may do it together. The forms you will need to prepare, the Motion to Convert, JDF 1321 and Order to Convert, JDF 1322 are available from

Notice of Change of Address Checklist

Directions: fill in according to your agreement:

Husband will notify the following of his change of address, if any:

Wife will notify the following of her change of address, if any:

We will handle the joint mail as follows:

Bradford Publishing. If only one of you is doing the conversion you must notify your spouse when you do this, and prove that you have done so by filling out the Certificate of Service at the bottom of the Motion form. This is another time when it is a good idea to use certified mail. The court will grant the conversion automatically, if there are not other requests with it.

It is assumed that you will continue the terms of the Separation Agreement which the court approved when you were granted the Decree of Legal Separation. If you want to amend some of these terms, then it is a good idea to treat the changes as a modification, and file a separate Motion to Modify or to specifically include the requested changes in the Motion to Convert. You should file new financial affidavits and child support worksheets if the changes concern money or children. These modifications may require a hearing unless you have both agreed to them in writing.

Making Things Happen: Enforcement

One or both of you may be less than reliable about making promised payments, or find yourself unable or unwilling to follow through with transfers of property or children. You may need to invoke the teeth you included in your agreement or may need to seek outside help in getting things back on track. For example, you may need to activate an income assignment you have already signed. You may need a court order transferring property to you, either to effect your agreement or to make up for something your agreement called for which did not happen.

INTERNAL ENFORCEMENT

If some element of your agreement does not work as planned, look first to the agreement itself. Did you anticipate this event and provide for what was to happen? For example, did you agree that a missed (late) payment of maintenance means a loss of the tax deductibility? Does a mortgage default mean the other spouse may take back the home? Does unpaid support mean the receiving spouse gets access to a bank account? Each of the separation agreement chapters (7-11) contains ideas for teeth and security. Chapter 12 contains sample wordings.

If you find that your agreement did not anticipate the present malfunction, try to find the least expensive, least damaging means of fixing it. The more of your agreement you leave intact, the more chance there is that the erring spouse will feel able to honor the rest of the provisions, once the immediate difficulty is resolved. As difficult as it may be, try to focus only on the thing which has

"Figuratively if not literally, the participants shall come to see themselves as working side by side, attacking the problem, not each other." Roger Fisher and William Ury, *Getting To Yes.*

"If it ain't broke, don't fix it."

gone wrong. If you allow your frustrations at the current break-down to lead you back into all the old resentments, you are apt to forget the harmony you found when you worked together.

Security

If you fear that one of you might not be able to keep the promises made, especially about large ticket items, see if there is some way to "secure" the action. For example, agree to withhold the transfer of title to an asset until the debt against it is paid. Record a Deed of Trust or Promissory Note against a future-paying asset, savings account, or the family home. Sometimes you can sign over title to the person who should receive an asset on the payment of certain money, but hold the signed paperwork in the file with the attorney or mediator until the money is paid.

Income Assignment

An income assignment is a formal arrangement between the employee and his or her employer to withhold a regular amount of money each payday and forward it to the other spouse. This removes the danger of memory lapse, as well as all temptation to spend the money other than in the way you agreed, by effectively making someone else responsible for making the payments for you. Income assignment for child support, or maintenance when combined with child support, was mandatory as of January 1, 1994, with some significant exceptions. You may also, now, do an income assignment for health insurance premiums for children. The forms and procedures for doing this at the time of the decree are in Chapter 12.

Some people set up their own private income assignment by creating an automatic transfer from the bank or credit union account of the paying spouse to an account of the receiving spouse. Check the cost of this beforehand.

If you did not do an income assignment at the time of the decree, because it was not possible then, or you did not think it was necessary, you may start one at any time. You may use the forms and instructions in the previous chapter.

ENFORCEMENT THROUGH THE COURT

The court may stand in the place of the non-cooperative spouse and transfer the property for him or her. The court can open the door for you to collect money owed directly from your spouse's assets and can punish the spouse for non-compliance, in order to make him or her comply.

"Commissioner's Deed" Enforcement of Property Transfers

This procedure contained in Rule 70 of the Colorado Rules of Civil Procedure gives the court the power to act in the place of a defaulting spouse to transfer the title of property that is presently in his or her name. This procedure may be used when you have a signed separation agreement incorporated into your Decree that spells out the agreement for the transfer of property and the spouse with title is unable or unwilling to transfer it.

This procedure is also the only way to transfer property which is in the name of an absent spouse. To set up this procedure, you must have specifically described the titled property in your summons and again in your final order of court. See Chapters 6 and 7 about how and why to do this. If you did not specifically name and request the property you are now seeking title to, in your first papers, you may now find that the court will find it lacks jurisdiction and will not issue this order for you. For this procedure, use JDF 1814 and 1815 available from Bradford Publishing.

Reduction to Judgment

When the court incorporates your separation agreement into your decree, it makes your agreement an order of the court. Everything you promised to do in the agreement is now ordered by the court and therefore more than a private contract. If one of you fails to keep any agreement about the payment of money, the court may simply *enter judgment* against you for the unpaid amount. This allows the *moving party* to collect by any means available for collection of judgments, including garnishment and remedies against property.

Any amounts in a judgment can be collected later if the person failing to pay has a positive change of fortune.

Contempt Citation

A contempt citation is based on the premise that anyone who does not comply with a court order *offends the dignity of the Court.* If your separation agreement has been made an order of the court *(incorporated into the decree),* this form of enforcement is available to you. The *aggrieved* person swears in an affidavit that the other has not done what the court said they should do. The court then orders the *offending* party to appear in court to "show cause" why they should not be *held in contempt.* In other words, the affidavit creates a presumption that the non-compliance happened, and the burden of proof is on the person who allegedly did not comply to prove that he or she either did comply or was unable to do so. This is one of the few times in law in which innocence is not presumed. It is a quasi-criminal

Judgment: A court order which acknowledges and fixes the amount past due, or action not completed, so that the person to whom the money is owed or for whose benefit the activity was to be done, can go directly after the income or assets of the person who failed to pay or act.

Every unpaid installment of child support automatically becomes a judgment enforceable by the spouse who was to receive the payment, or by the child being supported.

matter and if the aggrieved party is seeking punitive damages (jail/fine) as well as remedial damages (payment of what is owing), then the accused has a right to an attorney and a hearing.

If the court finds that the accused person did have the ability to keep the court order and did offend the court, then the court can enter fines and/or a jail sentence. In most cases, the court will suspend the jail time, and sometimes the fine, for a period of time to give the non-complying party a chance to comply. Contempt citations can thus come up for review after review, waiting for a promising party to come through with money or action. A contempt citation almost always requires a lawyer to prepare, argue, and defend. They are expensive and not always satisfactory.

If the court finds, at the hearing on contempt, that the person was unable to pay, you can no longer collect the amounts described in the motion for contempt citation by any means, including judgment.

Title IV D Federal Law Enforcement of Child Support and Maintenance, by the County Child Support Enforcement Unit (CSE)

Each County in Colorado has an office of Child Support Enforcement, whose job it is to enforce child support and maintenance when combined with child support orders, within the judicial district as well as between counties, states, and even countries. There is a small fee. This remedy is not swift, due to the volume of cases and the necessity of finding and personally serving the person who is not paying. If despite the friendly manner in which you worked out the child support and/or maintenance, it is not being paid, this is the least expensive means of collecting, especially across state lines. Like contempt citations and garnishments, the technical instructions for this kind of enforcement are beyond the scope of this book. If you need this kind of help, call your County Child Support Enforcement Office.

CSE actions to collect child support and maintenance result in a judgment and a lien "by operation of law" against any real or personal property of the defaulting spouse. The CSE unit may use these liens to get to income tax refunds and lottery winnings.

Federal Law Enforcement of Parenting Plans:
PKPA and UCCJA

There are two Federal laws that help enforce "custody" and "visitation" orders state to state. The Parental Kidnapping Prevention

Unless you have agreed to, and the Court orders, party-to-party payment, all child support and/or maintenance payments are made to the Family Support Registry, which in turn sends the payment on to the other parent. The records of this registry will be all the evidence necessary to establish failure to pay in a contempt action.

"The best laid schemes o' mice and men Gang aft a-gley." Robert Burns

Collecting unpaid child support is enforceable by the child in question, even after the child emancipates.

Act (PKPA) makes it a crime to violate a "custody" order, and permits the FBI and other Federal agencies to enforce them.

The Uniform Child Custody Jurisdiction Act (UCCJA) sets guidelines about which state is the best one to make decisions about a given child's "custody". This question comes up if the parents at the time of the divorce live in different states, or if one parent moved to another state after the divorce decree. This law helps prevent *forum shopping* in which a parent moves with the children from state to state until he/she can find one which will give him or her "custody" or will change an old custody order.

These federal laws do refer throughout to "custody". They may be used to enforce orders about children that use alternate words, as the Colorado law does now. Both laws are beyond the scope of this book. If you need enforcement under one of these laws, you should consult an attorney.

Can We Change Our Agreement After the Court Approves It?

This section concerns your ability to change your agreement after the court has entered it as an order. The legal term for this is *modification*. If you are agreeing to the changes, you and your ex-spouse have only to write them up and sign them. If you want to have them filed with the court so they become a new court order, you can follow the procedure in Chapter 4 for making an agreement into a court order—but delete the word "temporary" from that example.

If only one of you is asking the court to change the order, there are certain rules—burdens of proof—which you must follow in order for the court to do what you want. These rules differ from one area to another, i.e., from property to parental responsibilities, from child support to maintenance. Reading them now, as you settle the matters involved in your divorce, may help you phrase your agreement for the long run.

MODIFYING YOUR PROPERTY AND DEBT DIVISION

The court cannot change your agreement as to property and debts without the agreement of you and your former spouse. In practice, the only *grounds* for changing a property settlement without agreement is showing that the original separation agreement was obtained by fraud or duress. This is very hard to prove. The court will not modify or set aside your final division of property and debts even if you made mistakes in your interpretation of the tax consequences or made honest mistakes about the value

D **DEFINITION**

Modification: Formally changing a court order.

"If it ain't broke, don't fix it."

The court may, if requested by any party or on its own, order all parties to mediate requests for modification of parenting time, child support or maintneance.

of things or the balances due. It is therefore a good idea to approach the property and debts portion of your agreement as though it will be chiseled in stone.

MODIFYING PARENTAL RESPONSIBILITIES

The court keeps jurisdiction over children, parenting plans and child support arrangements until your children are emancipated. You always have the right to ask the court to modify your parental responsibilities arrangements. You must, however, have sufficient grounds, unless you both agree in writing to the change.

If you are asking the court to change your parenting plan in a way that substantially changes physical care between the parents, then the statute says the court shall not do so unless a) the parties agree to the change, b) the child has been integated into the new home with the consent of the other parent, c) the parent with primary physical care substantially relocates or d) the child would be endangered if the present plan continued. Win or lose, once such a request has been made, no other such request may be brought for two years.

If you share physical care and decision-making and ask the court to change your parenting plan, then you only need to show that such a change is in the best interest of the children.

If the "primary" physical care parent wishes to substantially relocate with the children, and the other parent is opposed, then recent law allows the court to consider many things (see sidebar). If you have shared physical care and decision-making, then it takes much more proof that such a change would be in the best interest of the children.

MODIFYING CHILD SUPPORT

The Child Support Guideline strongly suggests an annual review of the support amount based on an exchange between the parents of their previous year's tax returns, current income information, and verification of the children's medical insurance coverage and its costs. If you do not want to do this annually, you may say in your agreement that you will review incomes for the purpose of adjusting child support at the request of either one of you. This means you will always cooperate; neither of you can say no.

Fill in your new incomes on a new child support worksheet. If the bottom line amount (final *suggested support amount*) changes by more than 10%, either direction, then you *must* make the change.

What if I Wish to Move Away

Legislation in 2001 allows the court to consider several things if the parent with primary physical care is seeking to relocate with the child to a residence that "substantially changes the geographical ties between the child and the other party."

1. the reasons for relocation

2. the reasons for opposition

3. the history and quality of each parent's relationship with the child

4. educational opportunities of both locations

5. extended family at both locations

6. advantages of remaining with the present primary caregiver

7. the impact of the move on the child

8. a new, reasonable parenting time schedule is possible

9. any other factors in the best interest of the child

Another Note About Privacy

If you agree to exchange income tax returns annually to re-evaluate child support, then you will be likely to know a great deal more about your former spouse's new spouse's income than you or that spouse may be comfortable with. You might want to agree instead that if either of you re-marries, you will exchange W-2's, 1099's, Schedule C's (business profit & loss), K-1's, rental profit and loss statements, and Corporate tax returns, all concerning income and businesses of your former spouse only.

The easiest way is to file the new worksheet with the court, along with current financial affidavits and your signed agreement to pay and accept the new amount.

If you need a modification of your child support agreement, and have not worked out the terms ahead of time, you will need *grounds* to ask the court to change your agreement. The grounds for changing the support amount are "a change of circumstance so substantial and continuing" as to make the original agreement "unfair." The fact that the change(s) which have occurred change the bottom line on the same child support worksheet by more than 10% (up or down) is sufficient grounds.

If you change the physical care parenting plan for your children you will almost always need to change the child support accordingly—sometimes changing which worksheet you use. You can still do the kind of calculations suggested in Chapter 7 to avoid having the Child Support Guideline force you into an unworkable amount for either the paying or receiving parent.

MODIFYING MAINTENANCE

Modifying or changing maintenance generates more horror stories among lawyers and divorcing people than probably any other aspect of divorce. The misunderstandings are many, and the consequences sometimes unforeseen and unpleasant. It is vital that you review the chapters on maintenance and taxes if you are thinking of modifying your maintenance plan, or the terms of an old maintenance order.

The grounds for modifying maintenance in front of a court are that there have been "changed circumstances that are substantial and continuing" such that the original agreement or order as to maintenance is now "unfair." Case law has tightened that criteria further to require that the change not be voluntary or in the control of the person seeking the change (quit job, for example). The ability to modify a maintenance order is usually defined by the type of maintenance. See Chapter 10 for a complete discussion.

If maintenance is for a fixed amount for a fixed period of time, or a lump sum amount—any plan in which the total amount to be paid can be calculated in advance—then that maintenance is said to be *contractual* or *in gross* and is presumed to be not modifiable. If you want your fixed-term maintenance plan to be modifiable under certain circumstances, you must say so clearly in your agreement.

If you and your spouse waived your right to maintenance in your original agreement, then there is probably no hope of doing it now—even if you both agree. The IRS definition of maintenance requires that it be *under* or *incident to a divorce or separation instrument.* That is generally accepted to mean that it must be agreed to or at least contemplated at the time of the decree. If you want to leave the door open for maintenance at a later date (for a spouse with a chronic illness in remission or an injury which is not completely healed, for example) then that spouse must not waive maintenance at the final decree, and you should state in your agreement the condition which you agree might give rise to the need for maintenance in the future.

ONWARD

If you have used this Guidebook well, you have brought yourself and your family through a difficult transition, and saved a significant amount of money. If you have children, you have learned, or are learning, how to work together as parents without having to relate to each other as spouses.

You can take pride in how you have done your divorce or separation, and be pleased that you have completed the process without accumulating more baggage than you already had, and perhaps even gotten rid of some.

May your near and distant futures be better for your choices about how to complete a friendly divorce.

We welcome your comments. Please send them to:

Bradford Publishing Company
1743 Wazee Street
Denver, Colorado 80202
(303) 292-2500
www.bradfordpublishing.com

✦

M. Arden Hauer
Center for Non-Adversarial Divorce
603 Point Park Drive
Suite 120
Golden, CO 80401
(303) 526-7749
www.friendlydivorce.com

✦

Wendy Whicher
Dove Creek, CO 81328
(970) 533-1456

✦

BIBLIOGRAPHY

I. Books About the Divorce Process

BETWEEN LOVE AND HATE: A Guide to Civilized Divorce. Gold, Lois. New York: Plenum Publishing, 1992. A "road map for sane and civilized divorce" by a therapist/mediator. How to negotiate with your ex even in the difficult times after the final decree.

THE CASE AGAINST DIVORCE. Medved, Diane. New York: Ivy Books, 1990. Things to consider and reconsider before giving up on your marriage.

DANCING WITH LAWYERS: How to Take Charge and Get Results. Carroll, Nicholas. Lafayette, CA: Royce Baker Publishing, 1992, Guide to hiring a lawyer without giving up control of your life.

DIVORCE AND THE MYTH OF LAWYERS. Marlow, Leonard. Garden City, NY: Harlan Press, 1992. How some divorce lawyers have needlessly carried the market in the divorce business.

THE DIVORCE BOOK. McKay, Matthew; Peter D. Rogers, Joan Blades, and Richard Gosse. Oakland CA: New Harbinger Publications, 1984. Overview of the divorce process, including the emotional, legal and relationship divorces. Written by a lawyer and several mental health experts.

GETTING APART TOGETHER: The Couple's Guide to a Fair Divorce or Separation. Kranitz, Martin A. San Louis Obispo: Impact Publishers, 1987. How to use mediation and other non-adversarial routes.

GETTING DIVORCED WITHOUT RUINING YOUR LIFE. Margulies, Sam. New York: Fireside Books, Simon and Schuster, 1992. Advice to divorcing spouses about negotiating a wise and workable settlement.

THE GOOD DIVORCE: Keeping Your Family Together When Your Marriage Comes Apart, Ahrons, Constance R. PhD, NYC: Harper Collins, 1994. Advocates and anticipates a cultural shift from thinking of divorce as a failure, to thinking of divorce as a natural change of life. Think not of divorced or separated families, but of whole families with two nucleii – the bi-nuclear family. Shows how such a change in thinking can help children, especially, to heal.

A GUIDE TO DIVORCE MEDIATION: How to Reach a Fair, Legal Settlement at a Fraction of the Cost. Friedman, Gary J. New York: Workman Publishing, 1993. Story-filled guide to optimum use of mediation.

HANDBOOK OF COLORADO FAMILY LAW, Whicher, S.W., with Cheryl Loetscher, CLE of Colorado, Inc. 1978, 1996 edition. Cookbook for inexperienced lawyers and paralegals. Same information as this Guidebook, in greater depth and in legal format. Available in the reference section of most public libraries – especially those with a Law section.

SECOND CHANCES: Men, Women and Children a Decade After Divorce. Wallerstein, Judith, and Sandra Blakeslee. New York: Ticknor and Fields, 1990. Results of 10 and 15 year studies of California families following divorce, showing long-term effect of divorce on the children.

WOMAN'S GUIDE TO DIVORCE AND DECISION-MAKING: A Supportive Workbook for Women Facing the Process of Divorce. Robertson, Christina. New York: Fireside Books, Simon and Schuster, 1988. Workbook which teaches the decision-making process through examples of decisions which are encountered at divorce.

COLORADO REVISED STATUTES

10-16-104 as amended 1994	Health insurance for children
14-1-101 – 113	Marriage
14-2-101 – 210	Rights of married women
14-3-101 – 310	Pre-marriage agreements
14-4-101 – 105	Domestic abuse
14-5-101 – 145	Interstate support actions
14-6-101 – 104	Non-support in this state

II. Books About Your Other Divorces

Communication and Relationships

BUTTER BATTLE BOOK, Dr. Seuss. New York: Random House, 1984. Children's book about a simple disagreement which escalates into war.

CRAZY TIME: Surviving Divorce. Trafford, Abigail. New York: Bantam Books, 1982. For the newly separated. THE book to read when you feel this can't be happening to you.

DANCE OF ANGER. Lerner, Harriet. New York: Harper, 1989. Helpful guide to understanding anger and other emotions in close relationships.

THE DANCE OF INTIMACY: A Woman's Guide to Courageous Acts of Change in Key Relationships. Lerner, Harriet. New York: Harper Collins, 1989. A significant writing about "making responsible and lasting changes that enhance our capacity for genuine closeness *over the long haul.*"

FIGHTING FOR YOUR MARRIAGE: Positve Steps for Preventing Divorce And Preserving a Lasting Love. Markman, Howard; Scott Stanley and Susan L. Blumberg. San Fracisco, CA.: Jossey-Bass, 1994. Blueprint for how to celebrate and use differences between spouses to enable problem-solving and working communication. Since these are often the marriage-busting problems, this book and *We Can Work It Out* may well save many, many marriages.

FROM CONFLICT TO RESOLUTION: Skills and Strategies for Individual, Couple, and Family Therapy. Heitler, Susan M. New York: Norton, 1993. Negotiation and dispute resolution and how to do them. Written for professionals.

GETTING THE LOVE YOU WANT: A Guide for Couples. Hendrix, Harville. New York: Harper Collins, 1990. Practical, encouraging advice about how to help yourself find fulfillment within a relationship.

GETTING TO YES: Negotiating Agreement Without Giving In. Fisher, Roger, and William L. Ury. New York: Viking Penguin, 1982, Houghton Mifflin, 1981. Accessible, clear discussion of Win-Win negotiating for whenever an agreement is needed.

GETTING TOGETHER: Building a Relationship That Gets to Yes. Fischer, Roger, and Scott Brown. New York: Viking Penguin, 1989. Applies the Win-Win negotiation formula to relationships.

GROWING THROUGH DIVORCE. Smoke, Jim. New York: Bantam, 1986. Examples of how to learn from the ending of this relationship.

HOW TO SURVIVE THE LOSS OF A LOVE. Colgrove, Melba, Ph.D.; Harold H. Bloomfield, M.D., and Peter McWilliams. Published by Prelude Press, 8159 Santa Monica Boulevard, Los Angeles, CA 90046, 1-800-LIFE101. Tips for negotiating through the grief process.

JOURNEY OF THE HEART: Intimate Relationship and the Path of Love. Wellwood, John. New York: Harper Collins Publishers, 1990. Sensitive and visionary discussion of intimate relationship and its challenges as spiritual practice and path.

LEARNING TO LIVE WITHOUT VIOLENCE. Sonkin, Daniel J. and Michael Durphy. Volcano, CA: Volcano Press, 1989. Workbook for the person whose anger slips into rage.

LIFE LESSONS: 50 Things I Learned From My Divorce. Beth Joselow, Beth. NYC: Avon, 1994. Fifty pithy sayings, which are certain to become classics, such as: Face Problems Squarely and Only When Necessary, and Be Prepared: The Law Isn't Always Fair and It Doesn't Cover Everything. Each followed by witty, profound and helpful short discussions.

(THE) MAGIC OF CONFLICT: Turning a Life of Work Into a Work of Art. Crum, Thomas F. New York: Simon and Schuster, 1987. Wise, how-to book about how to use conflict – physical, emotional, or intellectual – to progress and grow.

REBUILDING, AND WHEN YOUR RELATIONSHIP ENDS: The Divorce Process Rebuilding Blocks. Fisher, Bruce, Boulder, Colorado, Family Relations Learning Center, 1978. Book and workbook from the Fisher Divorce Seminar. For the spouse who is ready to begin looking past the end of this relationship.

(DIVORCE) RIGHTS OF PASSAGE: A Guide Through the Emotional and Legal Realities. Alpern, Gerald. Aspen, CO: Phychological Development Publications, 1982. Clear, helpful descriptions of the stages of divorce and divorce recovery.

WE CAN WORK IT OUT: Making Sense of Marital Conflict, Notarius, Clifford PhD.; and Howard Markman PhD, San Francisco, CA: Jossey-Bass, 1993. Blueprint for how to celebrate and use differences between spouses to enable problem-solving and working communication. Since these are often the marriage-busting problems, this book and *Fighting for Your Marriage* may well save many, many marriages.

WIN-WIN NEGOTIATIONS FOR COUPLES; A Personal Guide to Joint Decision Making. Whitney, Charlotte. Gloucester, MA: Para Research, Inc., 1986. Cooperative bargaining within a relationship.

YOU CAN NEGOTIATE ANYTHING. Cohen, Herb. Secaucus, NJ: Lyle Stuart, Inc., 1980. Specific guidelines, personnal anecdotes, and practical advice for being a successful negotiator.

YOU JUST DON'T UNDERSTAND: Women and Men in Conversation. Tannen, Deborah. New York: Ballantine Books, 1990. Witty and pungent illustrations of how gender differences in communication styles may affect the success of relationships.

III. Books About Children and Divorce:

AT DADDY'S ON SATURDAYS. Girard, Linda W., Morton Grove, IL: Albert, Whitman and Company, 1987. Picture book about a young child with visitation in father's home.

BOYS AND GIRLS BOOK ABOUT DIVORCE. Gardner, Richard. New York: Bantam Books, 1985. Classic discussions of traditional custody with mother and father visiting. Helpful. See also Dr. Gardner's other books in this series: *PARENTS BOOK ABOUT DIVORCE, 1977. BOYS AND GIRLS BOOK ABOUT ONE-PARENT FAMILIES. BOYS AND GIRLS BOOK ABOUT STEP-FAMILIES.*

CAUGHT IN THE MIDDLE: Protecting the Children of High-Conflict Divorce. Garrity, Carla B., and Mitchell A. Baris. New York. *Lexington* Books, MacMillan Publishing Co., 1994. Readable discussion of the on-going effect of high-conflict divorce on children. Suggests the role of a Parenting Coordinator to help the family after the decree.

CHILDREN OF DIVORCE: A Developmental Approach to Residence and Visitation. Baris, Mitchell A., and Carla B. Garrity. DeKalb, IL: Psytek, 1988. Guide to healthy parenting plans based upon developmental ages of the children. Practical, how-to advice.

THE CHILDREN'S BOOK: A Communication Workbook for Separate Parenting After Divorce. For the Sake of the Children. Erickson, Marilyn and Stephen. West Concord, MN: CPI Publishing, 1992. A carry-with day book for keeping track of the children's appointments, inoculation records, primary pediatrician and day care provider. A very useful tool for shared-time parents.

DADDY'S ROOMMATE. Wilhoite, Michael. Boston: Alyson Publications, 1991. Story of school age boy visiting with father and father's gay lover.

DINOSAUR'S DIVORCE: A Guide for Changing Families. Brown, Laurence Krasney, and Marc Tolon Brown. Boston: Little Brown and Co., 1986. THE book for young children facing divorce. Picture book of likely situations, most of those encountered after the divorce.

DIVORCE WITHOUT VICTIMS: Helping Children Through Divorce with a Minimum of Pain and Trauma. Berger, Stuart M. New York: NAL/Dutton, 1986. Discussion of many common reactions and problems of children resulting from their parents' separation.

GROWING UP WITH DIVORCE: Helping Your Child Avoid Immediate and Later Emotional Problems. Kalter, Neil. New York: Fawcett Columbine, 1990. Compassionate and helpful discussion of the states of the divorce process for children at each developmental age.

HEATHER HAS TWO MOMMIES. Newman, Leslea. Boston: Alyson Publications, 1991. Story of school age girl who lives with her mother and mother's lesbian lover.

HOW IT FEELS WHEN PARENTS DIVORCE. Krementz, Jill. New York: Alfred A. Knopf, 1988. Collection of their own stories by kids 8-17 describing their parents' divorces. Some happy, some difficult. All enlightening.

IT'S NOT THE END OF THE WORLD. Blume, Judy. New York: MacMillan Publishing Co., 1982. Young adult novel about early adolescent girl who tries to cope with and prevent her parents' divorce. Re-printed recently due to popular demand.

MOM'S HOUSE, DAD'S HOUSE: Making Shared Custody Work. Ricci, Isolina. New York: MacMillan Publishing Co., 1980. Self-help guide for crafting a shared parenting plan, with sample language, examples and practical hints.

MY TWO HOMES, (THE) DIVORCE CALENDAR FOR KIDS. P.O. Box 7249, Albuquerque, NM 87104-7249; (800) 244-1761. With colorful stickers for Mom, Dad, combination days, holidays, and other special days, gives kids a fun way to know their schedules.

MY STORY. Boulden, Jim and Joan. Beaverville, CA: Boulden Publishing, 1991. Coloring and activity book for child and family to help the child find his or her place in the process.

101 WAYS TO BE A LONG-DISTANCE SUPER DAD: Don't Divorce Your Kids. Newman, George. Saratoga, CA: Blossom Valley Press, R & E Publishers, 1981. Creative, innovative communication routes which will keep the parent-child relationship going over long distance; for both mom and dad.

SHARING THE CHILDREN: How to Resolve Custody Problems and Get on With Your Life. Adler, Robert E. Bethesda, MD: Adler and Adler, 1988. Now out of print (last printing sold out), but worth seeking through your library or book shop. Most wise and caring guide to creating a lasting parenting plan which meets both parents' and children's needs.

TALKING ABOUT DIVORCE AND SEPARATION: A Dialogue Between Parent and Child. Grollman, Earl A. Boston: Beacon Press, 1975. Family activity book based on pictures to which participants may react. Adult guide to what children's reactions mean.

TOUCHPOINTS: Your Child's Emotional Behavioral Development. Brazelton, T. Berry, M.D. Menlo Park, CA: Addison-Wesley Publishing Company, 1992. An excellent basic reference for child emotional and behavioral development, with helpful discussion of a variety of challenges to development, including divorce.

WHEN YOUR PARENTS GET A DIVORCE. Banks, Ann. New York: Viking Penguin, Inc., 1990. Do-it-yourself workbook for school-age child. Particularly helpful for the child who can't open up and talk about feelings.

IV. Books About Financial Considerations and Tax at Divorce

BUYING AND SELLING A BUSINESS: A Step by Step Guide. Klueger, Robert F. New York: John Wiley and Sons, Inc., 1988. Steps for buying a business and one good chapter on preparing a business for sale.

BUYING & SELLING A SMALL BUSINESS. Coltman, Michael M. Seattle: Self-Counsel Press, Inc., 1991. Practical advice for either buying or selling, with a good chapter on valuation methods.

THE DEBT REDUCTION BOOK: A Fiscal Fitness Guide for the 1990's. Lang, Russell. Richmond, VA: Financial Marketing Associates, 1992. Practical, money-saving ideas for handling money, cutting costs, credit, borrowing, and planning.

DON'T GET MARRIED UNTIL YOU READ THIS: Layman's Guide to Prenuptial Agreements. Saltman, David, and Harry Schaffner. New York: Barron's Educational Services, 1989. The book to read if you plan to marry or re-marry and want to keep your present children, property and finances separate.

DIVORCE AND MONEY: How to Make the Best Financial Decisions During Divorce. Woodhouse, Violet, and Victoria Felton-Collins, with M.C. Blakeman. Berkeley, CA: Nolo Press, 1992, revised edition Dec. 1993. Workbook about all the financial issues in divorce. Updated regularly.

REMARRIAGE WITHOUT FINANCIAL RISK: How to Do It Right the Next Time. Gordon, Hartley, with Jane Daniel. Boston: Financial Planning Institute, 1992. An Overview of financial issues which are different – and yet the same – the second time around.

SURVIVAL MANUAL FOR WOMEN IN DIVORCE, 1990; revised 1993. *SURVIVAL MANUAL FOR MEN IN DIVORCE*, 1992. Schilling, Edwin III, and Carol Ann Wilson. Boulder, CO: Quantum Press. Answers to the most-asked, or should-be- most-asked, questions about financial issues at divorce.

THE WALL STREET JOURNAL GUIDE TO UNDERSTANDING PERSONAL FINANCE. Morris, Kenneth M. and Alan M. Siegel. New York: Simon and Schuster, 1992. Visually rich illustrated guide to all the financial terms you never understood, such as what is a mortgage, how does credit work, and how to read a credit report.

A HANDBOOK FOR ATTORNEYS ON COURT-ORDERED RETIREMENT AND HEALTH BENEFITS UNDER THE CIVIL SERVICE RETIREMENT SYSTEM, FEDERAL EMPLOYEES RETIREMENT SYSTEM AND FEDERAL EMPLOYEE HEALTH BENEFITS PROGRAM. U.S. Government Printing Office, #38-116, October 1992.

IRS Publications, updated annually, which you may find at your public library, or order directly from the IRS for free:

#504:   Tax information for Divorced or Separated Individuals
#523:   Tax information on selling your home.
#551:   Basis of assets
#590:   Individual Retirement Arrangements (IRA's)

Internal Revenue CODE, selected sections

Sec. 2   Definition of tax rates (head of household, married or single)
Sec. 21   Child care credit defined
Sec. 71   Alimony defined
Sec. 121   One-time capital gains exclusions at 55
Sec. 125   Cafeteria plans
Sec. 151   Personal exemptions defined
Sec. 152   Dependent defined
Sec. 1034   Roll over of gain on sale of principal residence
Sec. 1041   Transfers of property in divorce not taxes
Sec. 1221–1223   Capital Gain defined
Sec. 7703   Determination of marital status for filing

Your public library will have copies of the Internal Revenue Code, many with explanatory text and interpretive cases.

There are many tax workbooks published each year which highlight any changes in the Code during the previous year, for both consumers and tax professionals.

V. Computer Software

BRADFORMS, DOMESTIC RELATIONS GROUP, VERSION 2.5, (Computer Program). Bradford Publishing Company, 2003 Denver, CO. This software contains the forms for dissolution of marriage, legal separation, child support and modification in Word and Word Perfect. The financial affidavits include the ability to calculate totals. The child support worksheets are set up in Excel or QuattroPro spreadsheets that automatically calculate child support and create the appropriate Worksheet.

COLORADO CHILD SUPPORT GUIDELINES, VERSION 4.1 (Computer Program). Redak, William. Boulder, CO. Custom Legal Software Corporation, 1994. This computer software makes preparing child support worksheets easy, and provides a useful tax/maintenance analysis.

LEGAL MATH PAC: Version 3.1 (Computer program). Redak, William. Boulder, CO: Custom Legal Software Corporation, 1994. This computer program will help you determine the value of a pension plan or future income stream, calculate interest on irregular transactions, create an amortization schedule, along with other handy features.

FORMS

CHECKLISTS

EXAMPLES

Adams	Adams County Justice Center	1100 Judicial Center Drive	Brighton, Co 80601
Alamosa	Alamosa County Courthouse	4th and San Juan	Alamosa, CO 8ll0l
Arapahoe	Arapahoe County Justice Center	7325 South Potomac Street	Englewood, Co 80112
Archuleta	449 San Juan St	P.O. Box 148	Pagosa Springs, CO 81147
Baca	Baca Combined Court	741 Main Street	Springfield, CO 81073
Bent	Bent Combined Court	725 Bent	Las Animas, Colorado 81054
Boulder	Boulder County Justice Center	P.O. Box 4249, 1777 Sixth Street	Boulder, Colorado 80306-4249
Chaffee	Chaffee Combined Court	142 Crestone, P.O. Box 279	Salida, CO 81201
Cheyenne	P. O. Box 696	51 South First Street	Cheyenne Wells, CO 80810
Clear Creek	Clear Creek Combined Court	5th & Argentine, P.O. Box 367	Georgetown, CO 80444
Conejos	Conejos County Courthouse	Main Street, P.O. Box l28	Conejos, CO 81129
Costilla	Costilla County Court Complex	401 Church Complex, P. O. Box 301	San Luis, CO 8ll52
Crowley	Crowley Combined Court	110 East 6th	Ordway, Colorado 81063
Custer	Custer Combined Court	205 S. 6th St, P.O. Box 60	Westcliffe, Colorado 81252
Delta	Delta Combined Court	501 Palmer, Rm. 338	Delta, Colorado 81416
Denver	Denver City & County Building	1437 Bannock Street	Denver, Colorado 80202
Dolores	Dolores Combined Court	409 N. Main, P.O. Box 511	Dove Creek, CO 81324
Douglas	Douglas County Justice Center	4000 Justice Way, #2009	Castle Rock, Colorado 80104
Eagle	Eagle Combined Court	885 Chambers Ave, P.O. Box 597	Eagle, Colorado 81631
El Paso	El Paso County Judicial Building	20 East Vermijo, Suite 105	Colorado Springs, Colorado 80903
Elbert	Elbert Combined Court	P. O. Box 232, 751 Ute Street	Kiowa, CO 80117
Fremont	Fremont Combined Court	136 Justice Center Rd., Rm. 103	Canon City, CO 81212
Garfield	Garfield Combined Court	109 8th Street, Suite 104	Glenwood Springs, CO 81601
Gilpin	Gilpin Combined Court	2960 Dory Hill Road, Suite 200	Golden, Colorado 80403-8780
Grand	Grand Combined Court	308 Byers Street, P.O. Box 192	Hot Sulphur Springs, CO 80451
Gunnison	Gunnison Combined Court	200 E. Virginia Ave	Gunnison, Colorado 81230
Hinsdale	Hinsdale Combined Court	300 Henson, P.O. Box 245	Lake City, Colorado 81235
Huerfano	Huerfano County Courthouse	401 Main Street	Walsenburg, CO 81089
Jackson	Jackson County Combined Court	P. O. Box 308, 396 Lafever St	Walden, Colorado 80480
Jefferson	Jefferson Combined Court	100 Jefferson County Parkway	Golden, Colorado 80401-6002
Kiowa	P. O. Box 353	200 East 13th Street	Eads, CO 81036
Kit Carson	Kit Carson Combined Court	251 16th Street	Burlington, CO 80807
La Plata	1060 Second Ave	P.O. Box 759	Durango, Colorado 81302
Lake	Lake Combined Court	5th & harrison Ave, P.O. Box 55	Leadville, CO 80461
Larimer	Larimer County Justice Center	201 LaPorte Avenue, Suite 100	Fort Collins, Colorado 80521-2761
Las Animas	Las Animas County Courthouse	200 East First Street, Room 304	Trinidad, Colorado 81082
Lincoln	Lincoln County Court	P. O. Box 128, 103 Third Avenue	Hugo, Colorado 80821

Logan	Logan District Court	P. O. Box 71, Third and Ash	Sterling, CO 80751
Mesa	Mesa County Justice Center	P.O. Box 20,000	Grand Junction, Colorado 81502
Mineral	Mineral County Courthouse	North First Street	Creede, CO 81130
Moffat	Moffat Combined Court	221 West Victory Way	Craig, Colorado 81625
Montezuma	Montezuma District Court	109 W. Main, Rm. 210	Cortez, Colorado 81321
Montrose	Montrose Combined Court	1200 N. Grand Ave., Bin A	Montrose, Colorado 81401
Morgan	Morgan District Court	P. O. Box 130, 400 Warner	Fort Morgan, Co 80701
Otero	Otero Combined Court	13 West Third Street	LaJunta, Colorado 81050
Ouray	Ouray Combined Court	541 S. 4th St., P.O. Box 643	541 S. 4th St., P.O. Box 643
Park	Park Combined Court	300 Fourth St, P.O. Box 190	Fairplay, CO 80440
Phillips	Phillips Combined Court	221 South Interocean	Holyoke, CO 80734
Pitkin	Pitkin Combined Court	506 E. Main, Suite E	Aspen, Colorado 81611
Prowers	Prowers District Court	301 South Main, Suite 300	Lamar, CO 81052
Pueblo	Pueblo County Judicial Building	320 West 10th Street	Pueblo, Colorado 81003
Rio Blanco	Rio Blanco Combined Court	555 Main St, P.O. Box 1150	Meeker, CO 81641
Rio Grande	Rio Grande County Courthouse	6th and Cherry Streets	Del Norte, CO 81132
Routt	Routt Combined Court	522 Lincoln Ave, P.O. Box 773117	Steamboat Springs, CO 80477
Saguache	Saguache County Courthouse	4th and Christy	Saguache, CO 81149
San Juan	1447 Greene St	P.O. Box 441	Silverton, CO 81433
San Miguel	San Miguel Combined Court	305 W. Colorado, P.O. Box 919	Telluride, Colorado 81435
Sedgwick	Sedgwick Combined Court	Third and Pine	Julesburg, CO 80737
Summit	Summit Combined Court	501 N. Park Ave, P.O. Box 185	Breckenridge, CO 80424
Teller	County Courthouse	101 West Bennett Avenue, P.O. Box 997	Cripple Creek, Colorado 80813
Washington	Washington Combined Court	P. O. Box 455, 26861 Highway 34	Akron, CO 80720
Weld	Weld County Combined Court	901 9th Avenue, P. O. Box 2038	Greeley, Colorado 80632
Yuma	Yuma Combined Court	P. O. Box 347, 200 East Third	Wray, CO 80758

INDEX

FROM THE BRADFORD CATALOG

ABOUT BRADFORD PUBLISHING

Founded in 1881, Bradford Publishing Company is Colorado's oldest and most trusted publisher of legal forms, law books, and information. Bradford Publishing upholds high standards of quality in all of its products. Our forms and most of our books are written by Colorado attorneys and kept accurate and current by constantly monitoring legislation, court rules, and agency regulations. All of our forms are used by Colorado attorneys and accepted by Colorado Courts.

NEW AND FORTHCOMING BOOKS FROM BRADFORD PUBLISHING INCLUDE:

Bradford's CRS: Six volumes compiled for specific fields of practice

Preserving Your Wealth: A Guide to Colorado Probate & Estate Planner

Colorado Will and Estate Planner

Law of the Web: A Field Guide to Internet Publishing

Managing Your Wired Workforce: A Practical Guide

Employment Law: An Essential Guide for Colorado Employers

The Lawyers Winning Edge: Exceptional Courtroom Performance

Living With Wildfire: Preparation, Prevention, and Recovery

BRADFORD GUIDES AND KITS

Legal procedures can be very complicated and difficult to understand, whether you are trying to do something on your own, or you are working with a professional. Bradford Guides and books are specific to Colorado law, written in plain English, and available in kits with PDF forms that can be filled out on CD-ROM.

HERE ARE JUST A FEW OF THE MANY TOPICS FROM OUR CATALOG:

- Family matters (Wills, Probate, Divorce, Child Support, Adoption)
- Civil matters (County Court Civil forms, Eviction, Garnishment)
- Real Estate (Leases, Sales Contracts, Deeds, Mechanic's Liens)
- Personal Property (Bills of Sale, Powers of Attorney)
- A complete line of incorporation forms and corporate kits

HOW TO FIND US

We invite you to visit us in any of the following ways:

RETAIL STORE IN DOWNTOWN DENVER AT 1743 WAZEE STREET
8 to 5 Monday through Friday
303-292-2500

CUSTOMER SERVICE AND MAIL ORDER
303-202-2590 or 800-446-2831

OUR WEB SITE AT WWW.BRADFORDPUBLISHING.COM
Download most of our great forms and booklets.

www.bradfordpublishing.com